Contents

Introduction

List of Standard Tables by Number and Name

1. Demography: People, Family and Households

Age and Sex

Living Arrangements

Country of Birth

2. Health and Care

3. Education, Employment and Economic Activity

Highest Level of Qualification

Economic Activity

4. Housing and Transport

Access to a Car or Van

Tenure and Accommodation Type

Central Heating and Occupancy Rating

5. Irish Language

Alphabetical Index of Standard Tables

Amenities

Concealed Families

Country of Birth

Couples

Dependent Children

Distance Travelled

will be included in a future publication

Divorced

Dwelling Type

Economic Activity

Employee

Floor, More Than One

Full-time Working

Gender

See Sex

Health

Holiday Accommodation

Hours Worked

Household Composition

Household Type

Household Reference Person

Households

Household Space

Industry

Irish

Language

see Irish

Limiting Long-Term Illness

Looking After Home/family

Lowest Floor Level

see Floor Level, Lowest

Marital Status

Married or Re-Married

Method of Travel to Work

Migration

Additional Tables Will Be Included in a Future Publication

More Than One Floor

see Floor, More Than One

National Statistics Socio-economic Classification (NS-SeC)

Number of Floors

see Floor, More Than One

Number of People in Employment in Household

see People in Employment in Households, Number of

Number of People in Household

see People in Households, Number of

Number of Rooms

Occupancy Rating

Occupation Groups

Part-time Working

Pensioner

People in Employment in Household, Number of

People in Household, Number of

Permanently Sick/disabled

Persons Per Room

See Also Occupancy Rating

Provision of Care

see Care, Provision of Unpaid Care

Qualifications

Religion

Rented

Resident Type

Retired

Rooms

See Number of Rooms

Schoolchidren (and Students)

Second Residence

Self-Employed

Separated

Sex

Shared Dwelling

Shower

Step-Children

Tenure

Time Since Last Worked

Toilet

Travel to Work, Method of

Unemployed

Introduction

This publication is the third report from the 2001 Census of Population for Northern Ireland, produced in accordance with the provisions of the Census Act (Northern Ireland) 1969. The first report, published in September 2002, provided population counts by age and sex. The second report, published in December 2002, provided summary statistics for the majority of Census questions and topics. This report contains 121 tables and provides more detailed cross-tabular Census output covering a wide variety of Census variables as agreed with users during the consultation phase of the 2001 Census. The information is presented in this report for Northern Ireland only. These tables will be available in the Census section of the Northern Ireland Statistics and Research Agency (NISRA) website www.nisra.gov.uk. Similar tables for Local Government Districts, Health and Social Services Boards, Education and Library Boards, NUTS Level III Areas, Parliamentary Constituencies and Electoral Wards will be made available electronically in due course. As with all Census outputs, this report was made possible by the co-operation of members of the public in responding to the Census; the commitment of the Census field staff in delivering and collecting forms; and the assistance of many other people and organisations throughout all aspects of the Census. The Registrar General would like to thank all those who have contributed to this work.

Background to the 2001 Census

Legislation

The Census Act (Northern Ireland) 1969 allows for the carrying out of a Census no less than five years after the previous Census. However various other legislative requirements need to be fulfilled before a Census can be held. The first stage in this process was the publication of the White Paper 'The 2001 Census of Population' which set out the reasons for holding a Census, the proposed questions, operational methodology and format of results. The White Paper was produced in March 1999, two years before the Census, to ensure sufficient time for public discussion of proposals. Prior to every Census, a Census Order is required. This states the date of the Census, the people who are required to complete the form, those who are to be included on the form and the topics on which questions will be asked. The operational aspects of the Census also require legislative approval. This information was set out in the Census Regulations, which contained details of how the Census was to be conducted and included a copy of the Census form.

Fieldwork

The Census was designed to collect information on the usually resident population on Census Day, 29 April 2001. Ahead of this day enumerators delivered Census forms to every identified household space and communal establishment. Residents were asked to complete the forms with their information, as correct on Census Day, and to return the completed forms by post. Where Census Office did not receive a form through the post, the enumerator visited the address in order to collect the form by hand. Special arrangements were made to enumerate the Armed Forces and people sleeping rough.

Processing

Returned forms were fed through scanning machinery which captured all the ticked responses and stored written answers in digital form. The latter were coded into categories either by automatic systems which recognised text responses to questions, or by manual coding. These data then underwent an edit process to ensure that the data were consistent, and an imputation process to supply responses for questions which had not been completed on the original form.

Coverage of the Population

The results in this report all relate to the usually resident population of Northern Ireland on Census Day, 29 April 2001. Students have been recorded at their term-time address. In contrast to the 1991 Census, information on visitors has not been collected. The Census placed a legal obligation on every household in which someone was usually resident on Census Day, and on every person who was a usual resident of a communal establishment, to complete a Census form. As no Census of Population succeeds in collecting information from every resident, a methodology (the One Number Census) was developed to adjust the results to take account of any undercount and thus provide an accurate estimate of the total population and its characteristics. The One Number Census methodology was developed with the assistance of academic experts and was subject to consultation and peer review. The work involved matching the results of the Census enumeration with those of an independent large scale Census Coverage Survey of 10,000 households, conducted shortly after the Census. The response rate in the Census Coverage Survey was 92 per cent. This enabled the number and characteristics of those not enumerated in the Census to be estimated and this information was used to adjust the Census database. The figures presented here, as with all reports on the 2001 Census, have been adjusted to take account of under-enumeration. Administrative registers and demographic estimates were used to quality assure the final estimates. Further details on the methodology to adjust for under-enumeration can be found in the Census section of the NISRA website at www.nisra.gov.uk.

Comparability with 1991

The Census is designed to provide the most accurate possible picture of the population on the day the Census is taken. Comparisons of the 2001 Census results with counts from the 1991 Census will be affected by changes in the Local Government District boundaries, changes in definitions, and adjustment for under-enumeration in the 2001 Census figures. Where comparisons between 1991 and 2001 Census results are required, the effects of the differences noted above can be mitigated by comparing differences between percentages calculated from the respective bases in each Census, rather than measuring the difference between the actual counts at each Census. Users interested in changes in population size are advised to use the mid-year population estimates, which are designed to measure such changes. The mid-year population estimates can be found in the Demography and Methodology Branch section of the NISRA website at www.nisra.gov.uk.

Information in this Report

As outlined earlier, this report provides Census results for Northern Ireland on Census Day, 29 April 2001. These results are based on the information collected from the Census forms. Copies of the sample Census forms can be found in the Census section of the NISRA web site at www.nisra.gov.uk and will be contained in the forthcoming 2001 Census Definitions volume which will be published in mid 2003. All questions included in the 1991 Census were included in the 2001 Census with the exception of questions relating to usual address and whereabouts on Census Night, fertility and professional/ vocational qualifications and household accommodation questions on water supply and domestic sewage disposal. The answer categories in some questions, such as educational qualifications, were updated, while questions on religion and economic activity have been restructured. There were also new questions on ethnic group, general health, the provision of unpaid care, time since last paid employment, the size of the work force at a person's place of work, supervision of employees, lowest floor level of accommodation and whether all rooms in a household were located on a single floor.

The Census questions asked of all people covered:

- relationship to others in the household

- sex, age (date of birth) and marital status
- whether schoolchild/ full-time student
- term-time address (where applicable)
- Irish language
- religion or religion brought up in
- country of birth
- ethnic group
- general health
- provision of unpaid care
- long-term illness
- usual address one year ago

Whilst questions for those aged 16 to 74 also covered:
- educational qualifications
- economic activity and employment status
- number of employees at place of work
- occupation and industry of employment
- address of workplace
- means of travel to work
- hours worked

In addition, the person filling in the form in each household was asked about:
- type of accommodation and whether it was self-contained
- number of rooms
- availability of bath/shower and toilet
- lowest floor level and whether all rooms were on one level
- presence of central heating
- availability of cars or vans
- tenure
- landlord

Census Definitions

Key Census definitions on persons, households and communal establishments are given below, and details on all 2001 Census definitions and classifications can be found in the metadata component of the Census section of the NISRA web site www.nisra.gov.uk. This includes a Census glossary together with details on 2001 Census output classifications, differences between parts of the UK, comparability with the 1991 Census, Census concepts and definitions, data classifications, and standard derived variables. A printed Census Definitions volume will be available in mid 2003.

Persons: Results from the 2001 Census of Population relate to the usually resident population where a usual resident is defined as someone who resides at that address most of the time. The usually resident population includes persons temporarily away on Census Day (for example on holiday, on business, in hospital or visiting family), persons who work away from home for part of the time, students at their term-time address, babies born before Census Day even if still in hospital, and persons staying at that address if they have no other usual address.

Households: A household comprises one person living alone, or a group of persons not necessarily related but living at the same address with common housekeeping, that is, sharing either a living-room or sitting-room or at least one meal a day.

Communal establishments: A communal establishment is defined as an establishment providing managed residential accommodation, where managed means full-time or part-time supervision of the accommodation.

Finding Information in this Report

This report contains 121 tables which provide cross-tabular output on a wide variety of Census topics. The tables are arranged in themes (listed below) with tables cross-tabulated by Community Background, Religion and Ethnicity appearing under most of the themes.

1. Demography: People, Family and Households
- Age and Sex
- Living Arrangements
- Country of Birth

2. Health and Care

3. Education, Employment and Economic Activity
- Highest Level of Qualification
- Economic Activity
- Occupation
- Industry
- National Statistics Socio-economic Classification (NS-SeC)

- Social Grade
- Method of Travel to Work

4. Housing and Transport
- Access to a Car or Van
- Tenure and Accommodation Type
- Central Heating and Occupancy Rating

5. Irish Language

An additional index 'Alphabetical Index of Standard Tables' is included following the 'List of Standard Tables by number and name'. This lists all the tables relating to a particular topic or census variable, along with their page number.

If the cross tabular results you require are not within these tables ad hoc queries can be requested by contacting Census Customer Services:

Census Customer Services
McAuley House
2-14 Castle Street
Belfast, BT1 1SA

Telephone: +44 (0) 28 90348160
Fax: +44 (0) 28 90348161

E-mail: census.nisra@dfpni.gov.uk

The service to provide ad hoc analysis will be available in Summer 2003 after the delivery of Census Area Statistics.

Geographical Level of Tables

Within each table results are presented at the Northern Ireland level. In due course, similar tables will be available electronically for Northern Ireland's 26 Local Government Districts and 582 Electoral Wards in the Census section of the NISRA website at www.nisra.gov.uk or may be purchased on CD from Census Customer Services, (see address above). Although the majority of tables will be available at both Local Government District and Electoral Ward levels, some will be restricted to Local Government District or Northern Ireland level due to the large number of cells and the resultant small numbers at lower geographical levels and the need to preserve the confidentiality and utility of the

data. A complete list showing the availability of each of the tables at the lower geographical levels is given in Annex A. All tables available at Local Government District level will also be available for Health and Social Services Boards, Education and Library Boards, NUTS Level III Areas and Parliamentary Constituencies. Where tables are not available at lower geographical levels an equivalent less detailed table will usually be included as part of the Census Area Statistics due to be released in mid 2003. Requests for tables for specified Electoral Wards or specified Local Government Districts will be considered by way of an ad hoc request and produced, provided the utility of the data and associated disclosure risk is judged to be within acceptable limits. This service will be available in Summer 2003 after the delivery of Census Area Statistics.

Comparability of Tables Across the UK

Tables numbered S001 to S068 are tables with a common UK format and can be obtained for other parts of the UK. Tables numbered S301 to S375 are either NI specific tables or tables with a format unique to NI. Similar tables may be available for other parts of the UK, but it is unlikely that they will be directly comparable. Gaps in the numbering S001 to S068 series relate to tables which are available for England, Scotland and Wales but not for Northern Ireland. Annex B lists these tables and suggests an alternative Northern Ireland table. Table S118 is available for England, Wales and Northern Ireland.

Quality of the Results

The use of the One Number Census methodology means that the results of the 2001 Census cover the entire population of Northern Ireland and are the most reliable achievable. The results are nonetheless subject to potential errors from a variety of sources including incorrect information provided on forms, sampling error relating to estimates derived through the One Number Census process, and errors introduced during processing and imputation. Some elements of incorrect information have been corrected during an edit process and, following this, the results have undergone an extensive quality assurance process including checks against administrative sources. Further information on accuracy, coverage and imputation rates is provided in the Census section of the NISRA website. A detailed report on the quality of Census results will be published in 2003.

Community Background and Religion

A new output variable Community Background, based on religion and religion brought up in, was introduced for the 2001 Census. A religion question has always been included in the Census in Northern Ireland. Since 1971 a sizeable proportion of the population have declined to answer the question. In addition, the 1991 Census included a 'None' category and together with the 'Not Stated' responses these accounted for 11 per cent of the population. To facilitate statutory equality monitoring the 1999 Census White Paper announced that the religion question in the 2001 Census would be extended to include an additional question on religion brought up in, to be asked only of those without a current religion.

The Community Background variable records a person's current religion, if any, or the religion brought up in for those people who do not regard themselves as currently belonging to any religion. 'None' is a valid Community Background category. The other categories are 'Catholic', 'Protestant and Other Christian (including Christian related)' and 'Other religions and philosophies'. However, as for the use of all statistics, the choice of appropriate data should be informed by the objectives of the research, and there will be occasions when use of the religion variable is more appropriate than the use of the Community Background variable. This report includes several tables cross-tabulating

Community Background with other Census variables. Where a similar table is included for religion the same table number is used with the addition of an 'A' (e.g. S305 and S305A). For those tables in this report presented using Community Background only, equivalent tables by religion are available in the Census section of the NISRA website at www.nisra.gov.uk.

Confidentiality

The Registrar General has taken steps to ensure that the confidentiality of respondents is fully protected. All published results from the Census have been subject to statistical processes to ensure that individuals cannot be identified. One of these processes, small cell adjustment, may result in marginally different results between tables reporting the same statistic, however any differences between the figures will be small. An example of this is seen in table S015 of this report where the population differs slightly from other tables. A description of the steps taken to ensure confidentiality, including the small cell adjustment process, is available in the Census section of the NISRA website at www.nisra.gov.uk.

Further Output

Some of the proposed Standard Tables, including the migration and distance to place of work tables are not currently available. However, these will be included in a future publication and will have either a common UK format or will be unique to NI.

In addition further tables will be produced as part of the Census Area Statistics, due to be released in mid 2003. This release, which will be in electronic form only, will include less detailed versions of Standard Tables for small geographical areas. A range of other outputs from the 2001 Census is planned for release over the rest of 2003. This is detailed in the output prospectus which can be accessed in the Census section of the NISRA website at www.nisra.gov.uk

Further Information

All Census results are available in the Census section of the NISRA website at www.nisra.gov.uk. Electronic versions of the data may be purchased on CD from Census Customer Services, later in 2003.

Census Customer Services
McAuley House
2-14 Castle Street
Belfast, BT1 1SA

Telephone: +44 (0) 28 90348160
Fax: +44 (0) 28 90348161
E-mail: census.nisra@dfpni.gov.uk
Website: www.nisra.gov.uk

Reports published to date on the 2001 Census are:

Northern Ireland Census 2001 Population Report and Mid-Year Estimates
ISBN 0-339-40112-5 Price £15

Northern Ireland Census 2001 Key Statistics
ISBN 0-339-40192-3 Price £15

To order these publications contact The Stationery Office.

The Stationery Office
16 Arthur Street
Belfast, BT1 4GD

Telephone: +44 (0) 28 90238451
Fax: +44 (0) 28 90235401
Website: www.tso.co.uk

Other Censuses in the UK

Separate Censuses were carried out, on the same day and using similar methodologies, in England and Wales and Scotland, under the authority of the respective Registrar Generals. Information on these Censuses is available from:

England and Wales
Census Customer Services
ONS
Titchfield
Fareham
Hants PO15 5RR

Telephone: +44 (0) 1329 813800
Fax: +44 (0) 1329 813587
Minicom: +44 (0) 1329 813669
E-mail: census.customerservices@ons.gov.uk

Scotland
General Register Office for Scotland
Census Division
Ladywell House
Ladywell Road
Edinburgh, EH12 7TF

Telephone: +44 (0) 131 314 4254
E-mail: customer@gro-scotland.gov.uk

Copyright and reproduction of material from this report

This report (excluding agency logos) may be reproduced free of charge in any format or medium for research, private study or for internal circulation within an organisation. This is subject to it being reproduced accurately and not used in a misleading context. The material must be acknowledged as Crown Copyright and the title of the report specified. This report can also be found in the Census section of the Northern Ireland Statistics and Research Agency website www.nisra.gov.uk. For any other use of this material please apply for a Click-Use Licence on the HMSO website at http://www.hmso.gov.uk/click-use-home.htm, or by writing to HMSO:

The Licensing Division
St Clements House
2-16 Colegate
Norwich, NR3 1BQ

Fax: +44 (0)1603 723000
E-mail: hmsolicensing@cabinetoffice.x.gsi.gov.uk

1. Demography: People, Family and Households

1. Demography: People, Family and Households

Age and Sex

Table S001:   Age by Sex and Whether Living in a Household or Communal Establishment
Table S002:   Age by Sex and Marital Status
Table S301:   Sex and Type of Communal Establishment by Type of Resident and Age
Table S302:   Type of Communal Establishment by Type of Resident and Whether or Not Resident One Year Ago
Table S303:   Sex and Age by Ethnic Group
Table S304:   Sex and Type of Communal Establishment by Ethnic Group
Table S305:   Age by Sex and Community Background (Religion or Religion Brought Up In)
Table S305A: Age by Sex and Religion
Table S306:   Age by Community Background (Religion or Religion Brought Up In)
Table S306A: Age by Religion
Table S307:   Sex and Type of Communal Establishment by Community Background (Religion or Religion Brought Up In)
Table S308:   Religion by Sex

Living Arrangements

Table S003:   Age of Household Reference Person (HRP) by Sex and Marital Status ('Headship')
Table S005:   Age of Household Reference Person (HRP) by Sex and Living Arrangements
Table S006:   Age of Family Reference Person (FRP) and Age of Dependent Children by Family Type
Table S007:   Age of Family Reference Person (FRP) and Number and Age of Dependent Children by Family Type
Table S011:   Family Composition by Age of Family Reference Person (FRP)
Table S068:   Age and Dependent Children by Household Type (Household Reference Persons)
Table S309:   Age by Sex and Living Arrangements
Table S012:   Schoolchildren and Students in Full-time Education Living Away From Home in Term-Time: Sex by Age
Table S014:   Age and Dependent Children by Household Type (Adults)
Table S310:   Age of Full-time Schoolchildren and Students Aged 18 and Under by Household Type
Table S311:   Household Composition by Ethnic Group of Household Reference Person (HRP)
Table S312:   Household Composition by Community Background (Religion or Religion Brought Up In) of Household Reference Person (HRP)
Table S313:   Living Arrangements and Community Background (Religion or Religion Brought Up In) by Sex and Age

Country of Birth

Table S015:   Country of Birth by Sex and Age
Table S314:   Country of Birth by Ethnic Group

Table S001: Age by Sex and Whether Living in a Household or Communal Establishment

Table population: All persons

	All persons			Males			Females		
	Total	Household residents	Communal establishment residents	Total	Household residents	Communal establishment residents	Total	Household residents	Communal establishment residents
All persons	1685268	1658813	26455	821450	809276	12174	863818	849537	14281
0 to 4	**115239**	**115192**	**47**	**59214**	**59191**	**23**	**56025**	**56001**	**24**
0	21683	21667	16	11116	11107	9	10567	10560	7
1	22363	22355	8	11550	11546	4	10813	10809	4
2	23264	23253	11	11887	11884	3	11377	11369	8
3	23585	23577	8	12198	12195	3	11387	11382	5
4	24344	24340	4	12463	12459	4	11881	11881	-
5 to 9	**123050**	**122984**	**66**	**63147**	**63113**	**34**	**59903**	**59871**	**32**
5	23883	23866	17	12421	12411	10	11462	11455	7
6	24064	24058	6	12380	12377	3	11684	11681	3
7	24400	24390	10	12370	12367	3	12030	12023	7
8	24907	24898	9	12676	12671	5	12231	12227	4
9	25796	25772	24	13300	13287	13	12496	12485	11
10 to 14	**132664**	**132379**	**285**	**68014**	**67845**	**169**	**64650**	**64534**	**116**
10	26189	26165	24	13436	13420	16	12753	12745	8
11	25963	25937	26	13271	13255	16	12692	12682	10
12	26403	26323	80	13561	13510	51	12842	12813	29
13	26997	26923	74	13789	13742	47	13208	13181	27
14	27112	27031	81	13957	13918	39	13155	13113	42
15 to 19	**129201**	**126083**	**3118**	**65598**	**64085**	**1513**	**63603**	**61998**	**1605**
15	27104	27001	103	13887	13839	48	13217	13162	55
16	27182	27080	102	13857	13803	54	13325	13277	48
17	26276	26075	201	13303	13183	120	12973	12892	81
18	25392	24725	667	12998	12631	367	12394	12094	300
19	23247	21202	2045	11553	10629	924	11694	10573	1121
20 to 24	**109385**	**105729**	**3656**	**54913**	**52456**	**2457**	**54472**	**53273**	**1199**
20	22791	21763	1028	11648	11059	589	11143	10704	439
21	22449	21645	804	11478	10947	531	10971	10698	273
22	21717	20997	720	10785	10267	518	10932	10730	202
23	21166	20548	618	10442	9992	450	10724	10556	168
24	21262	20776	486	10560	10191	369	10702	10585	117

	All persons			Males			Females		
	Total	Household residents	Communal establishment residents	Total	Household residents	Communal establishment residents	Total	Household residents	Communal establishment residents
25 to 29	**114704**	**112934**	**1770**	**56628**	**55254**	**1374**	**58076**	**57680**	**396**
25	21621	21183	438	10799	10461	338	10822	10722	100
26	21684	21304	380	10655	10358	297	11029	10946	83
27	22933	22615	318	11366	11111	255	11567	11504	63
28	24021	23720	301	11794	11563	231	12227	12157	70
29	24445	24112	333	12014	11761	253	12431	12351	80
30 to 34	**127517**	**126402**	**1115**	**62487**	**61614**	**873**	**65030**	**64788**	**242**
30	25275	24980	295	12421	12196	225	12854	12784	70
31	24965	24736	229	12257	12079	178	12708	12657	51
32	25532	25319	213	12425	12247	178	13107	13072	35
33	25781	25608	173	12657	12522	135	13124	13086	38
34	25964	25759	205	12727	12570	157	13237	13189	48
35 to 39	**129639**	**128847**	**792**	**63430**	**62841**	**589**	**66209**	**66006**	**203**
35	26120	25977	143	12887	12771	116	13233	13206	27
36	26845	26687	158	13119	13001	118	13726	13686	40
37	26198	26021	177	12820	12696	124	13378	13325	53
38	25578	25402	176	12591	12465	126	12987	12937	50
39	24898	24760	138	12013	11908	105	12885	12852	33
40 to 44	**117335**	**116727**	**608**	**57432**	**57045**	**387**	**59903**	**59682**	**221**
40	24847	24707	140	12209	12119	90	12638	12588	50
41	24074	23961	113	11774	11698	76	12300	12263	37
42	23039	22920	119	11231	11156	75	11808	11764	44
43	23217	23102	115	11353	11284	69	11864	11818	46
44	22158	22037	121	10865	10788	77	11293	11249	44
45 to 49	**102464**	**101915**	**549**	**51686**	**51331**	**355**	**50778**	**50584**	**194**
45	21720	21599	121	10895	10818	77	10825	10781	44
46	20582	20475	107	10494	10424	70	10088	10051	37
47	20513	20405	108	10434	10361	73	10079	10044	35
48	20298	20202	96	10179	10118	61	10119	10084	35
49	19351	19234	117	9684	9610	74	9667	9624	43

Table S001: Age by Sex and Whether Living in a Household or Communal Establishment (continued)

	All persons			Males			Females		
	Total	Household residents	Communal establishment residents	Total	Household residents	Communal establishment residents	Total	Household residents	Communal establishment residents
50 to 54	**98426**	**97817**	**609**	**48484**	**48113**	**371**	**49942**	**49704**	**238**
50	19474	19338	136	9765	9682	83	9709	9656	53
51	19697	19584	113	9721	9653	68	9976	9931	45
52	19549	19421	128	9641	9558	83	9908	9863	45
53	19653	19532	121	9578	9508	70	10075	10024	51
54	20053	19942	111	9779	9712	67	10274	10230	44
55 to 59	**88732**	**88132**	**600**	**43585**	**43241**	**344**	**45147**	**44891**	**256**
55	18122	18007	115	9025	8950	75	9097	9057	40
56	18161	18041	120	8873	8807	66	9288	9234	54
57	18427	18312	115	9081	9019	62	9346	9293	53
58	18015	17872	143	8783	8701	82	9232	9171	61
59	16007	15900	107	7823	7764	59	8184	8136	48
60 to 64	**73587**	**72985**	**602**	**35401**	**35082**	**319**	**38186**	**37903**	**283**
60	14781	14670	111	7189	7131	58	7592	7539	53
61	14821	14715	106	7153	7093	60	7668	7622	46
62	14999	14885	114	7178	7113	65	7821	7772	49
63	14386	14259	127	6963	6896	67	7423	7363	60
64	14600	14456	144	6918	6849	69	7682	7607	75
65 to 69	**65341**	**64594**	**747**	**30406**	**30036**	**370**	**34935**	**34558**	**377**
65	13876	13763	113	6554	6501	53	7322	7262	60
66	13199	13046	153	6269	6193	76	6930	6853	77
67	12929	12786	143	6011	5928	83	6918	6858	60
68	12790	12657	133	5784	5719	65	7006	6938	68
69	12547	12342	205	5788	5695	93	6759	6647	112
70 to 74	**57852**	**56634**	**1218**	**25069**	**24562**	**507**	**32783**	**32072**	**711**
70	12477	12272	205	5490	5410	80	6987	6862	125
71	11999	11785	214	5275	5171	104	6724	6614	110
72	11415	11165	250	4964	4853	111	6451	6312	139
73	10938	10662	276	4618	4512	106	6320	6150	170
74	11023	10750	273	4722	4616	106	6301	6134	167

Table S001: Age by Sex and Whether Living in a Household or Communal Establishment (continued)

	All persons			Males			Females		
	Total	Household residents	Communal establishment residents	Total	Household residents	Communal establishment residents	Total	Household residents	Communal establishment residents
75 to 79	**46542**	**44386**	**2156**	**18562**	**17841**	**721**	**27980**	**26545**	**1435**
75	10486	10147	339	4317	4197	120	6169	5950	219
76	9761	9362	399	4058	3903	155	5703	5459	244
77	9245	8829	416	3712	3570	142	5533	5259	274
78	8723	8237	486	3324	3171	153	5399	5066	333
79	8327	7811	516	3151	3000	151	5176	4811	365
80 to 84	**30289**	**27405**	**2884**	**11090**	**10334**	**756**	**19199**	**17071**	**2128**
80	7893	7302	591	3036	2876	160	4857	4426	431
81	7298	6699	599	2743	2586	157	4555	4113	442
82	5821	5258	563	2157	1988	169	3664	3270	394
83	4820	4283	537	1647	1522	125	3173	2761	412
84	4457	3863	594	1507	1362	145	2950	2501	449
85 to 89	**16116**	**13039**	**3077**	**4707**	**4074**	**633**	**11409**	**8965**	**2444**
85	4086	3469	617	1270	1128	142	2816	2341	475
86	3786	3149	637	1140	986	154	2646	2163	483
87	3248	2639	609	952	817	135	2296	1822	474
88	2790	2161	629	789	669	120	2001	1492	509
89	2206	1621	585	556	474	82	1650	1147	503
90 to 94	**5734**	**3839**	**1895**	**1322**	**1025**	**297**	**4412**	**2814**	**1598**
90	1733	1214	519	413	329	84	1320	885	435
91	1375	940	435	323	249	74	1052	691	361
92	1133	766	367	265	211	54	868	555	313
93	866	564	302	169	131	38	697	433	264
94	627	355	272	152	105	47	475	250	225
95 to 99	**1302**	**739**	**563**	**257**	**185**	**72**	**1045**	**554**	**491**
95	474	275	199	106	76	30	368	199	169
96	342	192	150	59	37	22	283	155	128
97	212	118	94	42	34	8	170	84	86
98	155	92	63	28	22	6	127	70	57
99	119	62	57	22	16	6	97	46	51
100 and over	**149**	**51**	**98**	**18**	**8**	**10**	**131**	**43**	**88**

Note:
1   Communal establishment residents includes staff and their families, other residents and persons sleeping rough.

Table S002: Age by Sex and Marital Status

Table population: All persons

	All persons	Males							Females						
		Total	Single (never married)	Married (first marriage)	Re-married	Separated (but still legally married)	Divorced	Widowed	Total	Single (never married)	Married (first marriage)	Re-married	Separated (but still legally married)	Divorced	Widowed
All persons	1685260	821447	430361	310987	17935	19388	21909	20867	863813	393909	312671	16490	30031	31091	79621
0 to 15	398056	204261	204261	-	-	-	-	-	193795	193795	-	-	-	-	-
16	27180	13855	13852	3	-	-	-	-	13325	13322	3	-	-	-	-
17	26272	13302	13287	15	-	-	-	-	12970	12945	25	-	-	-	-
18	25393	13000	12972	25	-	3	-	-	12393	12350	43	-	-	-	-
19	23245	11552	11506	42	-	4	-	-	11693	11561	123	-	9	-	-
20 to 24	109385	54913	52628	2059	8	145	57	16	54472	48796	5045	8	523	68	32
25 to 29	114704	56628	39833	15277	89	1004	394	31	58076	32448	22010	260	2451	784	123
30 to 34	127517	62487	24815	32647	760	2418	1761	86	65030	18489	36933	1273	4982	3043	310
35 to 39	129639	63430	14853	40201	2009	3189	3017	161	66209	10798	41786	2337	5777	4943	568
40 to 44	117335	57432	9507	38138	2668	3102	3710	307	59903	7085	38506	2756	4962	5674	920
45 to 49	102464	51686	7119	34822	2748	2771	3694	532	50778	4748	33607	2538	3563	4841	1481
50 to 54	98426	48484	5709	34051	2599	2173	3123	829	49942	3952	34037	2372	2851	4254	2476
55 to 59	88732	43585	4599	31344	2167	1713	2471	1291	45147	3447	30672	1784	2017	3069	4158
60 to 64	73587	35401	3767	25442	1619	1130	1689	1754	38186	3205	24334	1222	1273	1898	6254
65 to 69	65341	30406	3556	21337	1184	816	1051	2462	34935	3498	19274	761	801	1168	9433
70 to 74	57852	25069	3296	16463	891	514	555	3350	32783	3970	13568	570	487	723	13465
75 to 79	46542	18562	2493	11070	625	246	245	3883	27980	3772	8060	378	204	371	15195
80 to 84	30289	11090	1454	5687	388	120	95	3346	19199	2820	3296	157	87	164	12675
85 to 89	16116	4707	618	1898	136	32	40	1983	11409	1832	1042	59	29	64	8383
90 and over	7185	1597	236	466	44	8	7	836	5588	1076	307	15	15	27	4148

Table S301: Sex and Type of Communal Establishment by Type of Resident and Age

Table population: All persons in communal establishments

	All persons	Residents (non-staff)											Residents (staff and their families)
		0 to 14	15	16 to 17	18 to 19	20 to 44	45 to 59	60 to 64	65 to 74	75 to 84	85 to 89	90 and over	
All persons	**26438**	**356**	**90**	**293**	**2702**	**7664**	**1562**	**510**	**1718**	**4353**	**2730**	**2260**	**2200**
Medical and care establishments	**15598**	**143**	**45**	**59**	**89**	**1309**	**1191**	**403**	**1471**	**4031**	**2612**	**2216**	**2029**
'NHS/HSSB' managed	**3531**	**78**	**35**	**41**	**59**	**618**	**440**	**118**	**355**	**764**	**408**	**326**	**289**
Psychiatric hospital/home	1114	9	3	13	9	292	273	63	148	173	45	47	39
General or other hospital	616	15	-	-	45	267	94	16	32	46	15	26	60
Children's home	123	47	32	25	-	-	-	-	-	-	-	-	19
Nursing home	99	-	-	-	-	3	12	4	15	24	22	19	-
Residential care home	1539	7	-	3	5	56	61	35	157	512	320	230	153
Other medical and care home	40	-	-	-	-	-	-	-	3	9	6	4	18
Non 'NHS/HSSB' managed	**12067**	**65**	**10**	**18**	**30**	**691**	**751**	**285**	**1116**	**3267**	**2204**	**1890**	**1740**
Psychiatric hospital/home	349	22	-	8	12	59	38	16	38	53	28	12	63
General or other hospital	12	-	-	-	-	-	-	-	3	3	6	-	-
Children's home	40	23	10	7	-	-	-	-	-	-	-	-	-
Nursing home	8151	3	-	-	6	222	321	146	774	2335	1564	1418	1362
Residential care home	3347	14	-	3	9	402	384	120	277	806	580	443	309
Other medical and care home	168	3	-	-	3	8	8	3	24	70	26	17	6
Other establishments	**10840**	**213**	**45**	**234**	**2613**	**6355**	**371**	**107**	**247**	**322**	**118**	**44**	**171**
Defence establishments (including ships)	4356	-	-	63	491	3779	23	-	-	-	-	-	3
Prison Service establishments	587	-	-	-	12	462	96	14	8	-	-	-	-
Probation/Bail hostel	38	-	-	-	-	16	10	4	8	-	-	-	-
Education establishment (including halls of residence)	4189	158	45	128	2072	1704	18	4	3	-	-	-	57
Hotel, boarding house, guest house	125	3	-	-	-	30	27	7	8	4	-	-	46
Religious community	385	3	-	-	3	19	39	37	86	108	40	11	39
Hostel (including youth hostels, hostels for the homeless and persons sleeping rough)	671	46	-	40	32	311	136	22	41	23	5	-	15
Civilian ship, boat or barge	8	-	-	-	-	4	4	-	-	-	-	-	-
Other	481	3	-	3	3	30	18	19	101	187	73	33	11

Table S301: Sex and Type of Communal Establishment by Type of Resident and Age (continued)

	All persons	Residents (non-staff)											Residents (staff and their families)
		0 to 14	15	16 to 17	18 to 19	20 to 44	45 to 59	60 to 64	65 to 74	75 to 84	85 to 89	90 and over	
Males	**12165**	**205**	**41**	**171**	**1287**	**5534**	**970**	**285**	**760**	**1280**	**563**	**326**	**743**
Medical and care establishments	**5196**	**84**	**16**	**33**	**32**	**758**	**689**	**218**	**660**	**1199**	**547**	**321**	**639**
'NHS/HSSB' managed	**1540**	**47**	**12**	**26**	**16**	**389**	**271**	**70**	**178**	**276**	**93**	**52**	**110**
Psychiatric hospital/home	664	9	-	10	6	206	174	41	86	87	18	12	15
General or other hospital	316	12	-	-	5	150	61	11	16	17	7	5	32
Children's home	55	22	12	13	-	-	-	-	-	-	-	-	8
Nursing home	36	-	-	-	-	3	9	4	8	9	3	-	-
Residential care home	463	4	-	3	5	30	27	14	68	163	62	35	52
Other medical and care home	6	-	-	-	-	-	-	-	-	-	3	-	3
Non 'NHS/HSSB' managed	**3656**	**37**	**4**	**7**	**16**	**369**	**418**	**148**	**482**	**923**	**454**	**269**	**529**
Psychiatric hospital/home	173	18	-	4	5	35	27	7	22	15	11	4	25
General or other hospital	6	-	-	-	-	-	-	-	-	3	3	-	-
Children's home	19	12	4	3	-	-	-	-	-	-	-	-	-
Nursing home	2363	-	-	-	3	119	180	82	341	704	324	198	412
Residential care home	1051	7	-	-	5	212	208	56	113	185	109	67	89
Other medical and care home	44	-	-	-	3	3	3	3	6	16	7	-	3
Other establishments	**6969**	**121**	**25**	**138**	**1255**	**4776**	**281**	**67**	**100**	**81**	**16**	**5**	**104**
Defence establishments (including ships)	3860	-	-	60	453	3327	20	-	-	-	-	-	-
Prison Service establishments	576	-	-	-	12	454	93	14	-	-	-	-	3
Probation/Bail hostel	38	-	-	-	-	16	10	4	8	-	-	-	-
Education establishment (including halls of residence)	1743	96	25	57	768	744	9	4	3	-	-	-	37
Hotel, boarding house, guest house	80	3	-	-	-	20	18	4	4	4	-	-	27
Religious community	89	-	-	-	-	9	11	8	19	19	3	-	20
Hostel (including youth hostels, hostels for the homeless and persons sleeping rough)	418	19	-	18	19	186	107	22	28	9	-	-	10
Civilian ship, boat or barge	8	-	-	-	-	4	4	-	-	-	-	-	-
Other	157	3	-	3	3	16	9	11	38	49	13	5	7

Table S301: Sex and Type of Communal Establishment by Type of Resident and Age (continued)

	All persons	Residents (non-staff)											Residents (staff and their families)
		0 to 14	15	16 to 17	18 to 19	20 to 44	45 to 59	60 to 64	65 to 74	75 to 84	85 to 89	90 and over	
Females	**14273**	**151**	**49**	**122**	**1415**	**2130**	**592**	**225**	**958**	**3073**	**2167**	**1934**	**1457**
Medical and care establishments	**10402**	**59**	**29**	**26**	**57**	**551**	**502**	**185**	**811**	**2832**	**2065**	**1895**	**1390**
'NHS/HSSB' managed	**1991**	**31**	**23**	**15**	**43**	**229**	**169**	**48**	**177**	**488**	**315**	**274**	**179**
Psychiatric hospital/home	450	-	3	3	3	86	99	22	62	86	27	35	24
General or other hospital	300	3	-	-	40	117	33	5	16	29	8	21	28
Children's home	68	25	20	12	-	-	-	-	-	-	-	-	11
Nursing home	63	-	-	-	-	-	3	-	-	15	19	19	-
Residential care home	1076	3	-	-	-	26	34	21	89	349	258	195	101
Other medical and care home	34	-	-	-	-	-	-	-	3	9	3	4	15
Non 'NHS/HSSB' managed	**8411**	**28**	**6**	**11**	**14**	**322**	**333**	**137**	**634**	**2344**	**1750**	**1621**	**1211**
Psychiatric hospital/home	176	4	-	4	7	24	11	9	16	38	17	8	38
General or other hospital	6	-	-	-	-	-	-	-	3	-	3	-	-
Children's home	21	11	6	4	-	-	-	-	-	-	-	-	-
Nursing home	5788	3	-	-	3	103	141	64	433	1631	1240	1220	950
Residential care home	2296	7	-	3	4	190	176	64	164	621	471	376	220
Other medical and care home	124	3	-	-	-	5	5	-	18	54	19	17	3
Other establishments	**3871**	**92**	**20**	**96**	**1358**	**1579**	**90**	**40**	**147**	**241**	**102**	**39**	**67**
Defence establishments (including ships)	496	-	-	3	38	452	3	-	-	-	-	-	-
Prison Service establishments	11	-	-	-	-	8	3	-	-	-	-	-	-
Probation/Bail hostel	-	-	-	-	-	-	-	-	-	-	-	-	-
Education establishment (including halls of residence)	2446	62	20	71	1304	960	9	-	-	-	-	-	20
Hotel, boarding house, guest house	45	-	-	-	-	10	9	3	4	-	-	-	19
Religious community	296	3	-	-	3	10	28	29	67	89	37	11	19
Hostel (including youth hostels, hostels for the homeless and persons sleeping rough)	253	27	-	22	13	125	29	-	13	14	5	-	5
Civilian ship, boat or barge	-	-	-	-	-	-	-	-	-	-	-	-	-
Other	324	-	-	-	-	14	9	8	63	138	60	28	4

Note:
1 'NHS/HSSB' refers to the Health and Personal Social Services in Northern Ireland.

Table S302: Type of Communal Establishment by Type of Resident and Whether or Not Resident One Year Ago

Table population: All persons who are resident in communal establishments

	All persons resident in communal establishments	All persons		Residents (non-staff)		Residents (staff and their families)	
		Lived at same communal establishment one year ago	Lived elsewhere one year ago	Lived at same communal establishment one year ago	Lived elsewhere one year ago	Lived at same communal establishment one year ago	Lived elsewhere one year ago
All persons	**26451**	**16728**	**9723**	**15121**	**9136**	**1607**	**587**
Medical and care establishments	**15596**	**11827**	**3769**	**10349**	**3223**	**1478**	**546**
'NHS/HSSB' managed	**3533**	**2715**	**818**	**2517**	**729**	**198**	**89**
Psychiatric hospital/home	1113	956	157	935	139	21	18
General or other hospital	616	388	228	363	193	25	35
Children's home	123	57	66	47	57	10	9
Nursing home	102	79	23	79	23	-	-
Residential care home	1540	1205	335	1075	312	130	23
Other medical and care home	39	30	9	18	5	12	4
Non 'NHS/HSSB' managed	**12063**	**9112**	**2951**	**7832**	**2494**	**1280**	**457**
Psychiatric hospital/home	352	322	30	269	20	53	10
General or other hospital	13	6	7	6	7	-	-
Children's home	38	22	16	22	16	-	-
Nursing home	8149	5902	2247	4925	1862	977	385
Residential care home	3347	2718	629	2468	570	250	59
Other medical and care home	164	142	22	142	19	-	3
Other establishments	**10855**	**4901**	**5954**	**4772**	**5913**	**129**	**41**
Defence establishments (including ships)	4354	2524	1830	2524	1830	-	-
Prison Service establishments	590	342	248	339	248	3	-
Probation/Bail hostel	41	14	27	14	27	-	-
Education establishments (including halls of residence)	4192	909	3283	875	3260	34	23
Hotel, boarding house, guest house	132	106	26	67	19	39	7
Religious community	385	351	34	320	26	31	8
Hostel (including youth hostels, hostels for the homeless and persons sleeping rough)	675	235	440	221	440	14	-
Civilian ship, boat or barge	8	8	-	8	-	-	-
Other	**478**	**412**	**66**	**404**	**63**	**8**	**3**

Notes:

1 'NHS/HSSB' refers to the Health and Personal Social Services in Northern Ireland.

2 Lived elsewhere one year ago includes persons aged 0 resident in a communal establishment.

Table S303: Sex and Age by Ethnic Group

Table population: All persons

	All persons	White	Irish Traveller	Mixed	Indian	Pakistani	Bangladeshi	Other Asian	Black Caribbean	Black African	Other Black	Chinese	Other ethnic group
All persons	**1685260**	**1670988**	**1710**	**3320**	**1569**	**668**	**251**	**190**	**256**	**491**	**381**	**4145**	**1291**
0 to 4	115238	113752	160	636	113	73	42	8	10	43	31	257	113
5 to 9	123050	121646	155	518	104	82	26	10	11	44	25	341	88
10 to 14	132664	131269	193	501	83	64	24	13	19	46	19	376	57
15	27101	26844	43	80	24	8	3	-	3	4	3	82	7
16 to 17	53455	52951	71	163	43	19	-	7	8	10	6	159	18
18 to 19	48639	48234	48	122	19	12	7	3	9	14	11	142	18
20 to 24	109385	108162	160	220	79	38	26	16	19	31	65	441	128
25 to 34	242221	239535	241	416	339	133	64	59	62	104	99	825	344
35 to 44	246974	244720	193	315	245	111	26	47	61	92	45	819	300
45 to 59	289622	288036	222	182	317	67	17	19	27	66	32	481	156
60 to 64	73587	73231	58	53	95	28	6	5	6	13	7	67	18
65 to 74	123192	122739	84	63	80	22	10	-	16	10	31	114	23
75 to 84	76829	76620	63	42	21	8	-	3	5	14	3	32	18
85 and over	23303	23249	19	9	7	3	-	-	-	-	4	9	3
Males	**821447**	**814015**	**894**	**1674**	**839**	**378**	**141**	**80**	**137**	**277**	**221**	**2193**	**598**
0 to 4	59213	58466	80	311	62	38	21	4	6	26	17	119	63
5 to 9	63147	62387	82	267	62	47	15	6	4	29	13	186	49
10 to 14	68014	67306	89	262	40	34	14	8	11	20	12	188	30
15	13886	13743	22	45	11	5	3	-	-	4	3	46	4
16 to 17	27159	26880	39	87	15	15	-	4	5	10	3	93	8
18 to 19	24550	24348	29	56	10	7	4	-	6	9	3	70	8
20 to 24	54913	54255	88	107	44	22	8	6	8	13	47	259	56
25 to 34	119115	117796	126	206	171	69	38	14	40	51	58	413	133
35 to 44	120862	119656	107	159	126	65	20	19	38	62	27	448	135
45 to 59	143755	142893	121	106	183	44	10	11	11	35	16	243	82
60 to 64	35402	35194	34	24	55	18	3	5	3	8	7	42	9
65 to 74	55475	55231	43	30	47	11	5	-	5	6	12	72	13
75 to 84	29654	29575	30	8	9	3	-	3	-	4	3	11	8
85 and over	6302	6285	4	6	4	-	-	-	-	-	-	3	-

Table S303: Sex and Age by Ethnic Group (continued)

	All persons	White	Irish Traveller	Mixed	Indian	Pakistani	Bangladeshi	Other Asian	Black Caribbean	Black African	Other Black	Chinese	Other ethnic group
Females	**863813**	**856973**	**816**	**1646**	**730**	**290**	**110**	**110**	**119**	**214**	**160**	**1952**	**693**
0 to 4	56025	55286	80	325	51	35	21	4	4	17	14	138	50
5 to 9	59903	59259	73	251	42	35	11	4	7	15	12	155	39
10 to 14	64650	63963	104	239	43	30	10	5	8	26	7	188	27
15	13215	13101	21	35	13	3	-	-	3	-	-	36	3
16 to 17	26296	26071	32	76	28	4	-	3	3	-	3	66	10
18 to 19	24089	23886	19	66	9	5	3	3	3	5	8	72	10
20 to 24	54472	53907	72	113	35	16	18	10	11	18	18	182	72
25 to 34	123106	121739	115	210	168	64	26	45	22	53	41	412	211
35 to 44	126112	125064	86	156	119	46	6	28	23	30	18	371	165
45 to 59	145867	145143	101	76	134	23	7	8	16	31	16	238	74
60 to 64	38185	38037	24	29	40	10	3	-	3	5	-	25	9
65 to 74	67717	67508	41	33	33	11	5	-	11	4	19	42	10
75 to 84	47175	47045	33	34	12	5	-	-	5	10	-	21	10
85 and over	17001	16964	15	3	3	3	-	-	-	-	4	6	3

Table S304: Sex and Type of Communal Establishment by Ethnic Group

Table population: All persons resident in communal establishments

	All persons	White	Irish Traveller	Mixed	Indian	Pakistani	Bangladeshi	Other Asian	Black Caribbean	Black African	Other Black	Chinese	Other ethnic group
All persons	26426	25643	35	87	51	21	-	14	17	24	52	366	116
Medical and care establishments	15584	15409	3	21	32	11	-	11	-	3	-	58	36
'NHS/HSSB' managed	3523	3393	-	8	32	5	-	3	-	3	-	52	27
Psychiatric hospital/home	1109	1106	-	-	-	-	-	-	-	-	-	-	3
General or other hospital	614	490	-	8	32	5	-	3	-	3	-	49	24
Children's home	121	121	-	-	-	-	-	-	-	-	-	-	-
Nursing home	102	102	-	-	-	-	-	-	-	-	-	-	-
Residential care home	1538	1535	-	-	-	-	-	-	-	-	-	3	-
Other medical and care home	39	39	-	-	-	-	-	-	-	-	-	-	-
Non 'NHS/HSSB' managed	12061	12016	3	13	-	6	-	8	-	-	-	6	9
Psychiatric hospital/home	353	342	-	6	-	-	-	5	-	-	-	-	-
General or other hospital	14	14	-	-	-	-	-	-	-	-	-	-	-
Children's home	38	38	-	-	-	-	-	-	-	-	-	-	-
Nursing home	8147	8131	3	4	-	3	-	3	-	-	-	3	-
Residential care home	3346	3328	-	3	-	3	-	-	-	-	-	3	9
Other medical and care home	163	163	-	-	-	-	-	-	-	-	-	-	-
Other establishments	10842	10234	32	66	19	10	-	3	17	21	52	308	80
Defence establishments (including ships)	4349	4238	3	33	3	-	-	-	10	4	46	-	12
Prison Service establishments	589	572	10	3	-	-	-	-	-	-	-	4	-
Probation/Bail hostel	41	41	-	-	-	-	-	-	-	-	-	-	-
Education establishment (including halls of residence)	4190	3737	10	30	13	7	-	3	4	17	3	301	65
Hotel, boarding house, guest house	131	131	-	-	-	-	-	-	-	-	-	-	-
Religious community	386	377	-	-	-	3	-	-	-	-	3	-	3
Hostel (including youth hostels, hostels for the homeless and persons sleeping rough)	670	655	9	-	3	-	-	-	3	-	-	-	-
Civilian ship, boat or barge	7	7	-	-	-	-	-	-	-	-	-	-	-
Other	479	476	-	-	-	-	-	-	-	-	-	3	-

Table S304: Sex and Type of Communal Establishment by Ethnic Group (continued)

	All persons	White	Irish Traveller	Mixed	Indian	Pakistani	Bangladeshi	Other Asian	Black Caribbean	Black African	Other Black	Chinese	Other ethnic group
Males	12153	11689	23	59	35	15	-	8	14	15	46	192	57
Medical and care establishments	5191	5098	-	8	22	8	-	8	-	3	-	33	11
'NHS/HSSB' managed	1539	1460	-	5	22	5	-	-	-	3	-	33	11
Psychiatric hospital/home	661	658	-	-	-	-	-	-	-	-	-	-	3
General or other hospital	315	242	-	5	22	5	-	-	-	3	-	30	8
Children's home	55	55	-	-	-	-	-	-	-	-	-	-	-
Nursing home	38	38	-	-	-	-	-	-	-	-	-	-	-
Residential care home	463	460	-	-	-	-	-	-	-	-	-	3	-
Other medical and care home	7	7	-	-	-	-	-	-	-	-	-	-	-
Non 'NHS/HSSB' managed	3652	3638	-	3	-	3	-	8	-	-	-	-	-
Psychiatric hospital/home	177	169	-	3	-	-	-	5	-	-	-	-	-
General or other hospital	7	7	-	-	-	-	-	-	-	-	-	-	-
Children's home	17	17	-	-	-	-	-	-	-	-	-	-	-
Nursing home	2359	2356	-	-	-	-	-	3	-	-	-	-	-
Residential care home	1051	1048	-	-	-	3	-	-	-	-	-	-	-
Other medical and care home	41	41	-	-	-	-	-	-	-	-	-	-	-
Other establishments	6962	6591	23	51	13	7	-	-	14	12	46	159	46
Defence establishments (including ships)	3856	3754	3	27	3	-	-	-	7	4	46	-	12
Prison Service establishments	578	561	10	3	-	-	-	-	-	-	-	4	-
Probation/Bail hostel	41	41	-	-	-	-	-	-	-	-	-	-	-
Education establishment (including halls of residence)	1741	1498	7	21	10	4	-	-	4	8	-	155	34
Hotel, boarding house, guest house	80	80	-	-	-	-	-	-	-	-	-	-	-
Religious community	91	88	-	-	-	3	-	-	-	-	-	-	-
Hostel (including youth hostels, hostels for the homeless and persons sleeping rough)	416	410	3	-	-	-	-	-	3	-	-	-	-
Civilian ship, boat or barge	7	7	-	-	-	-	-	-	-	-	-	-	-
Other	152	152	-	-	-	-	-	-	-	-	-	-	-

	All persons	White	Irish Traveller	Mixed	Indian	Pakistani	Bangladeshi	Other Asian	Black Caribbean	Black African	Other Black	Chinese	Other ethnic group
Females	**14273**	**13954**	**12**	**28**	**16**	**6**	**-**	**6**	**3**	**9**	**6**	**174**	**59**
Medical and care establishments	**10393**	**10311**	**3**	**13**	**10**	**3**	**-**	**3**	**-**	**-**	**-**	**25**	**25**
'NHS/HSSB' managed	**1984**	**1933**	**-**	**3**	**10**	**-**	**-**	**3**	**-**	**-**	**-**	**19**	**16**
Psychiatric hospital/home	448	448	-	-	-	-	-	-	-	-	-	-	-
General or other hospital	299	248	-	3	10	-	-	3	-	-	-	19	16
Children's home	66	66	-	-	-	-	-	-	-	-	-	-	-
Nursing home	64	64	-	-	-	-	-	-	-	-	-	-	-
Residential care home	1075	1075	-	-	-	-	-	-	-	-	-	-	-
Other medical and care home	32	32	-	-	-	-	-	-	-	-	-	-	-
Non 'NHS/HSSB' managed	**8409**	**8378**	**3**	**10**	**-**	**3**	**-**	**-**	**-**	**-**	**-**	**6**	**9**
Psychiatric hospital/home	176	173	-	3	-	-	-	-	-	-	-	-	-
General or other hospital	7	7	-	-	-	-	-	-	-	-	-	-	-
Children's home	21	21	-	-	-	-	-	-	-	-	-	-	-
Nursing home	5788	5775	3	4	-	3	-	-	-	-	-	3	-
Residential care home	2295	2280	-	3	-	-	-	-	-	-	-	3	9
Other medical and care home	122	122	-	-	-	-	-	-	-	-	-	-	-
Other establishments	**3880**	**3643**	**9**	**15**	**6**	**3**	**-**	**3**	**3**	**9**	**6**	**149**	**34**
Defence establishments (including ships)	493	484	-	6	-	-	-	-	3	-	-	-	-
Prison Service establishments	11	11	-	-	-	-	-	-	-	-	-	-	-
Probation/Bail hostel	-		-	-	-	-	-	-	-	-	-	-	-
Education establishment (including halls of residence)	2449	2239	3	9	3	3	-	3	-	9	3	146	31
Hotel, boarding house, guest house	51	51	-	-	-	-	-	-	-	-	-	-	-
Religious community	295	289	-	-	-	-	-	-	-	-	3	-	3
Hostel (including youth hostels, hostels for the homeless and persons sleeping rough)	254	245	6	-	3	-	-	-	-	-	-	-	-
Civilian ship, boat or barge	-		-	-	-	-	-	-	-	-	-	-	-
Other	327	324	-	-	-	-	-	-	-	-	-	3	-

Note:
1 'NHS/HSSB' refers to the Health and Personal Social Services in Northern Ireland.

Table S305: Age by Sex and Community Background (Religion or Religion Brought Up In)

Table population: All persons

	All persons	Males					Females				
		Total	Catholic	Protestant and Other Christian (including Christian related)	Other religions and philosophies	None	Total	Catholic	Protestant and Other Christian (including Christian related)	Other religions and philosophies	None
All persons	1685267	821449	357327	435152	3718	25252	863818	380085	460225	2851	20657
0 to 4	115238	59213	28844	25639	235	4495	56025	27702	24035	221	4067
0	21683	11116	5327	4706	44	1039	10567	5199	4375	46	947
1	22363	11550	5685	4879	46	940	10813	5256	4728	35	794
2	23264	11887	5731	5203	56	897	11377	5765	4722	40	850
3	23584	12197	6027	5293	41	836	11387	5599	4967	55	766
4	24344	12463	6074	5558	48	783	11881	5883	5243	45	710
5 to 9	123050	63147	31030	28379	238	3500	59903	29822	26891	188	3002
5	23883	12421	6154	5489	45	733	11462	5675	5124	43	620
6	24064	12380	6076	5528	52	724	11684	5781	5246	35	622
7	24400	12370	6070	5595	47	658	12030	6022	5380	44	584
8	24907	12676	6253	5682	42	699	12231	6069	5524	33	605
9	25796	13300	6477	6085	52	686	12496	6275	5617	33	571
10 to 14	132664	68014	34121	30863	193	2837	64650	32754	29269	188	2439
10	26189	13436	6688	6044	53	651	12753	6436	5759	31	527
11	25963	13271	6519	6118	36	598	12692	6383	5786	38	485
12	26403	13561	6854	6137	50	520	12842	6498	5804	39	501
13	26997	13789	6947	6247	22	573	13208	6692	5979	41	496
14	27112	13957	7113	6317	32	495	13155	6745	5941	39	430
15 to 19	129201	65598	33733	29528	212	2125	63603	32725	28818	181	1879
15	27104	13887	7194	6176	46	471	13217	6702	6008	32	475
16	27182	13857	7123	6225	38	471	13325	6795	6096	32	402
17	26276	13303	6855	6005	53	390	12973	6713	5832	44	384
18	25392	12998	6668	5842	38	450	12394	6429	5585	36	344
19	23247	11553	5893	5280	37	343	11694	6086	5297	37	274

© Crown copyright 2003

	All persons	Males					Females				
		Total	Catholic	Protestant and Other Christian (including Christian related)	Other religions and philosophies	None	Total	Catholic	Protestant and Other Christian (including Christian related)	Other religions and philosophies	None
20 to 24	**109385**	**54913**	**26721**	**26114**	**287**	**1791**	**54472**	**27389**	**25294**	**252**	**1537**
20	22791	11648	5684	5549	46	369	11143	5672	5141	35	295
21	22449	11478	5664	5412	49	353	10971	5641	4971	53	306
22	21717	10785	5218	5167	47	353	10932	5485	5124	56	267
23	21166	10442	5053	4966	54	369	10724	5347	4969	57	351
24	21262	10560	5102	5020	91	347	10702	5244	5089	51	318
25 to 29	114704	56628	25274	29094	390	1870	58076	27455	28738	293	1590
30 to 34	127517	62487	27033	33037	441	1976	65030	30020	33108	301	1601
35 to 39	129639	63430	27556	33751	371	1752	66209	30241	34386	265	1317
40 to 44	117335	57432	24481	31396	336	1219	59903	26810	31968	221	904
45 to 49	102464	51686	21226	29048	287	1125	50778	22061	27880	191	646
50 to 54	98426	48484	18932	28541	207	804	49942	20106	29151	139	546
55 to 59	88732	43585	15922	26908	175	580	45147	16563	28105	117	362
60 to 64	73587	35401	12630	22227	132	412	38186	13712	24148	99	227
65 to 69	65341	30406	10710	19305	85	306	34935	12239	22459	58	179
70 to 74	57852	25069	8350	16426	59	234	32783	10971	21612	51	149
75 to 79	46542	18562	5853	12560	32	117	27980	8944	18901	44	91
80 to 84	30289	11090	3254	7740	20	76	19199	5828	13285	22	64
85 to 89	16116	4707	1270	3400	15	22	11409	3299	8068	11	31
90 and over	7185	1597	387	1196	3	11	5588	1444	4109	9	26

Note:

1   The term 'Catholic' includes those respondents who gave their religion as Catholic or Roman Catholic.

S305

Table S305A: Age by Sex and Religion

Table population: All persons

	All persons	Males								Females							
		Total	Catholic	Presbyterian Church in Ireland	Church of Ireland	Methodist Church in Ireland	Other Christian (including Christian related)	Other religions and philosophies	No religion or religion not stated	Total	Catholic	Presbyterian Church in Ireland	Church of Ireland	Methodist Church in Ireland	Other Christian (including Christian related)	Other religions and philosophies	No religion or religion not stated
All persons	1685267	821449	326508	167478	122176	27130	48752	2815	126590	863818	351954	181264	135612	32043	53469	2213	107263
0 to 4	115238	59213	25580	9025	7090	1510	2829	175	13004	56025	24484	8461	6677	1441	2692	166	12104
0	21683	11116	4632	1527	1184	283	488	31	2971	10567	4474	1446	1244	232	441	33	2697
1	22363	11550	4976	1655	1367	262	508	29	2753	10813	4577	1584	1236	268	513	26	2609
2	23264	11887	5056	1907	1428	301	544	45	2606	11377	5085	1717	1302	281	500	31	2461
3	23584	12197	5381	1851	1480	329	627	33	2496	11387	4993	1805	1406	323	586	40	2234
4	24344	12463	5535	2085	1631	335	662	37	2178	11881	5355	1909	1489	337	652	36	2103
5 to 9	123050	63147	28745	10867	8455	1893	3417	189	9581	59903	27633	10374	7814	1875	3419	155	8633
5	23883	12421	5677	2050	1635	367	640	36	2016	11462	5224	1967	1506	305	662	34	1764
6	24064	12380	5601	2154	1627	348	696	41	1913	11684	5334	2004	1510	364	655	30	1787
7	24400	12370	5596	2134	1694	359	672	38	1877	12030	5609	2075	1568	427	667	37	1647
8	24907	12676	5845	2142	1716	412	663	30	1868	12231	5638	2151	1601	363	698	27	1753
9	25796	13300	6026	2387	1783	407	746	44	1907	12496	5828	2177	1629	416	737	27	1682
0 to 14	132664	68014	32072	12045	9364	2073	3710	163	8587	64650	30831	11538	8568	2123	3655	145	7790
10	26189	13436	6272	2332	1810	409	770	41	1802	12753	6062	2243	1693	427	710	23	1595
11	25963	13271	6126	2343	1858	422	770	31	1721	12692	5991	2274	1750	409	709	29	1530
12	26403	13561	6426	2381	1888	418	750	45	1653	12842	6110	2281	1706	430	726	32	1557
13	26997	13789	6551	2494	1892	397	725	19	1711	13208	6317	2399	1707	431	752	28	1574
14	27112	13957	6697	2495	1916	427	695	27	1700	13155	6351	2341	1712	426	758	33	1534
15 to 19	129201	65598	31376	11421	8442	1892	3364	167	8936	63603	30600	11141	8307	1957	3569	134	7895
15	27104	13887	6737	2451	1763	426	718	38	1754	13217	6317	2286	1790	450	730	25	1619
16	27182	13857	6672	2448	1875	422	689	28	1723	13325	6359	2425	1736	433	740	24	1608
17	26276	13303	6391	2352	1723	358	667	45	1767	12973	6320	2202	1757	416	735	31	1512
18	25392	12998	6186	2161	1712	377	654	26	1882	12394	6005	2226	1530	356	672	30	1575
19	23247	11553	5390	2009	1369	309	636	30	1810	11694	5599	2002	1494	302	692	24	1581

S 3 0 5 A

	All persons	Males								Females							
		Total	Catholic	Presbyterian Church in Ireland	Church of Ireland	Methodist Church in Ireland	Other Christian (including Christian related)	Other religions and philosophies	No religion or religion not stated	Total	Catholic	Presbyterian Church in Ireland	Church of Ireland	Methodist Church in Ireland	Other Christian (including Christian related)	Other religions and philosophies	No religion or religion not stated
20 to 24	103385	54913	24120	9560	6548	1460	3426	209	9590	54472	25132	9379	6986	1466	3325	194	7990
20	22791	11648	5080	2046	1410	299	708	36	2069	11143	5250	1968	1397	308	674	25	1521
21	22449	11478	5107	2031	1366	297	678	32	1967	10971	5132	1854	1299	320	655	41	1670
22	21717	10785	4760	1849	1310	288	723	34	1821	10932	5018	1887	1477	262	638	45	1605
23	21166	10442	4559	1835	1205	303	687	46	1807	10724	4903	1772	1443	271	678	41	1616
24	21262	10560	4614	1799	1257	273	630	61	1926	10702	4829	1898	1370	305	680	42	1578
25 to 29	114704	56628	22745	10529	7362	1564	3839	298	10291	58076	25208	10626	8153	1746	3637	233	8473
30 to 34	127517	62487	24252	12153	8691	1818	3902	342	11329	65030	27532	12338	9517	2085	4121	230	9207
35 to 39	129639	63430	24852	12542	8887	1971	3949	267	10962	66209	27818	13099	9919	2260	4095	203	8815
40 to 44	117335	57432	22069	11983	8523	1825	3347	255	9430	59903	24668	12324	9316	2224	3660	172	7539
45 to 49	102464	51686	19152	10864	7906	1729	3092	199	8744	50778	20421	10764	8131	1886	3227	140	6209
50 to 54	98426	48484	17203	10907	8105	1761	3008	157	7343	49942	18719	11456	8692	2076	3380	108	5511
55 to 59	88732	43585	14636	10676	7850	1784	2714	134	5791	45147	15617	11468	8575	2055	3253	93	4086
60 to 64	73587	35401	11763	8982	6676	1512	2330	99	4039	38186	12948	10080	7492	1748	2671	79	3168
65 to 69	65341	30406	10021	8134	5903	1336	1808	67	3137	34935	11590	9354	7189	1762	2323	50	2667
70 to 74	57852	25069	7828	6899	5076	1150	1556	39	2521	32783	10397	9272	6866	1657	2122	41	2428
75 to 79	46542	18562	5511	5506	3782	908	1162	25	1668	27980	8475	8270	5940	1535	1762	34	1964
80 to 84	30289	11090	3063	3366	2246	581	782	15	1037	19199	5491	5941	3879	1142	1321	17	1408
85 to 89	16116	4707	1170	1493	955	264	379	12	434	11409	3071	3560	2403	668	832	11	864
90 and over	7185	1597	350	526	315	99	138	3	166	5588	1319	1819	1188	337	405	8	512

Note:
1   The term 'Catholic' includes those respondents who gave their religion as Catholic or Roman Catholic.

Table S306: Age by Community Background (Religion or Religion Brought Up In)

Table population: All persons

	All persons	Catholic	Protestant and Other Christian (including Christian related)	Other religions and philosophies	None
All persons	**1685264**	**737412**	**895377**	**6566**	**45909**
0 to 4	**115238**	**56546**	**49674**	**456**	**8562**
0	21683	10526	9081	90	1986
1	22363	10941	9607	81	1734
2	23264	11496	9925	96	1747
3	23584	11626	10260	96	1602
4	24344	11957	10801	93	1493
5 to 9	**123050**	**60852**	**55270**	**426**	**6502**
5	23883	11829	10613	88	1353
6	24064	11857	10774	87	1346
7	24400	12092	10975	91	1242
8	24907	12322	11206	75	1304
9	25796	12752	11702	85	1257
10 to 14	**132664**	**66875**	**60132**	**381**	**5276**
10	26189	13124	11803	84	1178
11	25963	12902	11904	74	1083
12	26403	13352	11941	89	1021
13	26997	13639	12226	63	1069
14	27112	13858	12258	71	925
15 to 19	**129201**	**66458**	**58346**	**393**	**4004**
15	27104	13896	12184	78	946
16	27182	13918	12321	70	873
17	26276	13568	11837	97	774
18	25392	13097	11427	74	794
19	23247	11979	10577	74	617
20 to 24	**109385**	**54110**	**51408**	**539**	**3328**
20	22791	11356	10690	81	664
21	22449	11305	10383	102	659
22	21717	10703	10291	103	620
23	21166	10400	9935	111	720
24	21262	10346	10109	142	665

	All persons	Catholic	Protestant and Other Christian (including Christian related)	Other religions and philosophies	None
25 to 29	**114704**	**52729**	**57832**	**683**	**3460**
25	21621	10156	10676	128	661
26	21684	10173	10682	129	700
27	22933	10350	11749	139	695
28	24021	11026	12142	134	719
29	24445	11024	12583	153	685
30 to 34	**127517**	**57053**	**66145**	**742**	**3577**
30	25275	11205	13141	168	761
31	24965	11332	12801	144	688
32	25532	11392	13260	158	722
33	25781	11532	13433	121	695
34	25964	11592	13510	151	711
35 to 39	**129639**	**57797**	**68137**	**636**	**3069**
35	26120	11713	13604	108	695
36	26845	11822	14253	129	641
37	26198	11726	13739	115	618
38	25578	11394	13446	145	593
39	24898	11142	13095	139	522
40 to 44	**117335**	**51291**	**63364**	**557**	**2123**
40	24847	10942	13284	115	506
41	24074	10623	12909	99	443
42	23039	9993	12547	104	395
43	23217	10096	12600	126	395
44	22158	9637	12024	113	384
45 to 49	**102464**	**43287**	**56928**	**478**	**1771**
45	21720	9357	11885	96	382
46	20582	8826	11301	87	368
47	20513	8682	11339	116	376
48	20298	8391	11492	104	311
49	19351	8031	10911	75	334

Table S306: Age by Community Background (Religion or Religion Brought Up In) (continued)

	All persons	Catholic	Protestant and Other Christian (including Christian related)	Other religions and philosophies	None
50 to 54	**98426**	**39038**	**57692**	**346**	**1350**
50	19474	8099	11036	82	257
51	19697	7947	11434	51	265
52	19549	7850	11352	78	269
53	19653	7563	11742	61	287
54	20053	7579	12128	74	272
55 to 59	**88732**	**32485**	**55013**	**292**	**942**
55	18122	6865	10978	66	213
56	18161	6856	11047	58	200
57	18427	6678	11508	69	172
58	18015	6401	11385	45	184
59	16007	5685	10095	54	173
60 to 64	**73587**	**26342**	**46375**	**231**	**639**
60	14781	5413	9180	47	141
61	14821	5325	9308	47	141
62	14999	5320	9496	56	127
63	14386	5153	9067	41	125
64	14600	5131	9324	40	105
65 to 69	**65341**	**22949**	**41764**	**143**	**485**
65	13876	4902	8844	29	101
66	13199	4663	8390	29	117
67	12929	4637	8178	23	91
68	12790	4451	8212	32	95
69	12547	4296	8140	30	81
70 to 74	**57852**	**19321**	**38038**	**110**	**383**
70	12477	4259	8099	26	93
71	11999	4034	7862	24	79
72	11415	3860	7447	16	92
73	10938	3610	7250	23	55
74	11023	3558	7380	21	64

Table S306: Age by Community Background (Religion or Religion Brought Up In) (continued)

	All persons	Catholic	Protestant and Other Christian (including Christian related)	Other religions and philosophies	None
75 to 79	**46542**	**14797**	**31461**	**76**	**208**
75	10486	3397	7028	18	43
76	9761	3154	6546	23	38
77	9245	2993	6201	10	41
78	8723	2727	5941	14	41
79	8327	2526	5745	11	45
80 to 84	**30289**	**9082**	**21025**	**42**	**140**
80	7893	2359	5489	10	35
81	7298	2266	4989	7	36
82	5821	1770	4027	6	18
83	4820	1378	3407	9	26
84	4457	1309	3113	10	25
85 to 89	**16113**	**4569**	**11468**	**23**	**53**
85	4086	1166	2890	13	17
86	3786	1088	2685	7	6
87	3248	877	2355	3	13
88	2789	786	1991	-	12
89	2204	652	1547	-	5
90 and over	**7185**	**1831**	**5305**	**12**	**37**

Note:
1   The term 'Catholic' includes those respondents who gave their religion as Catholic or Roman Catholic.

S306

33

Table S306A: Age by Religion

Table population: All persons

	All persons	Catholic	Presbyterian Church in Ireland	Church of Ireland	Methodist Church in Ireland	Other Christian (including Christian related)	Other religions and philosophies	No religion or religion not stated
All persons	**1685265**	**678462**	**348742**	**257788**	**59173**	**102221**	**5026**	**233853**
0 to 4	**115238**	**50064**	**17486**	**13767**	**2951**	**5521**	**341**	**25108**
0	21683	9106	2973	2428	515	929	64	5668
1	22363	9553	3239	2603	530	1021	55	5362
2	23264	10141	3624	2730	582	1044	76	5067
3	23584	10374	3656	2886	652	1213	73	4730
4	24344	10890	3994	3120	672	1314	73	4281
5 to 9	**123050**	**56378**	**21241**	**16269**	**3768**	**6836**	**344**	**18214**
5	23883	10901	4017	3141	672	1302	70	3780
6	24064	10935	4158	3137	712	1351	71	3700
7	24400	11205	4209	3262	786	1339	75	3524
8	24907	11483	4293	3317	775	1361	57	3621
9	25796	11854	4564	3412	823	1483	71	3589
10 to 14	**132664**	**62903**	**23583**	**17932**	**4196**	**7365**	**308**	**16377**
10	26189	12334	4575	3503	836	1480	64	3397
11	25963	12117	4617	3608	831	1479	60	3251
12	26403	12536	4662	3594	848	1476	77	3210
13	26997	12868	4893	3599	828	1477	47	3285
14	27112	13048	4836	3628	853	1453	60	3234
15 to 19	**129201**	**61976**	**22562**	**16749**	**3849**	**6933**	**301**	**16831**
15	27104	13054	4737	3553	876	1448	63	3373
16	27182	13031	4873	3611	855	1429	52	3331
17	26276	12711	4554	3480	774	1402	76	3279
18	25392	12191	4387	3242	733	1326	56	3457
19	23247	10989	4011	2863	611	1328	54	3391

Table S306A: Age by Religion (continued)

	All persons	Catholic	Presbyterian Church in Ireland	Church of Ireland	Methodist Church in Ireland	Other Christian (including Christian related)	Other religions and philosophies	No religion or religion not stated
20 to 24	**109385**	**49252**	**18939**	**13534**	**2926**	**6751**	**403**	**17580**
20	22791	10330	4014	2807	607	1382	61	3590
21	22449	10239	3885	2665	617	1333	73	3637
22	21717	9778	3736	2787	550	1361	79	3426
23	21166	9462	3607	2648	574	1365	87	3423
24	21262	9443	3697	2627	578	1310	103	3504
25 to 29	**114704**	**47953**	**21155**	**15515**	**3310**	**7476**	**531**	**18764**
25	21621	9331	3895	2792	609	1413	98	3483
26	21684	9240	3950	2760	663	1379	95	3597
27	22933	9390	4209	3198	666	1567	108	3795
28	24021	9981	4441	3365	685	1515	111	3923
29	24445	10011	4660	3400	687	1602	119	3966
30 to 34	**127517**	**51784**	**24491**	**18208**	**3903**	**8023**	**572**	**20536**
30	25275	10197	4719	3583	760	1595	125	4296
31	24965	10285	4747	3608	719	1548	114	3944
32	25532	10329	4963	3581	807	1664	122	4066
33	25781	10452	5054	3679	774	1639	99	4084
34	25964	10521	5008	3757	843	1577	112	4146
35 to 39	**129639**	**52670**	**25641**	**18806**	**4231**	**8044**	**470**	**19777**
35	26120	10623	5195	3661	788	1647	76	4130
36	26845	10774	5252	3940	903	1696	94	4186
37	26198	10669	5140	3762	832	1666	83	4046
38	25578	10436	5024	3808	864	1552	114	3780
39	24898	10168	5030	3635	844	1483	103	3635
40 to 44	**117335**	**46737**	**24307**	**17839**	**4049**	**7007**	**427**	**16969**
40	24847	9943	5043	3690	859	1498	90	3724
41	24074	9694	4907	3721	791	1426	76	3459
42	23039	9078	4874	3497	779	1433	80	3298
43	23217	9205	4893	3509	878	1351	94	3287
44	22158	8817	4590	3422	742	1299	87	3201

S306A

Table S306A: Age by Religion (continued)

	All persons	Catholic	Presbyterian Church in Ireland	Church of Ireland	Methodist Church in Ireland	Other Christian (including Christian related)	Other religions and philosophies	No religion or religion not stated
45 to 49	**102464**	**39573**	**21628**	**16037**	**3615**	**6319**	**339**	**14953**
45	21720	8533	4482	3426	735	1287	67	3190
46	20582	8091	4225	3166	681	1288	66	3065
47	20513	7935	4296	3222	775	1239	87	2959
48	20298	7668	4488	3219	715	1255	67	2886
49	19351	7346	4137	3004	709	1250	52	2853
50 to 54	**98426**	**35922**	**22363**	**16797**	**3837**	**6388**	**265**	**12854**
50	19474	7426	4359	3044	749	1173	67	2656
51	19697	7272	4335	3318	775	1290	37	2670
52	19549	7223	4380	3304	754	1261	53	2574
53	19653	6948	4584	3489	759	1273	50	2550
54	20053	7053	4705	3642	800	1391	58	2404
55 to 59	**88732**	**30253**	**22144**	**16425**	**3839**	**5967**	**227**	**9877**
55	18122	6360	4413	3183	737	1218	49	2162
56	18161	6371	4380	3268	831	1181	48	2082
57	18427	6259	4575	3448	796	1256	55	2038
58	18015	5954	4601	3452	796	1221	35	1956
59	16007	5309	4175	3074	679	1091	40	1639
60 to 64	**73587**	**24711**	**19062**	**14168**	**3260**	**5001**	**178**	**7207**
60	14781	5098	3741	2784	672	970	37	1479
61	14821	4950	3853	2821	639	993	43	1522
62	14999	5002	3790	2917	683	1056	43	1508
63	14386	4831	3782	2742	622	1039	29	1341
64	14600	4830	3896	2904	644	943	26	1357
65 to 69	**65341**	**21611**	**17488**	**13092**	**3098**	**4131**	**117**	**5804**
65	13876	4612	3702	2736	659	883	23	1261
66	13199	4378	3509	2619	612	845	25	1211
67	12929	4364	3445	2554	608	777	16	1165
68	12790	4168	3434	2607	603	839	25	1114
69	12547	4089	3398	2576	616	787	28	1053

Table S306A: Age by Religion (continued)

	All persons	Catholic	Presbyterian Church in Ireland	Church of Ireland	Methodist Church in Ireland	Other Christian (including Christian related)	Other religions and philosophies	No religion or religion not stated
70 to 74	**57852**	**18225**	**16171**	**11942**	**2807**	**3678**	**80**	**4949**
70	12477	4030	3454	2550	585	793	20	1045
71	11999	3793	3338	2443	595	750	16	1064
72	11415	3637	3197	2288	550	719	11	1013
73	10938	3415	3033	2340	531	714	17	888
74	11023	3350	3149	2321	546	702	16	939
75 to 79	**46542**	**13986**	**13776**	**9722**	**2443**	**2924**	**59**	**3632**
75	10486	3214	3091	2214	522	616	14	815
76	9761	2991	2839	2012	516	604	19	780
77	9245	2820	2713	1926	492	601	8	685
78	8723	2577	2651	1785	468	568	12	662
79	8327	2384	2482	1785	445	535	6	690
80 to 84	**30289**	**8554**	**9307**	**6125**	**1723**	**2103**	**32**	**2445**
80	7893	2235	2382	1657	445	548	6	620
81	7298	2127	2151	1468	442	492	7	611
82	5821	1675	1850	1104	311	415	4	462
83	4820	1290	1528	984	285	324	7	402
84	4457	1227	1396	912	240	324	8	350
85 to 89	**16114**	**4241**	**5053**	**3358**	**932**	**1211**	**21**	**1298**
85	4086	1086	1266	835	248	321	12	318
86	3786	1025	1215	753	201	292	6	294
87	3248	807	1019	700	210	257	3	252
88	2789	719	902	607	136	178	-	247
89	2205	604	651	463	137	163	-	187
90 and over	**7185**	**1669**	**2345**	**1503**	**436**	**543**	**11**	**678**

Note:
1   The term 'Catholic' includes those respondents who gave their religion as Catholic or Roman Catholic.

S306A

Table S307: Sex and Type of Communal Establishment by Community Background (Religion or Religion Brought Up In)

Table population: All persons resident in communal establishments

	All persons	Catholic	Protestant and Other Christian (including Christian related)	Other religions and philosophies	None
All persons	**26460**	**8939**	**16016**	**331**	**1174**
Medical and care establishments	**15608**	**5168**	**10077**	**103**	**260**
'NHS/HSSB' managed	**3534**	**1345**	**2073**	**79**	**37**
Psychiatric hospital/home	1111	460	644	3	4
General or other hospital	617	315	215	76	11
Children's home	124	56	62	-	6
Nursing home	102	36	66	-	-
Residential care home	1539	469	1054	-	16
Other medical and care home	41	9	32	-	-
Non 'NHS/HSSB' managed	**12074**	**3823**	**8004**	**24**	**223**
Psychiatric hospital/home	354	105	209	3	37
General or other hospital	17	6	11	-	-
Children's home	38	17	13	-	8
Nursing home	8150	2673	5355	10	112
Residential care home	3347	989	2287	8	63
Other medical and care home	168	33	129	3	3
Other establishments	**10852**	**3771**	**5939**	**228**	**914**
Defence establishments (including ships)	4354	671	3080	45	558
Prison Service establishments	590	234	329	8	19
Probation/Bail hostel	41	24	17	-	-
Education establishment (including halls of residence)	4192	1923	1793	166	310
Hotel, boarding house, guest house	128	66	62	-	-
Religious community	385	369	16	-	-
Hostel (including youth hostels, hostels for the homeless and persons sleeping rough)	674	375	272	6	21
Civilian ship, boat or barge	6	-	6	-	-
Other	482	109	364	3	6

Table S307: Sex and Type of Communal Establishment by Community Background (Religion or Religion Brought Up In) (continued)

	All persons	Catholic	Protestant and Other Christian (including Christian related)	Other religions and philosophies	None
Males	**12176**	**3974**	**7182**	**225**	**795**
Medical and care establishments	**5203**	**1936**	**3075**	**69**	**123**
'NHS/HSSB' managed	**1545**	**636**	**827**	**61**	**21**
Psychiatric hospital/home	664	282	375	3	4
General or other hospital	317	136	120	58	3
Children's home	55	21	31	-	3
Nursing home	38	17	21	-	-
Residential care home	462	177	274	-	11
Other medical and care home	9	3	6	-	-
Non 'NHS/HSSB' managed	**3658**	**1300**	**2248**	**8**	**102**
Psychiatric hospital/home	175	42	114	-	19
General or other hospital	9	3	6	-	-
Children's home	17	7	7	-	3
Nursing home	2362	881	1426	3	52
Residential care home	1052	356	666	5	25
Other medical and care home	43	11	29	-	3
Other establishments	**6973**	**2038**	**4107**	**156**	**672**
Defence establishments (including ships)	3860	584	2736	41	499
Prison Service establishments	579	230	322	8	19
Probation/Bail hostel	41	24	17	-	-
Education establishment (including halls of residence)	1744	790	711	101	142
Hotel, boarding house, guest house	78	41	37	-	-
Religious community	91	86	5	-	-
Hostel (including youth hostels, hostels for the homeless and persons sleeping rough)	420	236	169	6	9
Civilian ship, boat or barge	6	-	6	-	-
Other	154	47	104	-	3

Table S307: Sex and Type of Communal Establishment by Community Background (Religion or Religion Brought Up In) (continued)

© Crown copyright 2003

	All persons	Catholic	Protestant and Other Christian (including Christian related)	Other religions and philosophies	None
Females	**14284**	**4965**	**8834**	**106**	**379**
Medical and care establishments	**10405**	**3232**	**7002**	**34**	**137**
'NHS/HSSB' managed	**1989**	**709**	**1246**	**18**	**16**
Psychiatric hospital/home	447	178	269	-	-
General or other hospital	300	179	95	18	8
Children's home	69	35	31	-	3
Nursing home	64	19	45	-	-
Residential care home	1077	292	780	-	5
Other medical and care home	32	6	26	-	-
Non 'NHS/HSSB' managed	**8416**	**2523**	**5756**	**16**	**121**
Psychiatric hospital/home	179	63	95	3	18
General or other hospital	8	3	5	-	-
Children's home	21	10	6	-	5
Nursing home	5788	1792	3929	7	60
Residential care home	2295	633	1621	3	38
Other medical and care home	125	22	100	3	-
Other establishments	**3879**	**1733**	**1832**	**72**	**242**
Defence establishments (including ships)	494	87	344	4	59
Prison Service establishments	11	4	7	-	-
Probation/Bail hostel	-	-	-	-	-
Education establishment (including halls of residence)	2448	1133	1082	65	168
Hotel, boarding house, guest house	50	25	25	-	-
Religious community	294	283	11	-	-
Hostel (including youth hostels, hostels for the homeless and persons sleeping rough)	254	139	103	-	12
Civilian ship, boat or barge	-	-	-	-	-
Other	328	62	260	3	3

Notes:

1 'NHS/HSSB' refers to the Health and Personal Social Services in Northern Ireland.

2 The term 'Catholic' includes those respondents who gave their religion as Catholic or Roman Catholic.

S307

Table S308: Religion by Sex

Table population: All persons

	All persons	Males	Females
All persons	**1685267**	**821449**	**863818**
Catholic	678462	326508	351954
Presbyterian Church in Ireland	348742	167478	181264
Church of Ireland	257788	122176	135612
Methodist Church in Ireland	59173	27130	32043
Other Christian (including Christian related)	**102221**	**48752**	**53469**
Baptist	18974	8806	10168
Free Presbyterian	11902	5893	6009
Brethren	8595	3891	4704
Christian	8502	4224	4278
Church of England	6417	3854	2563
Congregational Church	5701	2568	3133
Pentecostal	5533	2446	3087
Elim Church	5448	2421	3027
Protestant	3674	1837	1837
Reformed Presbyterian	2238	1098	1140
Jehovah's Witness	1993	850	1143
Church of Scotland	1901	1213	688
Independent Methodist	1771	823	948
Salvation Army	1640	682	958
Church of Jesus Christ of Latter Day Saints (Mormons)	1414	642	772
Non-Subscribing Presbyterian	1233	565	668
Evangelical	1229	553	676
Church of the Nazarene	1215	529	686
Non Denominational	1115	497	618
Christian Fellowship	1015	448	567
Church of God	990	457	533
Presbyterian	985	433	552
Religious Society of Friends (Quakers)	749	325	424
Moravian	691	317	374
Protestant (Mixed)	625	263	362
Evangelical Presbyterian Church	543	264	279
Whitewell Metropolitan Tabernacle	399	173	226

© Crown copyright 2003

	All persons	Males	Females
Methodist	379	214	165
Unitarian	342	173	169
Independent	305	157	148
Church of Christ	273	107	166
Free Methodist	266	113	153
Apostolic Church	237	106	131
Seventh Day Adventist	232	104	128
Assemblies of God	216	91	125
Church	194	96	98
Lutheran	186	63	123
City Mission	184	64	120
House Church	138	71	67
Interdenominational	131	61	70
Anglican	128	58	70
Metropolitan Church	125	48	77
Independent Evangelist	120	48	72
Orthodox Church	113	49	64
Christian Fellowship Church	111	53	58
Church in Wales	100	57	43
Other Christian denominations	1949	947	1002
Other religions and philosophies	**5028**	**2815**	**2213**
Muslim (Islam)	1943	1164	779
Hindu	825	438	387
Buddhist	533	295	238
Jewish	365	193	172
Baha'i	254	117	137
Sikh	219	115	104
Pagan	148	84	64
Atheist	106	81	25
Spiritualist	106	33	73
Other religious and philosophical groups	529	295	234
No religion or religion not stated	**233853**	**126590**	**107263**

Notes:
1   The term 'Catholic' includes those respondents who gave their religion as Catholic or Roman Catholic.
2   'Other Christian (including Christian related)' and 'Other religions and philosophies' include all other religions, religious denominations or religious bodies with less than 100 adherents in Northern Ireland.

S308

Table S003: Age of Household Reference Person (HRP) by Sex and Marital Status ('Headship')

Table population: All household reference persons (HRPs)

	All HRPs	Males						Females					
		Total	Single (never married)	Married or re-married	Separated (but still legally married)	Divorced	Widowed	Total	Single (never married)	Married or re-married	Separated (but still legally married)	Divorced	Widowed
All HRPs	**626715**	**372547**	**63288**	**258658**	**15214**	**17499**	**17888**	**254168**	**64873**	**69129**	**26409**	**26326**	**67431**
19 and under	3030	891	842	45	4	-	-	2139	2120	10	9	-	-
20 to 24	18263	7511	6062	1364	54	21	10	10752	9845	446	399	39	23
25 to 29	42688	24764	12511	11476	549	208	20	17924	12420	2885	1988	556	75
30 to 34	64345	41735	11425	27534	1542	1163	71	22610	10068	5571	4307	2401	263
35 to 39	69852	47524	6914	35868	2392	2212	138	22328	6077	6627	5111	4005	508
40 to 44	65781	44936	4529	34737	2476	2921	273	20845	3979	6745	4469	4818	834
45 to 49	59242	41280	3814	31621	2345	3013	487	17962	2585	6697	3185	4148	1347
50 to 54	57086	38807	3411	30075	1886	2666	769	18279	2261	7509	2553	3687	2269
55 to 59	52704	34468	3058	26608	1488	2129	1185	18236	2139	7803	1803	2702	3789
60 to 64	44001	26016	2686	19281	1000	1456	1593	17985	2158	7243	1155	1696	5733
65 to 69	41986	22723	2613	16244	704	929	2233	19263	2475	6310	718	1080	8680
70 to 74	45052	20506	2554	13994	442	482	3034	24546	3140	7919	441	659	12387
75 to 79	26962	9463	1499	4249	206	190	3319	17499	2303	1435	171	326	13264
80 to 84	21012	7566	884	3735	96	76	2775	13446	1780	1249	65	142	10210
85 to 89	10912	3346	362	1460	25	28	1471	7566	1052	536	25	48	5905
90 and over	3799	1011	124	367	5	5	510	2788	471	144	10	19	2144

Table S005: Age of Household Reference Person (HRP) by Sex and Living Arrangements

Table population: All household reference persons (HRPs)

	All HRPs	Males								Females							
			Living in a couple		Not living in a couple						Living in a couple		Not living in a couple				
		Total	Married or re-married	Cohabiting	Single (never married)	Married or re-married	Separated (but still legally married)	Divorced	Widowed	Total	Married or re-married	Cohabiting	Single (never married)	Married or re-married	Separated (but still legally married)	Divorced	Widowed
ALL HRPs	626722	372551	256513	19314	50418	2129	12582	14006	17589	254171	66274	7221	60352	2899	25471	24788	67166
19 and under	3035	895	43	169	673	3	4	3	-	2140	7	124	1998	-	8	-	3
20 to 24	18263	7511	1348	2138	3949	11	40	15	10	10752	411	879	8974	33	393	39	23
25 to 29	42688	24764	11393	4586	8163	65	425	119	13	17924	2760	1665	10872	91	1943	518	75
30 to 34	64345	41735	27413	3983	8199	141	1194	739	66	22610	5414	1298	9063	174	4164	2241	256
35 to 39	69852	47524	35756	2721	5386	163	1840	1537	121	22328	6391	878	5668	255	4919	3730	487
40 to 44	65781	44936	34640	1898	3844	158	1948	2200	248	20845	6602	733	3742	188	4294	4471	815
45 to 49	59242	41280	31427	1414	3476	187	1947	2377	452	17962	6538	586	2460	182	3033	3853	1310
50 to 54	57086	38807	29889	1016	3207	175	1573	2212	735	18279	7308	410	2192	200	2457	3464	2248
55 to 59	52704	34468	26402	673	2950	182	1288	1842	1131	18236	7646	270	2096	162	1731	2584	3747
60 to 64	44001	26016	19094	368	2615	154	914	1318	1553	17985	7067	171	2112	169	1133	1638	5695
65 to 69	41986	22723	16068	167	2581	152	668	882	2205	19263	6086	74	2462	222	698	1063	8658
70 to 74	45052	20506	13763	123	2519	211	417	467	3006	24546	7575	96	3112	331	428	652	12352
75 to 79	26962	9463	4026	26	1495	221	202	188	3305	17499	1068	15	2301	365	171	326	13253
80 to 84	21012	7566	3544	20	878	188	94	75	2767	13446	963	14	1778	285	64	142	10200
85 to 89	10912	3346	1366	9	359	93	24	28	1467	7566	363	5	1051	173	25	48	5901
90 and over	3801	1011	341	3	124	25	4	4	510	2790	75	3	471	69	10	19	2143

Notes:

1 Cohabiting couples includes same sex couples.

2 The living arrangements variable is different to marital status. It combines information from both marital status and the relationship matrix. Therefore a person living as part of a 'cohabiting couple' could in fact be married (to someone else) but will not appear as married or separated in this classification.

3 A person not living in a couple can be classified married (or re-married) but have no spouse or partner resident in the household.

Table S006: Age of Family Reference Person (FRP) and Age of Dependent Children by Family Type

Table population: All families

| | All families | Couple family | | | Lone parent family | | | | | | | | | | | |
| | | | | | Male Parent | | | | | | Female Parent | | | | | |
		Total	Married or re-married	Cohabiting	Total	Single (never married)	Married or re-married	Separated (but still legally married)	Divorced	Widowed	Total	Single (never married)	Married or re-married	Separated (but still legally married)	Divorced	Widowed
All families	**442580**	**351459**	**324609**	**26850**	**11516**	**888**	**614**	**2596**	**2262**	**5156**	**79605**	**24443**	**1423**	**19303**	**14725**	**19711**
Age of FRP 24 or under	**13870**	**5289**	**1847**	**3442**	**119**	**105**	**3**	**8**	**3**	**-**	**8462**	**8019**	**39**	**357**	**35**	**12**
- no children	3078	3078	837	2241	-	-	-	-	-	-	-	-	-	-	-	-
- youngest dependent child aged 0 to 4	9931	2037	940	1097	102	88	3	8	3	-	7792	7378	35	343	27	9
- youngest dependent child aged 5 to 7	731	88	40	48	14	14	-	-	-	-	629	600	4	14	8	3
- youngest dependent child aged 8 to 9	55	18	6	12	-	-	-	-	-	-	37	37	-	-	-	-
- youngest dependent child aged 10 to 11	18	14	5	9	-	-	-	-	-	-	4	4	-	-	-	-
- youngest dependent child aged 12 to 15	21	21	7	14	-	-	-	-	-	-	-	-	-	-	-	-
- youngest dependent child aged 16 to 18	9	9	3	6	-	-	-	-	-	-	-	-	-	-	-	-
- all children non-dependent	27	24	9	15	3	3	-	-	-	-	-	-	-	-	-	-
Age of FRP 25 to 34	**79162**	**58924**	**47271**	**11653**	**723**	**307**	**76**	**231**	**79**	**30**	**19515**	**11155**	**248**	**5511**	**2323**	**278**
- no children	20587	20587	13244	7343	-	-	-	-	-	-	-	-	-	-	-	-
- youngest dependent child aged 0 to 4	40954	30806	27631	3175	320	136	54	97	23	10	9828	5827	175	2962	755	109
- youngest dependent child aged 5 to 7	9911	4800	4232	568	167	68	12	59	18	10	4944	2728	37	1447	646	86
- youngest dependent child aged 8 to 9	3880	1489	1236	253	91	45	5	27	11	3	2300	1253	17	581	410	39
- youngest dependent child aged 10 to 11	2056	636	523	113	57	24	-	22	7	4	1363	760	11	297	265	30
- youngest dependent child aged 12 to 15	1533	457	325	132	70	23	5	22	17	3	1006	545	8	205	234	14
- youngest dependent child aged 16 to 18	114	53	38	15	5	5	-	-	-	-	56	36	-	13	7	-
- all children non-dependent	127	96	42	54	13	6	-	4	3	-	18	6	-	6	6	-

Table S006: Age of Family Reference Person (FRP) and Age of Dependent Children by Family Type (continued)

	All families	Couple family			Lone parent family											
					Male Parent						Female Parent					
		Total	Married or re-married	Cohabiting	Total	Single (never married)	Married or re-married	Separated (but still legally married)	Divorced	Widowed	Total	Single (never married)	Married or re-married	Separated (but still legally married)	Divorced	Widowed
Age of FRP 35 to 49	**160768**	**129795**	**121535**	**8260**	**3940**	**316**	**202**	**1534**	**1282**	**606**	**27033**	**4528**	**507**	**10625**	**9254**	**2119**
- no children	17102	17102	13794	3308	-	-	-	-	-	-	-	-	-	-	-	-
- youngest dependent child aged 0 to 4	36802	32920	31109	1811	293	64	63	78	53	35	3589	933	112	1529	889	126
- youngest dependent child aged 5 to 7	23537	19706	18924	782	315	48	23	130	63	51	3516	707	84	1661	896	168
- youngest dependent child aged 8 to 9	15939	12552	12122	430	317	43	21	118	65	70	3070	519	41	1373	930	207
- youngest dependent child aged 10 to 11	15736	11963	11509	454	359	35	16	145	104	59	3414	568	64	1383	1157	242
- youngest dependent child aged 12 to 15	27423	19650	18905	745	973	69	23	425	289	167	6800	948	107	2590	2572	583
- youngest dependent child aged 16 to 18	10465	7256	7008	248	468	14	21	211	158	64	2741	325	45	972	1094	305
- all children non-dependent	13764	8646	8164	482	1215	43	35	427	550	160	3903	528	54	1117	1716	488
Age of FRP 50 and over	**188780**	**157451**	**153956**	**3495**	**6734**	**160**	**333**	**823**	**898**	**4520**	**24595**	**741**	**629**	**2810**	**3113**	**17302**
- no children	86081	86081	83925	2156	-	-	-	-	-	-	-	-	-	-	-	-
- youngest dependent child aged 0 to 4	1854	1475	1328	147	94	17	8	16	18	35	285	66	11	60	49	99
- youngest dependent child aged 5 to 7	1814	1523	1433	90	78	15	10	14	12	27	213	32	6	38	42	95
- youngest dependent child aged 8 to 9	1843	1595	1533	62	63	8	4	18	8	25	185	13	5	46	49	72
- youngest dependent child aged 10 to 11	3047	2648	2566	82	100	6	7	23	22	42	299	26	15	89	81	88
- youngest dependent child aged 12 to 15	11160	9562	9318	244	382	13	19	72	95	183	1216	65	38	396	329	388
- youngest dependent child aged 16 to 18	10109	8603	8502	101	354	11	24	71	71	177	1152	48	36	339	302	427
- all children non-dependent	72872	45964	45351	613	5663	90	261	609	672	4031	21245	491	518	1842	2261	16133

Notes:

1 The family reference person may not be the oldest person in a couple, as economic activity is given priority over age.

2 Cohabiting couples includes same sex couples.

3 A dependent child is a person in a household aged 0 to 15 (whether or not in a family) or a person aged 16 to 18 who is a full-time student in a family with parent(s).

4 A lone parent can be classified as married (or re-married) if they denote their marital status as married (or re-married), but have no spouse or partner identified in the relationship matrix.

5 A family consists of a couple (married or cohabiting) with or without children, or a lone parent and their children. It also includes a married or cohabiting couple with their grandchildren or a lone grandparent with his or her grandchildren, if there is no parent in the intervening generation in the household. A family will also include step-children when their parent is part of the couple.

Table S007: Age of Family Reference Person (FRP) and Number and Age of Dependent Children by Family Type

Table population: All families

	All families	Lone parent family			Couple family					
		Total	Male parent	Female parent	Total	Married or re-married		Cohabiting		
						Without step-child(ren)	With step-child(ren)	Without step-child(ren)	With step-child(ren)	
All families	442586	91126	11519	79607	351460	315124	9482	22178	4676
Age of FRP 24 or under	**13873**	**8584**	**121**	**8463**	**5289**	**1732**	**114**	**3207**	**236**
- no dependent children	3105	3	3	-	3102	837	9	2241	15
- one dependent child aged 0 to 4	7589	6142	89	6053	1447	562	23	795	67
- one dependent child aged 5 to 7	665	607	16	591	58	21	5	19	13
- one dependent child aged 8 to 9	47	38	-	38	9	3	-	3	3
- one dependent child aged 10 to 11	10	4	-	4	6	-	3	-	3
- one dependent child aged 12 to 15	12	-	-	-	12	-	4	-	8
- one dependent child aged 16 to 18	8	-	-	-	8	-	3	-	5
- two dependent children, youngest aged 0 to 4	1962	1478	10	1468	484	263	37	133	51
- two dependent children, youngest aged 5 to 7	55	38	-	38	17	3	5	-	9
- two dependent children, youngest aged 8 to 9	6	-	-	-	6	-	3	-	3
- two dependent children, youngest aged 10 to 11	3	-	-	-	3	-	-	-	3
- two dependent children, youngest aged 12 to 15	8	-	-	-	8	-	3	-	5
- two dependent children, youngest aged 16 to 18	-	-	-	-	-	-	-	-	-
- three or more dependent children, youngest aged 0 to 4	380	274	3	271	106	43	12	16	35
- three or more dependent children, youngest aged 5 to 7	13	-	-	-	13	-	7	-	6
- three or more dependent children, youngest aged 8 to 9	3	-	-	-	3	-	-	-	3
- three or more dependent children, youngest aged 10 to 11	4	-	-	-	4	-	-	-	4
- three or more dependent children, youngest aged 12 to 15	3	-	-	-	3	-	-	-	3
- three or more dependent children, youngest aged 16 to 18	-	-	-	-	-	-	-	-	-

Table S007: Age of Family Reference Person (FRP) and Number and Age of Dependent Children by Family Type (continued)

	All families	Lone parent family			Couple family				
						Married or re-married		Cohabiting	
		Total	Male parent	Female parent	Total	Without step-child(ren)	With step-child(ren)	Without step-child(ren)	With step-child(ren)
Age of FRP 25 to 34	**79166**	**20241**	**725**	**19516**	**58925**	**45531**	**1738**	**10421**	**1235**
- no dependent children	20715	32	13	19	20683	13254	32	7348	49
- one dependent child aged 0 to 4	15466	3650	181	3469	11816	10062	65	1583	106
- one dependent child aged 5 to 7	3794	2377	96	2281	1417	1039	72	200	106
- one dependent child aged 8 to 9	1922	1333	68	1265	589	373	71	81	64
- one dependent child aged 10 to 11	1140	873	42	831	267	156	43	28	40
- one dependent child aged 12 to 15	1130	821	57	764	309	142	71	29	67
- one dependent child aged 16 to 18	113	63	7	56	50	14	22	6	8
- two dependent children, youngest aged 0 to 4	15695	3501	104	3397	12194	10820	425	687	262
- two dependent children, youngest aged 5 to 7	4085	1754	51	1703	2331	2039	120	93	79
- two dependent children, youngest aged 8 to 9	1389	736	16	720	653	526	54	38	35
- two dependent children, youngest aged 10 to 11	714	427	14	413	287	222	30	10	25
- two dependent children, youngest aged 12 to 15	347	215	11	204	132	76	22	3	31
- two dependent children, youngest aged 16 to 18	3	-	-	-	3	-	-	-	3
- three or more dependent children, youngest aged 0 to 4	9793	2997	35	2962	6796	5684	575	271	266
- three or more dependent children, youngest aged 5 to 7	2032	980	20	960	1052	873	89	33	57
- three or more dependent children, youngest aged 8 to 9	569	322	7	315	247	182	30	8	27
- three or more dependent children, youngest aged 10 to 11	204	122	3	119	82	60	12	3	7
- three or more dependent children, youngest aged 12 to 15	55	38	-	38	17	9	5	-	3
- three or more dependent children, youngest aged 16 to 18	-	-	-	-	-	-	-	-	-

Table S007: Age of Family Reference Person (FRP) and Number and Age of Dependent Children by Family Type (continued)

| | All families | Lone parent family | | | Total | Couple family | | | |
| | | Total | Male parent | Female parent | | Married or re-married | | Cohabiting | |
						Without step-child(ren)	With step-child(ren)	Without step-child(ren)	With step-child(ren)
Age of FRP 35 to 49	**160767**	**30972**	**3939**	**27033**	**129795**	**116770**	**4765**	**5716**	**2544**
- no dependent children	30866	5118	1215	3903	25748	21366	592	3415	375
- one dependent child aged 0 to 4	7355	950	121	829	6405	5628	123	594	60
- one dependent child aged 5 to 7	3626	1012	106	906	2614	2268	103	145	98
- one dependent child aged 8 to 9	2699	946	108	838	1753	1504	112	77	60
- one dependent child aged 10 to 11	3598	1333	122	1211	2265	1946	134	94	91
- one dependent child aged 12 to 15	12085	4504	621	3883	7581	6652	471	158	300
- one dependent child aged 16 to 18	9130	2888	428	2460	6242	5730	285	69	158
- two dependent children, youngest aged 0 to 4	12964	1163	107	1056	11801	10748	472	363	218
- two dependent children, youngest aged 5 to 7	9767	1347	137	1210	8420	7849	276	150	145
- two dependent children, youngest aged 8 to 9	7193	1308	111	1197	5885	5524	180	82	99
- two dependent children, youngest aged 10 to 11	7547	1619	166	1453	5928	5597	155	62	114
- two dependent children, youngest aged 12 to 15	12183	2662	290	2372	9521	8965	306	79	171
- two dependent children, youngest aged 16 to 18	1296	315	39	276	981	926	34	7	14
- three or more dependent children, youngest aged 0 to 4	16483	1769	65	1704	14714	13333	805	240	336
- three or more dependent children, youngest aged 5 to 7	10144	1472	72	1400	8672	8054	374	92	152
- three or more dependent children, youngest aged 8 to 9	6047	1133	98	1035	4914	4645	157	39	73
- three or more dependent children, youngest aged 10 to 11	4591	821	71	750	3770	3566	111	40	53
- three or more dependent children, youngest aged 12 to 15	3155	607	62	545	2548	2436	75	10	27
- three or more dependent children, youngest aged 16 to 18	38	5	-	5	33	33	-	-	-

Table S007: Age of Family Reference Person (FRP) and Number and Age of Dependent Children by Family Type (continued)

	All families	Lone parent family			Total	Couple family			
						Married or re-married		Cohabiting	
		Total	Male parent	Female parent		Without step-child(ren)	With step-child(ren)	Without step-child(ren)	With step-child(ren)
Age of FRP 50 and over	**188780**	**31329**	**6734**	**24595**	**157451**	**151091**	**2865**	**2834**	**661**
- no dependent children	158953	26908	5663	21245	132045	127630	1646	2443	326
- one dependent child aged 0 to 4	868	277	74	203	591	431	103	43	14
- one dependent child aged 5 to 7	683	213	57	156	470	385	50	25	10
- one dependent child aged 8 to 9	683	154	41	113	529	453	52	11	13
- one dependent child aged 10 to 11	1171	206	44	162	965	851	74	26	14
- one dependent child aged 12 to 15	6782	1146	261	885	5636	5208	263	89	76
- one dependent child aged 16 to 18	9308	1432	333	1099	7876	7544	243	46	43
- two dependent children, youngest aged 0 to 4	488	65	9	56	423	337	42	27	17
- two dependent children, youngest aged 5 to 7	583	48	13	35	535	473	33	16	13
- two dependent children, youngest aged 8 to 9	639	59	15	44	580	527	31	9	13
- two dependent children, youngest aged 10 to 11	1166	151	38	113	1015	943	43	20	9
- two dependent children, youngest aged 12 to 15	3541	386	105	281	3155	2988	104	31	32
- two dependent children, youngest aged 16 to 18	769	68	18	50	701	670	19	5	7
- three or more dependent children, youngest aged 0 to 4	498	37	11	26	461	372	43	14	32
- three or more dependent children, youngest aged 5 to 7	548	30	8	22	518	454	38	12	14
- three or more dependent children, youngest aged 8 to 9	521	35	7	28	486	449	21	8	8
- three or more dependent children, youngest aged 10 to 11	710	42	18	24	668	626	29	6	7
- three or more dependent children, youngest aged 12 to 15	837	66	16	50	771	728	27	3	13
- three or more dependent children, youngest aged 16 to 18	32	6	3	3	26	22	4	-	-

Notes:

1 The family reference person may not be the oldest person in a couple, as economic activity is given priority over age.

2 A family 'without step-child(ren)' is a family where all children are children of both members of the married or cohabiting couple.
   A family 'with step-child(ren)' is one where there is a child (or children) who belong to only one member of the married or cohabiting couple.
   Where a couple family contains no children, the family is recorded under 'without step-child(ren)'.

3 A dependent child is a person in a household aged 0 to 15 (whether or not in a family) or a person aged 16 to 18 who is a full-time student in a family with parent(s).

4 Families with no children are included under 'no dependent children'.

5 A family consists of a couple (married or cohabiting) with or without children, or a lone parent and their children.
   It also includes a married or cohabiting couple with their grandchildren or a lone grandparent with his or her grandchildren, if there is no parent in the intervening generation in the household.
   A family will also include step-children when their parent is part of the couple.

Table S011: Family Composition by Age of Family Reference Person (FRP)

Table population: All families

	All FRPs	24 or under	25 to 34	35 to 49	50 and over
All families	**442584**	**13873**	**79163**	**160768**	**188780**
Concealed families	**5751**	**1814**	**1391**	**631**	**1915**
Lone parent families	**3613**	**1643**	**981**	**420**	**569**
with dependent child(ren)	3070	1643	981	334	112
with non-dependent child(ren) only	543	-	-	86	457
Couple families	**2138**	**171**	**410**	**211**	**1346**
with no children	1314	127	244	64	879
with dependent child(ren)	466	41	166	133	126
with non-dependent child(ren) only	358	3	-	14	341
Unconcealed families	**436833**	**12059**	**77772**	**160137**	**186865**
with no children	125534	2951	20343	17038	85202
with dependent child(ren)	225412	9083	57305	129435	29589
with non-dependent child(ren) only	85887	25	124	13664	72074

Notes:

1 The family reference person may not be the oldest person in a couple, as economic activity is given priority over age.
2 A dependent child is a person in a household aged 0 to 15 (whether or not in a family) or a person aged 16 to 18 who is a full-time student in a family with parent(s).
3 A 'concealed family' is one that does not contain the Household Reference Person. This will occur where there is more than one family living in a household. The members of these families may or may not be related.
4 A family consists of a couple (married or cohabiting) with or without children, or a lone parent and their children.
   It also includes a married or cohabiting couple with their grandchildren or a lone grandparent with his or her grandchildren, if there is no parent in the intervening generation in the household.
   A family will also include step-children when their parent is part of the couple.

Table S068: Age and Dependent Children by Household Type (Household Reference Persons)

Table population: All household reference persons (HRPs)

	All HRPs	Living in a couple household	Not living in a couple household
All HRPs	**626718**	**350022**	**276696**
24 and under	**21296**	**5241**	**16055**
- no dependent children in household	11947	2919	9028
- dependent child(ren) in household, youngest aged 0 to 4	8456	2136	6320
- dependent child(ren) in household, youngest aged 5 to 9	744	130	614
- dependent child(ren) in household, youngest aged 10 to 15	139	46	93
- dependent child(ren) in household, youngest aged 16 to 18	10	10	-
25 to 34	**107033**	**58822**	**48211**
- no dependent children in household	49476	20320	29156
- dependent child(ren) in household, youngest aged 0 to 4	40555	30908	9647
- dependent child(ren) in household, youngest aged 5 to 9	13461	6375	7086
- dependent child(ren) in household, youngest aged 10 to 15	3426	1156	2270
- dependent child(ren) in household, youngest aged 16 to 18	115	63	52
35 to 44	**135633**	**89797**	**45836**
- no dependent children in household	38620	13140	25480
- dependent child(ren) in household, youngest aged 0 to 4	34029	30244	3785
- dependent child(ren) in household, youngest aged 5 to 9	32158	25831	6327
- dependent child(ren) in household, youngest aged 10 to 15	26597	18159	8438
- dependent child(ren) in household, youngest aged 16 to 18	4229	2423	1806
45 to 54	**116328**	**78642**	**37686**
- no dependent children in household	63642	33975	29667
- dependent child(ren) in household, youngest aged 0 to 4	5386	4803	583
- dependent child(ren) in household, youngest aged 5 to 9	9927	8779	1148
- dependent child(ren) in household, youngest aged 10 to 15	25665	21509	4156
- dependent child(ren) in household, youngest aged 16 to 18	11708	9576	2132
55 to pensionable age	**78720**	**54462**	**24258**
- no dependent children in household	68978	45786	23192
- dependent child(ren) in household, youngest aged 0 to 4	1046	911	135
- dependent child(ren) in household, youngest aged 5 to 9	1026	913	113
- dependent child(ren) in household, youngest aged 10 to 15	4011	3597	414
- dependent child(ren) in household, youngest aged 16 to 18	3659	3255	404
Pensionable age to 74	**105023**	**51206**	**53817**
75 and over	**62685**	**11852**	**50833**

Notes:

1. The Household Reference Person may not be the oldest person in a household, as economic activity is given priority over age.
2. A dependent child is a person in a household aged 0 to 15 (whether or not in a family) or a person aged 16 to 18 who is a full-time student in a family with parent(s). The dependent child may or may not be a child of the Household Reference Person.
3. A 'couple household' contains at least one couple family with or without other families or individuals. A Household Reference Person living in a 'couple household' may or may not be part of the couple.
4. Pensionable age at the time of the Census (29 April 2001) was 65 for men and 60 for women.

Table S309: Age by Sex and Living Arrangements

Table population: All persons aged 16 and over in households

	All persons	Males								Females							
			Living in a couple		Not living in a couple						Living in a couple		Not living in a couple				
		Total	Married or re-married	Cohabiting	Single (never married)	Married or re-married	Separated (but still legally married)	Divorced	Widowed	Total	Married or re-married	Cohabiting	Single (never married)	Married or re-married	Separated (but still legally married)	Divorced	Widowed
All persons	1261257	605288	324608	26988	199435	3085	15345	16638	19189	655969	324608	26691	174795	3944	26725	26305	72901
16 to 19	99082	50246	67	381	49776	13	6	3	-	48836	166	832	47802	23	10	-	3
20 to 24	105729	52456	1948	3428	46856	77	97	35	15	53273	4924	5479	42216	105	468	54	27
25 to 29	112934	55254	15053	6514	32491	200	755	219	22	57680	22010	6589	26017	225	2142	590	107
30 to 34	126402	61614	33088	5236	20013	284	1827	1094	72	64788	37968	4436	15057	318	4336	2396	277
35 to 39	128847	62841	41947	3561	12487	268	2420	2022	136	66006	43884	3061	9191	375	5069	3921	505
40 to 44	116727	57045	40612	2529	8314	246	2374	2701	269	59682	41075	2169	6237	289	4407	4659	846
45 to 49	101915	51331	37288	1895	6377	257	2212	2819	483	50584	35967	1512	4255	246	3153	4064	1387
50 to 54	97817	48113	36347	1330	5159	252	1754	2493	778	49704	36119	1027	3596	289	2586	3701	2386
55 to 59	88132	43241	33222	924	4206	237	1406	2030	1216	44891	32212	713	3121	232	1840	2760	4013
60 to 64	72985	35082	26779	537	3464	195	981	1449	1677	37903	25292	395	2909	214	1206	1760	6127
65 to 69	64594	30036	22229	293	3286	197	722	933	2376	34558	19719	190	3257	256	749	1123	9264
70 to 74	56634	24562	16976	185	2990	245	443	503	3220	32072	13610	154	3674	370	456	690	13118
75 to 79	44386	17841	11233	96	2190	258	218	217	3629	26545	7821	68	3334	412	189	354	14367
80 to 84	27405	10334	5645	52	1201	211	100	86	3039	17071	2936	40	2310	315	76	154	11240
85 to 89	13039	4074	1763	17	462	113	25	30	1664	8965	747	18	1252	193	26	56	6673
90 and over	4629	1218	411	10	163	32	5	4	593	3411	158	8	567	82	12	23	2561

Notes:

1 Cohabiting couples includes same sex couples.

2 The living arrangements variable is different to marital status. It combines information from both marital status and the relationship matrix. Therefore a person living as part of a 'cohabiting couple' could in fact be married (to someone else) but will not appear as married or separated in this classification.

3 A person not living in a couple can be classified married (or re-married) but have no spouse or partner resident in the household.

Table S012: Schoolchildren and Students in Full-time Education Living Away From Home in Term-Time: Sex by Age

Table population: All schoolchildren and students in full-time education whose home address is in the area, but they live away from home during term-time

	All schoolchildren and students	Under 10	10 to 11	12 to 14	15	16	17	18	19	20	21	22	23	24	25 to 34	35 and over
All schoolchildren and students	**24290**	**98**	**100**	**335**	**111**	**119**	**182**	**1068**	**4988**	**5445**	**4934**	**3521**	**1621**	**710**	**961**	**97**
Males	**10785**	50	44	182	51	58	109	438	2103	2262	2130	1607	767	379	558	47
Females	**13505**	48	56	153	60	61	73	630	2885	3183	2804	1914	854	331	403	50

Note:
1 This table only includes schoolchildren and students where information was provided at their home address.

S012

Table S014: Age and Dependent Children by Household Type (Adults)

Table population: All adults in households

| | All adults | Adults | |
		Living in a couple household	Not living in a couple household
All adults	**1205421**	**845275**	**360146**
16 to 24	**148975**	**100551**	**48424**
- no dependent children in household	80929	50052	30877
- dependent child(ren) in household, youngest aged 0 to 4	20596	12294	8302
- dependent child(ren) in household, youngest aged 5 to 9	9447	7040	2407
- dependent child(ren) in household, youngest aged 10 to 15	25754	20880	4874
- dependent child(ren) in household, youngest aged 16 to 18	12249	10285	1964
25 to 34	**239336**	**171320**	**68016**
- no dependent children in household	119847	73172	46675
- dependent child(ren) in household, youngest aged 0 to 4	81961	71597	10364
- dependent child(ren) in household, youngest aged 5 to 9	24933	17394	7539
- dependent child(ren) in household, youngest aged 10 to 15	9542	6536	3006
- dependent child(ren) in household, youngest aged 16 to 18	3053	2621	432
35 to 44	**245574**	**188085**	**57489**
- no dependent children in household	70448	34312	36136
- dependent child(ren) in household, youngest aged 0 to 4	57584	53429	4155
- dependent child(ren) in household, youngest aged 5 to 9	59000	52422	6578
- dependent child(ren) in household, youngest aged 10 to 15	50260	41531	8729
- dependent child(ren) in household, youngest aged 16 to 18	8282	6391	1891

S014

56

© Crown copyright 2003

| | All adults | Adults | |
		Living in a couple household	Not living in a couple household
45 to 54	**199732**	**154117**	**45615**
- no dependent children in household	111262	74338	36924
- dependent child(ren) in household, youngest aged 0 to 4	8427	7537	890
- dependent child(ren) in household, youngest aged 5 to 9	15323	14028	1295
- dependent child(ren) in household, youngest aged 10 to 15	43527	39206	4321
- dependent child(ren) in household, youngest aged 16 to 18	21193	19008	2185
55 to pensionable age	**123214**	**95281**	**27933**
- no dependent children in household	107801	81289	26512
- dependent child(ren) in household, youngest aged 0 to 4	2157	1864	293
- dependent child(ren) in household, youngest aged 5 to 9	1715	1511	204
- dependent child(ren) in household, youngest aged 10 to 15	5872	5373	499
- dependent child(ren) in household, youngest aged 16 to 18	5669	5244	425
Pensionable age to 74	**159131**	**101061**	**58070**
75 and over	**89459**	**34860**	**54599**

Notes:
1 A 'couple household' contains at least one couple family with or without other families or individuals. An adult living in a 'couple household' may or may not be part of the couple.
2 A dependent child is a person in a household aged 0 to 15 (whether or not in a family) or a person aged 16 to 18 who is a full-time student in a family with parent(s). The dependent child may or may not be a child of the adult.
3 An adult in a household is defined as a person who is not a dependent child i.e. an adult is someone aged 19 or over, or someone aged 16 to 18 who is not a full-time student living with their parent(s).

S014

Table S310: Age of Full-time Schoolchildren and Students Aged 18 and Under by Household Type

Table population: All full-time schoolchildren and students aged 18 and under at their term-time address

	All full-time schoolchildren and students	Living with parent(s)	Communal establishment	Other household type
All full-time schoolchildren and students	**365182**	**359086**	**1075**	**5021**
8 and under	**121521**	120270	46	1205
9 to 11	**77948**	77021	74	853
12 to 14	**80512**	79359	235	918
15	**27104**	26600	103	401
16	**25081**	24411	79	591
17	**18205**	17674	93	438
18	**14811**	13751	445	615

Table S311: Household Composition by Ethnic Group of Household Reference Person (HRP)

Table population: All households

	All HRPs	White	Irish Traveller	Mixed	Indian	Pakistani	Bangladeshi	Other Asian	Black Caribbean	Black African	Other Black	Chinese	Other ethnic group
All households	**626715**	**622346**	**665**	**646**	**602**	**178**	**73**	**70**	**124**	**184**	**122**	**1287**	**418**
One person	**171573**	**170463**	**281**	**196**	**125**	**29**	**10**	**11**	**59**	**54**	**38**	**219**	**88**
- pensioner	80486	80185	89	57	32	3	4	3	14	11	18	51	19
- other	91087	90278	192	139	93	26	6	8	45	43	20	168	69
One family and no others	**413706**	**411017**	**308**	**368**	**420**	**120**	**50**	**37**	**53**	**111**	**73**	**885**	**264**
All pensioner	40768	40662	14	23	26	-	-	-	3	4	4	23	9
Couple family households	293312	291185	165	256	358	109	47	33	38	89	52	755	225
- no children	79766	79218	38	73	120	17	11	9	18	18	16	174	54
- with dependent child(ren)	162118	160688	109	160	211	82	33	21	20	64	33	536	161
- all children non-dependent	51428	51279	18	23	27	10	3	3	-	7	3	45	10
Lone parent households	79626	79170	129	89	36	11	3	4	12	18	17	107	30
- with dependent child(ren)	50641	50288	106	71	25	6	3	4	8	18	13	72	27
- all children non-dependent	28985	28882	23	18	11	5	-	-	4	-	4	35	3
Other households	**41436**	**40866**	**76**	**82**	**57**	**29**	**13**	**22**	**12**	**19**	**11**	**183**	**66**
- with dependent child(ren)	15756	15497	45	32	35	21	9	5	4	3	3	88	14
- all student	1731	1672	4	12	3	-	-	3	-	-	-	27	10
- all pensioner	4292	4279	7	-	-	-	-	-	-	3	-	-	3
- other	19657	19418	20	38	19	8	4	14	8	13	8	68	39

Notes:

1 A dependent child is a person in a household aged 0 to 15 (whether or not in a family) or a person aged 16 to 18 who is a full-time student in a family with parent(s).

2 A family consists of a couple (married or cohabiting) with or without children, or a lone parent and their children.
   It also includes a married or cohabiting couple with their grandchildren or a lone grandparent with his or her grandchildren, if there is no parent in the intervening generation in the household.
   A family will also include step-children when their parent is part of the couple.

3 Pensionable age at the time of the Census (29 April 2001) was 65 for men and 60 for women

Table S312: Household Composition by Community Background (Religion or Religion Brought Up In) of Household Reference Person (HRP)

Table population: All households

	All HRPs	Catholic	Protestant and Other Christian (including Christian related)	Other religions and philosophies	None
All households	**626719**	**247568**	**364767**	**2668**	**11716**
One person	**171573**	**60524**	**106584**	**775**	**3690**
- pensioner	80486	24848	54994	145	499
- other	91087	35676	51590	630	3191
One family and no other	**413707**	**165764**	**239157**	**1609**	**7177**
All pensioners	**40769**	**10103**	**30335**	**77**	**254**
Married couple households	**269087**	**107164**	**156171**	**1213**	**4539**
- no children	66484	19440	45374	335	1335
- with one dependent child	50235	20624	28300	278	1033
- with two or more dependent children	101983	47343	52387	498	1755
- all children non-dependent	50385	19757	30110	102	416
Cohabiting couple households	**24224**	**9082**	**13998**	**116**	**1028**
- no children	13282	4710	7846	74	652
- with one dependent child	5116	2026	2902	21	167
- with two or more dependent children	4784	2006	2579	18	181
- all children non-dependent	1042	340	671	3	28
Lone parent households	**79627**	**39415**	**38653**	**203**	**1356**
- with one dependent child	24657	12104	11858	78	617
- with two or more dependent children	25984	14358	11098	68	460
- all children non-dependent	28986	12953	15697	57	279
Other households	**41439**	**21280**	**19026**	**284**	**849**
- with one dependent child	7319	3869	3271	40	139
- with two or more dependent children	8436	4865	3359	70	142
- all students	1732	1034	628	22	48
- all pensioners	4295	1881	2396	7	11
- other	19657	9631	9372	145	509

Notes:
1 A dependent child is a person in a household aged 0 to 15 (whether or not in a family) or a person aged 16 to 18 who is a full-time student in a family with parent(s).
2 A family consists of a couple (married or cohabiting) with or without children, or a lone parent and their children.
  It also includes a married or cohabiting couple with their grandchildren or a lone grandparent with his or her grandchildren, if there is no parent in the intervening generation in the household.
  A family will also include step-children when their parent is part of the couple.
3 Pensionable age at the time of the Census (29 April 2001) was 65 for men and 60 for women.
4 The term 'Catholic' includes those respondents who gave their religion as Catholic or Roman Catholic.

Table S313: Living Arrangements and Community Background (Religion or Religion Brought Up In) by Sex and Age

Table population: All persons aged 16 and over in households

	All persons	All persons						Males						Females					
		16 to 24	25 to 34	35 to 44	45 to 54	55 to 64	65 and over	16 to 24	25 to 34	35 to 44	45 to 54	55 to 64	65 and over	16 to 24	25 to 34	35 to 44	45 to 54	55 to 64	65 and over
All persons	1261250	204807	239333	245573	199732	161117	210688	102702	116866	119885	99444	78323	88065	102105	122467	125688	100288	82794	122623
Catholic	530478	104209	109031	108553	81825	58258	68602	52077	51775	51680	39852	28250	28621	52132	57256	56873	41973	30008	39981
Protestant and Other Christian (including Christian related)	702358	94079	122259	130738	114006	100787	140489	47227	60727	64599	57194	48798	58516	46852	61532	66139	56812	51989	81973
Other religions and philosophies	4906	707	1296	1168	819	521	395	355	740	686	489	306	210	352	556	482	330	215	185
None	23508	5812	6747	5114	3082	1551	1202	3043	3624	2920	1909	969	718	2769	3123	2194	1173	582	484
Living in a couple	702895	17225	130894	178838	151485	120074	104379	5824	59891	88649	76860	61462	58910	11401	71003	90189	74625	58612	45469
Married or re-married	649216	7105	108119	167518	145721	117505	103248	2015	48141	82559	73635	60001	58257	5090	59978	84959	72086	57504	44991
Catholic	251057	2341	46043	72695	58641	40603	30734	679	20145	35295	29162	20658	17457	1662	25898	37400	29479	19945	13277
Protestant and Other Christian (including Christian related)	385928	4358	58698	90929	84658	75545	71740	1207	26339	45034	42988	38473	40279	3151	32359	45895	41670	37072	31461
Other religions and philosophies	2739	108	686	819	561	358	207	34	339	480	334	223	140	74	347	339	227	135	67
None	9492	298	2692	3075	1861	999	567	95	1318	1750	1151	647	381	203	1374	1325	710	352	186
Cohabiting	53679	10120	22775	11320	5764	2569	1131	3809	11750	6090	3225	1461	653	6311	11025	5230	2539	1108	478
Catholic	20994	4164	9511	4211	1905	821	382	1610	4666	2235	1051	453	199	2554	4845	1976	854	368	183
Protestant and Other Christian (including Christian related)	30127	5508	12016	6556	3641	1688	718	2045	6365	3516	2029	966	433	3463	5651	3040	1612	722	285
Other religions and philosophies	246	42	90	65	30	11	8	13	53	43	21	7	5	29	37	22	9	4	3
None	2312	406	1158	488	188	49	23	141	666	296	124	35	16	265	492	192	64	14	7
Not living in a couple	558355	187582	108439	66735	48247	41043	106309	96878	56975	31236	22584	16861	29155	90704	51464	35499	25663	24182	77154
Single (never married)	374230	186650	93578	36229	19387	13700	24686	96632	52504	20801	11536	7670	10292	90018	41074	15428	7851	6030	14394
Catholic	188149	97329	46657	17641	8940	6234	11148	49679	25176	9754	5228	3559	4801	47650	21681	7887	3712	2675	6347
Protestant and Other Christian (including Christian related)	175802	83705	43809	17590	10019	7302	13377	43860	25556	10393	6003	4000	5386	39845	18253	7197	4016	3302	7991
Other religions and philosophies	1237	546	412	136	71	34	38	297	286	85	54	23	19	249	126	51	17	11	19
None	9042	5070	2500	862	357	130	123	2796	1486	569	251	88	86	2274	1014	293	106	42	37

Table S313: Living Arrangements and Community Background (Religion or Religion Brought Up In) by Sex and Age (continued)

	All persons	All persons						Males						Females					
		16 to 24	25 to 34	35 to 44	45 to 54	55 to 64	65 and over	16 to 24	25 to 34	35 to 44	45 to 54	55 to 64	65 and over	16 to 24	25 to 34	35 to 44	45 to 54	55 to 64	65 and over
Married or re-married	**7028**	**216**	**1027**	**1178**	**1044**	**878**	**2685**	**90**	**484**	**514**	**509**	**432**	**1056**	**126**	**543**	**664**	**535**	**446**	**1629**
Catholic	3184	97	551	599	502	396	1039	39	242	239	241	201	363	58	309	360	261	195	676
Protestant and Other Christian (including Christian related)	3497	99	408	476	454	439	1621	38	198	213	212	206	677	61	210	263	242	233	944
Other religions and philosophies	106	8	28	26	20	17	7	8	20	17	14	12	4	-	8	9	6	5	3
None	241	12	40	77	68	26	18	5	24	45	42	13	12	7	16	32	26	13	6
Separated (but still legally married)	**42070**	**581**	**9060**	**14270**	**9705**	**5433**	**3021**	**103**	**2582**	**4794**	**3966**	**2387**	**1513**	**478**	**6478**	**9476**	**5739**	**3046**	**1508**
Catholic	21076	218	4318	7458	5000	2726	1356	42	1072	2230	1871	1152	646	176	3246	5228	3129	1574	710
Protestant and Other Christian (including Christian related)	20021	348	4485	6491	4470	2624	1603	58	1409	2424	1953	1180	818	290	3076	4067	2517	1444	785
Other religions and philosophies	181	-	52	60	39	19	11	-	28	34	20	13	7	-	24	26	19	6	4
None	792	15	205	261	196	64	51	3	73	106	122	42	42	12	132	155	74	22	9
Divorced	**42944**	**93**	**4299**	**13303**	**13077**	**7999**	**4173**	**39**	**1313**	**4723**	**5312**	**3479**	**1773**	**54**	**2986**	**8580**	**7765**	**4520**	**2400**
Catholic	14347	33	1524	5100	4593	2293	804	17	436	1726	1747	1018	387	16	1088	3374	2846	1275	417
Protestant and Other Christian (including Christian related)	27311	46	2606	7831	8073	5490	3265	16	806	2826	3334	2330	1318	30	1800	5005	4739	3160	1947
Other religions and philosophies	223	3	28	54	72	44	22	3	14	27	41	23	10	-	14	27	31	21	12
None	1063	11	141	318	339	172	82	3	57	144	190	108	58	8	84	174	149	64	24
Widowed	**92083**	**42**	**475**	**1755**	**5034**	**13033**	**71744**	**14**	**92**	**404**	**1261**	**2893**	**14521**	**28**	**383**	**1351**	**3773**	**10140**	**57223**
Catholic	31671	27	227	849	2244	5185	23139	11	38	201	552	1209	4768	16	189	648	1692	3976	18371
Protestant and Other Christian (including Christian related)	59672	15	237	865	2691	7699	48165	3	54	193	675	1643	9605	12	183	672	2016	6056	38560
Other religions and philosophies	174	-	-	8	26	38	102	-	-	-	5	5	25	-	-	8	21	33	77
None	566	-	11	33	73	111	338	-	-	10	29	36	123	-	11	23	44	75	215

Notes:
1 Cohabiting couples includes same sex couples.
2 The living arrangements variable is different to marital status. It combines information from both marital status and the relationship matrix.
  Therefore a person living as part of a 'cohabiting couple' could in fact be married (to someone else) but will not appear as married or separated in this classification.
3 A person not living in a couple can be classified married (or re-married) but have no spouse or partner resident in the household.
4 The term 'Catholic' includes those respondents who gave their religion as Catholic or Roman Catholic.

S313

Table S015: Country of Birth by Sex and Age

Table population: All persons

	All persons				Males				Females			
	Total	0 to 15	16 to pensionable age	Pensionable age and over	Total	0 to 15	16 to 64	65 and over	Total	0 to 15	16 to 59	60 and over
All persons	**1685274**	**398058**	**1025700**	**261516**	**821453**	**204263**	**525757**	**91433**	**863821**	**193795**	**499943**	**170083**
Europe	**1666288**	**394741**	**1012210**	**259337**	**812165**	**202550**	**518996**	**90619**	**854123**	**192191**	**493214**	**168718**
United Kingdom	1615769	389766	980282	245721	792060	199948	505241	86871	823709	189818	475041	158850
England	61609	9983	44441	7185	32200	5154	24170	2876	29409	4829	20271	4309
Scotland	16772	1807	11611	3354	8406	898	6406	1102	8366	909	5205	2252
Northern Ireland	1534268	377631	921936	234701	749632	193717	473246	82669	784636	183914	448690	152032
Wales	3008	334	2210	464	1751	173	1363	215	1257	161	847	249
UK part not specified	112	11	84	17	71	6	56	9	41	5	28	8
Republic of Ireland	39051	2438	23826	12787	14522	1287	9743	3492	24529	1151	14083	9295
Ireland part not specified	3221	839	2129	253	1801	440	1266	95	1420	399	863	158
Channel Islands and Isle of Man	567	176	346	45	313	115	184	14	254	61	162	31
Other Western Europe	6970	1403	5102	465	3133	714	2309	110	3837	689	2793	355
EU countries	6455	1334	4712	409	2895	680	2126	89	3560	654	2586	320
France	750	86	622	42	291	44	239	8	459	42	383	34
Germany	3879	1001	2709	169	1750	503	1226	21	2129	498	1483	148
Italy	288	16	223	49	164	11	139	14	124	5	84	35
Netherlands	398	82	271	45	191	41	133	17	207	41	138	28
Spain	364	42	309	13	155	24	128	3	209	18	181	10
Other EU	776	107	578	91	344	57	261	26	432	50	317	65
Non EU countries in Western Europe	515	69	390	56	238	34	183	21	277	35	207	35
Eastern Europe	710	119	525	66	336	46	253	37	374	73	272	29
Poland	102	6	71	25	51	3	32	16	51	3	39	9
Other Eastern Europe	608	113	454	41	285	43	221	21	323	70	233	20

Table S015: Country of Birth by Sex and Age (continued)

	All persons				Males				Females			
	Total	0 to 15	16 to pensionable age	Pensionable age and over	Total	0 to 15	16 to 64	65 and over	Total	0 to 15	16 to 59	60 and over
Africa	**3118**	**590**	**2338**	**190**	**1645**	**307**	**1269**	**69**	**1473**	**283**	**1069**	**121**
North Africa	481	94	360	27	315	52	253	10	166	42	107	17
Central and Western Africa	300	39	247	14	171	20	143	8	129	19	104	6
Nigeria	169	24	139	6	101	16	82	3	68	8	57	3
Other Central and Western Africa	131	15	108	8	70	4	61	5	61	11	47	3
South and Eastern Africa	2337	457	1731	149	1159	235	873	51	1178	222	858	98
Kenya	228	29	187	12	122	16	100	6	106	13	87	6
South Africa	1301	339	863	99	644	183	425	36	657	156	438	63
Zimbabwe	289	44	229	16	132	15	113	4	157	29	116	12
Other South and Eastern Africa	519	45	452	22	261	21	235	5	258	24	217	17
Asia	**7006**	**846**	**5542**	**618**	**3565**	**418**	**2909**	**238**	**3441**	**428**	**2633**	**380**
Middle East	939	242	666	31	524	118	394	12	415	124	272	19
Cyprus	380	122	252	6	190	61	126	3	190	61	126	3
Iran	137	-	124	13	90	-	85	5	47	-	39	8
Other Middle East	422	120	290	12	244	57	183	4	178	63	107	8
Far East	4326	471	3616	239	2130	231	1797	102	2196	240	1819	137
China	756	72	636	48	375	39	314	22	381	33	322	26
Hong Kong	1746	217	1418	111	942	96	791	55	804	121	627	56
Japan	116	21	92	3	47	13	34	-	69	8	58	3
Malaysia	582	23	524	35	322	8	302	12	260	15	222	23
Singapore	271	9	249	13	142	4	135	3	129	5	114	10
Other Far East	855	129	697	29	302	71	221	10	553	58	476	19
South Asia	1741	133	1260	348	911	69	718	124	830	64	542	224
Bangladesh	142	11	123	8	77	3	69	5	65	8	54	3
India	1170	70	802	298	583	39	438	106	587	31	364	192
Pakistan	324	28	262	34	182	14	159	9	142	14	103	25
Other South Asia	105	24	73	8	69	13	52	4	36	11	21	4

© Crown copyright 2003

	All persons				Males				Females			
	Total	0 to 15	16 to pensionable age	Pensionable age and over	Total	0 to 15	16 to 64	65 and over	Total	0 to 15	16 to 59	60 and over
North America	**6093**	**1301**	**3667**	**1125**	**2761**	**687**	**1633**	**441**	**3332**	**614**	**2034**	**684**
Canada	2449	276	1643	530	1070	152	721	197	1379	124	922	333
Carribbean & West Indies	198	22	147	29	92	11	72	9	106	11	75	20
Jamaica	81	9	63	9	44	5	35	4	37	4	28	5
Other Caribbean & West Indies	117	13	84	20	48	6	37	5	69	7	47	15
U.S.A	3369	980	1826	563	1573	515	823	235	1796	465	1003	328
Other North America	77	23	51	3	26	9	17	-	51	14	34	3
South America	**374**	**47**	**284**	**43**	**140**	**22**	**112**	**6**	**234**	**25**	**172**	**37**
Oceania	**2166**	**470**	**1536**	**160**	**1070**	**246**	**774**	**50**	**1096**	**224**	**762**	**110**
Australia	1544	349	1084	111	712	176	501	35	832	173	583	76
New Zealand	448	72	327	49	236	36	185	15	212	36	142	34
Other Oceania	174	49	125	-	122	34	88	-	52	15	37	-
Other	**229**	**63**	**123**	**43**	**107**	**33**	**64**	**10**	**122**	**30**	**59**	**33**

Notes:

1   The European Union (EU) as defined on Census day (29 April 2001).

2   Pensionable age at the time of the Census (29 April 2001) was 65 for men and 60 for women.

3   'Other' consists of persons born at sea or in the air, or with country of birth not stated.

4   Persons born in Central America have been included in North America.

S015

Table S314: Country of Birth by Ethnic Group

Table population: All persons

	All persons	White	Irish Traveller	Mixed	Indian	Pakistani	Bangladeshi	Other Asian	Black Caribbean	Black African	Other Black	Chinese	Other ethnic group
All persons	**1685247**	**1670988**	**1715**	**3313**	**1572**	**661**	**246**	**191**	**254**	**491**	**381**	**4144**	**1291**
Europe	**1666278**	**1658718**	**1706**	**2691**	**578**	**343**	**117**	**22**	**160**	**157**	**222**	**1339**	**225**
United Kingdom	1615767	1608780	1440	2540	554	337	114	22	148	137	199	1294	202
Northern Ireland	1534268	1528516	1342	2022	441	249	70	10	82	110	150	1110	166
England	61609	60582	62	465	97	64	33	9	60	24	46	141	26
Scotland	16773	16614	33	39	13	20	-	-	3	3	3	40	5
Wales	3008	2962	3	14	3	4	8	3	3	-	-	3	5
UK part not specified	109	106	-	-	-	-	3	-	-	-	-	-	-
Republic of Ireland	39051	38672	257	55	18	6	3	-	4	10	3	18	5
Ireland part not specified	3217	3208	6	-	-	-	-	-	-	3	-	-	-
Channel Islands and Isle of Man	568	559	-	-	3	-	-	-	3	-	-	3	-
Other Western Europe	6967	6813	-	87	3	-	-	-	5	4	20	24	11
EU countries	6453	6314	-	76	3	-	-	-	5	4	20	24	7
Non EU countries	514	499	-	11	-	-	-	-	-	-	-	-	4
Eastern Europe	708	686	3	9	-	-	-	-	-	3	-	-	7
Africa	**3111**	**2346**	**3**	**196**	**68**	**3**	-	**3**	**4**	**323**	**33**	**8**	**124**
North Africa	481	188	3	101	-	-	-	-	4	65	16	4	100
Central and Western Africa	300	152	-	11	-	-	-	-	-	131	3	-	3
Nigeria	168	77	-	8	-	-	-	-	-	80	-	-	3
Other Central and Western Africa	132	75	-	3	-	-	-	-	-	51	3	-	-
South and Eastern Africa	2330	2006	-	84	68	3	-	3	-	127	14	4	21
Kenya	227	139	-	14	21	3	-	3	-	44	-	-	3
South Africa	1300	1246	-	18	13	-	-	-	-	19	4	-	-
Zimbabwe	288	243	-	14	3	-	-	-	-	22	6	-	-
Other South and Eastern Africa	515	378	-	38	31	-	-	-	-	42	4	4	18

Table S314: Country of Birth by Ethnic Group (continued)

	All persons	White	Irish Traveller	Mixed	Indian	Pakistani	Bangladeshi	Other Asian	Black Caribbean	Black African	Other Black	Chinese	Other ethnic group
Asia	**7003**	**1706**	**-**	**216**	**903**	**315**	**125**	**158**	**3**	**5**	**10**	**2766**	**796**
Middle East	936	639	-	77	10	3	-	13	-	5	3	3	183
Far East	4327	705	-	111	54	4	3	87	3	-	4	2758	598
China	756	25	-	4	-	-	-	-	-	-	-	727	-
Other Far East	3571	680	-	107	54	4	3	87	3	-	4	2031	598
South Asia	1740	362	-	28	839	308	122	58	-	-	3	5	15
Bangladesh	138	8	-	-	8	-	122	-	-	-	-	-	-
India	1172	298	-	20	815	28	-	3	-	-	-	5	3
Pakistan	324	28	-	8	8	280	-	-	-	-	-	-	-
Other South Asia	106	28	-	-	8	-	-	55	-	-	3	-	12
North America	**6091**	**5820**	**3**	**107**	**6**	**-**	**-**	**-**	**77**	**6**	**18**	**9**	**45**
Canada	2448	2423	-	20	-	-	-	-	-	-	-	-	5
Caribbean & West Indies	200	105	-	15	3	-	-	-	65	3	3	6	-
Jamaica	84	36	-	7	-	-	-	-	32	3	3	3	-
Other Caribbean & West Indies	116	69	-	8	3	-	-	-	33	-	-	3	-
U.S.A	3368	3264	3	55	-	-	-	-	5	3	15	3	20
Other North America	75	28	-	17	3	-	-	-	7	-	-	-	20
South America	375	260	-	52	6	-	-	5	5	-	3	3	41
Oceania	2161	1971	-	45	-	-	-	-	-	-	89	-	56
Other	228	167	3	6	11	-	4	3	5	-	6	19	4

Notes:

1 The European Union (EU) as defined on Census day (29 April 2001).

2 'Other' consists of persons born at sea or in the air, or with country of birth not stated.

3 Persons born in Central America have been included in North America.

S314

2. Health and Care

2. Health and Care

Table S016: Sex and Age by General Health and Limiting Long-Term Illness (Household Residents)

Table population: All persons in households

	All persons			Good health			Fairly good health			Not good health		
	Total	Limiting long-term illness	No limiting long-term illness	Total	Limiting long-term illness	No limiting long-term illness	Total	Limiting long-term illness	No limiting long-term illness	Total	Limiting long-term illness	No limiting long-term illness
All persons	1658813	327465	1331348	1167297	50596	1116701	318194	121916	196278	173322	154953	18369
0 to 2	67275	2362	64913	61021	1094	59927	5123	595	4528	1131	673	458
3 to 4	47917	2496	45421	43201	1008	42193	3898	869	3029	818	619	199
5 to 7	72314	4586	67728	65919	2028	63891	5259	1614	3645	1136	944	192
8 to 9	50670	3212	47458	46778	1495	45283	3206	1130	2076	686	587	99
10 to 14	132379	7859	124520	121994	3758	118236	8808	2817	5991	1577	1284	293
15	27001	1521	25480	24658	758	23900	1963	496	1467	380	267	113
16 to 17	53155	2930	50225	48052	1309	46743	4231	983	3248	872	638	234
18 to 19	45927	2712	43215	40228	1047	39181	4634	882	3752	1065	783	282
20 to 24	105729	7630	98099	89287	2352	86935	12728	2535	10193	3714	2743	971
25 to 29	112934	10070	102864	91060	2558	88502	16512	3398	13114	5362	4114	1248
30 to 34	126402	14322	112080	96599	2932	93667	21592	4823	16769	8211	6567	1644
35 to 39	128847	18392	110455	93574	3198	90376	24020	5890	18130	11253	9304	1949
40 to 44	116727	20249	96478	79767	3008	76759	24259	6480	17779	12701	10761	1940
45 to 49	101915	21488	80427	64753	2878	61875	23474	6668	16806	13688	11942	1746
50 to 54	97817	26975	70842	55654	2856	52798	24704	8360	16344	17459	15759	1700
55 to 59	88132	31478	56654	43659	2851	40808	24485	10070	14415	19988	18557	1431
60 to 64	72985	31588	41397	31708	3006	28702	23486	11779	11707	17791	16803	988
65 to 69	64594	30067	34527	25693	3064	22629	23932	12945	10987	14969	14058	911
70 to 74	56634	29325	27309	19580	2919	16661	23083	13236	9847	13971	13170	801
75 to 79	44386	26309	18077	13340	2903	10437	18782	11765	7017	12264	11641	623
80 to 84	27405	18513	8892	7027	2102	4925	12085	8475	3610	8293	7936	357
85 to 89	13039	9798	3241	2733	1046	1687	5844	4441	1403	4462	4311	151
90 and over	4629	3583	1046	1012	426	586	2086	1665	421	1531	1492	39

Table S016: Sex and Age by General Health and Limiting Long-Term Illness (Household Residents) (continued)

	All persons			Good health			Fairly good health			Not good health		
	Total	Limiting long-term illness	No limiting long-term illness	Total	Limiting long-term illness	No limiting long-term illness	Total	Limiting long-term illness	No limiting long-term illness	Total	Limiting long-term illness	No limiting long-term illness
Males	**809276**	**151057**	**658219**	**590608**	**26921**	**563687**	**141417**	**54722**	**86695**	**77251**	**69414**	**7837**
0 to 2	34537	1369	33168	30988	611	30377	2870	368	2502	679	390	289
3 to 4	24654	1467	23187	22104	591	21513	2069	501	1568	481	375	106
5 to 7	37155	2724	34431	33599	1193	32406	2865	941	1924	691	590	101
8 to 9	25958	1915	24043	23829	906	22923	1725	664	1061	404	345	59
10 to 14	67845	4538	63307	62365	2157	60208	4625	1656	2969	855	725	130
15	13839	812	13027	12742	401	12341	922	272	650	175	139	36
16 to 17	26986	1568	25418	24751	744	24007	1851	502	1349	384	322	62
18 to 19	23260	1446	21814	20823	601	20222	1934	444	1490	503	401	102
20 to 24	52456	3916	48540	45385	1280	44105	5280	1238	4042	1791	1398	393
25 to 29	55254	4965	50289	45886	1406	44480	7031	1666	5365	2337	1893	444
30 to 34	61614	6724	54890	48875	1623	47252	9259	2251	7008	3480	2850	630
35 to 39	62841	8529	54312	47199	1716	45483	10769	2740	8029	4873	4073	800
40 to 44	57045	9527	47518	40205	1586	38619	11138	3064	8074	5702	4877	825
45 to 49	51331	10530	40801	33724	1680	32044	11137	3207	7930	6470	5643	827
50 to 54	48113	12720	35393	28617	1564	27053	11452	3873	7579	8044	7283	761
55 to 59	43241	15147	28094	22345	1541	20804	11300	4699	6601	9596	8907	689
60 to 64	35082	16097	18985	15316	1646	13670	10523	5668	4855	9243	8783	460
65 to 69	30036	14263	15773	12438	1710	10728	10835	6169	4666	6763	6384	379
70 to 74	24562	12471	12091	9102	1477	7625	9725	5576	4149	5735	5418	317
75 to 79	17841	10013	7828	5982	1223	4759	7312	4476	2836	4547	4314	233
80 to 84	10334	6561	3773	3013	808	2205	4476	3039	1437	2845	2714	131
85 to 89	4074	2874	1200	992	339	653	1791	1295	496	1291	1240	51
90 and over	1218	881	337	328	118	210	528	413	115	362	350	12

Table S016: Sex and Age by General Health and Limiting Long-Term Illness (Household Residents) (continued)

	All persons			Good health			Fairly good health			Not good health		
	Total	Limiting long-term illness	No limiting long-term illness	Total	Limiting long-term illness	No limiting long-term illness	Total	Limiting long-term illness	No limiting long-term illness	Total	Limiting long-term illness	No limiting long-term illness
Females	**849537**	**176408**	**673129**	**576689**	**23675**	**553014**	**176777**	**67194**	**109583**	**96071**	**85539**	**10532**
0 to 2	32738	993	31745	30033	483	29550	2253	227	2026	452	283	169
3 to 4	23263	1029	22234	21097	417	20680	1829	368	1461	337	244	93
5 to 7	35159	1862	33297	32320	835	31485	2394	673	1721	445	354	91
8 to 9	24712	1297	23415	22949	589	22360	1481	466	1015	282	242	40
10 to 14	64534	3321	61213	59629	1601	58028	4183	1161	3022	722	559	163
15	13162	709	12453	11916	357	11559	1041	224	817	205	128	77
16 to 17	26169	1362	24807	23301	565	22736	2380	481	1899	488	316	172
18 to 19	22667	1266	21401	19405	446	18959	2700	438	2262	562	382	180
20 to 24	53273	3714	49559	43902	1072	42830	7448	1297	6151	1923	1345	578
25 to 29	57680	5105	52575	45174	1152	44022	9481	1732	7749	3025	2221	804
30 to 34	64788	7598	57190	47724	1309	46415	12333	2572	9761	4731	3717	1014
35 to 39	66006	9863	56143	46375	1482	44893	13251	3150	10101	6380	5231	1149
40 to 44	59682	10722	48960	39562	1422	38140	13121	3416	9705	6999	5884	1115
45 to 49	50584	10958	39626	31029	1198	29831	12337	3461	8876	7218	6299	919
50 to 54	49704	14255	35449	27037	1292	25745	13252	4487	8765	9415	8476	939
55 to 59	44891	16331	28560	21314	1310	20004	13185	5371	7814	10392	9650	742
60 to 64	37903	15491	22412	16392	1360	15032	12963	6111	6852	8548	8020	528
65 to 69	34558	15804	18754	13255	1354	11901	13097	6776	6321	8206	7674	532
70 to 74	32072	16854	15218	10478	1442	9036	13358	7660	5698	8236	7752	484
75 to 79	26545	16296	10249	7358	1680	5678	11470	7289	4181	7717	7327	390
80 to 84	17071	11952	5119	4014	1294	2720	7609	5436	2173	5448	5222	226
85 to 89	8965	6924	2041	1741	707	1034	4053	3146	907	3171	3071	100
90 and over	3411	2702	709	684	308	376	1558	1252	306	1169	1142	27

Notes:

1 General health refers to health over the 12 months prior to Census day (29 April 2001).

2 Limiting long-term illness covers any long-term illness, health problem or disability which limits daily activities or work.

S016

Table S316: Limiting Long-Term Illness and Age by Number of Floor Levels and Tenure

Table population: All persons in households

	All persons	Rooms on one floor					Rooms on more than one floor				
		All persons	Owner occupied	Rented from NIHE	Other social rented	Private rented	All persons	Owner occupied	Rented from NIHE	Other social rented	Private rented
All persons	**1658813**	**451466**	**330076**	**70350**	**13779**	**37261**	**1207347**	**903544**	**196102**	**15004**	**92697**
0 to 15	397556	87227	68001	10615	947	7664	310329	215790	64070	5227	25242
16 to 24	204811	50025	36637	7079	837	5472	154786	105864	27989	1919	19014
25 to 44	484910	120623	90198	15807	2064	12554	364287	281272	49480	4093	29442
45 to 59	287864	84420	65682	12376	1885	4477	203444	164762	28105	1896	8681
60 to 64	72985	24721	18206	4431	842	1242	48264	38670	7106	396	2092
65 to 74	121228	45051	30250	9721	2446	2634	76177	59900	11665	795	3817
75 to 84	71791	30967	17142	8079	3377	2369	40824	30622	6410	521	3271
85 and over	17668	8432	3960	2242	1381	849	9236	6664	1277	157	1138
With a limiting long-term illness	**327465**	**112645**	**63650**	**31589**	**8394**	**9012**	**214820**	**141294**	**53009**	**4000**	**16517**
0 to 15	22036	4627	2960	1005	149	513	17409	9219	5890	487	1813
16 to 24	13272	3520	2000	965	180	375	9752	5385	2950	217	1200
25 to 44	63033	18365	10113	5312	927	2013	44668	26376	12707	1100	4485
45 to 59	79941	25946	15749	7150	1237	1810	53995	35931	14108	933	3023
60 to 64	31588	11203	6954	3007	601	641	20385	14783	4342	276	984
65 to 74	59392	22675	13136	6482	1648	1409	36717	26716	7495	502	2004
75 to 84	44822	19853	9850	5858	2541	1604	24969	17931	4529	370	2139
85 and over	13381	6456	2888	1810	1111	647	6925	4953	988	115	869
Without a limiting long-term illness	**1331348**	**338821**	**266426**	**38761**	**5385**	**28249**	**992527**	**762250**	**143093**	**11004**	**76180**
0 to 15	375520	82600	65041	9610	798	7151	292920	206571	58180	4740	23429
16 to 24	191539	46505	34637	6114	657	5097	145034	100479	25039	1702	17814
25 to 44	421877	102258	80085	10495	1137	10541	319619	254896	36773	2993	24957
45 to 59	207923	58474	49933	5226	648	2667	149449	128831	13997	963	5658
60 to 64	41397	13518	11252	1424	241	601	27879	23887	2764	120	1108
65 to 74	61836	22376	17114	3239	798	1225	39460	33184	4170	293	1813
75 to 84	26969	11114	7292	2221	836	765	15855	12691	1881	151	1132
85 and over	4287	1976	1072	432	270	202	2311	1711	289	42	269

Notes:

1 The terms used to describe tenure are defined as:
   Owner occupied: either owns outright, owns with a mortgage or loan, or pays part rent and part mortgage (shared ownership).
   Rented from NIHE: rented from Northern Ireland Housing Executive.
   Other social rented: rented from Registered Social Landlord, Housing Association, Housing Co-operative or Charitable Trust.
   Private rented: rented from a private landlord or letting agency, employer of a household member, or relative or friend of a household member or other person.

2 'Rented from NIHE', 'Other social rented' and 'Private rented' include living in the household rent free.

3 Limiting long-term illness covers any long-term illness, health problem or disability which limits daily activities or work.

Table S018: Sex and Amenities and Central Heating by General Health and Limiting Long-Term Illness

Table population: All persons in households

	All persons			Good health			Fairly good health			Not good health		
	Total	Limiting long-term illness	No limiting long-term illness	Total	Limiting long-term illness	No limiting long-term illness	Total	Limiting long-term illness	No limiting long-term illness	Total	Limiting long-term illness	No limiting long-term illness
All persons	**1658813**	**327465**	**1331348**	**1167297**	**50596**	**1116701**	**318194**	**121916**	**196278**	**173322**	**154953**	**18369**
Has sole use of bath/shower and toilet	**1648959**	**324973**	**1323986**	**1161143**	**50262**	**1110881**	**315830**	**120964**	**194866**	**171986**	**153747**	**18239**
Central heating	1589527	307007	1282520	1127622	48060	1079562	300139	114276	185863	161766	144671	17095
No central heating	59432	17966	41466	33521	2202	31319	15691	6688	9003	10220	9076	1144
Does not have sole use of bath/shower and toilet	**9854**	**2492**	**7362**	**6154**	**334**	**5820**	**2364**	**952**	**1412**	**1336**	**1206**	**130**
Central heating	7178	1492	5686	4915	236	4679	1476	561	915	787	695	92
No central heating	2676	1000	1676	1239	98	1141	888	391	497	549	511	38
Males	**809276**	**151057**	**658219**	**590608**	**26921**	**563687**	**141417**	**54722**	**86695**	**77251**	**69414**	**7837**
Has sole use of bath/shower and toilet	**804092**	**149832**	**654260**	**587284**	**26755**	**560529**	**140244**	**54265**	**85979**	**76564**	**68812**	**7752**
Central heating	774546	141065	633481	570103	25597	544506	132860	51102	81758	71583	64366	7217
No central heating	29546	8767	20779	17181	1158	16023	7384	3163	4221	4981	4446	535
Does not have sole use of bath/shower and toilet	**5184**	**1225**	**3959**	**3324**	**166**	**3158**	**1173**	**457**	**716**	**687**	**602**	**85**
Central heating	3546	668	2878	2545	111	2434	639	252	387	362	305	57
No central heating	1638	557	1081	779	55	724	534	205	329	325	297	28
Females	**849537**	**176408**	**673129**	**576689**	**23675**	**553014**	**176777**	**67194**	**109583**	**96071**	**85539**	**10532**
Has sole use of bath/shower and toilet	**844867**	**175141**	**669726**	**573859**	**23507**	**550352**	**175586**	**66699**	**108887**	**95422**	**84935**	**10487**
Central heating	814981	165942	649039	557519	22463	535056	167279	63174	104105	90183	80305	9878
No central heating	29886	9199	20687	16340	1044	15296	8307	3525	4782	5239	4630	609
Does not have sole use of a bath/shower and toilet	**4670**	**1267**	**3403**	**2830**	**168**	**2662**	**1191**	**495**	**696**	**649**	**604**	**45**
Central heating	3632	824	2808	2370	125	2245	837	309	528	425	390	35
No central heating	1038	443	595	460	43	417	354	186	168	224	214	10

Notes:

1 General health refers to health over the 12 months prior to Census day (29 April 2001).

2 Limiting long-term illness covers any long-term illness, health problem or disability which limits daily activities or work.

S018

Table S317: Sex and Limiting Long-Term Illness and Type of Communal Establishment by Age (Residents (Non-Staff) in Communal Establishments)

Table population: All communal establishment residents (excluding staff and their families)

	All persons	0 to 4	5 to 9	10 to 11	12 to 14	15 to 17	18 to 19	20 to 44	45 to 59	60 to 64	65 to 74	75 to 84	85 to 89	90 and over
All persons	24258	35	41	37	219	397	2695	7669	1563	514	1722	4355	2735	2276
With a limiting long-term illness	13819	6	6	6	25	54	100	1595	1321	440	1533	4030	2549	2154
Medical and care establishments	12501	6	6	6	11	39	24	1074	1136	389	1402	3828	2462	2118
'NHS/HSSB' managed	2797	6	3	3	11	26	14	450	418	116	339	726	375	310
General, psychiatric or other hospital	1385	6	3	3	8	15	9	389	348	78	177	216	60	73
Nursing home	100	-	-	-	-	-	-	6	12	4	14	24	22	18
Residential care home	1273	-	-	-	-	3	5	52	58	34	145	477	287	212
Children's home	11	-	-	-	3	8	-	-	-	-	-	-	-	-
Other medical and care home	28	-	-	-	-	-	-	3	-	-	3	9	6	7
Non 'NHS/HSSB' managed	9704	-	3	3	-	13	10	624	718	273	1063	3102	2087	1808
Nursing home	6677	-	3	-	-	3	-	218	317	145	759	2294	1541	1397
Residential care home	2662	-	-	-	-	-	3	359	362	110	246	703	493	386
Children's home	6	-	-	3	-	3	-	-	-	-	-	-	-	-
Other	359	-	-	-	-	7	7	47	39	18	58	105	53	25
Other establishments	1318	-	-	-	14	15	76	521	185	51	131	202	87	36
Without a limiting long-term illness	10439	29	35	31	194	343	2595	6074	242	74	189	325	186	122
Medical and care establishments	1075	5	15	8	68	74	57	240	58	16	70	204	151	109
'NHS/HSSB' managed	454	5	4	3	39	52	44	173	22	-	18	38	33	23
General, psychiatric or other hospital	244	5	-	-	-	-	44	170	19	-	3	3	-	-
Nursing home	6	-	-	-	-	-	-	-	-	-	3	-	-	3
Residential care home	112	-	4	-	3	3	-	3	3	-	12	35	33	20
Children's home	92	-	-	3	36	49	-	-	-	-	-	-	-	-
Other medical and care home	-	-	-	-	-	-	-	-	-	-	-	-	-	-
Non 'NHS/HSSB' managed	621	-	11	5	29	22	13	67	36	16	52	166	118	86
Nursing home	116	-	-	-	-	-	3	4	6	3	15	41	23	21
Residential care home	368	-	6	-	3	3	3	43	22	10	31	103	87	57
Children's home	30	-	-	-	17	13	-	-	-	-	-	-	-	-
Other	107	-	5	5	9	6	7	20	8	3	6	22	8	8
Other establishments	9364	24	20	23	126	269	2538	5834	184	58	119	121	35	13

Table S317: Sex and Limiting Long-Term Illness and Type of Communal Establishment by Age (Residents (Non-Staff) in Communal Establishments) (continued)

	All persons	0 to 4	5 to 9	10 to 11	12 to 14	15 to 17	18 to 19	20 to 44	45 to 59	60 to 64	65 to 74	75 to 84	85 to 89	90 and over
Males	11433	17	20	28	131	214	1280	5536	972	286	763	1282	566	338
With a limiting long-term illness	**4917**	**3**	**-**	**6**	**15**	**24**	**62**	**1026**	**807**	**249**	**688**	**1191**	**525**	**321**
Medical and care establishments	4160	3	-	6	8	16	18	646	659	212	627	1139	510	316
NHS/HSSB' managed	1236	3	-	3	8	13	11	303	256	69	169	262	85	54
General, psychiatric or other hospital	816	3	-	3	8	10	6	268	221	52	101	102	25	17
Nursing home	35	-	-	-	-	-	-	3	9	4	7	9	3	-
Residential care home	373	-	-	-	-	-	5	29	26	13	61	151	54	34
Children's home	3	-	-	-	-	3	-	-	-	-	-	-	-	-
Other medical and care home	9	-	-	-	-	-	-	3	-	-	-	-	3	3
Non 'NHS/HSSB' managed	2924	-	-	3	-	3	7	343	403	143	458	877	425	262
Nursing home	1914	-	-	-	-	-	-	119	179	82	332	692	315	195
Residential care home	851	-	-	-	-	-	3	192	196	52	98	156	91	63
Children's home	3	-	-	3	-	-	-	-	-	-	-	-	-	-
Other	156	-	-	-	-	3	4	32	28	9	28	29	19	4
Other establishments	757	-	-	-	7	8	44	380	148	37	61	52	15	5
Without a limiting long-term illness	**6516**	**14**	**20**	**22**	**116**	**190**	**1218**	**4510**	**165**	**37**	**75**	**91**	**41**	**17**
Medical and care establishments	401	5	12	8	36	33	8	114	32	7	34	61	38	13
'NHS/HSSB' managed	198	5	4	3	18	25	5	88	14	-	10	15	8	3
General, psychiatric or other hospital	115	5	-	-	-	-	5	88	14	-	-	3	-	-
Nursing home	3	-	-	-	-	-	-	-	-	-	3	-	-	-
Residential care home	36	-	-	-	3	3	-	-	-	-	7	12	8	3
Children's home	44	-	4	3	15	22	-	-	-	-	-	-	-	-
Other medical and care home	-	-	-	-	-	-	-	-	-	-	-	-	-	-
Non 'NHS/HSSB' managed	203	-	8	5	18	8	3	26	18	7	24	46	30	10
Nursing home	36	-	-	-	-	-	-	-	3	-	9	12	9	3
Residential care home	108	-	3	-	3	-	-	20	12	4	15	29	18	4
Children's home	14	-	-	-	9	5	-	-	-	-	-	-	-	-
Other	45	-	5	5	6	3	3	6	3	3	-	5	3	3
Other establishments	6115	9	8	14	80	157	1210	4396	133	30	41	30	3	4

S317

Table S317: Sex and Limiting Long-Term Illness and Type of Communal Establishment by Age (Residents (Non-Staff) in Communal Establishments) (continued)

	All persons	0 to 4	5 to 9	10 to 11	12 to 14	15 to 17	18 to 19	20 to 44	45 to 59	60 to 64	65 to 74	75 to 84	85 to 89	90 and over
Females	**12825**	**18**	**21**	**9**	**88**	**183**	**1415**	**2133**	**591**	**228**	**959**	**3073**	**2169**	**1938**
With a limiting long-term illness	**8902**	**3**	**6**	**-**	**10**	**30**	**38**	**569**	**514**	**191**	**845**	**2839**	**2024**	**1833**
Medical and care establishments	8341	3	6	-	3	23	6	428	477	177	775	2689	1952	1802
'NHS/HSSB' managed	1561	3	3	-	3	13	3	147	162	47	170	464	290	256
General, psychiatric or other hospital	569	3	3	-	-	5	3	121	127	26	76	114	35	56
Nursing home	65	-	-	-	-	-	-	3	3	-	7	15	19	18
Residential care home	900	-	-	-	-	3	-	23	32	21	84	326	233	178
Children's home	8	-	-	-	3	5	-	-	-	-	-	-	-	-
Other medical and care home	19	-	-	-	-	-	-	-	-	-	3	9	3	4
Non 'NHS/HSSB' managed	6780	-	3	-	-	10	3	281	315	130	605	2225	1662	1546
Nursing home	4763	-	3	-	-	3	-	99	138	63	427	1602	1226	1202
Residential care home	1811	-	-	-	-	-	-	167	166	58	148	547	402	323
Children's home	3	-	-	-	-	3	-	-	-	-	-	-	-	-
Other	203	-	-	-	-	4	3	15	11	9	30	76	34	21
Other establishments	561	-	-	-	7	7	32	141	37	14	70	150	72	31
Without a limiting long-term illness	**3923**	**15**	**15**	**9**	**78**	**153**	**1377**	**1564**	**77**	**37**	**114**	**234**	**145**	**105**
Medical and care establishments	674	-	3	-	32	41	49	126	26	9	36	143	113	96
'NHS/HSSB' managed	256	-	-	-	21	27	39	85	8	-	8	23	25	20
General, psychiatric or other hospital	129	-	-	-	-	-	39	82	5	-	3	-	-	-
Nursing home	3	-	-	-	-	-	-	-	-	-	-	-	-	3
Residential care home	76	-	-	-	-	-	-	3	3	-	5	23	25	17
Children's home	48	-	-	-	21	27	-	-	-	-	-	-	-	-
Other medical and care home	-	-	-	-	-	-	-	-	-	-	-	-	-	-
Non 'NHS/HSSB' managed	418	-	3	-	11	14	10	41	18	9	28	120	88	76
Nursing home	80	-	-	-	-	-	3	4	3	3	6	29	14	18
Residential care home	260	-	3	-	-	3	3	23	10	6	16	74	69	53
Children's home	16	-	-	-	8	8	-	-	-	-	-	-	-	-
Other	62	-	-	-	3	3	4	14	5	-	6	17	5	5
Other establishments	3249	15	12	9	46	112	1328	1438	51	28	78	91	32	9

Notes:
1 'NHS/HSSB' refers to the Health and Personal Social Services in Northern Ireland.
2 Limiting long-term illness covers any long-term illness, health problem or disability which limits daily activities or work.

Table S065: Sex and Age by General Health and Limiting Long-Term Illness (Communal Establishment Residents)

Table population: All persons resident in communal establishments (excluding staff and their families)

	All persons			Good health			Fairly good health			Not good health		
	Total	Limiting long-term illness	No limiting long-term illness	Total	Limiting long-term illness	No limiting long-term illness	Total	Limiting long-term illness	No limiting long-term illness	Total	Limiting long-term illness	No limiting long-term illness
All persons	24248	13822	10426	11691	3026	8665	6983	5410	1573	5574	5386	188
0 to 2	29	3	26	20	-	20	3	-	3	6	3	3
3 to 4	9	3	6	6	-	6	3	3	-	-	-	-
5 to 7	27	6	21	21	-	21	3	3	-	3	3	-
8 to 9	22	3	19	19	-	19	3	3	-	-	-	-
10 to 11	43	9	34	34	3	31	6	3	3	3	3	-
12 to 14	218	24	194	172	8	164	42	12	30	4	4	-
15	97	6	91	74	3	71	20	-	20	3	3	-
16 to 17	295	46	249	214	20	194	69	19	50	12	7	5
18 to 19	2698	105	2593	2307	38	2269	339	39	300	52	28	24
20 to 24	3601	260	3341	3052	101	2951	457	108	349	92	51	41
25 to 29	1708	252	1456	1400	110	1290	226	80	146	82	62	20
30 to 34	1071	301	770	751	109	642	210	105	105	110	87	23
35 to 39	742	384	358	436	163	273	214	136	78	92	85	7
40 to 44	545	395	150	246	137	109	171	139	32	128	119	9
45 to 49	497	412	85	182	127	55	199	179	20	116	106	10
50 to 54	535	458	77	162	106	56	218	197	21	155	155	-
55 to 59	524	451	73	164	107	57	194	178	16	166	166	-
60 to 64	515	440	75	129	81	48	204	184	20	182	175	7
65 to 69	654	579	75	135	83	52	256	236	20	263	260	3
70 to 74	1062	952	110	165	110	55	470	418	52	427	424	3
75 to 79	1861	1709	152	437	359	78	710	642	68	714	708	6
80 to 84	2493	2321	172	523	444	79	960	879	81	1010	998	12
85 to 89	2733	2549	184	581	502	79	1104	1008	96	1048	1039	9
90 and over	2269	2154	115	461	415	46	902	839	63	906	900	6

S065

Table S065: Sex and Age by General Health and Limiting Long-Term Illness (Communal Establishment Residents) (continued)

	All persons			Good health			Fairly good health			Not good health		
	Total	Limiting long-term illness	No limiting long-term illness	Total	Limiting long-term illness	No limiting long-term illness	Total	Limiting long-term illness	No limiting long-term illness	Total	Limiting long-term illness	No limiting long-term illness
Males	**11427**	**4924**	**6503**	**6742**	**1167**	**5575**	**2705**	**1878**	**827**	**1980**	**1879**	**101**
0 to 2	13	3	10	10	-	10	-	-	-	3	3	-
3 to 4	3	-	3	3	-	3	-	-	-	-	-	-
5 to 7	11	-	11	11	-	11	-	-	-	-	-	-
8 to 9	15	3	12	12	-	12	3	3	-	-	-	-
10 to 11	32	9	23	23	3	20	6	3	3	3	3	-
12 to 14	130	15	115	103	4	99	23	7	16	4	4	-
15	43	-	43	35	-	35	8	-	8	-	-	-
16 to 17	170	25	145	135	11	124	31	10	21	4	4	-
18 to 19	1282	63	1219	1098	24	1074	159	25	134	25	14	11
20 to 24	2437	156	2281	2107	61	2046	279	68	211	51	27	24
25 to 29	1342	180	1162	1122	80	1042	168	62	106	52	38	14
30 to 34	847	194	653	611	64	547	159	72	87	77	58	19
35 to 39	559	262	297	343	115	228	150	88	62	66	59	7
40 to 44	351	233	118	164	75	89	107	84	23	80	74	6
45 to 49	329	257	72	120	75	45	134	117	17	75	65	10
50 to 54	333	278	55	104	65	39	128	112	16	101	101	-
55 to 59	306	272	34	82	59	23	112	101	11	112	112	-
60 to 64	285	249	36	66	45	21	106	95	11	113	109	4
65 to 69	324	289	35	61	43	18	122	108	14	141	138	3
70 to 74	438	399	39	76	57	19	177	157	20	185	185	-
75 to 79	624	586	38	140	122	18	227	207	20	257	257	-
80 to 84	656	605	51	131	108	23	250	225	25	275	272	3
85 to 89	564	525	39	120	96	24	229	214	15	215	215	-
90 and over	333	321	12	65	60	5	127	120	7	141	141	-

Table S065: Sex and Age by General Health and Limiting Long-Term Illness (Communal Establishment Residents) (continued)

	All persons			Good health			Fairly good health			Not good health		
	Total	Limiting long-term illness	No limiting long-term illness	Total	Limiting long-term illness	No limiting long-term illness	Total	Limiting long-term illness	No limiting long-term illness	Total	Limiting long-term illness	No limiting long-term illness
Females	**12821**	**8898**	**3923**	**4949**	**1859**	**3090**	**4278**	**3532**	**746**	**3594**	**3507**	**87**
0 to 2	**16**	-	16	**10**	-	10	**3**	-	3	**3**	-	3
3 to 4	**6**	3	3	**3**	-	3	**3**	3	-	**-**	-	-
5 to 7	**16**	6	10	**10**	-	10	**3**	3	-	**3**	3	-
8 to 9	**7**	-	7	**7**	-	7	**-**	-	-	**-**	-	-
10 to 11	**11**	-	11	**11**	-	11	**-**	-	-	**-**	-	-
12 to 14	**88**	9	79	**69**	4	65	**19**	5	14	**3**	3	-
15	**54**	6	48	**39**	3	36	**12**	-	12	**3**	3	-
16 to 17	**125**	21	104	**79**	9	70	**38**	9	29	**8**	3	5
18 to 19	**1416**	42	1374	**1209**	14	1195	**180**	14	166	**27**	14	13
20 to 24	**1164**	104	1060	**945**	40	905	**178**	40	138	**41**	24	17
25 to 29	**366**	72	294	**278**	30	248	**58**	18	40	**30**	24	6
30 to 34	**224**	107	117	**140**	45	95	**51**	33	18	**33**	29	4
35 to 39	**183**	122	61	**93**	48	45	**64**	48	16	**26**	26	-
40 to 44	**194**	162	32	**82**	62	20	**64**	55	9	**48**	45	3
45 to 49	**168**	155	13	**62**	52	10	**65**	62	3	**41**	41	-
50 to 54	**202**	180	22	**58**	41	17	**90**	85	5	**54**	54	-
55 to 59	**218**	179	39	**82**	48	34	**82**	77	5	**54**	54	-
60 to 64	**230**	191	39	**63**	36	27	**98**	89	9	**69**	66	3
65 to 69	**330**	290	40	**74**	40	34	**134**	128	6	**122**	122	-
70 to 74	**624**	553	71	**89**	53	36	**293**	261	32	**242**	239	3
75 to 79	**1237**	1123	114	**297**	237	60	**483**	435	48	**457**	451	6
80 to 84	**1837**	1716	121	**392**	336	56	**710**	654	56	**735**	726	9
85 to 89	**2169**	2024	145	**461**	406	55	**875**	794	81	**833**	824	9
90 and over	**1936**	1833	103	**396**	355	41	**775**	719	56	**765**	759	6

Notes:
1   This table includes 'residents' of communal establishments only, i.e. it excludes staff and their relatives living at the establishment.
2   General health refers to health over the 12 months prior to Census day (29 April 2001).
3   Limiting long-term illness covers any long-term illness, health problem or disability which limits daily activities or work.

S065

Table S019: General Health and Limiting Long-Term Illness and Occupancy Rating by Age

Table population: All persons in households

	All ages	0 to 2	3 to 4	5 to 7	8 to 9	10 to 14	15	16 to 17	18 to 19	20 to 24	25 to 34	35 to 44	45 to 49	50 to 54	55 to 59	60 to 64	65 to 74	75 to 84	85 to 89	90 and over
All persons	**1658814**	**67275**	**47917**	**72314**	**50670**	**132379**	**27001**	**53155**	**45927**	**105729**	**239336**	**245574**	**101915**	**97817**	**88132**	**72985**	**121228**	**71791**	**13039**	**4630**
With a limiting long-term illness	**327465**	**2362**	**2496**	**4586**	**3212**	**7859**	**1521**	**2930**	**2712**	**7630**	**24392**	**38641**	**21488**	**26975**	**31478**	**31588**	**59392**	**44822**	**9798**	**3583**
+2 or more	155087	781	818	1436	958	2199	431	769	703	2114	8918	14271	8620	12531	16826	17960	34430	24567	4985	1770
+1	83192	657	694	1276	869	1823	336	570	602	2080	7355	10390	5597	6961	7782	7426	14225	11152	2475	922
0	56696	577	669	1207	932	2250	412	766	693	1864	5312	8674	4275	4524	4315	4063	7282	6533	1708	640
-1 or less	32490	347	315	667	453	1587	342	825	714	1572	2807	5306	2996	2959	2555	2139	3455	2570	630	251
Without a limiting long-term illness	**1331349**	**64913**	**45421**	**67728**	**47458**	**124520**	**25480**	**50225**	**43215**	**98099**	**214944**	**206933**	**80427**	**70842**	**56654**	**41397**	**61836**	**26969**	**3241**	**1047**
+2 or more	650121	28919	20760	30121	20059	47174	9437	16569	13066	32544	108292	107824	43430	42162	37606	29273	43292	17237	1843	513
+1	302854	17864	12163	17137	11359	27101	5367	10017	9092	23844	55557	46645	16950	14298	10608	7055	11220	5607	729	241
0	229701	11846	8450	13663	10298	29736	5814	11465	10242	22534	34121	33852	11667	8604	5332	3347	5095	2911	509	215
-1 or less	148673	6284	4048	6807	5742	20509	4862	12174	10815	19177	16974	18612	8380	5778	3108	1722	2229	1214	160	78
Good health	**1167297**	**61021**	**43201**	**65919**	**46778**	**121994**	**24658**	**48052**	**40228**	**89287**	**187659**	**173341**	**64753**	**55654**	**43659**	**31708**	**45273**	**20367**	**2733**	**1012**
With a limiting long-term illness	**50596**	**1094**	**1008**	**2028**	**1495**	**3758**	**758**	**1309**	**1047**	**2352**	**5490**	**6206**	**2878**	**2856**	**2851**	**3006**	**5983**	**5005**	**1046**	**426**
+2 or more	24028	395	372	728	521	1176	244	396	309	759	2365	2753	1367	1533	1731	1910	3832	2867	565	205
+1	11808	306	269	527	383	827	172	258	233	607	1539	1554	659	596	578	583	1198	1190	222	107
0	8936	240	250	499	406	1018	175	314	254	538	1007	1188	496	428	325	325	599	623	187	64
-1 or less	5824	153	117	274	185	737	167	341	251	448	579	711	356	299	217	188	354	325	72	50
Without a limiting long-term illness	**1116701**	**59927**	**42193**	**63891**	**45283**	**118236**	**23900**	**46743**	**39181**	**86935**	**182169**	**167135**	**61875**	**52798**	**40808**	**28702**	**39290**	**15362**	**1687**	**586**
+2 or more	549312	27117	19647	28906	19453	45565	8992	15733	12032	29268	94501	90848	34744	32538	28144	21150	28883	10454	1032	305
+1	249917	16275	11132	15926	10736	25615	5015	9282	8121	20765	46233	36704	12564	10178	7157	4486	6365	2883	347	133
0	191585	10752	7710	12701	9702	27839	5375	10530	9214	19870	27516	25789	8463	6023	3487	2028	2854	1393	235	104
-1 or less	125887	5783	3704	6358	5392	19217	4518	11198	9814	17032	13919	13794	6104	4059	2020	1038	1188	632	73	44

Table S019: General Health and Limiting Long-Term Illness and Occupancy Rating by Age (continued)

	All ages	0 to 2	3 to 4	5 to 7	8 to 9	10 to 14	15	16 to 17	18 to 19	20 to 24	25 to 34	35 to 44	45 to 49	50 to 54	55 to 59	60 to 64	65 to 74	75 to 84	85 to 89	90 and over
Fairly good health	**318194**	**5123**	**3898**	**5259**	**3206**	**8808**	**1963**	**4231**	**4634**	**12728**	**38104**	**48279**	**23474**	**24704**	**24485**	**23486**	**47015**	**30867**	**5844**	**2086**
With a limiting long-term illness	**121916**	**595**	**869**	**1614**	**1130**	**2817**	**496**	**983**	**882**	**2535**	**8221**	**12370**	**6668**	**8360**	**10070**	**11779**	**26181**	**20240**	**4441**	**1665**
+2 or more	61963	191	283	490	299	750	124	239	217	707	3013	4789	2738	4063	5785	7138	16144	11786	2345	862
+1	29621	164	257	460	322	683	115	195	167	685	2489	3241	1721	2120	2299	2589	5854	4731	1110	419
0	19550	142	229	444	340	815	147	280	240	626	1799	2670	1272	1333	1280	1377	2824	2707	735	290
-1 or less	10782	98	100	220	169	569	110	269	258	517	920	1670	937	844	706	675	1359	1016	251	94
Without a limiting long-term illness	**196278**	**4528**	**3029**	**3645**	**2076**	**5991**	**1467**	**3248**	**3752**	**10193**	**29883**	**35909**	**16806**	**16344**	**14415**	**11707**	**20834**	**10627**	**1403**	**421**
+2 or more	92847	1624	1044	1157	585	1542	416	770	960	3014	12625	15343	7900	8800	8722	7552	13513	6346	741	193
+1	48101	1452	966	1152	588	1414	336	667	896	2790	8523	8931	3952	3707	3096	2362	4391	2442	341	95
0	34678	985	694	916	567	1802	416	889	955	2428	5965	7331	2888	2296	1639	1188	2025	1346	246	102
-1 or less	20652	467	325	420	336	1233	299	922	941	1961	2770	4304	2066	1541	958	605	905	493	75	31
Not good health	**173323**	**1131**	**818**	**1136**	**686**	**1577**	**380**	**872**	**1065**	**3714**	**13573**	**23954**	**13688**	**17459**	**19988**	**17791**	**28940**	**20557**	**4462**	**1532**
With a limiting long-term illness	**154953**	**673**	**619**	**944**	**587**	**1284**	**267**	**638**	**783**	**2743**	**10681**	**20065**	**11942**	**15759**	**18557**	**16803**	**27228**	**19577**	**4311**	**1492**
+2 or more	69096	195	163	218	138	273	63	134	177	648	3540	6729	4515	6935	9310	8912	14454	9914	2075	703
+1	41763	187	168	289	164	313	49	117	202	788	3327	5595	3217	4245	4905	4254	7173	5231	1143	396
0	28210	195	190	264	186	417	90	172	199	700	2506	4816	2507	2763	2710	2361	3859	3203	786	286
-1 or less	15884	96	98	173	99	281	65	215	205	607	1308	2925	1703	1816	1632	1276	1742	1229	307	107
Without a limiting long-term illness	**18370**	**458**	**199**	**192**	**99**	**293**	**113**	**234**	**282**	**971**	**2892**	**3889**	**1746**	**1700**	**1431**	**988**	**1712**	**980**	**151**	**40**
+2 or more	7962	178	69	58	21	67	29	66	74	262	1166	1633	786	824	740	571	896	437	70	15
+1	4836	137	65	59	35	72	16	68	75	289	801	1010	434	413	355	207	464	282	41	13
0	3438	109	46	46	29	95	23	46	73	236	640	732	316	285	206	131	216	172	28	9
-1 or less	2134	34	19	29	14	59	45	54	60	184	285	514	210	178	130	79	136	89	12	3

Notes:

1 The occupancy rating provides a measure of under-occupancy and overcrowding. For example a value of -1 implies that there is one room too few and that there is overcrowding in the household. The occupancy rating assumes that every household, including one person households, requires a minimum of two common rooms (excluding bathrooms).

2 Limiting long-term illness covers any long-term illness, health problem or disability which limits daily activities or work.

S019

Table S020: Limiting Long-Term Illness and Age by Accommodation Type and Lowest Floor Level of Accommodation

Table population: All persons in households

	All persons	Caravan or other mobile or temporary structure	Other Accommodation - lowest floor level of accommodation				
			Basement or semi-basement	Ground floor (street level)	First or second floor	Third or fourth floor	Fifth floor or higher
All persons	**1658812**	**4429**	**14781**	**1581359**	**53985**	**2548**	**1710**
0 to 2	67276	407	504	64519	1742	58	46
3 to 4	47916	198	395	46214	1056	29	24
5 to 7	72316	216	680	69825	1526	45	24
8 to 9	50669	126	480	48970	1062	26	5
10 to 14	132379	274	1354	127953	2714	60	24
15	27001	51	295	26116	523	12	4
16 to 17	53155	103	582	51328	1103	26	13
18 to 19	45927	75	434	43925	1418	51	24
20 to 24	105729	308	880	99630	4483	302	126
25 to 34	239336	979	1627	226553	9317	550	310
35 to 44	245574	543	2356	234389	7581	405	300
45 to 49	101915	267	1095	97268	3033	130	122
50 to 54	97817	171	1040	93386	2952	148	120
55 to 59	88132	111	867	84288	2618	122	126
60 to 64	72985	132	701	69571	2367	118	96
65 to 74	121228	244	921	114652	5011	215	185
75 to 84	71791	164	447	66622	4237	183	138
85 to 89	13039	40	97	11907	927	50	18
90 and over	4627	20	26	4243	315	18	5
With a limiting long-term illness	**327466**	**864**	**2361**	**307766**	**15046**	**808**	**621**
0 to 2	2363	11	22	2247	77	3	3
3 to 4	2495	17	18	2387	69	4	-
5 to 7	4588	9	41	4383	143	9	3
8 to 9	3211	8	31	3090	77	5	-
10 to 14	7859	19	75	7554	195	9	7
15	1521	7	17	1459	35	3	7
16 to 17	2930	7	24	2823	71	5	-
18 to 19	2712	6	24	2570	105	3	4
20 to 24	7630	24	72	7104	388	30	12
25 to 34	24392	104	165	22590	1373	103	57
35 to 44	38641	117	319	36126	1856	122	101
45 to 49	21488	64	195	20178	951	49	51
50 to 54	26975	62	215	25467	1128	51	52
55 to 59	31478	52	211	29886	1185	71	73
60 to 64	31588	65	225	29971	1212	55	60
65 to 74	59392	135	373	56040	2629	118	97
75 to 84	44822	113	250	41591	2666	121	81
85 to 89	9798	28	66	8987	665	37	15
90 and over	3583	16	18	3313	221	10	5

	All persons	Caravan or other mobile or temporary structure	Other Accommodation - lowest floor level of accommodation				
			Basement or semi-basement	Ground floor (street level)	First or second floor	Third or fourth floor	Fifth floor or higher
Without a limiting long-term illness	**1331346**	**3565**	**12420**	**1273593**	**38939**	**1740**	**1089**
0 to 2	64913	396	482	62272	1665	55	43
3 to 4	45421	181	377	43827	987	25	24
5 to 7	67728	207	639	65442	1383	36	21
8 to 9	47458	118	449	45880	985	21	5
10 to 14	124520	255	1279	120399	2519	51	17
15	25480	44	278	24657	488	9	4
16 to 17	50225	96	558	48505	1032	21	13
18 to 19	43215	69	410	41355	1313	48	20
20 to 24	98099	284	808	92526	4095	272	114
25 to 34	214944	875	1462	203963	7944	447	253
35 to 44	206933	426	2037	198263	5725	283	199
45 to 49	80427	203	900	77090	2082	81	71
50 to 54	70842	109	825	67919	1824	97	68
55 to 59	56654	59	656	54402	1433	51	53
60 to 64	41397	67	476	39600	1155	63	36
65 to 74	61836	109	548	58612	2382	97	88
75 to 84	26969	51	197	25031	1571	62	57
85 to 89	3241	12	31	2920	262	13	3
90 and over	1044	4	8	930	94	8	-

Notes:

1   Limiting long-term illness covers any long-term illness, health problem or disability which limits daily activities or work.

S020

Table S021: Economic Activity and Hours Worked by Sex and Limiting Long-Term Illness

Table population: All persons aged 16 to 74

	All persons			Males			Females		
	Total	Limiting long-term illness	No limiting long-term illness	Total	Limiting long-term illness	No limiting long-term illness	Total	Limiting long-term illness	No limiting long-term illness
All persons	**1187079**	**252773**	**934306**	**581232**	**121013**	**460219**	**605847**	**131760**	**474087**
Economically active	**739134**	**49897**	**689237**	**412035**	**29912**	**382123**	**327099**	**19985**	**307114**
Employed	**662004**	**42572**	**619432**	**367232**	**24952**	**342280**	**294772**	**17620**	**277152**
Employee	563770	34263	529507	288285	18217	270068	275485	16046	259439
1 to 15 hours	25760	2568	23192	3312	527	2785	22448	2041	20407
16 to 30 hours	92221	7113	85108	13860	1700	12160	78361	5413	72948
31 to 37 hours	128037	7702	120335	53305	3854	49451	74732	3848	70884
38 to 48 hours	266880	14095	252785	176299	9872	166427	90581	4223	86358
49 hours and over	50872	2785	48087	41509	2264	39245	9363	521	8842
Self-employed without employees	56808	5395	51413	46372	4448	41924	10436	947	9489
1 to 15 hours	3312	573	2739	1638	373	1265	1674	200	1474
16 to 30 hours	8419	1242	7177	5330	949	4381	3089	293	2796
31 to 37 hours	3768	349	3419	2910	296	2614	858	53	805
38 to 48 hours	22280	1555	20725	19352	1352	18000	2928	203	2725
49 hours and over	19029	1676	17353	17142	1478	15664	1887	198	1689
Self-employed with employees	41426	2914	38512	32575	2287	30288	8851	627	8224
1 to 15 hours	1032	159	873	409	88	321	623	71	552
16 to 30 hours	3194	373	2821	1315	233	1082	1879	140	1739
31 to 37 hours	2217	154	2063	1327	106	1221	890	48	842
38 to 48 hours	17069	1017	16052	13730	825	12905	3339	192	3147
49 hours and over	17914	1211	16703	15794	1035	14759	2120	176	1944
Unemployed	**49098**	**6264**	**42834**	**32957**	**4478**	**28479**	**16141**	**1786**	**14355**
Full-time student	**28032**	**1061**	**26971**	**11846**	**482**	**11364**	**16186**	**579**	**15607**
Economically inactive	**447945**	**202876**	**245069**	**169197**	**91101**	**78096**	**278748**	**111775**	**166973**
Retired	130313	58749	71564	53408	24938	28470	76905	33811	43094
Student	67623	3981	63642	30894	1936	28958	36729	2045	34684
Looking after home/family	88207	15355	72852	8398	1805	6593	79809	13550	66259
Permanently sick/disabled	110787	105248	5539	56421	53840	2581	54366	51408	2958
Other	51015	19543	31472	20076	8582	11494	30939	10961	19978

Notes:

1 For the Census, part-time is defined as working 30 hours or less a week. Full-time is defined as working 31 or more hours a week.

2 Hours worked is the average number of hours worked per week for the last four weeks before the Census (29 April 2001).

3 Limiting long-term illness covers any long-term illness, health problem or disability which limits daily activities or work.

Table S022: Sex and Number of Cars or Vans in Household by General Health and Limiting Long-Term Illness

Table population: All persons in households

	All persons			Good health			Fairly good health			Not good health		
	Total	Limiting long-term illness	No limiting long-term illness	Total	Limiting long-term illness	No limiting long-term illness	Total	Limiting long-term illness	No limiting long-term illness	Total	Limiting long-term illness	No limiting long-term illness
All persons	**1658813**	**327465**	**1331348**	**1167297**	**50596**	**1116701**	**318194**	**121916**	**196278**	**173322**	**154953**	**18369**
Cars or vans in household												
None	306822	106442	200380	163026	12871	150155	82043	37590	44453	61753	55981	5772
1	703922	148228	555694	481149	22288	458861	144818	55679	89139	77955	70261	7694
2 or more	648069	72795	575274	523122	15437	507685	91333	28647	62686	33614	28711	4903
Males	**809276**	**151057**	**658219**	**590608**	**26921**	**563687**	**141417**	**54722**	**86695**	**77251**	**69414**	**7837**
Cars or vans in household												
None	127454	41127	86327	73354	5688	67666	29453	12975	16478	24647	22464	2183
1	346941	72784	274157	242802	12297	230505	67351	27103	40248	36788	33384	3404
2 or more	334881	37146	297735	274452	8936	265516	44613	14644	29969	15816	13566	2250
Females	**849537**	**176408**	**673129**	**576689**	**23675**	**553014**	**176777**	**67194**	**109583**	**96071**	**85539**	**10532**
Cars or vans in household												
None	179368	65315	114053	89672	7183	82489	52590	24615	27975	37106	33517	3589
1	356981	75444	281537	238347	9991	228356	77467	28576	48891	41167	36877	4290
2 or more	313188	35649	277539	248670	6501	242169	46720	14003	32717	17798	15145	2653

Notes:

1 General health refers to health over the 12 months prior to Census day (29 April 2001).

2 Cars or vans includes company cars or vans if available for private use.

3 Limiting long-term illness covers any long-term illness, health problem or disability which limits daily activities or work.

S022

Table S315: Tenure and Age by General Health and Limiting Long-Term Illness

Table population: All persons in households

	All persons			Good health			Fairly good health			Not good health		
	Total	Limiting long-term illness	No limiting long-term illness	Total	Limiting long-term illness	No limiting long-term illness	Total	Limiting long-term illness	No limiting long-term illness	Total	Limiting long-term illness	No limiting long-term illness
All persons	**1658813**	**327465**	**1331348**	**1167297**	**50596**	**1116701**	**318194**	**121916**	**196278**	**173322**	**154953**	**18369**
0 to 4	115192	4858	110334	104222	2102	102120	9021	1464	7557	1949	1292	657
5 to 9	122984	7798	115186	112697	3523	109174	8465	2744	5721	1822	1531	291
10 to 15	159380	9380	150000	146652	4516	142136	10771	3313	7458	1957	1551	406
16 to 24	204811	13272	191539	177567	4708	172859	21593	4400	17193	5651	4164	1487
25 to 34	239336	24392	214944	187659	5490	182169	38104	8221	29883	13573	10681	2892
35 to 44	245574	38641	206933	173341	6206	167135	48279	12370	35909	23954	20065	3889
45 to 49	101915	21488	80427	64753	2878	61875	23474	6668	16806	13688	11942	1746
50 to 54	97817	26975	70842	55654	2856	52798	24704	8360	16344	17459	15759	1700
55 to 59	88132	31478	56654	43659	2851	40808	24485	10070	14415	19988	18557	1431
60 to 64	72985	31588	41397	31708	3006	28702	23486	11779	11707	17791	16803	988
65 to 74	121228	59392	61836	45273	5983	39290	47015	26181	20834	28940	27228	1712
75 to 84	71791	44822	26969	20367	5005	15362	30867	20240	10627	20557	19577	980
85 and over	17668	13381	4287	3745	1472	2273	7930	6106	1824	5993	5803	190
Owner occupied	**1233620**	**204944**	**1028676**	**912723**	**34683**	**878040**	**220154**	**81011**	**139143**	**100743**	**89250**	**11493**
0 to 4	80457	2527	77930	74290	1173	73117	5220	765	4455	947	589	358
5 to 9	87436	4261	83175	81959	2110	79849	4645	1454	3191	832	697	135
10 to 15	115898	5391	110507	108818	2802	106016	6149	1879	4270	931	710	221
16 to 24	142501	7385	135116	128005	3088	124917	11878	2388	9490	2618	1909	709
25 to 34	177734	13610	164124	146320	3614	142706	24279	4636	19643	7135	5360	1775
35 to 44	193736	22879	170857	146304	4417	141887	34166	7781	26385	13266	10681	2585
45 to 49	82009	13305	68704	56442	2155	54287	17673	4501	13172	7894	6649	1245
50 to 54	78083	17119	60964	48919	2134	46785	18916	5899	13017	10248	9086	1162
55 to 59	70352	21256	49096	38612	2218	36394	19124	7404	11720	12616	11634	982
60 to 64	56876	21737	35139	27430	2302	25128	18037	8708	9329	11409	10727	682
65 to 74	90150	39852	50298	37907	4535	33372	34559	18643	15916	17684	16674	1010
75 to 84	47764	27781	19983	15265	3259	12006	20696	13245	7451	11803	11277	526
85 and over	10624	7841	2783	2452	876	1576	4812	3708	1104	3360	3257	103

Table S315: Tenure and Age by General Health and Limiting Long-Term Illness (continued)

	All persons			Good health			Fairly good health			Not good health		
	Total	Limiting long-term illness	No limiting long-term illness	Total	Limiting long-term illness	No limiting long-term illness	Total	Limiting long-term illness	No limiting long-term illness	Total	Limiting long-term illness	No limiting long-term illness
Rented from NIHE	**266452**	**84598**	**181854**	**150565**	**10333**	**140232**	**63950**	**26962**	**36988**	**51937**	**47303**	**4634**
0 to 4	20586	1476	19110	17602	590	17012	2356	435	1921	628	451	177
5 to 9	23291	2522	20769	19880	981	18899	2666	917	1749	745	624	121
10 to 15	30808	2897	27911	26670	1240	25430	3385	1046	2339	753	611	142
16 to 24	35068	3915	31153	27314	1040	26274	5815	1332	4483	1939	1543	396
25 to 34	32223	6828	25395	19929	1071	18858	8160	2256	5904	4134	3501	633
35 to 44	33064	11191	21873	15746	1155	14591	9616	3216	6400	7702	6820	882
45 to 49	13732	6039	7693	5201	487	4714	4147	1540	2607	4384	4012	372
50 to 54	14073	7478	6595	4330	515	3815	4199	1833	2366	5544	5130	414
55 to 59	12676	7741	4935	3111	441	2670	3860	1947	1913	5705	5353	352
60 to 64	11537	7349	4188	2764	502	2262	3869	2184	1685	4904	4663	241
65 to 74	21386	13977	7409	4533	991	3542	8494	5153	3341	8359	7833	526
75 to 84	14489	10387	4102	2902	1059	1843	5873	3934	1939	5714	5394	320
85 and over	3519	2798	721	583	261	322	1510	1169	341	1426	1368	58
Other social rented	**28783**	**12394**	**16389**	**13578**	**1505**	**12073**	**8425**	**4570**	**3855**	**6780**	**6319**	**461**
0 to 4	1971	169	1802	1628	63	1565	265	50	215	78	56	22
5 to 9	1889	204	1685	1615	82	1533	220	76	144	54	46	8
10 to 15	2314	263	2051	1957	91	1866	278	97	181	79	75	4
16 to 24	2756	397	2359	2020	101	1919	525	136	389	211	160	51
25 to 34	3100	815	2285	1827	161	1666	815	272	543	458	382	76
35 to 44	3057	1212	1845	1388	151	1237	887	342	545	782	719	63
45 to 49	1319	661	658	459	79	380	440	199	241	420	383	37
50 to 54	1251	756	495	337	66	271	408	210	198	506	480	26
55 to 59	1211	753	458	307	58	249	383	205	178	521	490	31
60 to 64	1238	877	361	270	70	200	421	279	142	547	528	19
65 to 74	3241	2150	1091	726	146	580	1331	872	459	1184	1132	52
75 to 84	3898	2911	987	766	286	480	1742	1294	448	1390	1331	59
85 and over	1538	1226	312	278	151	127	710	538	172	550	537	13

S315

S315

Table S315: Tenure and Age by General Health and Limiting Long-Term Illness (continued)

	All persons			Good health			Fairly good health			Not good health		
	Total	Limiting long-term illness	No limiting long-term illness	Total	Limiting long-term illness	No limiting long-term illness	Total	Limiting long-term illness	No limiting long-term illness	Total	Limiting long-term illness	No limiting long-term illness
Private rented	**129958**	**25529**	**104429**	**90431**	**4075**	**86356**	**25665**	**9373**	**16292**	**13862**	**12081**	**1781**
0 to 4	12178	686	11492	10702	276	10426	1180	214	966	296	196	100
5 to 9	10368	811	9557	9243	350	8893	934	297	637	191	164	27
10 to 15	10360	829	9531	9207	383	8824	959	291	668	194	155	39
16 to 24	24486	1575	22911	20228	479	19749	3375	544	2831	883	552	331
25 to 34	26279	3139	23140	19583	644	18939	4850	1057	3793	1846	1438	408
35 to 44	15717	3359	12358	9903	483	9420	3610	1031	2579	2204	1845	359
45 to 49	4855	1483	3372	2651	157	2494	1214	428	786	990	898	92
50 to 54	4410	1622	2788	2068	141	1927	1181	418	763	1161	1063	98
55 to 59	3893	1728	2165	1629	134	1495	1118	514	604	1146	1080	66
60 to 64	3334	1625	1709	1244	132	1112	1159	608	551	931	885	46
65 to 74	6451	3413	3038	2107	311	1796	2631	1513	1118	1713	1589	124
75 to 84	5640	3743	1897	1434	401	1033	2556	1767	789	1650	1575	75
85 and over	1987	1516	471	432	184	248	898	691	207	657	641	16

Notes:
1 The terms used to describe tenure are defined as:
   Owner occupied: either owns outright, owns with a mortgage or loan, or pays part rent and part mortgage (shared ownership).
   Rented from NIHE: rented from Northern Ireland Housing Executive.
   Other social rented: rented from Registered Social Landlord, Housing Association, Housing Co-operative or Charitable Trust.
   Private rented: rented from a private landlord or letting agency, employer of a household member, or relative or friend of a household member or other person.
2 'Rented from NIHE', 'Other social rented' and 'Private rented' include living in the household rent free.
3 General health refers to health over the 12 months prior to Census day (29 April 2001).
4 Limiting long-term illness covers any long-term illness, health problem or disability which limits daily activities or work.

Table S318: Age and Limiting Long-Term Illness and General Health by Ethnic Group

Table population: All persons

	All persons	White	Irish Traveller	Mixed	Indian	Pakistani	Bangladeshi	Other Asian	Black Caribbean	Black African	Other Black	Chinese	Other ethnic group
All persons	1685258	1670988	1711	3318	1565	666	244	196	258	492	388	4145	1287
All persons aged 0 to 15 years	398049	393511	551	1735	322	226	92	33	44	137	79	1056	263
With limiting long-term illness	22088	21871	45	100	14	7	-	3	3	-	-	35	10
Good or fairly good health	17701	17524	29	82	11	7	-	3	3	-	-	32	10
Not good health	4387	4347	16	18	3	-	-	-	-	-	-	3	-
Without limiting long-term illness	375961	371640	506	1635	308	219	92	30	41	137	79	1021	253
Good or fairly good health	374607	370311	501	1631	308	213	92	30	38	137	76	1017	253
Not good health	1354	1329	5	4	-	6	-	-	3	-	3	4	-
All persons aged 16 to 44 years	700678	693602	713	1236	725	314	124	134	158	251	227	2386	808
With limiting long-term illness	78142	77531	182	143	56	33	13	6	14	16	30	85	33
Good or fairly good health	42774	42450	73	75	34	18	8	3	10	9	16	57	21
Not good health	35368	35081	109	68	22	15	5	3	4	7	14	28	12
Without limiting long-term illness	622536	616071	531	1093	669	281	111	128	144	235	197	2301	775
Good or fairly good health	614135	607781	497	1076	661	278	108	128	140	235	194	2268	769
Not good health	8401	8290	34	17	8	3	3	-	4	-	3	33	6
All persons aged 45 to 64 years	363208	361267	280	235	412	95	19	26	32	79	41	548	174
With limiting long-term illness	113480	112891	150	88	108	32	6	6	16	13	12	126	32
Good or fairly good health	49748	49492	48	28	49	16	6	3	7	7	4	73	15
Not good health	63732	63399	102	60	59	16	-	3	9	6	8	53	17
Without limiting long-term illness	249728	248376	130	147	304	63	13	20	16	66	29	422	142
Good or fairly good health	243844	242557	110	140	293	58	13	20	16	63	26	412	136
Not good health	5884	5819	20	7	11	5	-	-	-	3	3	10	6
All persons aged 65 and over	223323	222608	167	112	106	31	9	3	24	25	41	155	42
With limiting long-term illness	129393	129001	93	66	46	22	3	3	11	14	21	86	27
Good or fairly good health	71790	71594	45	35	24	10	-	-	8	8	13	40	13
Not good health	57603	57407	48	31	22	12	3	3	3	6	8	46	14
Without limiting long-term illness	93930	93607	74	46	60	9	6	-	13	11	20	69	15
Good or fairly good health	91002	90695	71	46	57	9	6	-	9	8	20	66	15
Not good health	2928	2912	3	-	3	-	-	-	4	3	-	3	-

Notes:

1 General health refers to health over the 12 months prior to Census day (29 April 2001).

2 Limiting long-term illness covers any long-term illness, health problem or disability which limits daily activities or work.

S318

Table S319: Sex and Age and Limiting Long-Term Illness and General Health by Community Background (Religion or Religion Brought Up In)

Table population: All persons

	All persons	Catholic	Protestant and Other Christian (including Christian related)	Other religions and philosophies	None
All persons					
All persons all ages	**1685263**	**737412**	**895377**	**6565**	**45909**
With limiting long-term illness	**343105**	**146896**	**190161**	**993**	**5055**
Good or fairly good health	182018	75268	103574	501	2675
Not good health	161087	71628	86587	492	2380
Without limiting long-term illness	**1342158**	**590516**	**705216**	**5572**	**40854**
Good or fairly good health	1323589	582731	695139	5458	40261
Not good health	18569	7785	10077	114	593
All persons aged 0 to 15 years	**398054**	**198169**	**177260**	**1339**	**21286**
With limiting long-term illness	**22090**	**11997**	**9006**	**53**	**1034**
Good or fairly good health	17702	9518	7314	44	826
Not good health	4388	2479	1692	9	208
Without limiting long-term illness	**375964**	**186172**	**168254**	**1286**	**20252**
Good or fairly good health	374607	185497	167713	1275	20122
Not good health	1357	675	541	11	130
All persons aged 16 to 44 years	**700677**	**325542**	**353048**	**3472**	**18615**
With limiting long-term illness	**78141**	**39547**	**36428**	**348**	**1818**
Good or fairly good health	42774	21286	20346	180	962
Not good health	35367	18261	16082	168	856
Without limiting long-term illness	**622536**	**285995**	**316620**	**3124**	**16797**
Good or fairly good health	614135	282301	312313	3061	16460
Not good health	8401	3694	4307	63	337
All persons aged 45 to 64 years	**363209**	**141152**	**216008**	**1347**	**4702**
With limiting long-term illness	**113480**	**50264**	**61383**	**377**	**1456**
Good or fairly good health	49748	20810	28226	161	551
Not good health	63732	29454	33157	216	905
Without limiting long-term illness	**249729**	**90888**	**154625**	**970**	**3246**
Good or fairly good health	243844	88499	151267	934	3144
Not good health	5885	2389	3358	36	102
All persons aged 65 and over	**223323**	**72549**	**149061**	**407**	**1306**
With limiting long-term illness	**129394**	**45088**	**83344**	**215**	**747**
Good or fairly good health	71794	23654	47688	116	336
Not good health	57600	21434	35656	99	411
Without limiting long-term illness	**93929**	**27461**	**65717**	**192**	**559**
Good or fairly good health	91003	26434	63846	188	535
Not good health	2926	1027	1871	4	24

Table S319: Sex and Age and Limiting Long-Term Illness and General Health by Community Background (Religion or Religion Brought Up In) (continue)

	All persons	Catholic	Protestant and Other Christian (including Christian related)	Other religions and philosophies	None
Males					
All males all ages	**821447**	**357327**	**435152**	**3716**	**25252**
With limiting long-term illness	**156540**	**68294**	**84786**	**569**	**2891**
Good or fairly good health	85013	35818	47369	295	1531
Not good health	71527	32476	37417	274	1360
Without limiting long-term illness	**664907**	**289033**	**350366**	**3147**	**22361**
Good or fairly good health	656963	285767	346041	3086	22069
Not good health	7944	3266	4325	61	292
All males aged 0 to 15 years	**204261**	**101189**	**91057**	**712**	**11303**
With limiting long-term illness	**12854**	**6993**	**5232**	**36**	**593**
Good or fairly good health	10282	5505	4277	27	473
Not good health	2572	1488	955	9	120
Without limiting long-term illness	**191407**	**94196**	**85825**	**676**	**10710**
Good or fairly good health	190685	93835	85526	670	10654
Not good health	722	361	299	6	56
All males aged 16 to 44 years	**346601**	**157604**	**176744**	**1991**	**10262**
With limiting long-term illness	**37839**	**18931**	**17720**	**193**	**995**
Good or fairly good health	21741	10578	10510	103	550
Not good health	16098	8353	7210	90	445
Without limiting long-term illness	**308762**	**138673**	**159024**	**1798**	**9267**
Good or fairly good health	305422	137251	157301	1761	9109
Not good health	3340	1422	1723	37	158
All males aged 45 to 64 years	**179156**	**68710**	**106724**	**801**	**2921**
With limiting long-term illness	**55645**	**24620**	**29913**	**228**	**884**
Good or fairly good health	24616	10299	13891	99	327
Not good health	31029	14321	16022	129	557
Without limiting long-term illness	**123511**	**44090**	**76811**	**573**	**2037**
Good or fairly good health	120759	42998	75235	555	1971
Not good health	2752	1092	1576	18	66
All males aged 65 and over	**91429**	**29824**	**60627**	**212**	**766**
With limiting long-term illness	**50202**	**17750**	**31921**	**112**	**419**
Good or fairly good health	28374	9436	18691	66	181
Not good health	21828	8314	13230	46	238
Without limiting long-term illness	**41227**	**12074**	**28706**	**100**	**347**
Good or fairly good health	40097	11683	27979	100	335
Not good health	1130	391	727	-	12

S 3 1 9

Table S319: Sex and Age and Limiting Long-Term Illness and General Health by Community Background (Religion or Religion Brought Up In) (continue)

	All persons	Catholic	Protestant and Other Christian (including Christian related)	Other religions and philosophies	None
Females					
All females all ages	**863816**	**380085**	**460225**	**2849**	**20657**
With limiting long-term illness	**186565**	**78602**	**105375**	**424**	**2164**
Good or fairly good health	97005	39450	56205	206	1144
Not good health	89560	39152	49170	218	1020
Without limiting long-term illness	**677251**	**301483**	**354850**	**2425**	**18493**
Good or fairly good health	666626	296964	349098	2372	18192
Not good health	10625	4519	5752	53	301
All females aged 0 to 15 years	**193793**	**96980**	**86203**	**627**	**9983**
With limiting long-term illness	**9236**	**5004**	**3774**	**17**	**441**
Good or fairly good health	7420	4013	3037	17	353
Not good health	1816	991	737	-	88
Without limiting long-term illness	**184557**	**91976**	**82429**	**610**	**9542**
Good or fairly good health	183922	91662	82187	605	9468
Not good health	635	314	242	5	74
All females aged 16 to 44 years	**354076**	**167938**	**176304**	**1481**	**8353**
With limiting long-term illness	**40302**	**20616**	**18708**	**155**	**823**
Good or fairly good health	21033	10708	9836	77	412
Not good health	19269	9908	8872	78	411
Without limiting long-term illness	**313774**	**147322**	**157596**	**1326**	**7530**
Good or fairly good health	308713	145050	155012	1300	7351
Not good health	5061	2272	2584	26	179
All females aged 45 to 64 years	**184053**	**72442**	**109284**	**546**	**1781**
With limiting long-term illness	**57835**	**25644**	**31470**	**149**	**572**
Good or fairly good health	25132	10511	14335	62	224
Not good health	32703	15133	17135	87	348
Without limiting long-term illness	**126218**	**46798**	**77814**	**397**	**1209**
Good or fairly good health	123085	45501	76032	379	1173
Not good health	3133	1297	1782	18	36
All females aged 65 and over	**131894**	**42725**	**88434**	**195**	**540**
With limiting long-term illness	**79192**	**27338**	**51423**	**103**	**328**
Good or fairly good health	43420	14218	28997	50	155
Not good health	35772	13120	22426	53	173
Without limiting long-term illness	**52702**	**15387**	**37011**	**92**	**212**
Good or fairly good health	50906	14751	35867	88	200
Not good health	1796	636	1144	4	12

Notes:

1 Limiting long-term illness covers any long-term illness, health problem or disability which limits daily activities or work.

2 General health refers to health over the 12 months prior to Census day (29 April 2001).

3 The term 'Catholic' includes those respondents who gave their religion as Catholic or Roman Catholic.

Table S025: Sex and Age by General Health and Provision of Unpaid Care

Table population: All persons in households

	All persons					Good health					Fairly good health					Not good health				
			Provides care					Provides care					Provides care					Provides care		
	Total	Provides no care	1 to 19 hours	20 to 49 hours	50 or more hours	Total	Provides no care	1 to 19 hours	20 to 49 hours	50 or more hours	Total	Provides no care	1 to 19 hours	20 to 49 hours	50 or more hours	Total	Provides no care	1 to 19 hours	20 to 49 hours	50 or more hours
All persons	1658815	1474381	109958	27933	46543	1167298	1054267	74802	16067	22162	318194	265828	27419	8823	16124	173323	154286	7737	3043	8257
0 to 4	115192	115192	-	-	-	104222	104222	-	-	-	9021	9021	-	-	-	1949	1949	-	-	-
5 to 7	72311	72019	228	19	45	65919	65671	193	16	39	5258	5227	28	-	3	1134	1121	7	3	3
8 to 9	50675	50190	393	34	58	46778	46382	330	26	40	3210	3138	56	8	8	687	670	7	-	10
10 to 11	52104	51247	691	77	89	48147	47391	616	69	71	3335	3246	69	8	12	622	610	6	-	6
12 to 14	80275	77725	2093	269	188	73847	71635	1856	218	138	5473	5156	223	48	46	955	934	14	3	4
15	27002	25823	959	146	74	24658	23663	818	114	63	1963	1797	129	26	11	381	363	12	6	-
16 to 17	53155	50166	2302	429	258	48052	45500	2006	338	208	4231	3847	267	80	37	872	819	29	11	13
18 to 19	45927	43074	2112	466	275	40228	37886	1776	367	199	4634	4190	304	82	58	1065	998	32	17	18
20 to 24	105729	98462	5142	1215	910	89287	83659	4096	927	605	12728	11378	881	251	218	3714	3425	165	37	87
25 to 34	239336	213931	15586	4227	5592	187659	169967	11407	2862	3423	38104	32100	3367	1104	1533	13573	11864	812	261	636
35 to 44	245574	201354	27167	7115	9938	173341	143847	19321	4437	5736	48279	37165	6233	2011	2870	23954	20342	1613	667	1332
45 to 49	101915	78799	14877	3266	4973	64753	50080	10135	1896	2642	23474	17221	3673	1033	1547	13688	11498	1069	337	784
50 to 54	97817	75907	13243	3234	5433	55654	42704	8687	1705	2558	24704	18280	3442	1120	1862	17459	14923	1114	409	1013
55 to 59	88132	70088	10107	2849	5088	43659	34027	6221	1391	2020	24485	18601	2948	1023	1913	19988	17460	938	435	1155
60 to 64	72985	61252	5975	1724	4034	31708	26145	3308	765	1490	23486	19171	2037	676	1602	17791	15936	630	283	942
65 to 74	121228	106200	6601	2027	6400	45273	39348	3118	700	2107	47015	40623	2598	942	2852	28940	26229	885	385	1441
75 to 84	71791	65966	2242	753	2830	20367	18585	833	210	739	30867	28059	1052	375	1381	20557	19322	357	168	710
85 to 89	13039	12478	194	73	294	2733	2583	66	19	65	5844	5573	94	36	141	4462	4322	34	18	88
90 and over	4628	4508	46	10	64	1013	972	15	7	19	2083	2035	18	-	30	1532	1501	13	3	15

S025

Table S025: Sex and Age by General Health and Provision of Unpaid Care (continued)

	All persons					Good health					Fairly good health					Not good health				
			Provides care					Provides care					Provides care					Provides care		
	Total	Provides no care	1 to 19 hours	20 to 49 hours	50 or more hours	Total	Provides no care	1 to 19 hours	20 to 49 hours	50 or more hours	Total	Provides no care	1 to 19 hours	20 to 49 hours	50 or more hours	Total	Provides no care	1 to 19 hours	20 to 49 hours	50 or more hours
Males	**809276**	**734164**	**46518**	**10890**	**17704**	**590608**	**543316**	**32342**	**6402**	**8548**	**141418**	**121492**	**10969**	**3267**	**5690**	**77250**	**69356**	**3207**	**1221**	**3466**
0 to 4	**59191**	59191	-	-	-	**53092**	53092	-	-	-	**4939**	4939	-	-	-	**1160**	1160	-	-	-
5 to 7	**37153**	37015	102	9	27	**33599**	33476	90	9	24	**2864**	2855	9	-	-	**690**	684	3	-	3
8 to 9	**25963**	25745	176	15	27	**23829**	23654	146	12	17	**1729**	1696	27	3	3	**405**	395	3	-	7
10 to 11	**26677**	26266	331	35	45	**24627**	24264	296	31	36	**1710**	1668	32	4	6	**340**	334	3	-	3
12 to 14	**41167**	40010	959	116	82	**37738**	36736	849	93	60	**2915**	2768	102	23	22	**514**	506	8	-	-
15	**13839**	13306	439	61	33	**12742**	12308	367	41	26	**922**	833	65	17	7	**175**	165	7	3	-
16 to 17	**26986**	25733	984	165	104	**24751**	23658	868	139	86	**1851**	1710	105	22	14	**384**	365	11	4	4
18 to 19	**23260**	22020	943	199	98	**20823**	19758	827	163	75	**1934**	1783	105	28	18	**503**	479	11	8	5
20 to 24	**52456**	49528	2093	564	271	**45385**	42981	1754	455	195	**5280**	4847	293	93	47	**1791**	1700	46	16	29
25 to 34	**116868**	107405	6151	1581	1731	**94761**	87784	4695	1154	1128	**16290**	14371	1177	334	408	**5817**	5250	279	93	195
35 to 44	**119886**	102591	10943	2669	3683	**87404**	75490	7967	1742	2205	**21907**	17822	2386	678	1021	**10575**	9279	590	249	457
45 to 49	**51331**	41811	6343	1187	1990	**33724**	27537	4381	683	1123	**11137**	8703	1510	382	542	**6470**	5571	452	122	325
50 to 54	**48113**	39180	5746	1155	2032	**28617**	23194	3855	597	971	**11452**	9034	1420	391	607	**8044**	6952	471	167	454
55 to 59	**43241**	35738	4498	1086	1919	**22345**	18255	2846	523	721	**11300**	9035	1207	391	667	**9596**	8448	445	172	531
60 to 64	**35082**	30223	2565	706	1588	**15316**	13014	1441	295	566	**10523**	8876	805	279	563	**9243**	8333	319	132	459
65 to 74	**54598**	48129	3015	904	2550	**21540**	18873	1460	326	881	**20560**	17946	1162	409	1043	**12498**	11310	393	169	626
75 to 84	**28175**	25318	1120	392	1345	**8995**	8029	457	122	387	**11788**	10441	518	195	634	**7392**	6848	145	75	324
85 to 89	**4074**	3792	92	42	148	**992**	902	39	13	38	**1791**	1665	37	18	71	**1291**	1225	16	11	39
90 and over	**1216**	1163	18	4	31	**328**	311	4	4	9	**526**	500	9	-	17	**362**	352	5	-	5

Table S025: Sex and Age by General Health and Provision of Unpaid Care (continued)

	All persons					Good health					Fairly good health					Not good health				
			Provides care					Provides care					Provides care					Provides care		
	Total	Provides no care	1 to 19 hours	20 to 49 hours	50 or more hours	Total	Provides no care	1 to 19 hours	20 to 49 hours	50 or more hours	Total	Provides no care	1 to 19 hours	20 to 49 hours	50 or more hours	Total	Provides no care	1 to 19 hours	20 to 49 hours	50 or more hours
Females	**849539**	**740217**	**63440**	**17043**	**28839**	**576690**	**510951**	**42460**	**9665**	**13614**	**176776**	**144336**	**16450**	**5556**	**10434**	**96073**	**84930**	**4530**	**1822**	**4791**
0 to 4	56001	56001	-	-	-	51130	51130	-	-	-	4082	4082	-	-	-	789	789	-	-	-
5 to 7	35158	35004	126	10	18	32320	32195	103	7	15	2394	2372	19	-	3	444	437	4	3	-
8 to 9	24712	24445	217	19	31	22949	22728	184	14	23	1481	1442	29	5	5	282	275	4	-	3
10 to 11	25427	24981	360	42	44	23520	23127	320	38	35	1625	1578	37	4	6	282	276	3	-	3
12 to 14	39108	37715	1134	153	106	36109	34899	1007	125	78	2558	2388	121	25	24	441	428	6	3	4
15	13163	12517	520	85	41	11916	11355	451	73	37	1041	964	64	9	4	206	198	5	3	-
16 to 17	26169	24433	1318	264	154	23301	21842	1138	199	122	2380	2137	162	58	23	488	454	18	7	9
18 to 19	22667	21054	1169	267	177	19405	18128	949	204	124	2700	2407	199	54	40	562	519	21	9	13
20 to 24	53273	48934	3049	651	639	43902	40678	2342	472	410	7448	6531	588	158	171	1923	1725	119	21	58
25 to 34	122468	106526	9435	2646	3861	92898	82183	6712	1708	2295	21814	17729	2190	770	1125	7756	6614	533	168	441
35 to 44	125688	98763	16224	4446	6255	85937	68357	11354	2695	3531	26372	19343	3847	1333	1849	13379	11063	1023	418	875
45 to 49	50584	36988	8534	2079	2983	31029	22543	5754	1213	1519	12337	8518	2163	651	1005	7218	5927	617	215	459
50 to 54	49704	36727	7497	2079	3401	27037	19510	4832	1108	1587	13252	9246	2022	729	1255	9415	7971	643	242	559
55 to 59	44891	34350	5609	1763	3169	21314	15772	3375	868	1299	13185	9566	1741	632	1246	10392	9012	493	263	624
60 to 64	37903	31029	3410	1018	2446	16392	13131	1867	470	924	12963	10295	1232	397	1039	8548	7603	311	151	483
65 to 74	66630	58071	3586	1123	3850	23733	20475	1658	374	1226	26455	22677	1436	533	1809	16442	14919	492	216	815
75 to 84	43616	40648	1122	361	1485	11372	10556	376	88	352	19079	17618	534	180	747	13165	12474	212	93	386
85 to 89	8965	8686	102	31	146	1741	1681	27	6	27	4053	3908	57	18	70	3171	3097	18	7	49
90 and over	3412	3345	28	6	33	685	661	11	3	10	1557	1535	9	-	13	1170	1149	8	3	10

Notes:
1 The term 'care' covers any unpaid help, looking after or supporting family members, friends, neighbours or others because of long-term physical or mental ill-health or disability or problems related to old age.
2 General health refers to health over the 12 months prior to Census day (29 April 2001).

S025

Table S026: Sex and Economic Activity by General Health and Provision of Unpaid Care

Table population: All persons aged 16 to 74 in households

	All persons					Good Health					Fairly good health					Not good health				
	Total	Provides no care	Provides care 1 to 19 hours	Provides care 20 to 49 hours	Provides care 50 or more hours	Total	Provides no care	Provides care 1 to 19 hours	Provides care 20 to 49 hours	Provides care 50 or more hours	Total	Provides no care	Provides care 1 to 19 hours	Provides care 20 to 49 hours	Provides care 50 or more hours	Total	Provides no care	Provides care 1 to 19 hours	Provides care 20 to 49 hours	Provides care 50 or more hours
All persons	1171799	999233	103112	26552	42902	779614	673163	70075	15388	20988	251140	202576	25750	8322	14492	141045	123494	7287	2842	7422
Economically active	732435	627928	75893	14258	14356	582543	507312	56053	9657	9521	127900	103092	17036	3881	3891	21992	17524	2804	720	944
Employee - Part-time	117687	94325	15965	3600	3797	88427	72217	11397	2370	2443	24877	18773	3943	1034	1127	4383	3335	625	196	227
Employee - Full-time	441159	381770	44574	7598	7217	359592	315818	33519	5268	4987	70219	56899	9547	1972	1801	11348	9053	1508	358	429
Self-employed - Part-time	15936	12793	2202	449	492	11319	9169	1543	290	317	3782	2951	550	137	144	835	673	109	22	31
Self-employed - Full-time	82160	71171	8180	1287	1522	65635	57446	6208	926	1055	14371	11941	1726	317	387	2154	1784	246	44	80
Unemployed	48927	43159	3430	1132	1206	33586	30240	2074	648	624	12373	10495	1074	391	413	2968	2424	282	93	169
Full-time student	26566	24710	1542	192	122	23984	22422	1312	155	95	2278	2033	196	30	19	304	255	34	7	8
Economically inactive	439364	371305	27219	12294	28546	197071	165851	14022	5731	11467	123240	99484	8714	4441	10601	119053	105970	4483	2122	6478
Retired	129621	110316	9392	2598	7315	52971	44426	4901	1031	2613	50637	42712	3489	1148	3288	26013	23178	1002	419	1414
Student	64951	61177	2954	511	309	58492	55382	2491	394	225	5217	4674	399	94	50	1242	1121	64	23	34
Looking after home/family	88134	59596	8495	6168	13875	53608	37841	5147	3472	7148	26942	16680	2696	2246	5320	7584	5075	652	450	1407
Permanently sick/disabled	106796	95469	4083	1922	5322	8813	7412	411	289	701	25292	22050	1325	559	1358	72691	66007	2347	1074	3263
Other	49862	44747	2295	1095	1725	23187	20790	1072	545	780	15152	13368	805	394	585	11523	10589	418	156	360
Males	571821	502358	43281	10216	15966	394666	350544	30094	6077	7951	112234	94127	10170	3007	4930	64921	57687	3017	1132	3085
Economically active	407177	358948	35185	6269	6775	326908	291830	26250	4307	4521	68280	57281	7634	1618	1747	11989	9837	1301	344	507
Employee - Part-time	16934	14731	1391	386	426	12856	11339	993	259	265	3323	2770	338	95	120	755	622	60	32	41
Employee - Full-time	267196	235519	23706	3885	4086	218894	195439	17905	2718	2332	41564	34582	5004	970	1008	6738	5498	797	197	246
Self-employed - Part-time	8681	7223	986	219	253	5813	4875	658	128	152	2322	1900	262	79	81	546	448	66	12	20
Self-employed - Full-time	70186	61426	6611	1001	1148	56310	49714	5053	729	814	12077	10207	1359	238	273	1799	1505	199	34	61
Unemployed	32837	29374	1935	713	815	22638	20639	1160	420	419	8161	7068	603	228	262	2038	1667	172	65	134
Full-time student	11343	10675	556	65	47	10397	9824	481	53	39	833	754	68	8	3	113	97	7	4	5
Economically inactive	164644	143410	8096	3947	9191	67758	58714	3844	1770	3430	43954	36846	2536	1389	3183	52932	47850	1716	788	2578
Retired	53113	45688	3720	1008	2697	22399	18991	2001	388	1019	20139	17266	1300	455	1118	10575	9431	419	165	560
Student	29737	28328	1122	171	116	27189	25986	972	146	85	2051	1885	128	19	19	497	457	22	6	12
Looking after home/family	8379	2969	538	1474	3398	4698	1722	310	878	1788	2858	908	181	489	1280	823	339	47	107	330
Permanently sick/disabled	54175	49090	1882	826	2377	4778	4204	192	121	261	13248	11772	646	256	574	36149	33114	1044	449	1542
Other	19240	17335	834	468	603	8694	7811	369	237	277	5658	5015	281	170	192	4888	4509	184	61	134

Table S026: Sex and Economic Activity by General Health and Provision of Unpaid Care (continued)

	All persons					Good Health					Fairly good health					Not good health				
			Provides care					Provides care					Provides care					Provides care		
	Total	Provides no care	1 to 19 hours	20 to 49 hours	50 or more hours	Total	Provides no care	1 to 19 hours	20 to 49 hours	50 or more hours	Total	Provides no care	1 to 19 hours	20 to 49 hours	50 or more hours	Total	Provides no care	1 to 19 hours	20 to 49 hours	50 or more hours
Females	**599978**	**496875**	**59831**	**16336**	**26936**	**384948**	**322619**	**39981**	**9311**	**13037**	**138906**	**108449**	**15580**	**5315**	**9562**	**76124**	**65807**	**4270**	**1710**	**4337**
Economically active	**325258**	**268980**	**40708**	**7989**	**7581**	**255635**	**215482**	**29803**	**5350**	**5000**	**59620**	**45811**	**9402**	**2263**	**2144**	**10003**	**7687**	**1503**	**376**	**437**
Employee - Part-time	100753	79594	14574	3214	3371	75571	60878	10404	2111	2178	21554	16003	3605	939	1007	3628	2713	565	164	186
Employee - Full-time	173963	146251	20868	3713	3131	140698	120379	15614	2550	2155	28655	22317	4543	1002	793	4610	3555	711	161	183
Self-employed - Part-time	7255	5570	1216	230	239	5506	4294	885	162	165	1460	1051	288	58	63	289	225	43	10	11
Self-employed - Full-time	11974	9745	1569	286	374	9325	7732	1155	197	241	2294	1734	367	79	114	355	279	47	10	19
Unemployed	16090	13785	1495	419	391	10948	9601	914	228	205	4212	3427	471	163	151	930	757	110	28	35
Full-time student	15223	14035	986	127	75	13587	12598	831	102	56	1445	1279	128	22	16	191	158	27	3	3
Economically inactive	**274720**	**227895**	**19123**	**8347**	**19355**	**129313**	**107137**	**10178**	**3961**	**8037**	**79286**	**62638**	**6178**	**3052**	**7418**	**66121**	**58120**	**2767**	**1334**	**3900**
Retired	76508	64628	5672	1590	4618	30572	25435	2900	643	1594	30498	25446	2189	693	2170	15438	13747	583	254	854
Student	35214	32849	1832	340	193	31303	29396	1519	248	140	3166	2789	271	75	31	745	664	42	17	22
Looking after home/family	79755	56627	7957	4694	10477	48910	36119	4837	2594	5360	24084	15772	2515	1757	4040	6761	4736	605	343	1077
Permanently sick/disabled	52621	46379	2201	1096	2945	4035	3208	219	168	440	12044	10278	679	303	784	36542	32893	1303	625	1721
Other	30622	27412	1461	627	1122	14493	12979	703	308	503	9494	8353	524	224	393	6635	6080	234	95	226

Notes:
1   The term 'care' covers any unpaid help, looking after or supporting family members, friends, neighbours or others because of long-term physical or mental ill-health or disability or problems related to old age.
2   For the Census, part-time is defined as working 30 hours or less a week. Full-time is defined as working 31 or more hours a week.
3   General health refers to health over the 12 months prior to Census day (29 April 2001).

S026

Table S027: Households with a Person with a Limiting Long-Term Illness (LLTI) and Their Age by Number of Carers in Household and Economic Activity

Table population: All households

	All households	No carer in household	One carer in household								Two or more carers in household
			Working					Unemployed	Economically active Full-time students	Economically inactive	
			Total	Part-time		Full-time					
				Outside the home	At home	Outside the home	At home				
All households	**626718**	**488922**	**48549**	**13675**	**1654**	**30095**	**3125**	**3437**	**562**	**47461**	**37787**
Households containing no persons with a LLTI	**367814**	**312915**	**26828**	**7709**	**873**	**16736**	**1510**	**1557**	**320**	**11080**	**15114**
Households with only one person with a LLTI who is also the only carer	**7351**	**-**	**2109**	**648**	**88**	**1201**	**172**	**303**	**17**	**4922**	**-**
Households with one person with a LLTI	**191221**	**144330**	**15233**	**4024**	**513**	**9646**	**1050**	**1099**	**179**	**17412**	**12968**
- aged 0 to 15	10596	5631	982	501	37	401	43	118	7	1697	2161
- aged 16 to 44	45801	33166	4519	1118	111	3030	260	312	73	3745	3986
- aged 45 to 59	46572	33566	4882	1275	161	3130	316	354	75	4071	3624
- aged 60 to 64	16803	13043	1199	412	52	660	75	83	9	1759	710
- aged 65 to 74	32561	26876	1432	348	56	899	129	99	7	3121	1026
- aged 75 and over	38888	32048	2219	370	96	1526	227	133	8	3019	1461
Household with two or more persons with a LLTI	**60332**	**31677**	**4379**	**1294**	**180**	**2512**	**393**	**478**	**46**	**14047**	**9705**

Notes:

1 The term 'care' covers any unpaid help, looking after or supporting family members, friends, neighbours or others because of long-term physical or mental ill-health or disability or problems related to old age.
2 For the Census, part-time is defined as working 30 hours or less a week. Full-time is defined as working 31 or more hours a week.
3 Economically inactive includes carers under 16 and over 74.
4 'Working' means all persons aged 16–74 who are working excluding full-time students.
5 A carer is a person who provides unpaid care.
6 Limiting long-term illness covers any long-term illness, health problem or disability which limits daily activities or work.
7 The category 'Households with one person with a LLTI' does not include 'Households with only one person with a LLTI who is also the only carer'.

3. Education, Employment and Economic Activity

3. Education, Employment and Economic Activity

Highest Level of Qualification

Table S320:   Sex and Age by Highest Level of Qualification
Table S321:   Sex and NS-SeC by Highest Level of Qualification
Table S322:   Sex and Highest Level of Qualification by Ethnic Group
Table S323:   Age and Highest Level of Qualification by Ethnic Group
Table S324:   Sex and Highest Level of Qualification by Community Background (Religion or
                 Religion Brought Up In)
Table S325:   Age and Highest Level of Qualification by Sex and Community Background (Religion
                 or Religion Brought Up In)
Table S325A: Age and Highest Level of Qualification by Sex and Religion
Table S326:   Sex and Occupation by Highest Level of Qualification

Economic Activity

Table S327:   Age of Household Reference Person (HRP) and Tenure by Economic Activity of HRP
Table S028:   Sex and Age by Economic Activity
Table S029:   Sex and Age by Hours Worked
Table S041:   Sex and Economic Activity and Year Last Worked by Age
Table S030:   Sex and Economic Activity by Living Arrangements
Table S031:   Family Composition and Number of Dependent Children by
                 Sex and Economic Activity
Table S032:   Sex and Age and Level of Qualifications by Economic Activity
Table S328:   Economic Activity by Ethnic Group
Table S329:   Sex and Economic Activity by Community Background
                 (Religion or Religion Brought Up In)
Table S330:   Age and Economic Activity by Sex and Community Background (Religion or Religion
                 Brought Up In)
Table S330A: Age and Economic Activity by Sex and Religion
Table S331:   Economic Activity and Age of Full-time Students by Household Type and Tenure

Occupation

Table S033:   Sex and Occupation by Age
Table S034:   Sex and Former Occupation by Age (UK Basis)
Table S332:   Sex and Former Occupation by Age (NI Basis)
Table S035:   Sex and Occupation by Employment Status and Hours Worked
Table S040:   Sex and Occupation by Hours Worked
Table S333:   Sex and Occupation by Ethnic Group
Table S334:   Occupation by Sex and Community Background (Religion or Religion Brought Up In)

Industry

Table S039:   Occupation by Industry
Table S036:   Sex and Industry by Age
Table S037:   Sex and Former Industry by Age (UK Basis)
Table S335:   Sex and Former Industry by Age (NI Basis)
Table S038:   Sex and Industry by Employment Status and Hours Worked
Table S336:   Sex and Industry by Ethnic Group
Table S337:   Industry by Sex and Community Background (Religion or Religion Brought Up In)

National Statistics Socio-economic Classification (NS-SeC)

Table S338:   Sex and NS-SeC by Age
Table S339:   Sex and Age and General Health by NS-SeC
Table S340:   Sex and Age and Limiting Long-Term Illness by NS-SeC
Table S341:   Sex and NS-SeC by Economic Activity
Table S342:   Sex and NS-SeC by Method of Travel to Work
Table S343:   NS-SeC by Tenure
Table S344:   Sex and NS-SeC of Household Reference Person (HRP) by Tenure
Table S345:   Sex and NS-SeC of Household Reference Person (HRP) by Household Composition
Table S346:   Sex and NS-SeC of Household Reference Person (HRP) by Age (of HRP)
Table S347:   NS-SeC of Household Reference Person (HRP) by Households with Full-time Students Living Away From Home and Age of Student
Table S348:   Sex and NS-SeC by Ethnic Group
Table S349:   NS-SeC by Sex and Community Background (Religion or Religion Brought Up In)

Social Grade

Table S066:   Sex and Approximated Social Grade by Age

Table S067:   Age of Household Reference Person (HRP) and Dependent Children by Approximated Social Grade

Method of Travel to Work

Table S118:   Number of Employed Persons and Method of Travel to Work by Number of Cars or Vans in Household
Table S350:   Sex and Age by Method of Travel to Work

Table S320: Sex and Age by Highest Level of Qualification

Table population: All persons aged 16 to 74

	All persons	No qualifications	Level 1	Level 2	Level 3	Level 4	Level 5
All persons	**1187079**	**494277**	**204478**	**194265**	**106548**	**129741**	**57770**
16 to 17 years	53458	20026	12338	19020	1631	303	140
18 to 19 years	48639	4893	10991	19471	12528	600	156
20 to 24 years	109385	11917	21673	23391	32965	15506	3933
25 to 29 years	114704	19044	29357	18734	13943	23358	10268
30 to 34 years	127517	30142	36153	22504	11079	18684	8955
35 to 39 years	129639	40745	32404	22325	9727	16409	8029
40 to 44 years	117335	46050	23360	18574	8054	14226	7071
45 to 49 years	102464	49328	14428	13540	6603	12455	6110
50 to 54 years	98426	58091	9987	11179	4468	9786	4915
55 to 59 years	88732	60955	5959	9200	2529	6866	3223
60 to 64 years	73587	54315	3625	7315	1481	4778	2073
65 to 69 years	65341	51494	2489	5121	882	3790	1565
70 to 74 years	57852	47277	1714	3891	658	2980	1332
Males	**581232**	**255134**	**100064**	**82703**	**47868**	**64019**	**31444**
16 to 17 years	27160	10847	7006	8378	721	136	72
18 to 19 years	24551	3229	6436	9586	4947	277	76
20 to 24 years	54913	7522	12500	11655	14985	6621	1630
25 to 29 years	56628	11634	14917	8293	6602	10563	4619
30 to 34 years	62487	17424	17710	9069	4930	8982	4372
35 to 39 years	63430	22918	15414	8494	4056	8231	4317
40 to 44 years	57432	24971	10569	7122	3540	7182	4048
45 to 49 years	51686	26485	6334	5549	3186	6450	3682
50 to 54 years	48484	29408	3962	4501	2140	5341	3132
55 to 59 years	43585	30129	2347	3828	1307	3840	2134
60 to 64 years	35401	26297	1365	2931	752	2651	1405
65 to 69 years	30406	23936	926	1940	408	2123	1073
70 to 74 years	25069	20334	578	1357	294	1622	884

Table S320: Sex and Age by Highest Level of Qualification (continued)

© Crown copyright 2003

	All persons	No qualifications	Level 1	Level 2	Level 3	Level 4	Level 5
Females	**605847**	**239143**	**104414**	**111562**	**58680**	**65722**	**26326**
16 to 17 years	26298	9179	5332	10642	910	167	68
18 to 19 years	24088	1664	4555	9885	7581	323	80
20 to 24 years	54472	4395	9173	11736	17980	8885	2303
25 to 29 years	58076	7410	14440	10441	7341	12795	5649
30 to 34 years	65030	12718	18443	13435	6149	9702	4583
35 to 39 years	66209	17827	16990	13831	5671	8178	3712
40 to 44 years	59903	21079	12791	11452	4514	7044	3023
45 to 49 years	50778	22843	8094	7991	3417	6005	2428
50 to 54 years	49942	28683	6025	6678	2328	4445	1783
55 to 59 years	45147	30826	3612	5372	1222	3026	1089
60 to 64 years	38186	28018	2260	4384	729	2127	668
65 to 69 years	34935	27558	1563	3181	474	1667	492
70 to 74 years	32783	26943	1136	2534	364	1358	448

Notes:
1. The levels for 'Highest level of qualification' are defined as follows:
   No qualifications: No qualifications
   Level 1: GCSE (grades D-G), CSE (grades 2-5), 1-4 CSEs (grade 1), 1-4 GCSEs (grades A-C), 1-4 'O' level passes, NVQ level 1, GNVQ Foundation or equivalents
   Level 2: 5+ CSEs (grade 1), 5+ GCSEs (grades A-C), 5+ 'O' level passes, Senior Certificate, 1 'A' level, 1-3 AS levels, Advanced Senior Certificate, NVQ level 2, GNVQ Intermediate or equivalents
   Level 3: 2+ 'A' levels, 4+ AS levels, NVQ level 3, GNVQ Advanced or equivalents
   Level 4: First Degree, NVQ level 4, HNC, HND or equivalents
   Level 5: Higher Degree, NVQ level 5 or equivalents

Table S321: Sex and NS-SeC by Highest Level of Qualification

Table population: All persons aged 16 to 74

	All persons	No qualifications	Level 1	Level 2	Level 3	Level 4	Level 5
All persons	**1187079**	**494277**	**204478**	**194265**	**106548**	**129741**	**57770**
1. Higher managerial and professional occupations	69973	7534	4253	7095	4629	26081	20381
1.1 Large employers and higher managerial occupations	25056	4788	2679	3906	2258	7417	4008
1.2 Higher professional occupations	44917	2746	1574	3189	2371	18664	16373
2. Lower managerial and professional occupations	229609	38896	31420	46511	24414	62730	25638
3. Intermediate occupations	131679	32543	29787	35445	16501	13855	3548
4. Small employers and own account workers	103648	58641	18690	13103	5578	5852	1784
5. Lower supervisory and technical occupations	104088	48384	23276	15386	9743	5865	1434
6. Semi-routine occupations	183131	96915	41310	25427	12199	5763	1517
7. Routine occupations	193187	133901	34836	15187	6305	2188	770
8. Never worked and long-term unemployed	77975	58138	9271	5424	2536	1818	788
L14.1 Never worked	58134	46314	5651	3291	1508	942	428
L14.2 Long-term unemployed	19841	11824	3620	2133	1028	876	360
Not classified	93789	19325	11635	30687	24643	5589	1910
L15 Full-time students	93789	19325	11635	30687	24643	5589	1910
Males	**581232**	**255134**	**100064**	**82703**	**47868**	**64019**	**31444**
1. Higher managerial and professional occupations	49488	5884	3124	4985	3260	18098	14137
1.1 Large employers and higher managerial occupations	18426	3808	2018	2718	1580	5380	2922
1.2 Higher professional occupations	31062	2076	1106	2267	1680	12718	11215
2. Lower managerial and professional occupations	102820	22388	14684	18002	10697	25550	11499
3. Intermediate occupations	37837	11024	7862	8206	4429	4986	1330
4. Small employers and own account workers	82029	49086	14588	9011	3908	4177	1259
5. Lower supervisory and technical occupations	72078	33708	16291	10124	6756	4233	966
6. Semi-routine occupations	60119	32717	13166	7702	3709	2233	592
7. Routine occupations	102160	66231	20701	9205	4147	1428	448
8. Never worked and long-term unemployed	32813	24069	4014	2257	1199	902	372
L14.1 Never worked	19115	15133	1876	1018	571	363	154
L14.2 Long-term unemployed	13698	8936	2138	1239	628	539	218
Not classified	41888	10027	5634	13211	9763	2412	841
L15 Full-time students	41888	10027	5634	13211	9763	2412	841

Table S321: Sex and NS-SeC by Highest Level of Qualification (continued)

	All persons	No qualifications	Level 1	Level 2	Level 3	Level 4	Level 5
Females	**605847**	**239143**	**104414**	**111562**	**58680**	**65722**	**26326**
1. Higher managerial and professional occupations	20485	1650	1129	2110	1369	7983	6244
1.1 Large employers and higher managerial occupations	6630	980	661	1188	678	2037	1086
1.2 Higher professional occupations	13855	670	468	922	691	5946	5158
2. Lower managerial and professional occupations	126789	16508	16736	28509	13717	37180	14139
3. Intermediate occupations	93842	21519	21925	27239	12072	8869	2218
4. Small employers and own account workers	21619	9555	4102	4092	1670	1675	525
5. Lower supervisory and technical occupations	32010	14676	6985	5262	2987	1632	468
6. Semi-routine occupations	123012	64198	28144	17725	8490	3530	925
7. Routine occupations	91027	67670	14135	5982	2158	760	322
8. Never worked and long-term unemployed	45162	34069	5257	3167	1337	916	416
L14.1 Never worked	39019	31181	3775	2273	937	579	274
L14.2 Long-term unemployed	6143	2888	1482	894	400	337	142
Not classified	**51901**	**9298**	**6001**	**17476**	**14880**	**3177**	**1069**
L15 Full-time students	51901	9298	6001	17476	14880	3177	1069

Notes:

1 NS-SeC stands for National Statistics Socio-economic Classification.

2 In the NS-SeC classification all full-time students are recorded in the 'full-time students' category regardless of whether they are economically active or inactive.

3 For long-term unemployed, year last worked is 1999 or earlier.

4 The levels for 'Highest level of qualification' are defined as follows:

No qualifications: No qualifications

Level 1: GCSE (grades D-G), CSE (grades 2-5), 1-4 CSEs (grade 1), 1-4 GCSEs (grades A-C), 1-4 'O' level passes, NVQ level 1, GNVQ Foundation or equivalents

Level 2: 5+ CSEs (grade 1), 5+ GCSEs (grades A-C), 5+ 'O' level passes, Senior Certificate, 1 'A' level, 1-3 AS levels, Advanced Senior Certificate, NVQ level 2, GNVQ Intermediate or equivalents

Level 3: 2+ 'A' levels, 4+ AS levels, NVQ level 3, GNVQ Advanced or equivalents

Level 4: First Degree, NVQ level 4, HNC, HND or equivalents

Level 5: Higher Degree, NVQ level 5 or equivalents

S321

Table S322: Sex and Highest Level of Qualification by Ethnic Group

Table population: All persons aged 16 to 74

	All persons	White	Irish Traveller	Mixed	Indian	Pakistani	Bangladeshi	Other Asian	Black Caribbean	Black African	Other Black	Chinese	Other ethnic group
All persons	**1187077**	**1177608**	**1077**	**1534**	**1217**	**430**	**154**	**158**	**206**	**342**	**298**	**3048**	**1005**
No qualifications	494277	490928	770	373	227	151	66	30	49	51	98	1323	211
Level 1	204478	203264	96	244	116	58	26	19	49	48	69	415	74
Level 2	194265	193189	78	305	110	41	24	11	28	55	60	275	89
Level 3	106546	105715	48	183	102	39	3	12	31	31	27	240	115
Level 4	129741	128328	54	235	254	53	13	39	27	68	23	418	229
Level 5	57770	56184	31	194	408	88	22	47	22	89	21	377	287
Males	**581230**	**576253**	**587**	**775**	**651**	**251**	**87**	**60**	**115**	**194**	**173**	**1640**	**444**
No qualifications	255134	253383	408	202	112	81	41	8	22	26	55	718	78
Level 1	100064	99434	57	126	56	38	14	4	28	19	42	217	29
Level 2	82703	82199	40	140	53	18	12	5	14	25	34	118	45
Level 3	47866	47451	26	88	50	23	-	3	17	14	16	128	50
Level 4	64019	63318	33	112	122	27	6	13	21	40	10	228	89
Level 5	31444	30468	23	107	258	64	14	27	13	70	16	231	153
Females	**605847**	**601355**	**490**	**759**	**566**	**179**	**67**	**98**	**91**	**148**	**125**	**1408**	**561**
No qualifications	239143	237545	362	171	115	70	25	22	27	25	43	605	133
Level 1	104414	103830	39	118	60	20	12	15	21	29	27	198	45
Level 2	111562	110990	38	165	57	23	12	6	14	30	26	157	44
Level 3	58680	58264	22	95	52	16	3	9	14	17	11	112	65
Level 4	65722	65010	21	123	132	26	7	26	6	28	13	190	140
Level 5	26326	25716	8	87	150	24	8	20	9	19	5	146	134

Notes:

1 The levels for 'Highest level of qualification' are defined as follows:

No qualifications : No qualifications

Level 1 : GCSE (grades D–G), CSE (grades 2-5), 1-4 CSEs (grade 1), 1-4 GCSEs (grades A-C), 1-4 'O' level passes, NVQ level 1, GNVQ Foundation or equivalents

Level 2 : 5+ CSEs (grade 1), 5+ GCSEs (grades A-C), 5+ 'O' level passes, Senior Certificate, 1 'A' level, 1-3 AS levels, Advanced Senior Certificate, NVQ level 2, GNVQ Intermediate or equivalents

Level 3 : 2+ 'A' levels, 4+ AS levels, NVQ level 3, GNVQ Advanced or equivalents

Level 4 : First Degree, NVQ level 4, HNC, HND or equivalents

Level 5 : Higher Degree, NVQ level 5 or equivalents

Table S323: Age and Highest Level of Qualification by Ethnic Group

Table population: All persons aged 16 to 74

	All persons	White	Irish Traveller	Mixed	Indian	Pakistani	Bangladeshi	Other Asian	Black Caribbean	Black African	Other Black	Chinese	Other ethnic group
All persons	**1187071**	**1177608**	**1077**	**1534**	**1217**	**428**	**157**	**153**	**204**	**342**	**298**	**3048**	**1005**
16 to 24	**211480**	**209347**	**279**	**505**	**141**	**69**	**34**	**26**	**32**	**57**	**84**	**742**	**164**
No qualifications	36834	36339	165	92	29	13	7	8	-	6	20	128	27
Level 1	45002	44618	31	100	23	13	8	4	10	16	23	148	8
Level 2	61882	61414	35	161	32	15	13	5	8	9	24	139	27
Level 3	47125	46651	27	97	35	18	3	3	11	14	11	185	70
Level 4	16407	16175	12	42	17	5	3	6	-	6	3	117	21
Level 5	4230	4150	9	13	5	5	-	-	3	6	3	25	11
25 to 44	**489195**	**484255**	**434**	**731**	**584**	**244**	**90**	**106**	**123**	**196**	**144**	**1644**	**644**
No qualifications	135981	134447	303	146	74	78	41	18	20	26	37	659	132
Level 1	121274	120602	50	115	57	33	17	14	36	27	44	231	48
Level 2	82137	81666	31	108	47	24	10	5	17	31	22	123	53
Level 3	42803	42556	13	61	34	16	3	6	12	12	13	42	35
Level 4	72677	71748	25	171	140	39	7	31	20	43	15	272	166
Level 5	34323	33236	12	130	232	54	12	32	18	57	13	317	210
45 to 74	**486396**	**48006**	**364**	**298**	**492**	**115**	**33**	**21**	**49**	**89**	**70**	**662**	**197**
No qualifications	321460	320142	302	135	124	60	18	4	27	19	41	536	52
Level 1	38201	38044	15	29	36	12	3	-	3	5	-	36	18
Level 2	50242	50109	12	36	31	-	-	-	3	15	14	13	9
Level 3	16621	16508	8	25	33	5	-	3	8	5	3	13	10
Level 4	40653	40405	17	22	97	9	3	-	5	19	5	29	42
Level 5	19219	18798	10	51	171	29	9	14	3	26	7	35	66

S 3 2 3

Notes:

1   The levels for 'Highest level of qualification' are defined as follows:

No qualifications: No qualifications

Level 1: GCSE (grades D-G), CSE (grades 2-5), 1-4 CSEs (grade 1), 1-4 GCSEs (grades A-C), 1-4 'O' level passes, NVQ level 1, GNVQ Foundation or equivalents

Level 2: 5+ CSEs (grade 1), 5+ GCSEs (grades A-C), 5+ 'O' level passes, Senior Certificate, 1 'A' level, 1-3 AS levels, Advanced Senior Certificate, NVQ level 2, GNVQ Intermediate or equivalents

Level 3: 2+ 'A' levels, 4+ AS levels, NVQ level 3, GNVQ Advanced or equivalents

Level 4: First Degree, NVQ level 4, HNC, HND or equivalents

Level 5: Higher Degree, NVQ level 5 or equivalents

Table S324: Sex and Highest Level of Qualification by Community Background (Religion or Religion Brought Up In)

Table population: All persons aged 16 to 74

	All persons	Catholic	Protestant and Other Christian (including Christian related)	Other religions and philosophies	None
All persons	**1187079**	**508964**	**648858**	**5072**	**24185**
No qualifications	494277	210113	276263	1243	6658
Level 1	204478	86060	113268	561	4589
Level 2	194265	82980	106025	675	4585
Level 3	106548	48106	55062	552	2828
Level 4	129741	54733	70645	926	3437
Level 5	57770	26972	27595	1115	2088
Males	**581232**	**245374**	**319199**	**2936**	**13723**
No qualifications	255134	110010	140386	733	4005
Level 1	100064	41686	55488	311	2579
Level 2	82703	34457	45430	374	2442
Level 3	47868	20726	25348	284	1510
Level 4	64019	25103	36473	504	1939
Level 5	31444	13392	16074	730	1248
Females	**605847**	**263590**	**329659**	**2136**	**10462**
No qualifications	239143	100103	135877	510	2653
Level 1	104414	44374	57780	250	2010
Level 2	111562	48523	60595	301	2143
Level 3	58680	27380	29714	268	1318
Level 4	65722	29630	34172	422	1498
Level 5	26326	13580	11521	385	840

Notes:
1   The levels for 'Highest level of qualification' are defined as follows:
No qualifications: No qualifications
Level 1: GCSE (grades D-G), CSE (grades 2-5), 1-4 CSEs (grade 1), 1-4 GCSEs (grades A-C), 1-4 'O' level passes, NVQ level 1, GNVQ Foundation or equivalents
Level 2: 5+ CSEs (grade 1), 5+ GCSEs (grades A-C), 5+ 'O' level passes, Senior Certificate, 1 'A' level, 1-3 AS levels, Advanced Senior Certificate, NVQ level 2, GNVQ Intermediate or equivalents
Level 3: 2+ 'A' levels, 4+ AS levels, NVQ level 3, GNVQ Advanced or equivalents
Level 4: First Degree, NVQ level 4, HNC, HND or equivalents
Level 5: Higher Degree, NVQ level 5 or equivalents
2   The term 'Catholic' includes those respondents who gave their religion as Catholic or Roman Catholic.

S324

Table S325: Age and Highest Level of Qualification by Sex and Community Background (Religion or Religion Brought Up In)

Table population: All persons aged 16 to 74

	All persons					Males					Females				
	Total	Catholic	Protestant and Other Christian (including Christian related)	Other religions and philosophies	None	Total	Catholic	Protestant and Other Christian (including Christian related)	Other religions and philosophies	None	Total	Catholic	Protestant and Other Christian (including Christian related)	Other religions and philosophies	None
All persons	**1187080**	**508964**	**648858**	**5073**	**24185**	**581233**	**245374**	**319199**	**2937**	**13723**	**605847**	**263590**	**329659**	**2136**	**10462**
16 to 24	**211482**	**106672**	**97570**	**854**	**6386**	**106624**	**53260**	**49466**	**453**	**3445**	**104858**	**53412**	**48104**	**401**	**2941**
No qualifications	36836	19293	16252	140	1151	21598	11478	9380	77	663	15238	7815	6872	63	488
Level 1	45002	22040	21477	127	1358	25942	12701	12372	68	801	19060	9339	9105	59	557
Level 2	61882	30922	28826	194	1940	29619	14706	13799	99	1015	32263	16216	15027	95	925
Level 3	47124	23932	21710	249	1233	20653	10151	9764	132	606	26471	13781	11946	117	627
Level 4	16409	8113	7642	103	551	7034	3264	3429	51	290	9375	4849	4213	52	261
Level 5	4229	2372	1663	41	153	1778	960	722	26	70	2451	1412	941	15	83
25 to 34	**242221**	**109782**	**123977**	**1425**	**7037**	**119115**	**52307**	**62131**	**831**	**3846**	**123106**	**57475**	**61846**	**594**	**3191**
No qualifications	49186	24484	23352	264	1086	29058	14289	13955	171	643	20128	10195	9397	93	443
Level 1	65510	27270	36372	181	1687	32627	13133	18495	92	907	32883	14137	17877	89	780
Level 2	41238	17787	22067	157	1227	17362	7173	9433	103	653	23876	10614	12634	54	574
Level 3	25022	10870	13126	117	909	11532	4808	6158	61	505	13490	6062	6968	56	404
Level 4	42042	19288	21059	333	1362	19545	8485	10165	182	713	22497	10803	10894	151	649
Level 5	19223	10083	8001	373	766	8991	4419	3925	222	425	10232	5664	4076	151	341
35 to 44	**246974**	**109088**	**131501**	**1193**	**5192**	**120862**	**52037**	**65147**	**707**	**2971**	**126112**	**57051**	**66354**	**486**	**2221**
No qualifications	86795	40768	44270	277	1480	47889	22164	24668	170	887	38906	18604	19602	107	593
Level 1	55764	22989	31610	129	1036	25983	10538	14799	80	566	29781	12451	16811	49	470
Level 2	40899	17454	22481	143	821	15616	6124	8975	82	435	25283	11330	13506	61	386
Level 3	17781	7299	9948	87	447	7596	3033	4267	44	252	10185	4266	5681	43	195
Level 4	30635	13235	16369	225	806	15413	6359	8468	123	463	15222	6876	7901	102	343
Level 5	15100	7343	6823	332	602	8365	3819	3970	208	368	6735	3524	2853	124	234
45 to 54	**200890**	**82325**	**114620**	**824**	**3121**	**100170**	**40158**	**57589**	**494**	**1929**	**100720**	**42167**	**57031**	**330**	**1192**
No qualifications	107419	47031	55802	227	1359	55893	24528	30391	132	842	51526	22503	28411	95	517
Level 1	24415	9266	14702	75	372	10296	3598	6429	49	220	14119	5668	8273	26	152
Level 2	24719	9136	15119	87	377	10050	3520	6276	44	210	14669	5616	8843	43	167
Level 3	11071	4081	6754	64	172	5326	1815	3376	29	106	5745	2266	3378	35	66
Level 4	22241	8349	13265	159	468	11791	4126	7265	87	313	10450	4223	6000	72	155
Level 5	11025	4462	5978	212	373	6814	2571	3852	153	238	4211	1891	2126	59	135

Table S325: Age and Highest Level of Qualification by Sex and Community Background (Religion or Religion Brought Up In) (continued)

	All persons					Males					Females				
	Total	Catholic	Protestant and Other Christian (including Christian related)	Other religions and philosophies	None	Total	Catholic	Protestant and Other Christian (including Christian related)	Other religions and philosophies	None	Total	Catholic	Protestant and Other Christian (including Christian related)	Other religions and philosophies	None
55 to 59	**88732**	**32485**	**55013**	**292**	**942**	**43585**	**15922**	**26908**	**175**	**580**	**45147**	**16563**	**28105**	**117**	**362**
No qualifications	60955	23684	36637	95	539	30129	11873	17877	55	324	30826	11811	18760	40	215
Level 1	5959	1938	3929	21	71	2347	783	1517	10	37	3612	1155	2412	11	34
Level 2	9200	2738	6317	43	102	3828	1092	2650	20	66	5372	1646	3667	23	36
Level 3	2529	897	1586	17	29	1307	434	841	10	22	1222	463	745	7	7
Level 4	6866	2146	4574	41	105	3840	1088	2667	23	62	3026	1058	1907	18	43
Level 5	3223	1082	1970	75	96	2134	652	1356	57	69	1089	430	614	18	27
60 to 64	**73588**	**26342**	**46375**	**232**	**639**	**35402**	**12630**	**22227**	**133**	**412**	**38186**	**13712**	**24148**	**99**	**227**
No qualifications	54315	20255	33535	107	418	26297	9923	16045	61	268	28018	10332	17490	46	150
Level 1	3625	1181	2401	14	29	1365	447	891	6	21	2260	734	1510	8	8
Level 2	7315	2174	5068	24	49	2931	829	2058	12	32	4384	1345	3010	12	17
Level 3	1482	520	930	10	22	753	262	479	3	9	729	258	451	7	13
Level 4	4778	1516	3162	34	66	2651	748	1844	18	41	2127	768	1318	16	25
Level 5	2073	696	1279	43	55	1405	421	910	33	41	668	275	369	10	14
65 to 74	**123193**	**42270**	**79802**	**253**	**868**	**55475**	**19060**	**35731**	**144**	**540**	**67718**	**23210**	**44071**	**109**	**328**
No qualifications	98771	34598	63415	133	625	44270	15755	28070	67	378	54501	18843	35345	66	247
Level 1	4203	1376	2777	14	36	1504	486	985	6	27	2699	890	1792	8	9
Level 2	9012	2769	6147	27	69	3297	1013	2239	14	31	5715	1756	3908	13	38
Level 3	1540	507	1008	9	16	702	223	463	6	10	838	284	545	3	6
Level 4	6770	2086	4574	31	79	3745	1033	2635	20	57	3025	1053	1939	11	22
Level 5	2897	934	1881	39	43	1957	550	1339	31	37	940	384	542	8	6

Notes:

1 The levels for 'Highest level of qualification' are defined as follows:

No qualifications: No qualifications

Level 1: GCSE (grades D–G), CSE (grades 2–5), 1–4 CSEs (grade 1), 1–4 GCSEs (grades A–C), 1–4 'O' level passes, NVQ level 1, GNVQ Foundation or equivalents

Level 2: 5+ CSEs (grade 1), 5+ GCSEs (grades A–C), 5+ 'O' level passes, Senior Certificate, 1 'A' level, 1–3 AS levels, Advanced Senior Certificate, NVQ level 2, GNVQ Intermediate or equivalents

Level 3: 2+ 'A' levels, 4+ AS levels, NVQ level 3, GNVQ Advanced or equivalents

Level 4: First Degree, NVQ level 4, HNC, HND or equivalents

Level 5: Higher Degree, NVQ level 5 or equivalents

2 The term 'Catholic' includes those respondents who gave their religion as Catholic or Roman Catholic.

S325

Table S325A: Age and Highest Level of Qualification by Sex and Religion

Table population: All persons aged 16 to 74

	All persons								Males								Females							
	Total	Catholic	Presbyterian Church in Ireland	Church of Ireland	Methodist Church in Ireland	Other Christian (including Christian related)	Other religions and philosophies	No religion or religion not stated	Total	Catholic	Presbyterian Church in Ireland	Church of Ireland	Methodist Church in Ireland	Other Christian (including Christian related)	Other religions and philosophies	No religion or religion not stated	Total	Catholic	Presbyterian Church in Ireland	Church of Ireland	Methodist Church in Ireland	Other Christian (including Christian related)	Other religions and philosophies	No religion or religion not stated
All persons	1187080	467613	251214	185559	41848	74270	3848	162728	581233	223280	122199	88206	19376	35617	2196	90359	605847	244333	129015	97353	22472	38653	1652	72369
16 to 24	211482	98174	36764	26730	5899	12236	641	31038	106624	48759	18530	13227	2926	6072	338	16772	104858	49415	18234	13503	2973	6164	303	14266
No quals.	36836	17737	6061	4937	968	1675	104	5354	21598	10541	3502	2927	554	910	55	3109	15238	7196	2559	2010	414	765	49	2245
Level 1	45002	20319	7668	6341	1292	2319	88	6975	25942	11754	4421	3556	725	1389	45	4052	19060	8565	3247	2785	567	930	43	2923
Level 2	61882	28698	10939	7822	1733	3721	148	8821	29619	13572	5275	3495	816	1759	81	4621	32263	15126	5664	4327	917	1962	67	4200
Level 3	47124	21911	8505	5321	1307	3197	201	6682	20653	9130	3803	2265	549	1413	103	3390	26471	12781	4702	3056	758	1784	98	3292
Level 4	16409	7343	2941	1871	491	1114	74	2575	7034	2895	1268	813	227	505	39	1287	9375	4448	1673	1058	264	609	35	1288
Level 5	4229	2166	650	438	108	210	26	631	1778	867	261	171	55	96	15	313	2451	1299	389	267	53	114	11	318
25 to 34	242221	99737	45646	33723	7213	15499	1103	39300	119115	46997	22682	16053	3382	7741	640	21620	123106	52740	22964	17670	3831	7758	463	17680
No quals.	49186	22495	8646	7599	1270	2092	208	6876	29058	13128	5338	4369	726	1265	131	4101	20128	9367	3308	3230	544	827	77	2775
Level 1	65510	25049	13547	10278	2203	4191	134	10108	32627	11993	6988	4876	1028	2223	71	5448	32883	13056	6559	5402	1175	1968	63	4660
Level 2	41238	16178	8093	5779	1321	2944	116	6807	17362	6372	3286	2339	531	1286	73	3475	23876	9806	4807	3440	790	1658	43	3332
Level 3	25022	9739	4819	3113	769	1881	87	4614	11532	4232	2152	1361	322	861	48	2556	13490	5507	2667	1752	447	1020	39	2058
Level 4	42042	17318	7671	5056	1218	3200	256	7323	19545	7414	3588	2230	561	1523	142	4087	22497	9904	4083	2826	657	1677	114	3236
Level 5	19223	8958	2870	1898	432	1191	302	3572	8991	3858	1330	878	214	583	175	1953	10232	5100	1540	1020	218	608	127	1619
35 to 44	246974	99407	49948	36645	8280	15051	897	36746	120862	46921	24525	17410	3796	7296	522	20392	126112	52486	25423	19235	4484	7755	375	16354
No quals.	86795	37665	16886	14485	2674	3905	199	10981	47889	20434	9689	7708	1384	2173	123	6378	38906	17231	7197	6777	1290	1732	76	4603
Level 1	55764	21238	12406	8559	2181	3677	87	7616	25983	9645	5766	3833	922	1685	51	4081	29781	11593	6640	4726	1259	1992	36	3535
Level 2	40899	15951	8730	5747	1437	2854	111	6069	15616	5456	3365	2117	550	1092	57	2979	25283	10495	5365	3630	887	1762	54	3090
Level 3	17781	6468	3629	2452	652	1346	61	3173	7596	2592	1437	1033	264	542	28	1700	10185	3876	2192	1419	388	804	33	1473
Level 4	30635	11689	6029	3832	965	2299	169	5652	15413	5503	2996	1879	459	1207	94	3275	15222	6186	3033	1953	506	1092	75	2377
Level 5	15100	6396	2268	1570	371	970	270	3255	8365	3291	1272	840	217	597	169	1979	6735	3105	996	730	154	373	101	1276
45 to 54	200890	75495	43991	32834	7452	12707	604	27807	100170	36355	21771	16011	3490	6100	356	16087	100720	39140	22220	16823	3962	6607	248	11720
No quals.	107419	43905	22892	18592	3813	6006	145	12066	55893	22708	11865	9351	1819	2976	84	7090	51526	21197	11027	9241	1994	3030	61	4976
Level 1	24415	8485	5667	4045	999	1757	48	3414	10296	3219	2421	1679	409	715	29	1824	14119	5266	3246	2366	590	1042	19	1590
Level 2	24719	8329	5894	4026	998	1857	64	3551	10050	3119	2315	1612	389	715	31	1869	14669	5210	3579	2414	609	1142	33	1682
Level 3	11071	3586	2525	1650	452	796	50	2012	5326	1559	1208	825	207	338	21	1168	5745	2027	1317	825	245	458	29	844
Level 4	22241	7413	4995	3123	844	1566	127	4173	11791	3583	2658	1714	437	846	70	2483	10450	3830	2337	1409	407	720	57	1690
Level 5	11025	3777	2018	1398	346	725	170	2591	6814	2167	1304	830	229	510	121	1653	4211	1610	714	568	117	215	49	938

	All persons								Males								Females							
	Total	Catholic	Presbyterian Church in Ireland	Church of Ireland	Methodist Church in Ireland	Other Christian (including Christian related)	Other religions and philosophies	No religion or religion not stated	Total	Catholic	Presbyterian Church in Ireland	Church of Ireland	Methodist Church in Ireland	Other Christian (including Christian related)	Other religions and philosophies	No religion or religion not stated	Total	Catholic	Presbyterian Church in Ireland	Church of Ireland	Methodist Church in Ireland	Other Christian (including Christian related)	Other religions and philosophies	No religion or religion not stated
55 to 59	**88732**	**30253**	**22144**	**16425**	**3839**	**5967**	**227**	**9877**	**43585**	**14636**	**10676**	**7850**	**1784**	**2714**	**134**	**5791**	**45147**	**15617**	**11468**	**8575**	**2055**	**3253**	**93**	**4086**
No quals.	60955	22275	14884	11477	2522	3934	64	5799	30129	11077	7190	5553	1166	1778	36	3329	30826	11198	7694	5924	1356	2156	28	2470
Level 1	**5959**	1801	1568	1085	304	493	16	692	**2347**	701	597	374	105	195	7	368	**3612**	1100	971	711	199	298	9	324
Level 2	9200	2514	2639	1710	486	670	36	1145	3828	984	1083	670	197	269	16	609	5372	1530	1556	1040	289	401	20	536
Level 3	2529	801	575	421	115	179	14	424	**1307**	375	277	222	58	95	8	272	**1222**	426	298	199	57	84	6	152
Level 4	6866	1929	1822	1219	283	461	34	1118	3840	948	1068	682	171	227	19	725	3026	981	754	537	112	234	15	393
Level 5	3223	933	656	513	129	230	63	699	2134	551	461	349	87	150	48	488	1089	382	195	164	42	80	15	211
60 to 64	**73588**	**24711**	**19062**	**14168**	**3260**	**5001**	**179**	**7207**	**35402**	**11763**	**8982**	**6676**	**1512**	**2330**	**100**	**4039**	**38186**	**12948**	**10080**	**7492**	**1748**	**2671**	**79**	**3168**
No quals.	54315	19075	13980	10484	2340	3592	80	4764	26297	9285	6633	4981	1066	1655	40	2637	28018	9790	7347	5503	1274	1937	40	2127
Level 1	**3625**	1102	960	693	182	291	11	386	**1365**	406	349	245	61	104	6	194	**2260**	696	611	448	121	187	5	192
Level 2	7315	2029	2133	1456	367	502	17	811	2931	769	842	567	161	184	9	399	4384	1260	1291	889	206	318	8	412
Level 3	**1482**	480	334	272	71	114	10	201	**753**	240	167	139	34	54	3	116	**729**	240	167	133	37	60	7	85
Level 4	4778	1401	1208	888	242	360	24	655	2651	678	669	495	144	228	14	423	2127	723	539	393	98	132	10	232
Level 5	2073	624	447	375	58	142	37	390	1405	385	322	249	46	105	28	270	668	239	125	126	12	37	9	120
65 to 74	**123193**	**39836**	**33659**	**25034**	**5905**	**7809**	**197**	**10753**	**55475**	**17849**	**15033**	**10979**	**2486**	**3364**	**106**	**5658**	**67718**	**21987**	**18626**	**14055**	**3419**	**4445**	**91**	**5095**
No quals.	98771	32677	26735	20137	4739	6283	110	8090	44270	14793	11877	8765	1945	2655	51	4184	54501	17884	14858	11372	2794	3628	59	3906
Level 1	**4203**	1273	1172	821	220	293	13	411	**1504**	454	396	280	90	98	5	181	**2699**	819	776	541	130	195	8	230
Level 2	9012	2612	2740	1842	428	505	18	867	3297	941	995	656	145	171	8	381	5715	1671	1745	1186	283	334	10	486
Level 3	**1540**	467	395	295	80	104	7	192	**702**	203	174	126	34	55	4	106	**838**	264	221	169	46	49	3	86
Level 4	6770	1955	1903	1359	330	426	24	773	3745	963	1078	750	193	253	17	491	3025	992	825	609	137	173	7	282
Level 5	2897	852	714	580	108	198	25	420	1957	495	513	402	79	132	21	315	940	357	201	178	29	66	4	105

Notes:

1 The levels for 'Highest level of qualification' are defined as follows:

No quals: No qualifications

Level 1: GCSE (grades D-G), CSE (grades 2-5), 1-4 CSEs (grade 1), 1-4 GCSEs (grades A-C), 1-4 'O' level passes, NVQ level 1, GNVQ Foundation or equivalents

Level 2: 5+ CSEs (grade 1), 5+ GCSEs (grades A-C), 5+ 'O' level passes, Senior Certificate, NVQ level 2, GNVQ Intermediate or equivalents

Level 3: 2+ 'A' levels, 4+ AS levels, NVQ level 3, GNVQ Advanced or equivalents

Level 4: First Degree, NVQ level 4, HNC, HND or equivalents

Level 5: Higher Degree, NVQ level 5 or equivalents

2 The term 'Catholic' includes those respondents who gave their religion as Catholic or Roman Catholic.

S 3 2 5 A

Table S326: Sex and Occupation by Highest Level of Qualification

Table population: All persons aged 16 to 74 in employment the week before the census

	All persons	No qualifications	Level 1	Level 2	Level 3	Level 4	Level 5
All persons	**686644**	**190303**	**139800**	**127771**	**76416**	**104089**	**48265**
1. Managers and senior officials	72772	14274	12395	13940	8155	16563	7445
2. Professional occupations	72509	1851	1812	4354	3870	34965	25657
3. Associate professional and technical occupations	86007	10150	15078	19687	11627	22203	7262
4. Administrative and secretarial occupations	100098	11786	22974	30759	16513	14118	3948
5. Skilled trades occupations	106900	46146	27603	16760	10055	5161	1175
6. Personal service occupations	45773	13657	10217	10219	8070	2877	733
7. Sales and customer service occupations	50359	13454	12687	11889	8420	3158	751
8. Process, plant and machine operatives	71288	36565	18530	9012	3769	2700	712
9. Elementary occupations	80938	42420	18504	11151	5937	2344	582
Males	**377391**	**124253**	**78376**	**59085**	**36042**	**52900**	**26735**
1. Managers and senior officials	47686	10391	7900	8429	5003	10883	5080
2. Professional occupations	38150	1380	1224	2327	2085	16747	14387
3. Associate professional and technical occupations	44482	7331	8869	9048	5788	10212	3234
4. Administrative and secretarial occupations	27064	4351	4947	6588	4494	5002	1682
5. Skilled trades occupations	96914	42023	25348	14779	9163	4607	994
6. Personal service occupations	6608	2777	1324	1194	620	515	178
7. Sales and customer service occupations	14069	3371	3214	3453	2637	1138	256
8. Process, plant and machine operatives	58496	30603	14789	7043	3081	2387	593
9. Elementary occupations	43922	22026	10761	6224	3171	1409	331
Females	**309253**	**66050**	**61424**	**68686**	**40374**	**51189**	**21530**
1. Managers and senior officials	25086	3883	4495	5511	3152	5680	2365
2. Professional occupations	34359	471	588	2027	1785	18218	11270
3. Associate professional and technical occupations	41525	2819	6209	10639	5839	11991	4028
4. Administrative and secretarial occupations	73034	7435	18027	24171	12019	9116	2266
5. Skilled trades occupations	9986	4123	2255	1981	892	554	181
6. Personal service occupations	39165	10880	8893	9025	7450	2362	555
7. Sales and customer service occupations	36290	10083	9473	8436	5783	2020	495
8. Process, plant and machine operatives	12792	5962	3741	1969	688	313	119
9. Elementary occupations	37016	20394	7743	4927	2766	935	251

S326

Notes:
1   The occupation classification is SOC2000 (Standard Occupation Classification).
2   The levels for 'Highest level of qualification' are defined as follows:
    No qualifications: No qualifications
    Level 1: GCSE (grades D–G), CSE (grades 2–5), 1-4 CSEs (grade 1), 1-4 GCSEs (grades A-C), 1-4 'O' level passes, NVQ level 1, GNVQ Foundation or equivalents
    Level 2: 5+ CSEs (grade 1), 5+ GCSEs (grades A-C), 5+ 'O' level passes, Senior Certificate, 1 'A' level, 1-3 AS levels, Advanced Senior Certificate, NVQ level 2, GNVQ Intermediate or equivalents
    Level 3: 2+ 'A' levels, 4+ AS levels, NVQ level 3, GNVQ Advanced or equivalents
    Level 4: First Degree, NVQ level 4, HNC, HND or equivalents
    Level 5: Higher Degree, NVQ level 5 or equivalents
3   'In employment' includes economically active full-time students in employment.

S 3 2 7

Table S327: Age of Household Reference Person (HRP) and Tenure by Economic Activity of HRP

Table population: All households with HRP aged 16 to 74

	All HRPs	Economically active					Economically inactive					
		Total	Employee	Self-employed	Unemployed	Full-time students	Total	Retired	Student	Looking after home/family	Permanently sick/disabled	Other
All households	**563972**	**378892**	**285304**	**69628**	**21515**	**2245**	**185280**	**85327**	**1974**	**26863**	**49202**	**21914**
Age of HRP 24 or under	**21234**	**14312**	**10418**	**481**	**1806**	**1607**	**6922**	**3**	**1066**	**3460**	**685**	**1708**
Owner occupied	5518	4895	4219	289	186	201	623	-	181	223	59	160
Rented from NIHE	7163	3712	2569	41	993	109	3451	3	145	1994	385	924
Other social rented	841	433	273	3	119	38	408	-	42	174	83	109
Private rented	7712	5272	3357	148	508	1259	2440	-	698	1069	158	515
Age of HRP 25 to 34	**107033**	**90468**	**73705**	**11365**	**5105**	**293**	**16565**	**31**	**523**	**8168**	**3903**	**3940**
Owner occupied	69858	67284	56327	9765	1090	102	2574	16	128	900	748	782
Rented from NIHE	18873	9769	6867	492	2354	56	9104	10	135	4997	1968	1994
Other social rented	2057	1085	783	53	241	8	972	-	33	457	285	197
Private rented	16245	12330	9728	1055	1420	127	3915	5	227	1814	902	967
Age of HRP 35 to 44	**135635**	**114492**	**87614**	**20723**	**5897**	**258**	**21143**	**182**	**292**	**7802**	**8534**	**4333**
Owner occupied	100160	94680	74009	18897	1627	147	5480	120	124	1786	2237	1213
Rented from NIHE	22318	11109	7399	700	2935	75	11209	44	96	4408	4397	2264
Other social rented	2226	1091	766	83	239	3	1135	3	9	362	606	155
Private rented	10931	7612	5440	1043	1096	33	3319	15	63	1246	1294	701

Table S327: Age of Household Reference Person (HRP) and Tenure by Economic Activity of HRP (continued)

	All HRPs	Economically active					Total	Economically inactive				Other
		Total	Employee	Self-employed	Unemployed	Full-time students		Retired	Student	Looking after home/family	Permanently sick/ disabled	
Age of HRP 45 to 54	**116326**	**93772**	**69178**	**19184**	**5323**	**87**	**22554**	**1283**	**80**	**4229**	**12940**	**4022**
Owner occupied	88785	80033	60041	17864	2064	64	8752	1033	39	1656	4502	1522
Rented from NIHE	19099	8613	5598	554	2446	15	10486	173	25	2026	6355	1907
Other social rented	1881	881	611	77	193	-	1000	23	-	153	698	126
Private rented	6561	4245	2928	689	620	8	2316	54	16	394	1385	467
Age of HRP 55 to pensionable age	**78719**	**50763**	**35066**	**12625**	**3072**	**-**	**27956**	**7583**	**6**	**2116**	**14551**	**3700**
Owner occupied	60342	44010	30585	11916	1509	-	16332	6216	3	1143	7265	1705
Rented from NIHE	13008	4214	2778	258	1178	-	8794	949	3	782	5512	1548
Other social rented	1338	404	287	31	86	-	934	119	-	49	645	121
Private rented	4031	2135	1416	420	299	-	1896	299	-	142	1129	326
Age of HRP pensionable age to 74	**105025**	**14885**	**9323**	**5250**	**312**	**-**	**90140**	**76245**	**7**	**1088**	**8589**	**4211**
Owner occupied	74452	12734	7625	4905	204	-	61718	54810	4	742	3958	2204
Rented from NIHE	21310	1252	1072	110	70	-	20058	14778	3	270	3497	1510
Other social rented	3229	164	140	17	7	-	3065	2364	-	15	510	176
Private rented	6034	735	486	218	31	-	5299	4293	-	61	624	321

Notes:
1   The terms used to describe tenure are defined as:
   Owner occupied: either owns outright, owns with a mortgage or loan, or pays part rent and part mortgage (shared ownership).
   Rented from NIHE: rented from Northern Ireland Housing Executive.
   Other social rented: rented from Registered Social Landlord, Housing Association, Housing Co-operative or Charitable Trust.
   Private rented: rented from a private landlord or letting agency, employer of a household member, or relative or friend of a household member or other person.
2   'Rented from NIHE', 'Other social rented' and 'Private rented' include living in the household rent free.
3   Pensionable age at the time of the Census (29 April 2001) was 65 for men and 60 for women.

S327

Table S028: Sex and Age by Economic Activity

Table population: All persons aged 16 to 74

	All persons	Economically active										Economically inactive					
		Total	Employee		Self employed				Unemployed	Full-time student	Total	Retired	Student	Looking after home/family	Permanently sick/disabled	Other
					With employees		Without employees									
			Part-time	Full-time	Part-time	Full-time	Part-time	Full-time								
All persons	1187082	739136	117981	445789	4227	37198	11734	45076	49098	28033	447946	130312	67625	88207	110787	51015
16	27184	5661	290	959	-	5	3	11	380	4013	21523	-	21209	39	43	232
17	26277	11950	1239	4455	3	29	9	32	1172	5011	14327	-	13392	224	168	543
18	25389	13835	1147	6129	-	34	11	55	1838	4621	11554	-	10326	374	232	622
19	23247	15723	1396	8017	7	77	19	142	2033	4032	7524	-	5775	624	376	749
20 to 24	109385	83263	7884	56244	73	1034	229	1775	7707	8317	26122	11	13264	5243	2857	4747
25 to 29	114704	94878	9734	70280	167	2782	630	4156	6297	832	19826	14	1650	8947	4477	4738
30 to 34	127517	100982	15476	66676	435	4852	1143	5882	6100	418	26535	48	756	13567	6921	5243
35 to 39	129639	99975	19282	59937	584	5997	1605	6469	5781	320	29664	132	530	14270	9346	5386
40 to 44	117335	89338	17187	52942	548	5769	1510	6118	5006	258	27997	316	389	11425	11077	4790
45 to 49	102464	75733	13562	44989	480	5229	1406	5604	4258	205	26731	720	235	9056	12249	4471
50 to 54	98427	65261	12620	36673	555	4629	1383	5443	3952	6	33166	2394	63	9494	16222	4993
55 to 59	88732	48273	9968	25331	526	3590	1400	4407	3051	-	40459	6347	15	9196	19655	5246
60 to 64	73588	23070	5184	10616	370	1856	1023	2786	1235	-	50518	28750	9	3175	14547	4037
65 to 69	65342	7197	1955	1717	277	865	794	1418	171	-	58145	47668	3	1429	6638	2407
70 to 74	57852	3997	1057	824	202	450	569	778	117	-	53855	43912	9	1144	5979	2811

S028

Table S028: **Sex and Age by Economic Activity (continued)**

	All persons	Economically active			Self employed						Economically inactive					
		Total	Employee		With employees		Without employees		Unemployed	Full-time student	Total	Retired	Student	Looking after home/family	Permanently sick/disabled	Other
			Part-time	Full-time	Part-time	Full-time	Part-time	Full-time								
Males	**581234**	**412037**	**17172**	**271113**	**1725**	**30851**	**6968**	**39404**	**32957**	**11847**	**169197**	**53407**	**30895**	**8398**	**56421**	**20076**
16	13857	3026	176	724	-	5	-	11	249	1861	10831	-	10663	7	24	137
17	13304	6959	740	3276	3	21	6	32	789	2092	6345	-	5909	32	104	300
18	12997	7959	524	4278	-	34	8	50	1153	1912	5038	-	4579	33	131	295
19	11553	8616	506	5027	3	64	14	128	1245	1629	2937	-	2386	29	216	306
20 to 24	54913	45048	2138	32028	40	872	142	1547	4941	3340	9865	3	5900	278	1563	2121
25 to 29	56628	51023	1641	38673	80	2175	330	3573	4159	392	5605	7	743	603	2317	1935
30 to 34	62487	55812	1776	40043	139	3939	521	5148	4042	204	6675	36	290	957	3317	2075
35 to 39	63430	55213	1836	37871	171	4937	799	5697	3738	164	8217	83	182	1408	4432	2112
40 to 44	57432	48662	1646	32292	173	4827	828	5422	3346	128	8770	161	115	1337	5292	1865
45 to 49	51686	42152	1320	27435	165	4385	803	4947	2975	122	9534	403	88	1163	6017	1863
50 to 54	48485	36613	1266	22893	191	3901	818	4731	2810	3	11872	1333	19	1033	7677	1810
55 to 59	43585	28188	1303	16755	226	2987	875	3810	2232	-	15397	2982	6	869	9785	1755
60 to 64	35401	15388	1084	8224	213	1590	753	2412	1112	-	20013	7249	6	557	10052	2149
65 to 69	30407	4760	762	1134	184	723	623	1221	113	-	25647	21840	3	50	3074	680
70 to 74	25069	2618	454	460	137	391	448	675	53	-	22451	19310	6	42	2420	673

S028

Table S028: Sex and Age by Economic Activity (continued)

	All persons	Economically active									Economically inactive					
		Total	Employee		Self employed				Unemployed	Full-time student	Total	Retired	Student	Looking after home/family	Permanently sick/ disabled	Other
					With employees		Without employees									
			Part-time	Full-time	Part-time	Full-time	Part-time	Full-time								
Females	**605848**	**327099**	**100809**	**174676**	**2502**	**6347**	**4766**	**5672**	**16141**	**16186**	**278749**	**76905**	**36730**	**79809**	**54366**	**30939**
16	13327	2635	114	235	-	-	3	-	131	2152	10692	-	10546	32	19	95
17	12973	4991	499	1179	-	8	3	-	383	2919	7982	-	7483	192	64	243
18	12392	5876	623	1851	-	-	3	5	685	2709	6516	-	5747	341	101	327
19	11694	7107	890	2990	4	13	5	14	788	2403	4587	-	3389	595	160	443
20 to 24	54472	38215	5746	24216	33	162	87	228	2766	4977	16257	8	7364	4965	1294	2626
25 to 29	58076	43855	8093	31607	87	607	300	583	2138	440	14221	7	907	8344	2160	2803
30 to 34	65030	45170	13700	26633	296	913	622	734	2058	214	19860	12	466	12610	3604	3168
35 to 39	66209	44762	17446	22066	413	1060	806	772	2043	156	21447	49	348	12862	4914	3274
40 to 44	59903	40676	15541	20650	375	942	682	696	1660	130	19227	155	274	10088	5785	2925
45 to 49	50778	33581	12242	17554	315	844	603	657	1283	83	17197	317	147	7893	6232	2608
50 to 54	49942	28648	11354	13780	364	728	565	712	1142	3	21294	1061	44	8461	8545	3183
55 to 59	45147	20085	8665	8576	300	603	525	597	819	-	25062	3365	9	8327	9870	3491
60 to 64	38187	7682	4100	2392	157	266	270	374	123	-	30505	21501	3	2618	4495	1888
65 to 69	34935	2437	1193	583	93	142	171	197	58	-	32498	25828	-	1379	3564	1727
70 to 74	32783	1379	603	364	65	59	121	103	64	-	31404	24602	3	1102	3559	2138

Notes:
1 For the Census, part-time is defined as working 30 hours or less a week. Full-time is defined as working 31 or more hours a week.

S028

Table S029: Sex and Age by Hours Worked

Table population: All persons aged 16 to 74 in employment the week before the Census

	All persons	Part-time					Full-time				
		Total	1 to 2 hours	3 to 5 hours	6 to 15 hours	16 to 30 hours	Total	31 to 37 hours	38 to 48 hours	49 to 59 hours	60 or more hours
All persons	**686644**	**153250**	**580**	**5033**	**37887**	**109750**	**533394**	**135604**	**309446**	**47573**	**40771**
16	4405	2625	8	192	1614	811	1780	397	1274	46	63
17	10150	4874	11	281	2607	1975	5276	1301	3648	179	148
18	11538	4809	7	259	2624	1919	6729	1511	4699	245	274
19	13250	4551	6	167	2217	2161	8699	1954	6057	358	330
20 to 24	74884	14036	43	428	4831	8734	60848	14186	41012	3065	2585
25 to 29	88442	10887	34	265	1587	9001	77555	18860	48206	5890	4599
30 to 34	94813	17195	50	416	2575	14154	77618	18766	46177	7325	5350
35 to 39	94145	21569	53	541	3672	17303	72576	18333	40962	7319	5962
40 to 44	84292	19314	54	528	3505	15227	64978	17641	35582	6333	5422
45 to 49	71455	15507	50	436	3050	11971	55948	15555	29406	6023	4964
50 to 54	61307	14558	73	431	3122	10932	46749	12982	24373	5048	4346
55 to 59	45222	11894	67	480	2885	8462	33328	9261	17334	3336	3397
60 to 64	21835	6577	60	310	1984	4223	15258	3743	8004	1596	1915
65 to 69	7026	3026	39	186	994	1807	4000	762	1803	509	926
70 to 74	3880	1828	25	113	620	1070	2052	352	909	301	490
Males	**377390**	**33053**	**139**	**1003**	**8944**	**22967**	**344337**	**58194**	**211349**	**39736**	**35058**
16	2323	1100	3	55	625	417	1223	200	936	41	46
17	5882	2108	3	92	944	1069	3774	748	2751	157	118
18	6573	1923	-	69	982	872	4650	794	3413	210	233
19	7171	1694	3	64	784	843	5477	876	4029	299	273
20 to 24	39771	4375	21	127	1619	2608	35396	5368	25399	2463	2166
25 to 29	46788	2214	16	59	353	1786	44574	6697	29361	4629	3887
30 to 34	51731	2489	7	45	357	2080	49242	7341	31057	6163	4681
35 to 39	51449	2835	3	67	365	2400	48614	7929	29082	6317	5286
40 to 44	45294	2663	12	52	378	2221	42631	7598	24886	5367	4780
45 to 49	39162	2315	6	64	366	1879	36847	6991	20677	4912	4267
50 to 54	33802	2275	9	57	385	1824	31527	5970	17701	4183	3673
55 to 59	25956	2404	13	85	470	1836	23552	4642	13213	2869	2828
60 to 64	14276	2050	18	64	509	1459	12226	2390	6786	1437	1613
65 to 69	4647	1569	13	56	473	1027	3078	464	1399	432	783
70 to 74	2565	1039	12	47	334	646	1526	186	659	257	424

Table S029: Sex and Age by Hours Worked (continued)

	All persons	Total	Part-time				Total	Full-time			
			1 to 2 hours	3 to 5 hours	6 to 15 hours	16 to 30 hours		31 to 37 hours	38 to 48 hours	49 to 59 hours	60 or more hours
Females	**309254**	**120197**	**441**	**4030**	**28943**	**86783**	**189057**	**77410**	**98097**	**7837**	**5713**
16	2082	1525	5	137	989	394	557	197	338	5	17
17	4268	2766	8	189	1663	906	1502	553	897	22	30
18	4965	2886	7	190	1642	1047	2079	717	1286	35	41
19	6079	2857	3	103	1433	1318	3222	1078	2028	59	57
20 to 24	35113	9661	22	301	3212	6126	25452	8818	15613	602	419
25 to 29	41654	8673	18	206	1234	7215	32981	12163	18845	1261	712
30 to 34	43082	14706	43	371	2218	12074	28376	11425	15120	1162	669
35 to 39	42696	18734	50	474	3307	14903	23962	10404	11880	1002	676
40 to 44	38998	16651	42	476	3127	13006	22347	10043	10696	966	642
45 to 49	32293	13192	44	372	2684	10092	19101	8564	8729	1111	697
50 to 54	27505	12283	64	374	2737	9108	15222	7012	6672	865	673
55 to 59	19266	9490	54	395	2415	6626	9776	4619	4121	467	569
60 to 64	7559	4527	42	246	1475	2764	3032	1353	1218	159	302
65 to 69	2379	1457	26	130	521	780	922	298	404	77	143
70 to 74	1315	789	13	66	286	424	526	166	250	44	66

Notes:
1 Hours worked is the average number of hours per week worked for the last four weeks before the Census (29 April 2001).
2 'In employment' includes economically active full-time students in employment.

S029

Table S041: Sex and Economic Activity and Year Last Worked by Age

Table population: All persons aged 16 to 74

	All persons	16 to 19	20	21	22	23 to 24	25 to 34	35 to 44	45 to 49	50 to 54	55 to 59	60 to 64	65 to 74
All persons	1187079	102098	22789	22449	21717	42428	242221	246974	102464	98427	88732	73588	123192
In employment	662004	24068	11232	12207	13370	30430	182213	177948	71270	61303	45222	21835	10906
Economically active full-time student	28033	17677	3254	2412	1482	1169	1250	578	205	6	-	-	-
Unemployed	49097	5424	1757	1669	1570	2709	12397	10787	4258	3952	3051	1236	287
Never worked	6164	2128	375	298	213	381	1331	865	218	167	103	31	54
Last worked in 2001	10576	1503	558	562	587	804	2833	1806	664	632	432	156	39
Last worked in 2000	12517	1392	553	517	479	903	3475	2449	903	933	630	245	38
Last worked in 1999	5441	311	169	176	159	313	1513	1316	548	428	333	151	24
Last worked in 1998	2659	71	75	67	67	144	754	706	279	215	172	95	14
Last worked in 1997	1602	16	19	35	32	69	492	422	170	158	114	60	15
Last worked in 1996	1329	3	8	10	25	45	448	329	181	116	112	41	11
Last worked in 1991 to 1995	3742	-	-	4	8	50	1128	1133	427	395	396	168	33
Last worked before 1991	5067	-	-	-	-	-	423	1761	868	908	759	289	59
Economically Inactive	447945	54929	6546	6161	5295	8120	46361	57661	26731	33166	40459	50517	11999
Never worked	102855	46309	3428	2815	2163	2750	9250	9124	3396	3577	3734	4254	12055
Last worked in 2001	17049	2850	804	736	543	905	3252	2429	1079	1286	1178	1041	946
Last worked in 2000	34951	4530	1373	1441	1286	1665	6399	4723	1915	2432	2900	3260	3027
Last worked in 1999	25006	928	485	565	551	954	4568	3846	1572	2043	2505	3296	3693
Last worked in 1998	21837	259	274	316	321	669	3832	3322	1363	1844	2244	3403	3990
Last worked in 1997	17954	47	132	183	219	397	2915	2676	1035	1446	2030	2941	3933
Last worked in 1996	18025	6	43	86	135	340	2514	2641	1078	1448	2180	2750	4804
Last worked in 1991 to 1995	76891	-	7	19	77	440	9053	10290	4286	5423	7850	10638	28808
Last worked before 1991	133377	-	-	-	-	-	4578	18610	11007	13667	15838	18934	50743

S041

133

Table S041: Sex and Economic Activity and Year Last Worked by Age (continued)

	All persons	16 to 19	20	21	22	23 to 24	25 to 34	35 to 44	45 to 49	50 to 54	55 to 59	60 to 64	65 to 74
Males	**581231**	**51711**	**11646**	**11478**	**10785**	**21002**	**119115**	**120862**	**51686**	**48485**	**43585**	**35401**	**55475**
In employment	**367232**	**15629**	**6619**	**7017**	**7217**	**15914**	**98038**	**96499**	**39055**	**33800**	**25956**	**14276**	**7212**
Economically active full-time student	**11847**	**7494**	**1206**	**968**	**617**	**549**	**596**	**292**	**122**	**3**	**-**	**-**	**-**
Unemployed	**32955**	**3436**	**1123**	**1111**	**969**	**1736**	**8201**	**7084**	**2975**	**2810**	**2232**	**1112**	**166**
Never worked	3986	1366	234	212	138	252	922	549	123	97	51	23	19
Last worked in 2001	6696	927	376	342	338	520	1812	1091	420	421	294	128	27
Last worked in 2000	8577	895	345	366	325	586	2371	1672	655	666	446	227	23
Last worked in 1999	3903	204	115	123	102	217	1046	943	417	309	269	141	17
Last worked in 1998	1801	34	40	38	34	71	523	491	197	150	127	86	10
Last worked in 1997	1132	10	10	22	16	37	330	312	132	117	89	46	11
Last worked in 1996	918	-	3	4	11	25	283	233	147	79	84	38	11
Last worked in 1991 to 1995	2556	-	-	4	5	28	695	730	319	311	293	152	19
Last worked before 1991	3386	-	-	-	-	-	219	1063	565	660	579	271	29
Economically inactive	**169197**	**25152**	**2698**	**2382**	**1982**	**2803**	**12280**	**16987**	**9534**	**11872**	**15397**	**20013**	**48097**
Never worked	38767	21639	1449	1159	917	1053	3283	3074	1127	1045	885	901	2235
Last worked in 2001	7300	1166	318	299	208	370	1274	909	447	661	619	469	560
Last worked in 2000	14854	1966	613	605	527	633	1855	1717	903	1176	1409	1579	1871
Last worked in 1999	10078	305	166	173	165	315	1065	1287	694	847	1232	1591	2238
Last worked in 1998	8758	64	73	80	79	179	1018	1052	539	728	1005	1578	2363
Last worked in 1997	7358	12	61	42	48	92	662	876	443	583	899	1355	2285
Last worked in 1996	7303	-	14	16	23	62	516	824	422	542	939	1244	2701
Last worked in 1991 to 1995	33974	-	4	8	15	99	1848	3128	1833	2292	3528	5123	16096
Last worked before 1991	40805	-	-	-	-	-	759	4120	3126	3998	4881	6173	17748

Table S041: Sex and Economic Activity and Year Last Worked by Age (continued)

	All persons	16 to 19	20	21	22	23 to 24	25 to 34	35 to 44	45 to 49	50 to 54	55 to 59	60 to 64	65 to 74
Females	**605848**	**50387**	**11143**	**10971**	**10932**	**21426**	**123106**	**126112**	**50778**	**49942**	**45147**	**38187**	**67717**
In employment	**294772**	**8439**	**4613**	**5190**	**6153**	**14516**	**84175**	**81449**	**32215**	**27503**	**19266**	**7559**	**3694**
Economically active full-time student	**16186**	**10183**	**2048**	**1444**	**865**	**620**	**654**	**286**	**83**	**3**	**-**	**-**	**-**
Unemployed	**16142**	**1988**	**634**	**558**	**601**	**973**	**4196**	**3703**	**1283**	**1142**	**819**	**124**	**121**
Never worked	2178	762	141	86	75	129	409	316	95	70	52	8	35
Last worked in 2001	3880	576	182	220	249	284	1021	715	244	211	138	28	12
Last worked in 2000	3940	497	208	151	154	317	1104	777	248	267	184	18	15
Last worked in 1999	1538	107	54	53	57	96	467	373	131	119	64	10	7
Last worked in 1998	858	37	35	29	33	73	231	215	82	65	45	9	4
Last worked in 1997	470	6	9	13	16	32	162	110	38	41	25	14	4
Last worked in 1996	411	3	5	6	14	20	165	96	34	37	28	3	-
Last worked in 1991 to 1995	1186	-	-	-	3	22	433	403	108	84	103	16	14
Last worked before 1991	1681	-	-	-	-	-	204	698	303	248	180	18	30
Economically inactive	**278748**	**29777**	**3848**	**3779**	**3313**	**5317**	**34081**	**40674**	**17197**	**21294**	**25062**	**30504**	**63902**
Never worked	64088	24670	1979	1656	1246	1697	5967	6050	2269	2532	2849	3353	9820
Last worked in 2001	9749	1684	486	437	335	535	1978	1520	632	625	559	572	386
Last worked in 2000	20097	2564	760	836	759	1032	4544	3006	1012	1256	1491	1681	1156
Last worked in 1999	14928	623	319	392	386	639	3503	2559	878	1196	1273	1705	1455
Last worked in 1998	13079	195	201	236	242	490	2814	2270	824	1116	1239	1825	1627
Last worked in 1997	10596	35	71	141	171	305	2253	1800	592	863	1131	1586	1648
Last worked in 1996	10722	6	29	70	112	278	1998	1817	656	906	1241	1506	2103
Last worked in 1991 to 1995	42917	-	3	11	62	341	7205	7162	2453	3131	4322	5515	12712
Last worked before 1991	92572	-	-	-	-	-	3819	14490	7881	9669	10957	12761	32995

S 0 4 1

Notes:

1 'Last worked in 2001' means last worked in the four months before Census day (29 April 2001).

2 This table includes all full-time students aged 16 to 74, whether economically active or inactive.

135

Table S030: Sex and Economic Activity by Living Arrangements

Table population: All persons aged 16 to 74 in households

	All persons	Living in a couple			Single (never married)	Married or re-married	Not living in a couple		
		Married	Re-married	Cohabiting			Separated (but still legally married)	Divorced	Widowed
All persons	**1171798**	**586437**	**32065**	**53370**	**362751**	**5413**	**41419**	**42019**	**48324**
Economically active	**732434**	**379521**	**20183**	**42698**	**234499**	**2882**	**21235**	**22141**	**9275**
Employee - Part-time	117687	76900	3626	4621	19623	471	5155	4088	3203
Employee - Full-time	441159	220708	12201	30844	148202	1710	10976	12567	3951
Self-employed with employees	41340	30252	1479	1580	5608	213	760	855	593
Self-employed without employees	56756	37534	1909	2302	11267	255	1210	1403	876
Unemployed	48927	13581	937	2780	24584	211	3051	3148	635
Full-time student	26565	546	31	571	25215	22	83	80	17
Economically inactive	**439364**	**206916**	**11882**	**10672**	**128252**	**2531**	**20184**	**19878**	**39049**
Retired	129621	78596	4197	1120	13223	926	2659	3932	24968
Student	64951	1007	57	609	62826	53	219	144	36
Looking after home/family	88134	55165	2851	3802	13081	501	6361	3915	2458
Permanently sick/disabled	106796	52550	3753	2887	23308	656	7473	8744	7425
Other	49862	19598	1024	2254	15814	395	3472	3143	4162
Males	**571821**	**289097**	**16459**	**26813**	**195419**	**2471**	**14997**	**16301**	**10264**
Economically active	**407177**	**213007**	**11632**	**22897**	**136611**	**1596**	**9155**	**9469**	**2810**
Employee - Part-time	16934	8183	473	821	6414	73	378	367	225
Employee - Full-time	267196	141124	7862	17018	87568	1018	5513	5609	1484
Self-employed with employees	32523	23865	1152	1230	4673	155	549	602	297
Self-employed without employees	46344	30507	1504	1839	9880	206	918	1013	477
Unemployed	32837	9078	629	1752	17295	133	1773	1858	319
Full-time student	11343	250	12	237	10781	11	24	20	8
Economically inactive	**164644**	**76090**	**4827**	**3916**	**58808**	**875**	**5842**	**6832**	**7454**
Retired	53113	36957	2241	585	5502	355	1118	1536	4819
Student	29737	303	14	233	29093	19	36	28	11
Looking after home/family	8379	4544	344	541	1936	44	401	379	190
Permanently sick/disabled	54175	27226	1863	1560	14178	329	3232	3845	1942
Other	19240	7060	365	997	8099	128	1055	1044	492

Table S030: Sex and Economic Activity by Living Arrangements (continued)

	All persons	Living in a couple			Single (never married)	Married or re-married	Not living in a couple		
		Married	Re-married	Cohabiting			Separated (but still legally married)	Divorced	Widowed
Females	**599977**	**297340**	**15606**	**26557**	**167332**	**2942**	**26422**	**25718**	**38060**
Economically active	**325257**	**166514**	**8551**	**19801**	**97888**	**1286**	**12080**	**12672**	**6465**
Employee - Part-time	100753	68717	3153	3800	13209	398	4777	3721	2978
Employee - Full-time	173963	79584	4339	13826	60634	692	5463	6958	2467
Self-employed with employees	8817	6387	327	350	935	58	211	253	296
Self-employed without employees	10412	7027	405	463	1387	49	292	390	399
Unemployed	16090	4503	308	1028	7289	78	1278	1290	316
Full-time student	15222	296	19	334	14434	11	59	60	9
Economically inactive	**274720**	**130826**	**7055**	**6756**	**69444**	**1656**	**14342**	**13046**	**31595**
Retired	76508	41639	1956	535	7721	571	1541	2396	20149
Student	35214	704	43	376	33733	34	183	116	25
Looking after home/family	79755	50621	2507	3261	11145	457	5960	3536	2268
Permanently sick/disabled	52621	25324	1890	1327	9130	327	4241	4899	5483
Other	30622	12538	659	1257	7715	267	2417	2099	3670

Notes:

1 For the Census, part-time is defined as working 30 hours or less a week. Full-time is defined as working 31 or more hours a week.

2 Cohabiting couples includes same sex couples.

3 The living arrangements variable is different to marital status. It combines information from both marital status and the relationship matrix.

Therefore a person living as part of a 'cohabiting couple' could in fact be married (to someone else) but will not appear as married or separated in this classification.

4 A person not living in a couple can be classified married (or re-married) but have no spouse or partner resident in the household.

S030

Table S031: Family Composition and Number of Dependent Children by Sex and Economic Activity

Table population: All parents aged 16 to 74 with dependent children

| | All parents | Males | | | | Females | | | |
| | | Employed | | Unemployed | Economically inactive | Employed | | Unemployed | Economically inactive |
		Part-time	Full-time			Part-time	Full-time		
All parents	**398150**	**8775**	**135670**	**7599**	**22120**	**65743**	**64040**	**6812**	**87391**
Both parents working	**198164**	**4039**	**95035**	**-**	**-**	**49476**	**49614**	**-**	**-**
Couple family	198164	4039	95035	-	-	49476	49614	-	-
1 dependent child	71084	1454	34083	-	-	14912	20635	-	-
2 or more dependent children	127080	2585	60952	-	-	34564	28979	-	-
One parent working	**128128**	**4736**	**40635**	**2449**	**6709**	**16267**	**14426**	**2586**	**40320**
Lone parent family	23842	316	2077	-	-	11461	9988	-	-
1 dependent child	14135	191	1260	-	-	6168	6516	-	-
2 or more dependent children	9707	125	817	-	-	5293	3472	-	-
Couple family	104286	4420	38558	2449	6709	4806	4438	2586	40320
1 dependent child	32741	1142	11429	914	2875	1843	1990	888	11660
2 or more dependent children	71545	3278	27129	1535	3834	2963	2448	1698	28660
No working parents	**71858**	**-**	**-**	**5150**	**15411**	**-**	**-**	**4226**	**47071**
Lone parent family	34940	-	-	482	1691	-	-	3163	29604
1 dependent child	16638	-	-	316	1057	-	-	1809	13456
2 or more dependent children	18302	-	-	166	634	-	-	1354	16148
Couple family	36918	-	-	4668	13720	-	-	1063	17467
1 dependent child	13795	-	-	1372	5493	-	-	387	6543
2 or more dependent children	23123	-	-	3296	8227	-	-	676	10924

Notes:
1 Couple families include both married couple families and cohabiting couple families.
2 Employed includes employees, the self-employed and economically active full-time students.
3 A dependent child is a person in a household aged 0 to 15 (whether or not in a family) or a person aged 16 to 18 who is a full-time student in a family with parent(s).
4 For the Census, part-time is defined as working 30 hours or less a week. Full-time is defined as working 31 or more hours a week.
5 A family consists of a couple (married or cohabiting) with or without children, or a lone parent and their children.
  It also includes a married or cohabiting couple with their grandchildren or a lone grandparent with his or her grandchildren, if there is no parent in the intervening generation in the household.
  A family will also include step-children when their parent is part of the couple.

Table S032: Sex and Age and Level of Qualifications by Economic Activity

Table population: All persons aged 16 to 74

	All persons	Economically active					Economically inactive					
		Total	Employee	Self-employed	Unemployed	Full-time student	Total	Retired	Student	Looking after home/family	Permanently sick or disabled	Other
All persons	**1187074**	**739135**	**563770**	**98234**	**49098**	**28033**	**447939**	**130312**	**67618**	**88207**	**110787**	**51015**
16 to 24	**211480**	**130431**	**87760**	**3547**	**13130**	**25994**	**81049**	**10**	**63966**	**6504**	**3676**	**6893**
No qualifications	36834	14161	7997	470	3528	2166	22673	-	16742	1713	1866	2352
Lower level qualifications	154009	99766	66514	2663	8690	21899	54243	6	43877	4637	1737	3986
Higher level qualifications	20637	16504	13249	414	912	1929	4133	4	3347	154	73	555
25 to 34	**242222**	**195860**	**162166**	**20047**	**12397**	**1250**	**46362**	**63**	**2406**	**22514**	**11398**	**9981**
No qualifications	49186	30137	20521	4612	4892	112	19049	20	219	7965	6008	4837
Lower level qualifications	131770	108689	90637	11460	6028	564	23081	33	851	13070	4890	4237
Higher level qualifications	61266	57034	51008	3975	1477	574	4232	10	1336	1479	500	907
35 to 49	**349438**	**265046**	**207899**	**41319**	**15045**	**783**	**84392**	**1168**	**1154**	**34751**	**32672**	**14647**
No qualifications	136123	84079	58063	16708	9082	226	52044	504	285	18918	22249	10088
Lower level qualifications	149015	121934	99923	16849	4790	372	27081	470	480	13431	8947	3753
Higher level qualifications	64300	59033	49913	7762	1173	185	5267	194	389	2402	1476	806
50 to 59	**187159**	**113534**	**84592**	**21933**	**7003**	**6**	**73625**	**8741**	**78**	**18690**	**35877**	**10239**
No qualifications	119044	62539	43794	13683	5062	-	56505	4084	14	14184	29648	8575
Lower level qualifications	43323	30910	24589	4974	1344	3	12413	2761	31	3646	4761	1214
Higher level qualifications	24792	20085	16209	3276	597	3	4707	1896	33	860	1468	450
60 to 64	**73582**	**23070**	**15800**	**6035**	**1235**	**-**	**50512**	**28750**	**3**	**3175**	**14547**	**4037**
No qualifications	54313	15705	10666	4102	937	-	38608	19743	3	2523	12761	3578
Lower level qualifications	12420	4476	3185	1113	178	-	7944	5808	-	536	1271	329
Higher level qualifications	6849	2889	1949	820	120	-	3960	3199	-	116	515	130
65 to 74	**123193**	**11194**	**5553**	**5353**	**288**	**-**	**111999**	**91580**	**11**	**2573**	**12617**	**5218**
No qualifications	98769	8013	3923	3926	164	-	90756	72605	5	2069	11441	4636
Lower level qualifications	14755	1750	976	692	82	-	13005	11463	3	393	797	349
Higher level qualifications	9669	1431	654	735	42	-	8238	7512	3	111	379	233

S032

S032

140

Table S032: Sex and Age and Level of Qualifications by Economic Activity (continued)

	All persons	Economically active					Economically inactive					
		Total	Employee	Self-employed	Unemployed	Full-time student	Total	Retired	Student	Looking after home/family	Permanently sick or disabled	Other
Males	**581229**	**412033**	**288285**	**78947**	**32957**	**11844**	**169196**	**53407**	**30894**	**8398**	**56421**	**20076**
16 to 24	**106623**	**71607**	**49417**	**2979**	**8377**	**10834**	**35016**	**3**	**29437**	**379**	**2038**	**3159**
No qualifications	21597	10214	6048	441	2653	1072	11383	-	8794	208	1133	1248
Lower level qualifications	76215	54338	37780	2285	5276	8997	21877	3	19176	165	869	1664
Higher level qualifications	8811	7055	5589	253	448	765	1756	-	1467	6	36	247
25 to 34	**119915**	**106835**	**82133**	**15905**	**8201**	**596**	**12280**	**43**	**1033**	**1560**	**5634**	**4010**
No qualifications	29058	22506	14423	4236	3777	70	6552	16	79	856	3568	2033
Lower level qualifications	61521	57127	44229	9035	3606	257	4394	20	320	642	1847	1565
Higher level qualifications	28536	27202	23481	2634	818	269	1334	7	634	62	219	412
35 to 49	**172548**	**146027**	**102400**	**33154**	**10059**	**414**	**26521**	**647**	**385**	**3908**	**15741**	**5840**
No qualifications	74374	55297	33681	14836	6638	142	19077	319	115	2787	11676	4180
Lower level qualifications	64264	58304	42734	12627	2752	191	5960	234	125	936	3385	1280
Higher level qualifications	33910	32426	25985	5691	669	81	1484	94	145	185	680	380
50 to 59	**92067**	**64798**	**42217**	**17539**	**5042**	**-**	**27269**	**4315**	**25**	**1902**	**17462**	**3565**
No qualifications	59535	38183	22937	11467	3779	-	21352	2056	6	1594	14693	3003
Lower level qualifications	18085	14161	9816	3488	857	-	3924	1291	8	242	2011	372
Higher level qualifications	14447	12454	9464	2584	406	-	1993	968	11	66	758	190
60 to 64	**35398**	**15388**	**9308**	**4968**	**1112**	**-**	**20010**	**7249**	**3**	**557**	**10052**	**2149**
No qualifications	26297	10868	6508	3492	868	-	15429	4207	3	490	8803	1926
Lower level qualifications	5047	2444	1499	804	141	-	2603	1555	-	46	846	156
Higher level qualifications	4054	2076	1301	672	103	-	1978	1487	-	21	403	67
65 to 74	**55478**	**7378**	**2810**	**4402**	**166**	**-**	**48100**	**41150**	**11**	**92**	**5494**	**1353**
No qualifications	44270	5396	2013	3278	105	-	38874	32651	5	78	4936	1204
Lower level qualifications	5504	931	385	511	35	-	4573	4153	3	5	352	60
Higher level qualifications	5704	1051	412	613	26	-	4653	4346	3	9	206	89

Table S032: Sex and Age and Level of Qualifications by Economic Activity (continued)

	All persons	Economically active					Economically inactive					
		Total	Employee	Self-employed	Unemployed	Full-time student	Total	Retired	Student	Looking after home/family	Permanently sick or disabled	Other
Females	**605845**	**327102**	**275485**	**19287**	**16141**	**16189**	**278743**	**76905**	**36724**	**79809**	**54366**	**30939**
16 to 24	**104857**	**58824**	**38343**	**568**	**4753**	**15160**	**46033**	**7**	**34529**	**6125**	**1638**	**3734**
No qualifications	15237	3947	1949	29	875	1094	11290	-	7948	1505	733	1104
Lower level qualifications	77794	45428	28734	378	3414	12902	32366	3	24701	4472	868	2322
Higher level qualifications	11826	9449	7660	161	464	1164	2377	4	1880	148	37	308
25 to 34	**123107**	**89025**	**80033**	**4142**	**4196**	**654**	**34082**	**20**	**1373**	**20954**	**5764**	**5971**
No qualifications	20128	7631	6098	376	1115	42	12497	4	140	7109	2440	2804
Lower level qualifications	70249	51562	46408	2425	2422	307	18687	13	531	12428	3043	2672
Higher level qualifications	32730	29832	27527	1341	659	305	2898	3	702	1417	281	495
35 to 49	**176890**	**119019**	**105499**	**8165**	**4986**	**369**	**57871**	**521**	**769**	**30843**	**16931**	**8807**
No qualifications	61749	28782	24382	1872	2444	84	32967	185	170	16131	10573	5908
Lower level qualifications	84751	63630	57189	4222	2038	181	21121	236	355	12495	5562	2473
Higher level qualifications	30390	26607	23928	2071	504	104	3783	100	244	2217	796	426
50 to 59	**95092**	**48736**	**42375**	**4394**	**1961**	**6**	**46356**	**4426**	**53**	**16788**	**18415**	**6674**
No qualifications	59509	24356	20857	2216	1283	-	35153	2028	8	12590	14955	5572
Lower level qualifications	25238	16749	14773	1486	487	3	8489	1470	23	3404	2750	842
Higher level qualifications	10345	7631	6745	692	191	3	2714	928	22	794	710	260
60 to 64	**38184**	**7682**	**6492**	**1067**	**123**	**-**	**30502**	**21501**	**-**	**2618**	**4495**	**1888**
No qualifications	28016	4837	4158	610	69	-	23179	15536	-	2033	3958	1652
Lower level qualifications	7373	2032	1686	309	37	-	5341	4253	-	490	425	173
Higher level qualifications	2795	813	648	148	17	-	1982	1712	-	95	112	63
65 to 74	**67715**	**3816**	**2743**	**951**	**122**	**-**	**63899**	**50430**	**-**	**2481**	**7123**	**3865**
No qualifications	54499	2617	1910	648	59	-	51882	39954	-	1991	6505	3432
Lower level qualifications	9251	819	591	181	47	-	8432	7310	-	388	445	289
Higher level qualifications	3965	380	242	122	16	-	3585	3166	-	102	173	144

S032

Notes:
1 The term 'no qualifications' describes persons without any qualifications. The term 'lower level qualifications' is used to describe persons with level 1 to 3 qualifications and the term 'higher level qualifications' refers to qualifications of levels 4 and 5.

Level 1: GCSE (grades D-G), CSE (grades 2-5), 1-4 CSEs (grade 1), 1-4 GCSEs (grades A-C), 1-4 'O' level passes, NVQ level 1, GNVQ Foundation or equivalents

Level 2: 5+ CSEs (grade 1), 5+ GCSEs (grades A-C), 5+ 'O' level passes, Senior Certificate, NVQ level 2, GNVQ Intermediate or equivalents

Level 3: 2+ 'A' levels, 4+ AS levels, NVQ level 3, GNVQ Advanced or equivalents

Level 4: First Degree, NVQ level 4, HNC, HND or equivalents

Level 5: Higher Degree, NVQ level 5 or equivalents

Table S328: Economic Activity by Ethnic Group

Table population: All persons aged 16 to 74

	All persons	White	Irish Traveller	Mixed	Indian	Pakistani	Bangladeshi	Other Asian	Black Caribbean	Black African	Other Black	Chinese	Other ethnic group
All persons	1187076	1177608	1077	1534	1217	430	155	158	206	341	297	3048	1005
Economically active	739133	733603	377	939	787	255	96	106	145	228	178	1835	584
Employee - Part-time	117981	117340	49	103	69	31	14	15	16	26	24	221	73
Employee - Full-time	445789	442902	144	543	468	119	45	78	86	139	120	776	369
Self-employed - Part-time	15955	15789	12	29	31	6	-	-	8	6	-	63	11
Self-employed - Full-time	82278	81253	45	82	155	64	23	3	11	15	6	578	43
Unemployed	49098	48651	102	80	41	20	10	3	15	28	18	66	64
Full-time student	28032	27668	25	102	23	15	4	7	9	14	10	131	24
Economically inactive	447943	444005	700	595	430	175	59	52	61	113	119	1213	421
Retired	130312	129831	69	65	95	17	6	-	10	12	31	150	26
Student	67623	66320	49	229	86	32	4	24	11	43	15	649	161
Looking after home/family	88207	87312	159	100	124	69	22	12	11	25	17	216	140
Permanently sick/disabled	110786	110278	198	107	64	22	4	3	13	-	19	57	21
Other	51015	50264	225	94	61	35	23	13	16	33	37	141	73

Note:
1   For the Census, part-time is defined as working 30 hours or less a week. Full-time is defined as working 31 or more hours a week.

S328

Table S329: Sex and Economic Activity by Community Background (Religion or Religion Brought Up In)

Table population: All persons aged 16 to 74

	All persons	Catholic	Protestant and Other Christian (including Christian related)	Other religions and philosophies	None
All persons	**1187079**	**508964**	**648858**	**5072**	**24185**
Economically active	**739134**	**305125**	**414233**	**3185**	**16591**
Employee - Part-time	117981	47168	68585	344	1884
Employee - Full-time	445789	176157	257179	1779	10674
Self-employed - Part-time	15957	5966	9512	136	343
Self-employed - Full-time	82277	34997	45135	531	1614
Unemployed	49098	26681	20930	253	1234
Full-time student	28032	14156	12892	142	842
Economically inactive	**447945**	**203839**	**234625**	**1887**	**7594**
Retired	130313	42120	86873	300	1020
Student	67623	36383	28289	574	2377
Looking after home/family	88207	43730	42346	438	1693
Permanently sick/disabled	110787	54976	53976	289	1546
Other	51015	26630	23141	286	958
Males	**581232**	**245374**	**319199**	**2936**	**13723**
Economically active	**412035**	**168434**	**231165**	**2132**	**10304**
Employee - Part-time	17172	8232	8423	121	396
Employee - Full-time	271113	101958	160679	1243	7233
Self-employed - Part-time	8692	3658	4766	70	198
Self-employed - Full-time	70255	30494	38053	434	1274
Unemployed	32957	18226	13732	181	818
Full-time student	11846	5866	5512	83	385
Economically inactive	**169197**	**76940**	**88034**	**804**	**3419**
Retired	53408	17050	35604	156	598
Student	30894	16229	13078	315	1272
Looking after home/family	8398	4917	3296	33	152
Permanently sick/disabled	56421	28164	27157	179	921
Other	20076	10580	8899	121	476

Table S329: Sex and Economic Activity by Community Background (Religion or Religion Brought Up In) (continued)

	All persons	Catholic	Protestant and Other Christian (including Christian related)	Other religions and philosophies	None
Females	**605847**	**263590**	**329659**	**2136**	**10462**
Economically active	**327099**	**136691**	**183068**	**1053**	**6287**
Employee - Part-time	100809	38936	60162	223	1488
Employee - Full-time	174676	74199	96500	536	3441
Self-employed - Part-time	7265	2308	4746	66	145
Self-employed - Full-time	12022	4503	7082	97	340
Unemployed	16141	8455	7198	72	416
Full-time student	16186	8290	7380	59	457
Economically inactive	**278748**	**126899**	**146591**	**1083**	**4175**
Retired	76905	25070	51269	144	422
Student	36729	20154	15211	259	1105
Looking after home/family	79809	38813	39050	405	1541
Permanently sick/disabled	54366	26812	26819	110	625
Other	30939	16050	14242	165	482

Notes:
1   The term 'Catholic' includes those respondents who gave their religion as Catholic or Roman Catholic.
2   For the Census, part-time is defined as working 30 hours or less a week. Full-time is defined as working 31 or more hours a week.

S329

Table S330: Age and Economic Activity by Sex and Community Background (Religion or Religion Brought Up In)

Table population: All persons aged 16 to 74

	All persons	Males					Females				
		Total	Catholic	Protestant and Other Christian (including Christian related)	Other religions and philosophies	None	Total	Catholic	Protestant and Other Christian (including Christian related)	Other religions and philosophies	None
All persons	**1187077**	**581227**	**245372**	**319197**	**2935**	**13723**	**605850**	**263589**	**329659**	**2140**	**10462**
Economically active	**739138**	**412036**	**168434**	**231165**	**2133**	**10304**	**327102**	**136691**	**183068**	**1056**	**6287**
Employee - Part-time	117981	17172	8232	8423	121	396	100809	38936	60162	223	1488
Employee - Full-time	445789	271113	101958	160679	1243	7233	174676	74199	96500	536	3441
Self-employed - Part-time	15959	8693	3658	4766	71	198	7266	2308	4746	67	145
Self-employed - Full-time	82278	70255	30494	38053	434	1274	12023	4503	7082	98	340
Unemployed	49098	32957	18226	13732	181	818	16141	8455	7198	72	416
Full-time student	28033	11846	5866	5512	83	385	16187	8290	7380	60	457
Economically inactive	**447939**	**169191**	**76938**	**88032**	**802**	**3419**	**278748**	**126898**	**146591**	**1084**	**4175**
Retired	130307	53402	17048	35602	154	598	76905	25069	51269	145	422
Student	67623	30894	16229	13078	315	1272	36729	20154	15211	259	1105
Looking after home/family	88207	8398	4917	3296	33	152	79809	38813	39050	405	1541
Permanently sick/disabled	110787	56421	28164	27157	179	921	54366	26812	26819	110	625
Other	51015	20076	10580	8899	121	476	30939	16050	14242	165	482
Aged 16 to 24 years	**211479**	**106621**	**53258**	**49464**	**454**	**3445**	**104858**	**53411**	**48104**	**403**	**2940**
Economically active	**130434**	**71608**	**34476**	**34752**	**215**	**2165**	**58826**	**28230**	**28867**	**152**	**1577**
Employee - Part-time	11956	4084	2183	1761	13	127	7872	3795	3799	20	258
Employee - Full-time	75804	45333	20496	23349	101	1387	30471	13786	15865	64	756
Self-employed - Part-time	352	216	99	105	3	9	136	46	82	3	5
Self-employed - Full-time	3198	2764	1556	1138	16	54	434	187	230	3	14
Unemployed	13130	8377	4783	3312	27	255	4753	2680	1931	17	125
Full-time student	25994	10834	5359	5087	55	333	15160	7736	6960	45	419
Economically inactive	**81045**	**35013**	**18782**	**14712**	**239**	**1280**	**46032**	**25181**	**19237**	**251**	**1363**
Retired	6	-	-	-	-	-	6	-	6	-	-
Student	63966	29437	15573	12543	207	1114	34529	19015	14366	180	968
Looking after home/family	6504	379	220	145	3	11	6125	3106	2733	38	248
Permanently sick/disabled	3676	2038	1203	777	7	51	1638	945	648	3	42
Other	6893	3159	1786	1247	22	104	3734	2115	1484	30	105

Table S330: Age and Economic Activity by Sex and Community Background (Religion or Religion Brought Up In) (continued)

	All persons	Males					Females				
		Total	Catholic	Protestant and Other Christian (including Christian related)	Other religions and philosophies	None	Total	Catholic	Protestant and Other Christian (including Christian related)	Other religions and philosophies	None
Aged 25 to 34 years	**242221**	**119115**	**52307**	**62131**	**831**	**3846**	**123106**	**57475**	**61846**	**594**	**3191**
Economically active	**195860**	**106835**	**45519**	**57222**	**673**	**3421**	**89025**	**39848**	**46638**	**318**	**2221**
Employee - Part-time	25210	3417	1772	1485	45	115	21793	9006	12267	50	470
Employee - Full-time	136956	78716	31059	44538	443	2676	58240	26505	30089	204	1442
Self-employed - Part-time	2375	1070	526	494	8	42	1305	471	776	10	48
Self-employed - Full-time	17672	14835	7162	7285	84	304	2837	1262	1453	16	106
Unemployed	12397	8201	4706	3174	72	249	4196	2242	1797	26	131
Full-time student	1250	596	294	246	21	35	654	362	256	12	24
Economically inactive	**46361**	**12280**	**6788**	**4909**	**158**	**425**	**34081**	**17627**	**15208**	**276**	**970**
Retired	62	43	17	26	-	-	19	4	15	-	-
Student	2406	1033	467	355	96	115	1373	715	498	59	101
Looking after home/family	22514	1560	955	556	5	44	20954	10515	9684	156	599
Permanently sick/disabled	11398	5634	3143	2330	15	146	5764	3103	2523	16	122
Other	9981	4010	2206	1642	42	120	5971	3290	2488	45	148
Aged 35 to 44 years	**246975**	**120860**	**52037**	**65147**	**705**	**2971**	**126115**	**57051**	**66354**	**488**	**2222**
Economically active	**189314**	**103875**	**42891**	**57771**	**621**	**2592**	**85439**	**35668**	**47955**	**295**	**1521**
Employee - Part-time	36469	3432	1899	1473	30	80	32987	13038	19387	80	482
Employee - Full-time	112879	70163	25884	42064	371	1844	42716	18447	23369	138	762
Self-employed - Part-time	4247	1971	1045	847	17	62	2276	794	1420	17	45
Self-employed - Full-time	24353	20883	9783	10511	151	438	3470	1384	1931	40	115
Unemployed	10787	7084	4132	2752	45	155	3703	1852	1727	17	107
Full-time student	579	292	148	124	7	13	287	153	121	3	10
Economically inactive	**57661**	**16985**	**9146**	**7376**	**84**	**379**	**40676**	**21383**	**18399**	**193**	**701**
Retired	448	242	91	146	-	5	206	95	105	3	3
Student	919	297	132	122	9	34	622	327	247	16	32
Looking after home/family	25695	2745	1654	1032	13	46	22950	11964	10447	112	427
Permanently sick/disabled	20423	9724	5128	4375	34	187	10699	5552	4973	26	148
Other	10176	3977	2141	1701	28	107	6199	3445	2627	36	91

Table S330: Age and Economic Activity by Sex and Community Background (Religion or Religion Brought Up In) (continued)

	All persons	Males					Females				
		Total	Catholic	Protestant and Other Christian (including Christian related)	Other religions and philosophies	None	Total	Catholic	Protestant and Other Christian (including Christian related)	Other religions and philosophies	None
Aged 45 to 74 years	**486402**	**234631**	**87770**	**142455**	**945**	**3461**	**251771**	**95652**	**153355**	**655**	**2109**
Economically active	**223530**	**129718**	**45548**	**81420**	**624**	**2126**	**93812**	**32945**	**59608**	**291**	**968**
Employee - Part-time	44346	6189	2378	3704	33	74	38157	13097	24709	73	278
Employee - Full-time	120150	76901	24519	50728	328	1326	43249	15461	27177	130	481
Self-employed - Part-time	8985	5436	1988	3320	43	85	3549	997	2468	37	47
Self-employed - Full-time	37055	31773	11993	19119	183	478	5282	1670	3468	39	105
Unemployed	12784	9295	4605	4494	37	159	3489	1681	1743	12	53
Full-time student	210	124	65	55	-	4	86	39	43	-	4
Economically inactive	**262872**	**104913**	**42222**	**61035**	**321**	**1335**	**157959**	**62707**	**93747**	**364**	**1141**
Retired	129791	53117	16940	35430	154	593	76674	24970	51143	142	419
Student	332	127	57	58	3	9	205	97	100	4	4
Looking after home/family	33494	3714	2088	1563	12	51	29780	13228	16186	99	267
Permanently sick/disabled	75290	39025	18690	19675	123	537	36265	17212	18675	65	313
Other	23965	8930	4447	4309	29	145	15035	7200	7643	54	138

Notes:

1 For the Census, part-time is defined as working 30 hours or less a week. Full-time is defined as working 31 or more hours a week.

2 The term 'Catholic' includes those respondents who gave their religion as Catholic or Roman Catholic.

S330

149

S330A

Table S330A: Age and Economic Activity by Sex and Religion

Table population: All persons aged 16 to 74

	All persons	Males								Females							
		Total	Catholic	Presbyterian Church in Ireland	Church of Ireland	Methodist Church in Ireland	Other Christian (including Christian related)	Other religions and philosophies	No religion or religion not stated	Total	Catholic	Presbyterian Church in Ireland	Church of Ireland	Methodist Church in Ireland	Other Christian (including Christian related)	Other religions and philosophies	No religion or religion not stated
All persons	1187070	581228	223279	122197	88206	19376	35617	2192	90361	605842	244333	129014	97353	22467	38653	1652	72370
Economically active	739130	412034	152933	88714	61114	13743	27047	1589	66894	327096	125987	72156	51965	12342	21564	792	42290
Employee - Part-time	117981	17172	7452	2919	2379	558	959	91	2814	100809	36198	24046	17025	4396	7631	179	11334
Employee - Full-time	445789	271113	92047	60312	42719	9874	18738	925	46498	174676	68361	37789	27886	6399	10479	388	23374
Self-employed - Part-time	15952	8691	3359	1848	1200	259	614	48	1363	7261	2091	1958	1095	254	797	48	1018
Self-employed - Full-time	82278	70255	28454	16842	9152	1917	4958	326	8606	12023	4093	3020	1818	379	938	75	1700
Unemployed	49098	32957	16352	4719	4266	759	1072	138	5651	16141	7632	2476	2178	404	735	59	2657
Full-time student	28032	11846	5269	2074	1398	376	706	61	1962	16186	7612	2867	1963	510	984	43	2207
Economically inactive	447940	169194	70346	33483	27092	5633	8570	603	23467	278746	118346	56858	45388	10125	17089	860	30080
Retired	130308	53406	15826	14503	11089	2511	3215	114	6148	76902	23773	21702	16166	3986	5213	117	5945
Student	67625	30895	14843	5051	3524	803	1662	249	4763	36730	18773	6054	4137	940	2149	189	4488
Looking after home/family	88205	8396	4521	1067	1026	192	309	22	1259	79809	36011	14475	11555	2479	5208	338	9743
Permanently sick/disabled	110787	56421	25745	9790	8782	1647	2536	134	7787	54366	25036	9534	8987	1836	3099	88	5786
Other	51015	20076	9411	3072	2671	480	848	84	3510	30939	14753	5093	4543	884	1420	128	4118
Aged 16 to 24 years	211474	106620	48758	18528	13227	2927	6072	334	16774	104854	49415	18233	13503	2971	6164	302	14266
Economically active	130427	71606	31622	12872	9203	2027	4295	146	11441	58821	26105	10857	8152	1826	3586	106	8189
Employee - Part-time	11956	4084	1970	589	462	116	215	7	725	7872	3524	1312	1075	238	513	16	1194
Employee - Full-time	75804	45333	18900	8606	6161	1315	2963	64	7324	30471	12805	6085	4502	982	1919	40	4138
Self-employed - Part-time	345	214	97	33	29	3	22	-	30	131	41	33	17	-	18	-	22
Self-employed - Full-time	3198	2764	1474	518	246	58	174	11	283	434	172	69	98	13	28	3	51
Unemployed	13130	8377	4340	1181	1009	185	282	21	1359	4753	2427	639	608	95	181	12	791
Full-time student	25994	10834	4841	1945	1296	350	639	43	1720	15160	7136	2719	1852	498	927	35	1993
Economically inactive	81047	35014	17136	5656	4024	900	1777	188	5333	46033	23310	7376	5351	1145	2578	196	6077
Retired	10	3	-	-	-	-	-	-	3	7	-	-	-	-	-	-	7
Student	63966	29437	14297	4890	3416	785	1552	168	4329	34529	17778	5798	3923	892	2012	133	3993
Looking after home/family	6502	377	199	66	38	10	18	-	46	6125	2774	869	789	135	343	36	1179
Permanently sick/disabled	3676	2038	1090	275	221	47	70	4	331	1638	841	224	195	38	75	3	262
Other	6893	3159	1550	425	349	58	137	16	624	3734	1917	485	444	80	148	24	636

Table S330A: Age and Economic Activity by Sex and Religion (continued)

	All persons	Males								Females							
		Total	Catholic	Presbyterian Church in Ireland	Church of Ireland	Methodist Church in Ireland	Other Christian (including Christian related)	Other religions and philosophies	No religion or religion not stated	Total	Catholic	Presbyterian Church in Ireland	Church of Ireland	Methodist Church in Ireland	Other Christian (including Christian related)	Other religions and philosophies	No religion or religion not stated
Aged 25 to 34 years	242218	119113	46997	22682	16053	3380	7741	640	21620	123105	52740	22964	17670	3829	7758	463	17681
Economically active	195860	106835	40966	21002	14652	3142	7226	520	19327	89025	36611	17910	13147	2908	5659	238	12552
Employee - Part-time	25210	3417	1572	461	401	85	186	34	678	21793	8280	4690	3364	812	1690	39	2918
Employee - Full-time	136956	78716	27845	16142	11367	2517	5593	342	14910	58240	24442	11629	8648	1878	3415	148	8080
Self-employed - Part-time	2375	1070	483	169	122	17	79	7	193	1305	424	286	165	44	151	9	226
Self-employed - Full-time	17672	14835	6668	3093	1698	343	1087	67	1879	2837	1155	613	371	67	171	14	446
Unemployed	12397	8201	4162	1064	1013	164	240	57	1501	4196	2006	602	535	98	195	23	737
Full-time student	1250	596	236	73	51	16	41	13	166	654	304	90	64	9	37	5	145
Economically inactive	46358	12278	6031	1680	1401	238	515	120	2293	34080	16129	5054	4523	921	2099	225	5129
Retired	59	41	14	6	6	-	6	-	9	18	4	5	6	-	-	-	3
Student	2406	1033	387	107	67	9	77	75	311	1373	623	142	129	26	84	43	326
Looking after home/family	22514	1560	855	189	150	24	61	3	278	20954	9656	3199	2844	596	1437	134	3088
Permanently sick/disabled	11398	5634	2816	819	707	110	221	13	948	5764	2846	885	784	154	328	14	753
Other	9981	4010	1959	559	471	95	150	29	747	5971	3000	823	760	145	250	34	959
Aged 35 to 44 years	246975	120863	46921	24525	17410	3796	7296	523	20392	126112	52486	25423	19235	4484	7755	375	16354
Economically active	189314	103875	38694	22062	15124	3403	6591	456	17545	85439	32745	18948	13518	3325	5475	227	11201
Employee - Part-time	36469	3482	1730	468	437	92	175	23	557	32987	12114	7781	5430	1445	2442	64	3711
Employee - Full-time	112879	70163	23078	15752	11136	2607	4732	271	12587	42716	16891	9171	6795	1582	2305	104	5868
Self-employed - Part-time	4247	1971	914	297	207	51	121	11	370	2276	701	574	295	82	256	12	356
Self-employed - Full-time	24353	20883	9116	4574	2456	509	1348	110	2770	3470	1234	768	461	123	263	31	590
Unemployed	10787	7084	3722	927	859	138	197	36	1205	3703	1667	610	503	90	194	13	626
Full-time student	579	292	134	44	29	6	18	5	56	287	138	44	34	3	15	3	50
Economically inactive	57661	16988	8227	2463	2286	393	705	67	2847	40673	19741	6475	5717	1159	2280	148	5153
Retired	448	245	78	45	44	7	17	3	51	203	87	34	35	8	10	-	29
Student	919	297	111	32	25	6	25	3	95	622	280	75	65	14	41	10	137
Looking after home/family	25695	2745	1524	302	333	50	93	10	433	22950	11105	3819	3105	581	1440	89	2811
Permanently sick/disabled	20423	9724	4613	1503	1393	241	402	29	1543	10699	5133	1644	1662	373	553	19	1315
Other	10176	3977	1901	581	491	89	168	22	725	6199	3136	903	850	183	236	30	861

S330A

Table S330A: Age and Economic Activity by Sex and Religion (continued)

	All persons	Males								Females							
		Total	Catholic	Presbyterian Church in Ireland	Church of Ireland	Methodist Church in Ireland	Other Christian (including Christian related)	Other religions and philosophies	No religion or religion not stated	Total	Catholic	Presbyterian Church in Ireland	Church of Ireland	Methodist Church in Ireland	Other Christian (including Christian related)	Other religions and philosophies	No religion or religion not stated
Aged 45 to 74 years	**486403**	**234632**	**80603**	**56462**	**41516**	**9273**	**14508**	**695**	**31575**	**251771**	**89692**	**62394**	**46945**	**11183**	**16976**	**512**	**24069**
Economically active	**223529**	**129718**	**41651**	**32778**	**22135**	**5171**	**8935**	**467**	**18581**	**93811**	**30526**	**24441**	**17148**	**4283**	**6844**	**221**	**10348**
Employee - Part-time	44346	6189	2180	1401	1079	265	383	27	854	38157	12280	10263	7156	1901	2986	60	3511
Employee - Full-time	120150	76901	22224	19812	14055	3435	5450	248	11677	43249	14223	10904	7941	1957	2840	96	5288
Self-employed - Part-time	8985	5436	1865	1349	842	188	392	30	770	3549	925	1065	618	128	372	27	414
Self-employed - Full-time	37055	31773	11196	8657	4752	1007	2349	138	3674	5282	1532	1570	888	176	476	27	613
Unemployed	12784	9295	4128	1547	1385	272	353	24	1586	3489	1532	625	532	121	165	11	503
Full-time student	209	124	58	12	22	4	8	-	20	85	34	14	13	-	5	-	19
Economically inactive	**262874**	**104914**	**38952**	**23684**	**19381**	**4102**	**5573**	**228**	**12994**	**157960**	**59166**	**37953**	**29797**	**6900**	**10132**	**291**	**13721**
Retired	129791	53117	15734	14452	11039	2504	3192	111	6085	76674	23682	21663	16125	3978	5203	117	5906
Student	334	128	48	22	16	3	8	3	28	206	92	39	20	8	12	3	32
Looking after home/family	33494	3714	1943	510	505	108	137	9	502	29780	12476	6588	4817	1167	1988	79	2665
Permanently sick/disabled	75290	39025	17226	7193	6461	1249	1843	88	4965	36265	16216	6781	6346	1271	2143	52	3456
Other	23965	8930	4001	1507	1360	238	393	17	1414	15035	6700	2882	2489	476	786	40	1662

Notes:

1 For the Census, part-time is defined as working 30 hours or less a week. Full-time is defined as working 31 or more hours a week.

2 The term 'Catholic' includes those respondents who gave their religion as Catholic or Roman Catholic.

Table S331: Economic Activity and Age of Full-time Students by Household Type and Tenure

Table population: All full-time schoolchildren and students aged 16 and over at their term-time address

	All full-time students	Living with parent(s)	Communal establishment	All student group household				Student living alone				Other household type			
				Owner occupied	Rented from NIHE	Other social rented	Private rented	Owner occupied	Rented from NIHE	Other social rented	Private rented	Owner occupied	Rented from NIHE	Other social rented	Private rented
All full-time students	**93782**	**74786**	**4087**	**698**	**212**	**76**	**5776**	**287**	**131**	**53**	**391**	**3358**	**854**	**99**	**2974**
16	25077	24411	79	4	9	-	4	-	6	-	4	292	193	13	66
17	18205	17674	93	13	4	4	14	3	9	3	6	242	85	6	49
18	14808	13751	445	26	-	3	160	3	9	3	20	224	69	10	85
19	9657	6144	1691	235	6	15	987	38	3	-	27	162	60	12	277
20	7423	4402	579	68	8	14	1660	24	10	3	53	177	42	9	374
21	5901	3324	353	65	8	10	1319	18	11	14	56	157	49	9	508
22 to 24	7620	3899	532	127	20	9	1334	48	28	11	102	455	67	15	973
25 and over	5091	1181	315	160	157	21	298	153	55	19	127	1649	289	25	642
Economically active	**28027**	**20641**	**1467**	**249**	**71**	**29**	**2260**	**126**	**59**	**25**	**179**	**1347**	**310**	**26**	**1238**
16	4011	3874	11	-	5	-	-	-	3	-	-	62	34	3	19
17	5007	4851	21	-	-	-	6	-	4	-	3	78	27	-	17
18	4619	4181	207	19	-	-	80	-	3	3	15	65	11	3	32
19	4032	2544	731	32	3	7	447	22	3	-	17	55	22	3	146
20	3255	1910	217	36	3	6	737	5	5	3	34	66	16	4	213
21	2412	1388	95	40	3	3	516	11	5	9	26	60	27	4	225
22 to 24	2653	1443	134	37	4	3	379	24	12	6	34	189	31	3	354
25 and over	2038	450	51	85	53	10	95	64	24	4	50	772	142	6	232
Economically inactive	**65755**	**54145**	**2620**	**449**	**141**	**47**	**3516**	**161**	**72**	**28**	**212**	**2011**	**544**	**73**	**1736**
16	21066	20537	68	4	4	-	4	-	3	-	-	230	159	10	47
17	13198	12823	72	13	4	4	8	3	5	3	3	164	58	6	32
18	10189	9570	238	7	-	3	80	3	6	-	5	159	58	7	53
19	5625	3600	960	203	3	8	540	16	-	-	10	107	38	9	131
20	4168	2492	362	32	5	8	923	19	5	-	19	111	26	5	161
21	3489	1936	258	25	5	7	803	7	6	5	30	97	22	5	283
22 to 24	4967	2456	398	90	16	6	955	24	16	5	68	266	36	12	619
25 and over	3053	731	264	75	104	11	203	89	31	15	77	877	147	19	410

Notes:

1 The terms used to describe tenure are defined as:
   Owner occupied: either owns outright, owns with a mortgage or loan, or pays part rent and part mortgage (shared ownership).
   Rented from NIHE: rented from Northern Ireland Housing Executive.
   Other social rented: rented from Registered Social Landlord, Housing Association, Housing Co-operative or Charitable Trust.
   Private rented: rented from a private landlord or letting agency, employer of a household member, or relative or friend of a household member or other person.

2 'Rented from NIHE', 'Other social rented' and 'Private rented' include living in the household rent free.

3 'Other household type' covers students living in a household with others, where one or more of them is not a student. This includes households where the student forms part of the 'parent' generation.

4 All students aged over 74 are classified as economically inactive though some may be economically active.

S331

Table S033: Sex and Occupation by Age

Table population: All persons aged 16 to 74 in employment the week before the Census

	All persons	16 to 17	18 to 19	20 to 24	25 to 29	30 to 39	40 to 49	50 to 54	55 to 59	60 to 64	65 to 69	70 to 74
All persons	**686643**	**14553**	**24789**	**74884**	**88442**	**188958**	**155747**	**61307**	**45222**	**21834**	**7028**	**3879**
1. Managers and senior officials	**72772**	**238**	**535**	**3762**	**8443**	**23297**	**19508**	**7562**	**5506**	**2580**	**854**	**487**
11. Corporate managers	52107	147	309	2661	6513	17430	14035	5151	3621	1548	448	244
12. Managers and proprietors in agriculture and services	20665	91	226	1101	1930	5867	5473	2411	1885	1032	406	243
2. Professional occupations	**72508**	**135**	**266**	**4491**	**11523**	**20230**	**19590**	**8168**	**4821**	**2079**	**784**	**421**
21. Science and technology professionals	13665	63	149	1736	3289	4118	2357	798	595	290	163	107
22. Health professionals	6895	6	12	311	1263	2325	1682	558	368	213	114	43
23. Teaching and research professionals	35546	52	55	1524	4679	8872	11118	5222	2739	971	212	102
24. Business and public service professionals	16402	14	50	920	2292	4915	4433	1590	1119	605	295	169
3. Associate professional and technical occupations	**86004**	**545**	**1361**	**8535**	**13665**	**27830**	**20495**	**6608**	**4402**	**1857**	**480**	**226**
31. Science and technology associate professionals	11443	148	274	1749	2069	3172	2407	792	542	249	29	12
32. Health and social welfare associate professionals	27655	47	147	1550	3398	9444	8249	2511	1548	558	138	65
33. Protective service occupations	11817	90	489	1832	2004	4477	2170	482	221	48	4	-
34. Culture, media and sports occupations	8332	71	144	899	1517	2493	1799	602	437	219	94	57
35. Business and public service associate professionals	26757	189	307	2505	4677	8244	5870	2221	1654	783	215	92
4. Administrative and secretarial occupations	**100098**	**883**	**2491**	**12231**	**14285**	**29321**	**23641**	**8327**	**5850**	**2142**	**616**	**311**
4.1. Administrative occupations	79189	658	1913	9960	11526	23441	18848	6235	4357	1578	444	229
42. Secretarial and related occupations	20909	225	578	2271	2759	5880	4793	2092	1493	564	172	82
5. Skilled trades occupations	**106899**	**3355**	**5289**	**12459**	**12535**	**26964**	**23019**	**9096**	**6874**	**4162**	**1957**	**1189**
51. Skilled agricultural trades	19362	108	200	750	1445	4044	4283	2243	2166	1769	1404	950
52. Skilled metal and electrical trades	36277	1193	2042	5063	4897	8616	8214	2946	2025	1012	193	76
53. Skilled construction and building trades	33164	1598	2252	4340	3924	8983	6689	2574	1648	862	216	78
54. Textiles, printing and other skilled trades	18096	456	795	2306	2269	5321	3833	1333	1035	519	144	85
6. Personal service occupations	**45773**	**1167**	**2018**	**5958**	**5503**	**11550**	**10145**	**4421**	**3155**	**1312**	**345**	**199**
61. Caring personal service occupations	32743	611	1215	4192	3721	8416	8053	3289	2190	779	185	92
62. Leisure and other personal service occupations	13030	556	803	1766	1782	3134	2092	1132	965	533	160	107
7. Sales and customer service occupations	**50363**	**3728**	**5784**	**10431**	**6001**	**10139**	**7117**	**3034**	**2427**	**1084**	**404**	**214**
71. Sales occupations	45875	3645	5476	9177	5077	9119	6508	2881	2330	1053	398	211
72. Customer service occupations	4488	83	308	1254	924	1020	609	153	97	31	6	3
8. Process, plant and machine operatives	**71288**	**1152**	**2125**	**7364**	**8930**	**20677**	**15745**	**6398**	**5378**	**2767**	**530**	**222**
81. Process, plant and machine operatives	42804	1033	1841	5796	6012	11745	8703	3341	2652	1304	247	130
82. Transport and mobile machine drivers and operatives	28484	119	284	1568	2918	8932	7042	3057	2726	1463	283	92
9. Elementary occupations	**80938**	**3350**	**4920**	**9653**	**7557**	**18950**	**16487**	**7693**	**6809**	**3851**	**1058**	**610**
91. Elementary trades, plant and storage related occupations	28442	901	1573	3915	3494	7549	5323	2198	1946	1111	279	153
92. Elementary administration and service occupations	52496	2449	3347	5738	4063	11401	11164	5495	4863	2740	779	457

S033

Table S033: Sex and Occupation by Age (continued)

	All persons	16 to 17	18 to 19	20 to 24	25 to 29	30 to 39	40 to 49	50 to 54	55 to 59	60 to 64	65 to 69	70 to 74
Males	**377389**	**8203**	**13746**	**39771**	**46788**	**103180**	**84456**	**33802**	**25956**	**14276**	**4648**	**2563**
1. Managers and senior officials	**47686**	**159**	**313**	**2082**	**4725**	**14961**	**13261**	**5265**	**3985**	**1986**	**613**	**336**
11. Corporate managers	34568	102	194	1464	3650	11374	9720	3629	2693	1231	333	178
12. Managers and proprietors in agriculture and services	13118	57	119	618	1075	3587	3541	1636	1292	755	280	158
2. Professional occupations	**38149**	**86**	**188**	**2320**	**5496**	**10271**	**9992**	**4492**	**2934**	**1447**	**606**	**317**
21. Science and technology professionals	11251	59	136	1347	2561	3376	2043	712	518	266	136	97
22. Health professionals	3971	-	4	113	573	1226	1073	403	272	171	101	35
23. Teaching and research professionals	12368	19	18	380	1138	2764	3956	2187	1257	513	101	35
24. Business and public service professionals	10559	8	30	480	1224	2905	2920	1190	887	497	268	150
3. Associate professional and technical occupations	**44480**	**397**	**976**	**4809**	**6817**	**13798**	**10111**	**3492**	**2456**	**1185**	**298**	**141**
31. Science and technology associate professionals	8683	127	228	1278	1531	2381	1888	628	403	191	19	9
32. Health and social welfare associate professionals	3734	13	32	203	425	1268	1096	347	206	101	25	18
33. Protective service occupations	10480	86	459	1620	1702	3948	1968	446	199	48	4	-
34. Culture, media and sports occupations	5241	43	91	557	888	1479	1199	410	310	158	65	41
35. Business and public service associate professionals	16342	128	166	1151	2271	4722	3960	1661	1338	687	185	73
4. Administrative and secretarial occupations	**27064**	**219**	**586**	**3088**	**3618**	**7864**	**6705**	**2279**	**1700**	**726**	**186**	**93**
41. Administrative occupations	26331	206	565	3016	3539	7679	6532	2200	1641	689	175	89
42. Secretarial and related occupations	733	13	21	72	79	185	173	79	59	37	11	4
5. Skilled trades occupations	**96914**	**3232**	**5061**	**11636**	**11675**	**24232**	**20566**	**8060**	**6002**	**3647**	**1743**	**1060**
51. Skilled agricultural trades	17775	101	189	721	1404	3805	3954	2025	1909	1537	1261	869
52. Skilled metal and electrical trades	35518	1178	2003	4933	4759	8412	8074	2901	1994	1000	188	76
53. Skilled construction and building trades	32835	1583	2236	4315	3898	8897	6623	2533	1614	850	213	73
54. Textiles, printing and other skilled trades	10786	370	633	1667	1614	3118	1915	601	485	260	81	42
6. Personal service occupations	**6608**	**133**	**212**	**644**	**673**	**1621**	**1484**	**722**	**595**	**393**	**78**	**53**
61. Caring personal service occupations	2829	56	79	322	365	862	652	231	162	82	9	9
62. Leisure and other personal service occupations	3779	77	133	322	308	759	832	491	433	311	69	44
7. Sales and customer service occupations	**14070**	**1185**	**1909**	**3456**	**1784**	**2356**	**1498**	**680**	**631**	**372**	**132**	**67**
71. Sales occupations	12782	1155	1801	3079	1509	2115	1342	640	591	354	129	67
72. Customer service occupations	1288	30	108	377	275	241	156	40	40	18	3	-
8. Process, plant and machine operatives	**58496**	**939**	**1641**	**5626**	**7048**	**17172**	**12995**	**5410**	**4581**	**2482**	**430**	**172**
81. Process, plant and machine operatives	30877	827	1374	4142	4253	8538	6150	2423	1902	1031	153	84
82. Transport and mobile machine drivers and operatives	27619	112	267	1484	2795	8634	6845	2987	2679	1451	277	88
9. Elementary occupations	**43922**	**1853**	**2860**	**6110**	**4952**	**10905**	**7844**	**3402**	**3072**	**2038**	**562**	**324**
91. Elementary trades, plant and storage related occupations	24169	783	1378	3385	2998	6482	4490	1828	1582	948	198	97
92. Elementary administration and service occupations	19753	1070	1482	2725	1954	4423	3354	1574	1490	1090	364	227

S033

© Crown copyright 2003

	All persons	16 to 17	18 to 19	20 to 24	25 to 29	30 to 39	40 to 49	50 to 54	55 to 59	60 to 64	65 to 69	70 to 74
Females	**309254**	**6350**	**11043**	**35113**	**41654**	**85778**	**71291**	**27505**	**19266**	**7558**	**2380**	**1316**
1. Managers and senior officials	**25086**	**79**	**222**	**1680**	**3718**	**8336**	**6247**	**2297**	**1521**	**594**	**241**	**151**
11. Corporate managers	17539	45	115	1197	2863	6056	4315	1522	928	317	115	66
12. Managers and proprietors in agriculture and services	7547	34	107	483	855	2280	1932	775	593	277	126	85
2. Professional occupations	**34359**	**49**	**78**	**2171**	**6027**	**9959**	**9598**	**3676**	**1887**	**632**	**178**	**104**
21. Science and technology professionals	2414	4	13	389	728	742	314	86	77	24	27	10
22. Health professionals	2924	6	8	198	690	1099	609	155	96	42	13	8
23. Teaching and research professionals	23178	33	37	1144	3541	6108	7162	3035	1482	458	111	67
24. Business and public service professionals	5843	6	20	440	1068	2010	1513	400	232	108	27	19
3. Associate professional and technical occupations	**41524**	**148**	**385**	**3726**	**6848**	**14032**	**10384**	**3116**	**1946**	**672**	**182**	**85**
31. Science and technology associate professionals	2760	21	46	471	538	791	519	164	139	58	10	3
32. Health and social welfare associate professionals	23921	34	115	1347	2973	8176	7153	2164	1342	457	113	47
33. Protective service occupations	1337	4	30	212	302	529	202	36	22	-	-	-
34. Culture, media and sports occupations	3091	28	53	342	629	1014	600	192	127	61	29	16
35. Business and public service associate professionals	10415	61	141	1354	2406	3522	1910	560	316	96	30	19
4. Administrative and secretarial occupations	**73034**	**664**	**1905**	**9143**	**10667**	**21457**	**16936**	**6048**	**4150**	**1416**	**430**	**218**
41. Administrative occupations	52858	452	1348	6944	7987	15762	12316	4035	2716	889	269	140
42. Secretarial and related occupations	20176	212	557	2199	2680	5695	4620	2013	1434	527	161	78
5. Skilled trades occupations	**9985**	**123**	**228**	**823**	**860**	**2732**	**2453**	**1036**	**872**	**515**	**214**	**129**
51. Skilled agricultural trades	1587	7	11	29	41	239	329	218	257	232	143	81
52. Skilled metal and electrical trades	759	15	39	130	138	204	140	45	31	12	5	-
53. Skilled construction and building trades	329	15	16	25	26	86	66	41	34	12	3	5
54. Textiles, printing and other skilled trades	7310	86	162	639	655	2203	1918	732	550	259	63	43
6. Personal service occupations	**39165**	**1034**	**1806**	**5314**	**4830**	**9929**	**8661**	**3699**	**2560**	**919**	**267**	**146**
61. Caring personal service occupations	29914	555	1136	3870	3356	7554	7401	3058	2028	697	176	83
62. Leisure and other personal service occupations	9251	479	670	1444	1474	2375	1260	641	532	222	91	63
7. Sales and customer service occupations	**36293**	**2543**	**3875**	**6975**	**4217**	**7783**	**5619**	**2354**	**1796**	**712**	**272**	**147**
71. Sales occupations	33093	2490	3675	6098	3568	7004	5166	2241	1739	699	269	144
72. Customer service occupations	3200	53	200	877	649	779	453	113	57	13	3	3
8. Process, plant and machine operatives	**12792**	**213**	**484**	**1738**	**1882**	**3505**	**2750**	**988**	**797**	**285**	**100**	**50**
81. Process, plant and machine operatives	11927	206	467	1654	1759	3207	2553	918	750	273	94	46
82. Transport and mobile machine drivers and operatives	865	7	17	84	123	298	197	70	47	12	6	4
9. Elementary occupations	**37016**	**1497**	**2060**	**3543**	**2605**	**8045**	**8643**	**4291**	**3737**	**1813**	**496**	**286**
91. Elementary trades, plant and storage related occupations	4273	118	195	530	496	1067	833	370	364	163	81	56
92. Elementary administration and service occupations	32743	1379	1865	3013	2109	6978	7810	3921	3373	1650	415	230

Notes:
1 The occupation classification is SOC2000 (Standard Occupation Classification).
2 'In employment' includes economically active full-time students in employment.

S033

157

Table S034: Sex and Former Occupation by Age (UK Basis)

Table population: All persons aged 16 to 64 not in employment the week before the Census

	All persons	16 to 17	18 to 19	20 to 24	25 to 29	30 to 39	40 to 49	50 to 54	55 to 59	60 to 64
All persons	**388150**	**38906**	**23850**	**34501**	**26262**	**68198**	**64052**	**37119**	**43510**	**51752**
Unemployed in the week before the Census	**52204**	**3055**	**4772**	**8379**	**6436**	**11999**	**9324**	**3953**	**3051**	**1235**
1. Managers and senior officials	1975	28	56	177	264	522	456	201	184	87
2. Professional occupations	1301	9	34	138	232	289	250	150	148	51
3. Associate professional and technical occupations	2875	44	118	435	467	710	613	263	152	73
4. Administrative and secretarial occupations	2955	74	215	623	465	620	463	263	175	57
5. Skilled trades occupations	7016	230	514	1221	988	1774	1301	477	330	181
6. Personal service occupations	2120	71	223	490	281	521	317	117	85	15
7. Sales and customer service occupations	3568	313	601	1036	450	607	303	138	91	29
8. Process, plant and machine operatives	5274	114	375	983	812	1363	868	366	279	114
9. Elementary occupations	8797	484	951	1778	1156	2034	1397	508	349	140
Never worked or last worked before 1996	16323	1688	1685	1498	1321	3559	3356	1470	1258	488
Economically inactive in the week before the Census	**335946**	**35851**	**19078**	**26122**	**19826**	**56199**	**54728**	**33166**	**40459**	**50517**
1. Managers and senior officials	7234	60	73	315	576	1291	1087	859	1350	1623
2. Professional occupations	7281	24	44	590	549	1040	943	814	1425	1852
3. Associate professional and technical occupations	10005	93	181	1010	829	2024	1678	1008	1424	1758
4. Administrative and secretarial occupations	14606	159	391	1562	1421	3158	2281	1385	1705	2544
5. Skilled trades occupations	12529	183	320	1177	1070	2670	2219	1349	1554	1987
6. Personal service occupations	10876	191	396	1601	1473	2594	1697	966	945	1013
7. Sales and customer service occupations	14745	1355	1813	3101	1621	2846	1394	811	798	1006
8. Process, plant and machine operatives	13609	153	425	1672	1652	3059	2080	1223	1459	1886
9. Elementary occupations	23544	1199	1560	3395	1995	4358	3554	2084	2377	3022
Never worked or last worked before 1996	221517	32434	13875	11699	8640	33159	37795	22667	27422	33826

S 0 3 4

Table S034: Sex and Former Occupation by Age (UK Basis) (continued)

	All persons	16 to 17	18 to 19	20 to 24	25 to 29	30 to 39	40 to 49	50 to 54	55 to 59	60 to 64
Males	**155578**	**18956**	**10805**	**15142**	**9840**	**22737**	**24662**	**14682**	**17629**	**21125**
Unemployed in the week before the Census	**34478**	**1779**	**2830**	**5277**	**4235**	**7845**	**6358**	**2810**	**2232**	**1112**
1. Managers and senior officials	1376	16	36	101	161	348	318	155	161	80
2. Professional occupations	768	6	26	86	151	156	132	81	90	40
3. Associate professional and technical occupations	1993	35	82	303	297	449	450	197	119	61
4. Administrative and secretarial occupations	1092	22	78	232	156	192	162	128	80	42
5. Skilled trades occupations	6586	208	485	1149	904	1645	1242	455	320	178
6. Personal service occupations	451	14	31	77	69	104	77	38	29	12
7. Sales and customer service occupations	1256	116	212	408	176	167	81	37	36	23
8. Process, plant and machine operatives	4153	86	276	745	616	1083	711	299	228	109
9. Elementary occupations	6185	280	619	1209	853	1494	1011	352	246	121
Never worked or last worked before 1996	10618	996	985	967	852	2207	2174	1068	923	446
Economically inactive in the week before the Census	**121100**	**17177**	**7975**	**9865**	**5605**	**14892**	**18304**	**11872**	**15397**	**20013**
1. Managers and senior officials	3666	28	41	125	147	375	527	483	873	1067
2. Professional occupations	2838	8	17	328	232	224	271	304	557	897
3. Associate professional and technical occupations	4132	54	91	506	276	513	672	505	700	815
4. Administrative and secretarial occupations	3480	60	85	351	195	376	559	495	596	763
5. Skilled trades occupations	9919	152	252	954	821	1928	1806	1091	1315	1600
6. Personal service occupations	1051	36	51	149	75	178	192	115	105	150
7. Sales and customer service occupations	2595	471	517	679	165	218	175	87	118	165
8. Process, plant and machine operatives	7176	95	194	676	559	1306	1228	783	1001	1334
9. Elementary occupations	8776	617	744	1393	702	1472	1311	674	838	1025
Never worked or last worked before 1996	77467	15656	5983	4704	2433	8302	11563	7335	9294	12197

S034

Table S034: Sex and Former Occupation by Age (UK Basis) (continued)

	All persons	16 to 17	18 to 19	20 to 24	25 to 29	30 to 39	40 to 49	50 to 54	55 to 59	60 to 64
Females	**232572**	**19950**	**13045**	**19359**	**16422**	**45461**	**39390**	**22437**	**25881**	**30627**
Unemployed in the week before the Census	**17726**	**1276**	**1942**	**3102**	**2201**	**4154**	**2966**	**1143**	**819**	**123**
1. Managers and senior officials	599	12	20	76	103	174	138	46	23	7
2. Professional occupations	533	3	8	52	81	133	118	69	58	11
3. Associate professional and technical occupations	882	9	36	132	170	261	163	66	33	12
4. Administrative and secretarial occupations	1863	52	137	391	309	428	301	135	95	15
5. Skilled trades occupations	430	22	29	72	84	129	59	22	10	3
6. Personal service occupations	1669	57	192	413	212	417	240	79	56	3
7. Sales and customer service occupations	2312	197	389	628	274	440	222	101	55	6
8. Process, plant and machine operatives	1121	28	99	238	196	280	157	67	51	5
9. Elementary occupations	2612	204	332	569	303	540	386	156	103	19
Never worked or last worked before 1996	5705	692	700	531	469	1352	1182	402	335	42
Economically inactive in the week before the Census	**214846**	**18674**	**11103**	**16257**	**14221**	**41307**	**36424**	**21294**	**25062**	**30504**
1. Managers and senior officials	3568	32	32	190	429	916	560	376	477	556
2. Professional occupations	4443	16	27	262	317	816	672	510	868	955
3. Associate professional and technical occupations	5873	39	90	504	553	1511	1006	503	724	943
4. Administrative and secretarial occupations	11126	99	306	1211	1226	2782	1722	890	1109	1781
5. Skilled trades occupations	2610	31	68	223	249	742	413	258	239	387
6. Personal service occupations	9825	155	345	1452	1398	2416	1505	851	840	863
7. Sales and customer service occupations	12150	884	1296	2422	1456	2628	1219	724	680	841
8. Process, plant and machine operatives	6433	58	231	996	1093	1753	852	440	458	552
9. Elementary occupations	14768	582	816	2002	1293	2886	2243	1410	1539	1997
Never worked or last worked before 1996	144050	16778	7892	6995	6207	24857	26232	15332	18128	21629

Notes:
1 The occupation classification is SOC2000 (Standard Occupation Classification).
2 'Not in employment' includes all full-time students who are not in employment.
3 This table gives the former occupation of all persons aged 16-64 who last worked between 1996 and 2001.

Table S332: Sex and Former Occupation by Age (NI Basis)

Table population: All persons aged 16 to 74 not in employment the week before the Census

	All persons	16 to 17	18 to 19	20 to 24	25 to 29	30 to 39	40 to 49	50 to 54	55 to 59	60 to 64	65 to 69	70 to 74
All persons	**500436**	**38906**	**23850**	**34501**	**26262**	**68198**	**64052**	**37119**	**43510**	**51752**	**58311**	**53975**
Unemployed in the week before the Census	**52491**	**3055**	**4772**	**8379**	**6436**	**11999**	**9324**	**3953**	**3051**	**1235**	**167**	**120**
1. Managers and senior officials	2347	28	56	179	284	604	546	245	257	123	18	7
2. Professional occupations	1469	9	34	138	241	320	295	175	183	61	7	6
3. Associate professional and technical occupations	3426	44	118	438	509	825	804	339	226	94	14	15
4. Administrative and secretarial occupations	3599	74	215	627	504	787	670	343	265	71	24	19
5. Skilled trades occupations	8934	230	514	1242	1108	2280	1930	747	567	293	14	9
6. Personal service occupations	2513	71	223	493	331	659	410	169	122	24	8	3
7. Sales and customer service occupations	4140	313	601	1041	523	775	494	210	142	38	-	3
8. Process, plant and machine operatives	7119	114	375	993	923	1804	1428	681	541	223	25	12
9. Elementary occupations	11324	484	951	1795	1297	2742	2207	877	645	277	29	20
Never worked	7620	1688	1685	1433	716	1203	540	167	103	31	28	26
Economically inactive in the week before the Census	**447945**	**35851**	**19078**	**26122**	**19826**	**56199**	**54728**	**33166**	**40459**	**50517**	**58144**	**53855**
1. Managers and senior officials	20049	60	73	320	657	2036	2087	1593	2490	3284	3908	3541
2. Professional occupations	19316	24	44	595	598	1418	1652	1421	2340	3465	4122	3637
3. Associate professional and technical occupations	26812	93	181	1028	989	3306	3817	2212	3083	4064	4439	3600
4. Administrative and secretarial occupations	46891	159	391	1593	1836	6012	6799	3888	4786	6527	7653	7247
5. Skilled trades occupations	42447	183	320	1256	1478	5063	5984	3813	4557	5731	7395	6667
6. Personal service occupations	24899	191	396	1697	2153	4980	3648	2204	2482	2492	2571	2085
7. Sales and customer service occupations	33907	1355	1813	3198	2286	6129	4205	2488	2631	3180	3373	3249
8. Process, plant and machine operatives	56533	153	425	1788	2584	8210	8818	5393	6332	7558	8120	7152
9. Elementary occupations	74236	1199	1560	3491	2827	9134	10277	6577	8024	9962	11100	10085
Never worked	102855	32434	13875	11156	4418	9911	7441	3577	3734	4254	5463	6592

S332

Table S332: Sex and Former Occupation by Age (NI Basis) (continued)

	All persons	16 to 17	18 to 19	20 to 24	25 to 29	30 to 39	40 to 49	50 to 54	55 to 59	60 to 64	65 to 69	70 to 74
Males	**203842**	**18956**	**10805**	**15142**	**9840**	**22737**	**24662**	**14682**	**17629**	**21125**	**25759**	**22505**
Unemployed in the week before the Census	**34645**	**1779**	**2830**	**5277**	**4235**	**7845**	**6358**	**2810**	**2232**	**1112**	**113**	**54**
1. Managers and senior officials	1659	16	36	103	171	393	386	192	226	115	18	3
2. Professional occupations	879	6	26	86	158	176	156	101	110	50	7	3
3. Associate professional and technical occupations	2388	35	82	306	334	525	571	255	180	80	10	10
4. Administrative and secretarial occupations	1284	22	78	234	160	229	215	167	113	50	11	5
5. Skilled trades occupations	8381	208	485	1168	1016	2107	1823	715	552	290	11	6
6. Personal service occupations	556	14	31	77	77	127	107	60	43	17	3	-
7. Sales and customer service occupations	1412	116	212	410	199	198	136	69	46	26	-	-
8. Process, plant and machine operatives	5362	86	276	750	678	1312	1049	537	431	212	22	9
9. Elementary occupations	8007	280	619	1216	944	1969	1603	617	480	249	17	13
Never worked	4717	996	985	927	498	809	312	97	51	23	14	5
Economically inactive in the week before the Census	**169197**	**17177**	**7975**	**9865**	**5605**	**14892**	**18304**	**11872**	**15397**	**20013**	**25646**	**22451**
1. Managers and senior officials	11344	28	41	125	161	557	920	828	1491	2054	2714	2425
2. Professional occupations	7983	8	17	328	255	312	441	460	883	1448	2026	1805
3. Associate professional and technical occupations	10778	54	91	515	320	840	1266	914	1279	1680	2122	1697
4. Administrative and secretarial occupations	9565	60	85	352	221	600	1024	825	1088	1550	1995	1765
5. Skilled trades occupations	32564	152	252	1007	1091	3463	4582	2935	3558	4440	5866	5218
6. Personal service occupations	3108	36	51	153	101	305	382	237	288	384	660	511
7. Sales and customer service occupations	4566	471	517	693	213	389	377	216	275	387	523	505
8. Process, plant and machine operatives	24242	95	194	695	684	2210	3073	2217	2908	3812	4543	3811
9. Elementary occupations	26280	617	744	1419	916	2865	3749	2195	2742	3357	4083	3593
Never worked	38767	15656	5983	4578	1643	3351	2490	1045	885	901	1114	1121

S332

162

Table S332: Sex and Former Occupation by Age (NI Basis) (continued)

	All persons	16 to 17	18 to 19	20 to 24	25 to 29	30 to 39	40 to 49	50 to 54	55 to 59	60 to 64	65 to 69	70 to 74
Females	**296594**	**19950**	**13045**	**19359**	**16422**	**45461**	**39390**	**22437**	**25881**	**30627**	**32552**	**31470**
Unemployed in the week before the Census	**17846**	**1276**	**1942**	**3102**	**2201**	**4154**	**2966**	**1143**	**819**	**123**	**54**	**66**
1. Managers and senior officials	688	12	20	76	113	211	160	53	31	8	-	4
2. Professional occupations	590	3	8	52	83	144	139	74	73	11	-	3
3. Associate professional and technical occupations	1038	9	36	132	175	300	233	84	46	14	4	5
4. Administrative and secretarial occupations	2315	52	137	393	344	558	455	176	152	21	13	14
5. Skilled trades occupations	553	22	29	74	92	173	107	32	15	3	3	3
6. Personal service occupations	1957	57	192	416	254	532	303	109	79	7	5	3
7. Sales and customer service occupations	2728	197	389	631	324	577	358	141	96	12	-	3
8. Process, plant and machine operatives	1757	28	99	243	245	492	379	144	110	11	3	3
9. Elementary occupations	3317	204	332	579	353	773	604	260	165	28	12	7
Never worked	2903	692	700	506	218	394	228	70	52	8	14	21
Economically inactive in the week before the Census	**278748**	**18674**	**11103**	**16257**	**14221**	**41307**	**36424**	**21294**	**25062**	**30504**	**32498**	**31404**
1. Managers and senior officials	8705	32	32	195	496	1479	1167	765	999	1230	1194	1116
2. Professional occupations	11333	16	27	267	343	1106	1211	961	1457	2017	2096	1832
3. Associate professional and technical occupations	16034	39	90	513	669	2466	2551	1298	1804	2384	2317	1903
4. Administrative and secretarial occupations	37326	99	306	1241	1615	5412	5775	3063	3698	4977	5658	5482
5. Skilled trades occupations	9883	31	68	249	387	1600	1402	878	999	1291	1529	1449
6. Personal service occupations	21791	155	345	1544	2052	4675	3266	1967	2194	2108	1911	1574
7. Sales and customer service occupations	29341	884	1296	2505	2073	5740	3828	2272	2356	2793	2850	2744
8. Process, plant and machine operatives	32291	58	231	1093	1900	6000	5745	3176	3424	3746	3577	3341
9. Elementary occupations	47956	582	816	2072	1911	6269	6528	4382	5282	6605	7017	6492
Never worked	64088	16778	7892	6578	2775	6560	4951	2532	2849	3353	4349	5471

S332

Notes:
1   The occupation classification is SOC2000 (Standard Occupation Classification).
2   'Not in employment' includes all full-time students who are not in employment.
3   This table gives the former occupation of all persons aged 16-74 who have ever worked.

Table S035: Sex and Occupation by Employment Status and Hours Worked

Table population: All persons aged 16 to 74 in employment the week before the Census

| | All persons | Employee | | Self-employed | | | |
| | | | | Without employees | | With employees | |
		Part-time	Full-time	Part-time	Full-time	Part-time	Full-time
All persons	**686640**	**137141**	**450941**	**11847**	**45155**	**4260**	**37296**
1. Managers and senior officials	**72772**	**3853**	**51618**	**890**	**3530**	**1363**	**11518**
11. Corporate managers	52107	2795	43072	263	956	494	4527
12. Managers and proprietors in agriculture and services	20665	1058	8546	627	2574	869	6991
2. Professional occupations	**72509**	**7895**	**55010**	**1418**	**3269**	**456**	**4461**
21. Science and technology professionals	13665	384	11508	265	981	39	488
22. Health professionals	6896	484	3898	245	427	252	1590
23. Teaching and research professionals	35546	5885	28679	510	255	62	155
24. Business and public service professionals	16402	1142	10925	398	1606	103	2228
3. Associate professional and technical occupations	**86006**	**13381**	**64635**	**1956**	**3695**	**309**	**2030**
31. Science and technology associate professionals	11442	793	10256	53	236	6	98
32. Health and social welfare associate professionals	27655	9325	17448	381	257	73	171
33. Protective service occupations	11820	333	11437	10	19	3	18
34. Culture, media and sports occupations	8332	855	4565	925	1329	120	538
35. Business and public service associate professionals	26757	2075	20929	587	1854	107	1205
4. Administrative and secretarial occupations	**100099**	**21924**	**75926**	**561**	**566**	**401**	**721**
41. Administrative occupations	79189	15226	62248	432	489	255	539
42. Secretarial and related occupations	20910	6698	13678	129	77	146	182
5. Skilled trades occupations	**106899**	**7011**	**58999**	**3354**	**24780**	**709**	**12046**
51. Skilled agricultural trades	19362	418	2716	1686	11177	276	3089
52. Skilled metal and electrical trades	36277	1135	29484	412	3128	91	2027
53. Skilled construction and building trades	33164	1272	15755	992	9576	200	5369
54. Textiles, printing and other skilled trades	18096	4186	11044	264	899	142	1561
6. Personal service occupations	**45773**	**19085**	**21920**	**1201**	**1858**	**346**	**1363**
61. Caring personal service occupations	32743	15325	15261	759	1126	108	164
62. Leisure and other personal service occupations	13030	3760	6659	442	732	238	1199
7. Sales and customer service occupations	**50356**	**26860**	**21196**	**388**	**992**	**191**	**729**
71. Sales occupations	45875	25455	18137	385	988	191	719
72. Customer service occupations	4481	1405	3059	3	4	-	10
8. Process, plant and machine operatives	**71288**	**5026**	**57124**	**1197**	**4467**	**229**	**3245**
81. Process, plant and machine operatives	42804	3155	36062	220	1292	72	2003
82. Transport and mobile machine drivers and operatives	28484	1871	21062	977	3175	157	1242
9. Elementary occupations	**80938**	**32106**	**44513**	**882**	**1998**	**256**	**1183**
91. Elementary trades, plant and storage related occupations	28442	3375	22671	368	1330	79	619
92. Elementary administration and service occupations	52496	28731	21842	514	668	177	564

| | All persons | Employee | | Self-employed | | | |
| | | | | Without employees | | With employees | |
		Part-time	Full-time	Part-time	Full-time	Part-time	Full-time
Males	**377390**	**24296**	**273937**	**7021**	**39468**	**1737**	**30931**
1. Managers and senior officials	**47686**	**1000**	**34544**	**403**	**2601**	**439**	**8699**
11. Corporate managers	34568	645	29261	128	768	160	3606
12. Managers and proprietors in agriculture and services	13118	355	5283	275	1833	279	5093
2. Professional occupations	**38150**	**1705**	**29111**	**702**	**2665**	**196**	**3771**
21. Science and technology professionals	11251	169	9514	192	896	32	448
22. Health professionals	3972	78	2209	83	252	73	1277
23. Teaching and research professionals	12368	1244	10774	153	127	14	56
24. Business and public service professionals	10559	214	6614	274	1390	77	1990
3. Associate professional and technical occupations	**44483**	**1632**	**37002**	**1033**	**3002**	**153**	**1661**
31. Science and technology associate professionals	8683	251	8069	42	224	6	91
32. Health and social welfare associate professionals	3734	271	3168	86	122	14	73
33. Protective service occupations	10483	248	10185	10	19	3	18
34. Culture, media and sports occupations	5241	331	2934	514	993	65	404
35. Business and public service associate professionals	16342	531	12646	381	1644	65	1075
4. Administrative and secretarial occupations	**27065**	**1173**	**25011**	**149**	**310**	**43**	**379**
41. Administrative occupations	26331	1105	24387	146	305	40	348
42. Secretarial and related occupations	734	68	624	3	5	3	31
5. Skilled trades occupations	**96914**	**3360**	**54965**	**2817**	**23786**	**546**	**11440**
51. Skilled agricultural trades	17775	328	2571	1354	10430	210	2882
52. Skilled metal and electrical trades	35518	1059	28833	406	3119	91	2010
53. Skilled construction and building trades	32835	1220	15628	953	9544	179	5311
54. Textiles, printing and other skilled trades	10786	753	7933	104	693	66	1237
6. Personal service occupations	**6608**	**1004**	**4857**	**82**	**274**	**38**	**353**
61. Caring personal service occupations	2829	438	2292	23	57	-	19
62. Leisure and other personal service occupations	3779	566	2565	59	217	38	334
7. Sales and customer service occupations	**14066**	**4479**	**8062**	**199**	**763**	**47**	**516**
71. Sales occupations	12782	4259	7001	199	763	47	513
72. Customer service occupations	1284	220	1061	-	-	-	3
8. Process, plant and machine operatives	**58496**	**2726**	**47070**	**1046**	**4337**	**187**	**3130**
81. Process, plant and machine operatives	30877	1094	26435	146	1224	52	1926
82. Transport and mobile machine drivers and operatives	27619	1632	20635	900	3113	135	1204
9. Elementary occupations	**43922**	**7217**	**33315**	**590**	**1730**	**88**	**982**
91. Elementary trades, plant and storage related occupations	24169	2278	19917	248	1129	32	565
92. Elementary administration and service occupations	19753	4939	13398	342	601	56	417

S035

S035

Table S035: Sex and Occupation by Employment Status and Hours Worked (continued)

| | All persons | Employee | | Self-employed | | | |
| | | | | Without employees | | With employees | |
		Part-time	Full-time	Part-time	Full-time	Part-time	Full-time
Females	**309250**	**112845**	**177004**	**4826**	**5687**	**2523**	**6365**
1. Managers and senior officials	**25086**	**2853**	**17074**	**487**	**929**	**924**	**2819**
11. Corporate managers	17539	2150	13811	135	188	334	921
12. Managers and proprietors in agriculture and services	7547	703	3263	352	741	590	1898
2. Professional occupations	**34359**	**6190**	**25899**	**716**	**604**	**260**	**690**
21. Science and technology professionals	2414	215	1994	73	85	7	40
22. Health professionals	2924	406	1689	162	175	179	313
23. Teaching and research professionals	23178	4641	17905	357	128	48	99
24. Business and public service professionals	5843	928	4311	124	216	26	238
3. Associate professional and technical occupations	**41523**	**11749**	**27633**	**923**	**693**	**156**	**369**
31. Science and technology associate professionals	2759	542	2187	11	12	-	7
32. Health and social welfare associate professionals	23921	9054	14280	295	135	59	98
33. Protective service occupations	1337	85	1252	-	-	-	-
34. Culture, media and sports occupations	3091	524	1631	411	336	55	134
35. Business and public service associate professionals	10415	1544	8283	206	210	42	130
4. Administrative and secretarial occupations	**73034**	**20751**	**50915**	**412**	**256**	**358**	**342**
41. Administrative occupations	52858	14121	37861	286	184	215	191
42. Secretarial and related occupations	20176	6630	13054	126	72	143	151
5. Skilled trades occupations	**9985**	**3651**	**4034**	**537**	**994**	**163**	**606**
51. Skilled agricultural trades	1587	90	145	332	747	66	207
52. Skilled metal and electrical trades	759	76	651	6	9	-	17
53. Skilled construction and building trades	329	52	127	39	32	21	58
54. Textiles, printing and other skilled trades	7310	3433	3111	160	206	76	324
6. Personal service occupations	**39165**	**18081**	**17063**	**1119**	**1584**	**308**	**1010**
61. Caring personal service occupations	29914	14887	12969	736	1069	108	145
62. Leisure and other personal service occupations	9251	3194	4094	383	515	200	865
7. Sales and customer service occupations	**36290**	**22381**	**13134**	**189**	**229**	**144**	**213**
71. Sales occupations	33093	21196	11136	186	225	144	206
72. Customer service occupations	3197	1185	1998	3	4	-	7
8. Process, plant and machine operatives	**12792**	**2300**	**10054**	**151**	**130**	**42**	**115**
81. Process, plant and machine operatives	11927	2061	9627	74	68	20	77
82. Transport and mobile machine drivers and operatives	865	239	427	77	62	22	38
9. Elementary occupations	**37016**	**24889**	**11198**	**292**	**268**	**168**	**201**
91. Elementary trades, plant and storage related occupations	4273	1097	2754	120	201	47	54
92. Elementary administration and service occupations	32743	23792	8444	172	67	121	147

© Crown copyright 2003

Notes:
1   The occupation classification is SOC2000 (Standard Occupation Classification).
2   For the Census, part-time is defined as working 30 hours or less a week. Full-time is defined as working 31 or more hours a week.
3   'In employment' includes economically active full-time students in employment.

Table S040: Sex and Occupation by Hours Worked

Table population: All persons aged 16 to 74 in employment the week before the Census

	All persons	Part-time					Full-time				
		Total	1 to 2 hours	3 to 5 hours	6 to 15 hours	16 to 30 hours	Total	31 to 37 hours	38 to 48 hours	49 to 59 hours	60 or more hours
All persons	**686641**	**153247**	**577**	**5033**	**37887**	**109750**	**533394**	**135604**	**309446**	**47573**	**40771**
1. Managers and senior officials	**72772**	**6106**	**24**	**141**	**1099**	**4842**	**66666**	**10060**	**37402**	**11333**	**7871**
11. Corporate managers	52107	3552	9	78	557	2908	48555	7938	28408	8048	4161
12. Managers and proprietors in agriculture and services	20665	2554	15	63	542	1934	18111	2122	8994	3285	3710
2. Professional occupations	**72509**	**9769**	**156**	**431**	**2560**	**6622**	**62740**	**18062**	**31674**	**7678**	**5326**
21. Science and technology professionals	13665	688	12	24	132	520	12977	3283	8019	1033	642
22. Health professionals	6896	981	6	27	200	748	5915	652	2379	1188	1696
23. Teaching and research professionals	35546	6457	128	326	1946	4057	29089	10191	14187	3519	1192
24. Business and public service professionals	16402	1643	10	54	282	1297	14759	3936	7089	1938	1796
3. Associate professional and technical occupations	**86008**	**15647**	**73**	**355**	**2204**	**13015**	**70361**	**22449**	**38171**	**5359**	**4382**
31. Science and technology associate professionals	11444	854	3	20	136	695	10590	3762	6210	408	210
32. Health and social welfare associate professionals	27657	9781	24	128	1068	8561	17876	10052	7221	388	215
33. Protective service occupations	11820	345	5	18	102	220	11475	623	7002	1654	2196
34. Culture, media and sports occupations	8332	1900	33	113	473	1281	6432	1561	3662	688	521
35. Business and public service associate professionals	26755	2767	8	76	425	2258	23988	6451	14076	2221	1240
4. Administrative and secretarial occupations	**100098**	**22885**	**70**	**389**	**3562**	**18864**	**77213**	**34292**	**39217**	**2417**	**1287**
41. Administrative occupations	79189	15913	49	282	2425	13157	63276	27227	32767	2153	1129
42. Secretarial and related occupations	20909	6972	21	107	1137	5707	13937	7065	6450	264	158
5. Skilled trades occupations	**106897**	**11072**	**33**	**191**	**2165**	**8683**	**95825**	**12965**	**60339**	**9105**	**13416**
51. Skilled agricultural trades	19362	2380	16	53	687	1624	16982	955	4512	2195	9320
52. Skilled metal and electrical trades	36280	1641	11	39	208	1383	34639	6774	23449	2938	1478
53. Skilled construction and building trades	33161	2461	-	30	261	2170	30700	2767	23677	2625	1631
54. Textiles, printing and other skilled trades	18094	4590	6	69	1009	3506	13504	2469	8701	1347	987
6. Personal service occupations	**45773**	**20632**	**50**	**449**	**3829**	**16304**	**25141**	**11220**	**12091**	**1034**	**796**
61. Caring personal service occupations	32744	16193	43	301	2865	12984	16551	8592	6840	613	506
62. Leisure and other personal service occupations	13029	4439	7	148	964	3320	8590	2628	5251	421	290
7. Sales and customer service occupations	**50357**	**27439**	**30**	**928**	**9933**	**16548**	**22918**	**6251**	**14827**	**1081**	**759**
71. Sales occupations	45875	26031	30	915	9558	15528	19844	5076	13031	1008	729
72. Customer service occupations	4482	1408	-	13	375	1020	3074	1175	1796	73	30
8. Process, plant and machine operatives	**71289**	**6453**	**17**	**144**	**959**	**5333**	**64836**	**10106**	**44079**	**6319**	**4332**
81. Process, plant and machine operatives	42804	3447	8	77	554	2808	39357	7524	28090	2342	1401
82. Transport and mobile machine drivers and operatives	28485	3006	9	67	405	2525	25479	2582	15989	3977	2931
9. Elementary occupations	**80938**	**33244**	**124**	**2005**	**11576**	**19539**	**47694**	**10199**	**31646**	**3247**	**2602**
91. Elementary trades, plant and storage related occupations	28442	3822	14	118	855	2835	24620	3876	18172	1537	1035
92. Elementary administration and service occupations	52496	29422	110	1887	10721	16704	23074	6323	13474	1710	1567

S040

Table S040: Sex and Occupation by Hours Worked (continued)

	All persons	Part-time					Full-time				
		Total	1 to 2 hours	3 to 5 hours	6 to 15 hours	16 to 30 hours	Total	31 to 37 hours	38 to 48 hours	49 to 59 hours	60 or more hours
Males	**377389**	**33052**	**138**	**1003**	**8944**	**22967**	**344337**	**58194**	**211349**	**39736**	**35058**
1. Managers and senior officials	**47686**	**1842**	**10**	**42**	**418**	**1372**	**45844**	**4631**	**24984**	**9572**	**6657**
11. Corporate managers	34568	933	3	22	196	712	33635	3547	19402	6977	3709
12. Managers and proprietors in agriculture and services	13118	909	7	20	222	660	12209	1084	5582	2595	2948
2. Professional occupations	**38150**	**2603**	**54**	**139**	**712**	**1698**	**35547**	**7978**	**18273**	**5260**	**4036**
21. Science and technology professionals	11251	393	7	17	102	267	10858	2612	6699	968	579
22. Health professionals	3972	234	3	12	68	151	3738	283	1423	858	1174
23. Teaching and research professionals	12368	1411	34	76	394	907	10957	3168	5390	1760	639
24. Business and public service professionals	10559	565	10	34	148	373	9994	1915	4761	1674	1644
3. Associate professional and technical occupations	**44484**	**2819**	**16**	**124**	**645**	**2034**	**41665**	**8681**	**24594**	**4521**	**3869**
31. Science and technology associate professionals	8685	301	3	12	63	223	8384	2790	5039	373	182
32. Health and social welfare associate professionals	3736	373	3	19	74	277	3363	1510	1617	155	81
33. Protective service occupations	10482	260	5	12	92	151	10222	480	6162	1506	2074
34. Culture, media and sports occupations	5241	910	5	44	235	626	4331	910	2456	548	417
35. Business and public service associate professionals	16340	975	-	37	181	757	15365	2991	9320	1939	1115
4. Administrative and secretarial occupations	**27064**	**1364**	**3**	**51**	**346**	**964**	**25700**	**7935**	**15194**	**1727**	**844**
41. Administrative occupations	26331	1291	3	48	329	911	25040	7788	14818	1628	806
42. Secretarial and related occupations	733	73	-	3	17	53	660	147	376	99	38
5. Skilled trades occupations	**96910**	**6719**	**21**	**121**	**1139**	**5438**	**90191**	**11452**	**57336**	**8674**	**12729**
51. Skilled agricultural trades	17775	1892	13	38	559	1282	15883	853	4151	2029	8850
52. Skilled metal and electrical trades	35518	1556	8	36	194	1318	33962	6580	22999	2917	1466
53. Skilled construction and building trades	32833	2350	-	27	232	2091	30483	2740	23522	2608	1613
54. Textiles, printing and other skilled trades	10784	921	-	20	154	747	9863	1279	6664	1120	800
6. Personal service occupations	**6608**	**1124**	**3**	**46**	**224**	**851**	**5484**	**2143**	**2806**	**298**	**237**
61. Caring personal service occupations	2830	462	3	23	97	339	2368	995	1151	109	113
62. Leisure and other personal service occupations	3778	662	-	23	127	512	3116	1148	1655	189	124
7. Sales and customer service occupations	**14069**	**4727**	**6**	**169**	**2307**	**2245**	**9342**	**1670**	**6413**	**786**	**473**
71. Sales occupations	12782	4505	6	163	2219	2117	8277	1322	5745	752	458
72. Customer service occupations	1287	222	-	6	88	128	1065	348	668	34	15
8. Process, plant and machine operatives	**58496**	**3959**	**11**	**89**	**599**	**3260**	**54537**	**7759**	**36496**	**6089**	**4193**
81. Process, plant and machine operatives	30877	1292	5	35	262	990	29585	5307	20812	2163	1303
82. Transport and mobile machine drivers and operatives	27619	2667	6	54	337	2270	24952	2452	15684	3926	2890
9. Elementary occupations	**43922**	**7895**	**14**	**222**	**2554**	**5105**	**36027**	**5945**	**25253**	**2809**	**2020**
91. Elementary trades, plant and storage related occupations	24169	2558	8	75	569	1906	21611	3262	16093	1406	850
92. Elementary administration and service occupations	19753	5337	6	147	1985	3199	14416	2683	9160	1403	1170

Table S040: Sex and Occupation by Hours Worked (continued)

	All persons	Part-time					Full-time				
		Total	1 to 2 hours	3 to 5 hours	6 to 15 hours	16 to 30 hours	Total	31 to 37 hours	38 to 48 hours	49 to 59 hours	60 or more hours
Females	**309252**	**120195**	**439**	**4030**	**28943**	**86783**	**189057**	**77410**	**98097**	**7837**	**5713**
1. Managers and senior officials	**25086**	**4264**	**14**	**99**	**681**	**3470**	**20822**	**5429**	**12418**	**1761**	**1214**
11. Corporate managers	17539	2619	6	56	361	2196	14920	4391	9006	1071	452
12. Managers and proprietors in agriculture and services	7547	1645	8	43	320	1274	5902	1038	3412	690	762
2. Professional occupations	**34359**	**7166**	**102**	**292**	**1848**	**4924**	**27193**	**10084**	**13401**	**2418**	**1290**
21. Science and technology professionals	2414	295	5	7	30	253	2119	671	1320	65	63
22. Health professionals	2924	747	3	15	132	597	2177	369	956	330	522
23. Teaching and research professionals	23178	5046	94	250	1552	3150	18132	7023	8797	1759	553
24. Business and public service professionals	5843	1078	-	20	134	924	4765	2021	2328	264	152
3. Associate professional and technical occupations	**41524**	**12828**	**57**	**231**	**1559**	**10981**	**28696**	**13768**	**13577**	**838**	**513**
31. Science and technology associate professionals	2759	553	-	8	73	472	2206	972	1171	35	28
32. Health and social welfare associate professionals	23921	9408	21	109	994	8284	14513	8542	5604	233	134
33. Protective service occupations	1338	85	-	6	10	69	1253	143	840	148	122
34. Culture, media and sports occupations	3091	990	28	69	238	655	2101	651	1206	140	104
35. Business and public service associate professionals	10415	1792	8	39	244	1501	8623	3460	4756	282	125
4. Administrative and secretarial occupations	**73034**	**21521**	**67**	**338**	**3216**	**17900**	**51513**	**26357**	**24023**	**690**	**443**
41. Administrative occupations	52858	14622	46	234	2096	12246	38236	19439	17949	525	323
42. Secretarial and related occupations	20176	6899	21	104	1120	5654	13277	6918	6074	165	120
5. Skilled trades occupations	**9987**	**4353**	**12**	**70**	**1026**	**3245**	**5634**	**1513**	**3003**	**431**	**687**
51. Skilled agricultural trades	1587	488	3	15	128	342	1099	102	361	166	470
52. Skilled metal and electrical trades	762	85	3	3	14	65	677	194	450	21	12
53. Skilled construction and building trades	328	111	-	3	29	79	217	27	155	17	18
54. Textiles, printing and other skilled trades	7310	3669	6	49	855	2759	3641	1190	2037	227	187
6. Personal service occupations	**39165**	**19508**	**47**	**403**	**3605**	**15453**	**19657**	**9077**	**9285**	**736**	**559**
61. Caring personal service occupations	29914	15731	40	278	2768	12645	14183	7597	5689	504	393
62. Leisure and other personal service occupations	9251	3777	7	125	837	2808	5474	1480	3596	232	166
7. Sales and customer service occupations	**36288**	**22712**	**24**	**759**	**7626**	**14303**	**13576**	**4581**	**8414**	**295**	**286**
71. Sales occupations	33093	21526	24	752	7339	13411	11567	3754	7286	256	271
72. Customer service occupations	3195	1186	-	7	287	892	2009	827	1128	39	15
8. Process, plant and machine operatives	**12793**	**2494**	**6**	**55**	**360**	**2073**	**10299**	**2347**	**7583**	**230**	**139**
81. Process, plant and machine operatives	11927	2155	3	42	292	1818	9772	2217	7278	179	98
82. Transport and mobile machine drivers and operatives	866	339	3	13	68	255	527	130	305	51	41
9. Elementary occupations	**37016**	**25349**	**110**	**1783**	**9022**	**14434**	**11667**	**4254**	**6393**	**438**	**582**
91. Elementary trades, plant and storage related occupations	4273	1264	6	43	286	929	3009	614	2079	131	185
92. Elementary administration and service occupations	32743	24085	104	1740	8736	13505	8658	3640	4314	307	397

S040

Notes:
1 The occupation classification is SOC2000 (Standard Occupation Classification).
2 Hours worked is the average number of hours worked per week for the last four weeks before the Census (29 April 2001).
3 'In employment' includes economically active full-time students in employment.

Table S333: Sex and Occupation by Ethnic Group

Table population: All persons aged 16 to 74 in employment the week before the Census

	All persons	White	Irish Traveller	Mixed	Indian	Pakistani	Bangladeshi	Other Asian	Black Caribbean	Black African	Other Black	Chinese	Other ethnic group
All persons	**686604**	**681653**	**260**	**840**	**739**	**222**	**80**	**99**	**124**	**190**	**157**	**1739**	**501**
1. Managers and senior officials	**72768**	**72038**	**17**	**80**	**144**	**44**	**26**	**6**	**9**	**16**	**14**	**302**	**72**
11. Corporate managers	52107	51825	11	42	69	13	8	6	6	12	8	61	46
12. Managers and proprietors in agriculture and services	20661	20213	6	38	75	31	18	-	3	4	6	241	26
2. Professional occupations	**72506**	**71516**	**11**	**121**	**317**	**60**	**6**	**30**	**15**	**56**	**18**	**243**	**113**
21. Science and technology professionals	13664	13487	4	17	43	7	-	13	4	10	4	56	19
22. Health professionals	6900	6442	-	41	197	45	3	6	-	29	7	83	47
23. Teaching and research professionals	35539	35262	3	46	62	8	3	8	8	11	4	87	40
24. Business and public service professionals	16403	16325	4	17	15	-	3	3	3	6	3	17	7
3. Associate professional and technical occupations	**85991**	**85334**	**18**	**163**	**69**	**16**	**3**	**39**	**30**	**35**	**61**	**74**	**149**
31. Science and technology associate professionals	11437	11384	3	8	8	-	3	-	7	-	-	16	8
32. Health and social welfare associate professionals	27651	27392	3	36	15	3	-	36	8	18	5	23	112
33. Protective service occupations	11821	11688	3	39	4	3	-	-	10	4	53	3	14
34. Culture, media and sports occupations	8328	8241	5	40	12	-	-	-	-	6	3	16	5
35. Business and public service associate professionals	26754	26629	4	40	30	10	-	3	5	7	-	16	10
4. Administrative and secretarial occupations	**100093**	**99768**	**19**	**100**	**45**	**14**	**-**	**-**	**15**	**16**	**10**	**83**	**23**
41. Administrative occupations	79185	78920	16	78	29	14	-	-	12	13	10	76	17
42. Secretarial and related occupations	20908	20848	3	22	16	-	-	-	3	3	-	7	6
5. Skilled trades occupations	**106898**	**105916**	**56**	**94**	**33**	**22**	**23**	**3**	**13**	**12**	**9**	**664**	**53**
51. Skilled agricultural trades	19365	19334	9	7	-	-	-	-	3	3	-	6	3
52. Skilled metal and electrical trades	36270	36179	12	28	13	-	-	-	4	5	3	11	15
53. Skilled construction and building trades	33165	33096	22	30	4	-	-	-	-	-	3	7	3
54. Textiles, printing and other skilled trades	18098	17307	13	29	16	22	23	3	6	4	3	640	32
6. Personal service occupations	**45768**	**45594**	**33**	**43**	**20**	**6**	**-**	**6**	**9**	**17**	**8**	**18**	**14**
61. Caring personal service occupations	32741	32612	24	32	17	3	-	3	9	14	8	9	10
62. Leisure and other personal service occupations	13027	12982	9	11	3	3	-	3	-	3	-	9	4
7. Sales and customer service occupations	**50359**	**50035**	**25**	**81**	**55**	**27**	**4**	**6**	**13**	**6**	**8**	**87**	**12**
71. Sales occupations	45875	45582	25	65	52	24	4	3	10	6	8	84	12
72. Customer service occupations	4484	4453	-	16	3	3	-	3	3	-	-	3	-
8. Process, plant and machine operatives	**71285**	**71053**	**46**	**60**	**18**	**16**	**3**	**-**	**3**	**11**	**6**	**29**	**40**
81. Process, plant and machine operatives	42802	42633	28	38	12	11	3	-	3	8	6	23	37
82. Transport and mobile machine drivers and operatives	28483	28420	18	22	6	5	-	-	-	3	-	6	3
9. Elementary occupations	**80936**	**80399**	**35**	**98**	**38**	**17**	**15**	**9**	**17**	**21**	**23**	**239**	**25**
91. Elementary trades, plant and storage related occupations	28441	28352	14	18	6	5	3	-	3	3	13	24	-
92. Elementary administration and service occupations	52495	52047	21	80	32	12	12	9	14	18	10	215	25

	All persons	White	Irish Traveller	Mixed	Indian	Pakistani	Bangladeshi	Other Asian	Black Caribbean	Black African	Other Black	Chinese	Other ethnic group
Males	**377378**	**374380**	**172**	**472**	**469**	**165**	**65**	**39**	**80**	**122**	**113**	**1028**	**273**
1. Managers and senior officials	**47685**	**47168**	**14**	**54**	**101**	**41**	**20**	**6**	**6**	**12**	**8**	**192**	**63**
11. Corporate managers	34568	34357	8	29	50	13	5	6	3	8	5	42	42
12. Managers and proprietors in agriculture and services	13117	12811	6	25	51	28	15	-	3	4	3	150	21
2. Professional occupations	**38149**	**37457**	**11**	**68**	**223**	**46**	**6**	**21**	**8**	**56**	**12**	**166**	**75**
21. Science and technology professionals	11249	11105	4	12	39	7	-	10	4	10	4	38	16
22. Health professionals	3975	3648	-	31	137	34	3	3	-	29	4	50	36
23. Teaching and research professionals	12366	12186	3	17	41	5	-	8	4	11	4	68	19
24. Business and public service professionals	10559	10518	4	8	6	-	3	-	-	6	-	10	4
3. Associate professional and technical occupations	**44473**	**44150**	**15**	**88**	**34**	**10**	**-**	**6**	**23**	**15**	**53**	**27**	**52**
31. Science and technology associate professionals	8682	8642	3	8	5	-	-	-	7	4	-	9	8
32. Health and social welfare associate professionals	3730	3681	-	8	-	-	-	3	4	4	53	6	24
33. Protective service occupations	10486	10362	3	33	4	3	-	-	7	3	-	3	14
34. Culture, media and sports occupations	5236	5195	5	24	5	-	-	-	-	4	-	4	-
35. Business and public service associate professionals	16339	16270	4	15	20	7	-	3	5	5	3	5	6
4. Administrative and secretarial occupations	**27062**	**26964**	**7**	**36**	**14**	**6**	**-**	**-**	**9**	**5**	**3**	**14**	**4**
41. Administrative occupations	26330	26235	7	36	11	6	-	-	9	5	3	14	4
42. Secretarial and related occupations	732	729	-	-	3	-	-	-	-	-	-	-	-
5. Skilled trades occupations	**96919**	**96139**	**49**	**88**	**29**	**22**	**20**	**3**	**7**	**12**	**9**	**502**	**39**
51. Skilled agricultural trades	17777	17752	9	7	-	-	-	-	-	3	-	3	3
52. Skilled metal and electrical trades	35431	35431	12	28	13	-	-	-	4	5	3	6	15
53. Skilled construction and building trades	32837	32771	19	30	4	-	-	-	-	-	3	7	3
54. Textiles, printing and other skilled trades	10788	10185	9	23	12	22	20	3	3	4	3	486	18
6. Personal service occupations	**6602**	**6575**	**3**	**11**	**3**	**-**	**-**	**-**	**4**	**3**	**3**	**-**	**-**
61. Caring personal service occupations	2829	2809	-	7	3	-	-	-	4	3	3	-	-
62. Leisure and other personal service occupations	3773	3766	3	4	-	-	-	-	-	-	-	-	-
7. Sales and customer service occupations	**14070**	**13951**	**15**	**24**	**29**	**14**	**4**	**-**	**7**	**-**	**3**	**18**	**5**
71. Sales occupations	12782	12672	15	21	29	14	4	-	4	-	3	15	5
72. Customer service occupations	1288	1279	-	3	-	-	-	-	3	-	-	3	-
8. Process, plant and machine operatives	**58496**	**58316**	**39**	**49**	**14**	**13**	**3**	**3**	**3**	**8**	**6**	**16**	**29**
81. Process, plant and machine operatives	30878	30758	21	27	8	8	3	-	3	5	6	13	26
82. Transport and mobile machine drivers and operatives	27618	27558	18	22	6	5	-	-	-	3	-	3	3
9. Elementary occupations	**43922**	**43660**	**19**	**54**	**22**	**13**	**12**	**3**	**13**	**11**	**16**	**93**	**6**
91. Elementary trades, plant and storage related occupations	24168	24106	11	15	3	5	-	-	3	3	10	12	-
92. Elementary administration and service occupations	19754	19554	8	39	19	8	12	3	10	8	6	81	6

S333

S 3 3 3

Table S333: Sex and Occupation by Ethnic Group (continued)

	All persons	White	Irish Traveller	Mixed	Indian	Pakistani	Bangladeshi	Other Asian	Black Caribbean	Black African	Other Black	Chinese	Other ethnic group
Females	**309226**	**307273**	**88**	**368**	**270**	**57**	**15**	**60**	**44**	**68**	**44**	**711**	**228**
1. Managers and senior officials	**25083**	**24870**	**3**	**26**	**43**	**3**	**6**	-	**3**	**4**	**6**	**110**	**9**
11. Corporate managers	17539	17468	3	13	19	-	3	-	3	4	3	19	4
12. Managers and proprietors in agriculture and services	7544	7402	-	13	24	3	3	-	-	-	3	91	5
2. Professional occupations	**34357**	**34059**	-	**53**	**94**	**14**	-	**9**	**7**	-	**6**	**77**	**38**
21. Science and technology professionals	2415	2382	-	5	4	-	-	3	-	-	-	18	3
22. Health professionals	2925	2794	-	10	60	11	-	3	-	-	3	33	11
23. Teaching and research professionals	23173	23076	-	29	21	3	-	-	4	-	3	19	21
24. Business and public service professionals	5844	5807	-	9	9	-	-	3	3	-	3	7	3
3. Associate professional and technical occupations	**41518**	**41184**	**3**	**75**	**35**	**6**	**3**	**33**	**7**	**20**	**8**	**47**	**97**
31. Science and techology associate professionals	2755	2742	-	-	3	-	3	-	-	-	-	7	7
32. Health and social welfare associate professionals	23921	23711	3	28	15	3	-	33	4	14	5	17	88
33. Protective service occupations	1335	1326	-	6	-	-	-	-	3	-	-	-	-
34. Culture, media and sports occupations	3092	3046	-	16	7	-	-	-	-	3	3	12	5
35. Business and public service associate professionals	10415	10359	-	25	10	3	-	-	-	3	-	11	4
4. Administrative and secretarial occupations	**73031**	**72804**	**12**	**64**	**31**	**8**	-	-	**6**	**11**	**7**	**69**	**19**
41. Administrative occupations	52855	52685	9	42	18	8	-	-	3	8	7	62	13
42. Secretarial and related occupations	20176	20119	3	22	13	-	-	-	3	3	-	7	6
5. Skilled trades occupations	**9979**	**9777**	**7**	**6**	**4**	-	**3**	-	**6**	-	-	**162**	**14**
51. Skilled agricultural trades	1588	1582	-	-	-	-	-	-	3	-	-	3	3
52. Skilled metal and electrical trades	753	748	-	-	-	-	-	-	-	-	-	5	5
53. Skilled construction and building trades	328	325	3	-	-	-	-	-	-	-	-	-	-
54. Textiles, printing and other skilled trades	7310	7122	4	6	4	-	3	-	3	-	-	154	14
6. Personal service occupations	**39166**	**39019**	**30**	**32**	**17**	**6**	-	**6**	**5**	**14**	**5**	**18**	**14**
61. Caring personal service occupations	29912	29803	24	25	14	3	-	3	5	11	5	9	10
62. Leisure and other personal service occupations	9254	9216	6	7	3	3	-	3	-	3	-	9	4
7. Sales and customer service occupations	**36289**	**36084**	**10**	**57**	**26**	**13**	-	**6**	**6**	**6**	**5**	**69**	**7**
71. Sales occupations	33093	32910	10	44	23	10	-	3	6	6	5	69	7
72. Customer service occupations	3196	3174	-	13	3	3	-	3	-	-	-	-	-
8. Process, plant and machine operatives	**12789**	**12737**	**7**	**11**	**4**	**3**	**3**	-	-	**3**	-	**13**	**11**
81. Process, plant and machine operatives	11924	11875	7	11	4	3	3	-	-	3	-	10	11
82. Transport and mobile machine drivers and operatives	865	862	-	-	-	-	-	-	-	-	-	3	-
9. Elementary occupations	**37014**	**36739**	**16**	**44**	**16**	**4**	**3**	**6**	**4**	**10**	**7**	**146**	**19**
91. Elementary trades, plant and storage related occupations	4273	4246	3	3	3	-	3	-	-	-	3	12	-
92. Elementary administration and service occupations	32741	32493	13	41	13	4	-	6	4	10	4	134	19

Notes:

1   The occupation classification is SOC2000 (Standard Occupation Classification).
2   'In employment' includes economically active full-time students in employment.

Table S334: Occupation by Sex and Community Background (Religion or Religion Brought Up In)

Table population: All persons aged 16 to 74 in employment the week before the Census

	All persons	Males					Females				
		Total	Catholic	Protestant and Other Christian (including Christian related)	Other religions and philosophies	None	Total	Catholic	Protestant and Other Christian (including Christian related)	Other religions and philosophies	None
All persons	**686645**	**377391**	**149273**	**216776**	**1923**	**9419**	**309254**	**127253**	**175222**	**971**	**5808**
1. Managers and senior officials	**72772**	**47686**	**17421**	**28578**	**355**	**1332**	**25086**	**10020**	**14348**	**130**	**588**
11. Corporate managers	52107	34568	11936	21505	179	948	17539	7095	10014	53	377
12. Managers and proprietors in agriculture and services	20665	13118	5485	7073	176	384	7547	2925	4334	77	211
2. Professional occupations	**72509**	**38150**	**15879**	**20627**	**534**	**1110**	**34359**	**16257**	**17226**	**212**	**664**
21. Science and technology professionals	13665	11251	4261	6483	113	394	2414	1129	1189	13	83
22. Health professionals	6896	3972	1520	2105	245	102	2924	1228	1523	95	78
23. Teaching and research professionals	35546	12368	5879	5962	127	400	23178	10993	11716	83	386
24. Business and public service professionals	16402	10559	4219	6077	49	214	5843	2907	2798	21	117
3. Associate professional and technical occupations	**86007**	**44482**	**14312**	**28023**	**237**	**1910**	**41525**	**18280**	**22256**	**138**	**851**
31. Science and technology associate professionals	11443	8683	3232	5119	46	286	2760	1118	1562	10	70
32. Health and social welfare associate professionals	27655	3734	2072	1557	24	81	23921	11535	12052	58	276
33. Protective service occupations	11820	10482	1602	7959	56	865	1338	217	1006	8	107
34. Culture, media and sports occupations	8332	5241	1913	3005	43	280	3091	1175	1740	33	143
35. Business and public service associate professionals	26757	16342	5493	10383	68	398	10415	4235	5896	29	255
4. Administrative and secretarial occupations	**100098**	**27064**	**9539**	**16590**	**104**	**831**	**73034**	**28519**	**43090**	**151**	**1274**
41. Administrative occupations	79189	26331	9285	16132	100	814	52858	20829	30914	101	1014
42. Secretarial and related occupations	20909	733	254	458	4	17	20176	7690	12176	50	260
5. Skilled trades occupations	**106900**	**96914**	**41309**	**53575**	**294**	**1736**	**9986**	**3592**	**6090**	**52**	**252**
51. Skilled agricultural trades	19361	17775	5522	12110	11	132	1586	388	1194	-	4
52. Skilled metal and electrical trades	36280	35518	12751	21989	67	711	762	294	443	3	22
53. Skilled construction and building trades	33163	32835	18571	13897	12	355	328	127	192	-	9
54. Textiles, printing and other skilled trades	18096	10786	4465	5579	204	538	7310	2783	4261	49	217
6. Personal service occupations	**45773**	**6608**	**3221**	**3212**	**30**	**145**	**39165**	**16202**	**22255**	**66**	**642**
61. Caring personal service occupations	32743	2829	1435	1307	18	69	29914	12185	17221	47	461
62. Leisure and other personal service occupations	13030	3779	1786	1905	12	76	9251	4017	5034	19	181
7. Sales and customer service occupations	**50359**	**14069**	**5785**	**7807**	**87**	**390**	**36290**	**14572**	**20888**	**109**	**721**
71. Sales occupations	45875	12782	5253	7114	81	334	33093	13328	19044	93	628
72. Customer service occupations	4484	1287	532	693	6	56	3197	1244	1844	16	93
8. Process, plant and machine operatives	**71289**	**58496**	**23977**	**33399**	**142**	**978**	**12793**	**5055**	**7526**	**33**	**179**
81. Process, plant and machine operatives	42804	30877	12510	17746	90	531	11927	4713	7026	30	158
82. Transport and mobile machine drivers and operatives	28485	27619	11467	15653	52	447	866	342	500	3	21
9. Elementary occupations	**80938**	**43922**	**17830**	**24965**	**140**	**987**	**37016**	**14756**	**21543**	**80**	**637**
91. Elementary trades, plant and storage related occupations	28442	24169	9978	13769	28	394	4273	1650	2547	9	67
92. Elementary administration and service occupations	52496	19753	7852	11196	112	593	32743	13106	18996	71	570

Notes:

1 The occupation classification is SOC2000 (Standard Occupation Classification).

2 'In employment' includes economically active full-time students in employment.

S3334

Table S039: Occupation by Industry

Table population: All persons aged 16 to 74 in employment the week before the Census

	All persons	Agriculture, hunting and forestry	Fishing	Mining and quarrying	Manufacturing	Electricity, gas and water supply	Construction	Wholesale and retail trade, repairs	Hotels and restaurants	Transport, storage and communications	Financial intermediaries	Real estate, renting and business activities	Public administration and defence, social security	Education	Health and social work	Other
All persons	**686646**	**20068**	**659**	**2569**	**97365**	**4776**	**61751**	**114721**	**31033**	**37206**	**20386**	**53842**	**64025**	**60490**	**87502**	**30253**
1. Managers and senior officials	**72772**	**711**	**35**	**276**	**11013**	**455**	**3321**	**23171**	**5876**	**4352**	**3555**	**6235**	**5025**	**712**	**5065**	**2970**
11. Corporate managers	52107	135	4	246	9992	435	3076	16271	578	3423	3403	4154	4404	557	4402	1027
12. Managers and proprietors in agriculture and services	20665	576	31	30	1021	20	245	6900	5298	929	152	2081	621	155	663	1943
2. Professional occupations	**72512**	**472**	**7**	**58**	**3959**	**450**	**1940**	**1176**	**156**	**1066**	**619**	**11930**	**4630**	**33250**	**9654**	**3145**
21. Science and technology professionals	13665	405	4	45	3371	362	1187	376	63	896	396	4318	1065	424	516	237
22. Health professionals	6896	12	-	-	64	7	15	511	24	10	21	222	316	270	5382	59
23. Teaching and research professionals	35547	14	-	3	187	31	28	61	62	43	26	638	1230	31946	831	485
24. Business and public service professionals	16404	41	3	10	337	50	710	228	7	117	176	6752	2019	610	2925	2364
3. Associate professional and technical occupations	**86005**	**161**	**16**	**96**	**9423**	**564**	**1753**	**6797**	**481**	**2074**	**3499**	**9200**	**17593**	**3876**	**25763**	**4709**
31. Science and technology associate professionals	11443	38	-	37	3174	298	645	625	62	508	156	2190	1111	1691	646	262
32. Health and social welfare associate professionals	27653	14	-	-	322	11	45	382	84	44	165	1016	1075	688	23086	721
33. Protective service occupations	11820	9	-	-	75	8	5	66	13	150	20	150	11185	28	79	32
34. Culture, media and sports occupations	8332	13	-	6	1732	20	109	494	97	87	86	1546	480	397	423	2842
35. Business and public service associate professionals	26757	87	16	53	4120	227	949	5230	225	1285	3072	4298	3742	1072	1529	852
4. Administrative and secretarial occupations	**100098**	**407**	**14**	**185**	**6652**	**810**	**3199**	**8731**	**1199**	**4702**	**10462**	**12716**	**29107**	**5682**	**11979**	**4253**
41. Administrative occupations	79189	291	11	148	5142	745	2100	6795	731	4257	10000	8030	27075	3726	7102	3036
42. Secretarial and related occupations	20909	116	3	37	1510	65	1099	1936	468	445	462	4686	2032	1956	4877	1217
5. Skilled trades occupations	**106900**	**14385**	**522**	**315**	**23728**	**1147**	**35168**	**12816**	**7019**	**3028**	**338**	**2291**	**1211**	**1785**	**1480**	**1667**
51. Skilled agricultural trades	19362	12953	446	15	855	25	2258	1002	272	112	4	209	194	223	111	683
52. Skilled metal and electrical trades	36278	452	20	256	13870	1020	7431	7064	257	2647	299	1276	577	320	268	521
53. Skilled construction and building trades	33164	763	46	36	3708	89	24997	1554	284	178	20	492	180	368	217	232
54. Textiles, printing and other skilled trades	18096	217	10	8	5295	13	482	3196	6206	91	15	314	260	874	884	231
6. Personal service occupations	**45772**	**230**	**-**	**-**	**127**	**10**	**70**	**406**	**720**	**1897**	**59**	**979**	**1146**	**8279**	**24116**	**7733**
61. Caring personal service occupations	32743	176	-	-	51	7	35	189	162	175	45	567	728	6315	23154	1139
62. Leisure and other personal service occupations	13029	54	-	-	76	3	35	217	558	1722	14	412	418	1964	962	6594
7. Sales and customer service occupations	**50361**	**60**	**3**	**16**	**1148**	**237**	**221**	**40397**	**1665**	**1917**	**1281**	**1631**	**397**	**172**	**415**	**801**
71. Sales occupations	45875	57	3	13	903	137	200	39079	1526	549	777	1226	257	154	314	680
72. Customer service occupations	4486	3	-	3	245	100	21	1318	139	1368	504	405	140	18	101	121
8. Process, plant and machine operatives	**71288**	**498**	**25**	**1500**	**31710**	**778**	**9231**	**8681**	**497**	**12143**	**140**	**2043**	**1324**	**774**	**784**	**1160**
81. Process, plant and machine operatives	42804	156	13	683	27960	618	5547	3711	295	1120	106	1038	648	172	317	420
82. Transport and mobile machine drivers and operatives	28484	342	12	817	3750	160	3684	4970	202	11023	34	1005	676	602	467	740
9. Elementary occupations	**80938**	**3144**	**37**	**123**	**9605**	**325**	**6848**	**12546**	**13420**	**6027**	**433**	**6817**	**3592**	**5960**	**8246**	**3815**
91. Elementary trades, plant and storage related occupations	28442	2924	37	93	7937	234	6120	6007	577	1481	89	1046	750	227	480	440
92. Elementary administration and service occupations	52496	220	-	30	1668	91	728	6539	12843	4546	344	5771	2842	5733	7766	3375

Notes:

1 The industry categorisation is based on the 'UK Standard Industrial Classifications of Economic Activities 1992' (SIC92).

2 'Other' industry includes other community, social and personal service activities, private households with employed persons and extra-territorial organisations and bodies.

3 The occupation classification is SOC2000 (Standard Occupation Classification).

4 'In employment' includes economically active full-time students in employment.

S039

Table S036: Sex and Industry by Age

Table population: All persons aged 16 to 74 in employment the week before the Census

	All persons	16 to 17	18 to 19	20 to 24	25 to 29	30 to 39	40 to 49	50 to 54	55 to 59	60 to 64	65 to 69	70 to 74
All persons	**686642**	**14556**	**24789**	**74882**	**88444**	**188958**	**155747**	**61307**	**45220**	**21834**	**7025**	**3880**
A. Agriculture, hunting and forestry	20066	246	378	1212	1792	4249	4296	2080	2071	1689	1234	819
B. Fishing	654	10	14	46	80	203	146	64	51	26	6	8
C. Mining and quarrying	2572	20	51	194	295	709	585	254	248	160	37	19
D. Manufacturing	97365	1606	3146	11819	14643	28196	20043	7608	6114	3061	736	393
E. Electricity, gas and water supply	4776	40	95	374	416	1232	1484	544	398	148	31	14
F. Construction	61751	2105	3398	7532	7500	16466	12889	5240	3729	1922	646	324
G. Wholesale and retail trade, repairs	114721	5087	8187	17087	14641	28638	20379	8534	6734	3472	1261	701
H. Hotels and restaurants	31033	1952	2452	4703	3346	7587	5853	2261	1695	786	249	149
I. Transport, storage and communications	37206	303	777	3659	5193	11342	8516	3426	2454	1178	233	125
J. Financial intermediaries	20386	134	457	3072	3532	5623	5037	1262	823	322	90	34
K. Real estate, renting and business activities	53842	518	1187	6528	8849	14613	11484	4550	3434	1743	637	299
L. Public administration and defence, social security	64025	297	1166	5591	7662	21749	16827	5388	3721	1219	266	139
M. Education	60490	761	643	3160	6419	14751	17992	8314	5280	2324	542	304
N. Health and social work	87502	687	1574	6596	10330	25689	23756	9167	6241	2594	587	281
O,P,Q. Other	30253	790	1264	3309	3746	7911	6460	2615	2227	1190	470	271
Males	**377391**	**8204**	**13746**	**39771**	**46788**	**103180**	**84456**	**33802**	**25956**	**14276**	**4647**	**2565**
A. Agriculture, hunting and forestry	17185	218	331	1118	1629	3725	3685	1721	1663	1353	1032	710
B. Fishing	633	10	14	46	77	196	138	61	51	26	6	8
C. Mining and quarrying	2341	17	45	167	253	636	547	240	235	153	33	15
D. Manufacturing	72348	1291	2455	8620	10375	20911	15062	5692	4617	2520	525	280
E. Electricity, gas and water supply	3931	33	76	252	288	971	1281	502	347	139	28	14
F. Construction	57502	2041	3261	7036	6942	15314	11969	4819	3425	1808	594	293
G. Wholesale and retail trade, repairs	59812	2330	3827	8347	7618	15232	10753	4572	3711	2267	748	407
H. Hotels and restaurants	12384	865	1073	2158	1549	2963	2010	739	560	287	116	64
I. Transport, storage and communications	27537	179	431	2073	3312	8475	6888	2803	2072	1031	178	95
J. Financial intermediaries	8159	41	124	902	1179	2182	2240	673	498	235	62	23
K. Real estate, renting and business activities	29989	247	519	3030	4622	8063	6712	2774	2143	1237	446	196
L. Public administration and defence, social security	37605	178	752	3259	4266	12368	10123	3311	2295	786	183	84
M. Education	18091	411	243	679	1496	3900	5266	2871	1890	975	225	135
N. Health and social work	15676	114	202	911	1764	4656	4394	1617	1140	652	154	72
O,P,Q. Other	14198	229	393	1173	1418	3588	3388	1407	1309	807	317	169

© Crown copyright 2003

	All persons	16 to 17	18 to 19	20 to 24	25 to 29	30 to 39	40 to 49	50 to 54	55 to 59	60 to 64	65 to 69	70 to 74
Females	**309251**	**6352**	**11043**	**35111**	**41656**	**85778**	**71291**	**27505**	**19264**	**7558**	**2378**	**1315**
A. Agriculture, hunting and forestry	2881	28	47	94	163	524	611	359	408	336	202	109
B. Fishing	21	-	-	-	3	7	8	3	-	-	-	-
C. Mining and quarrying	231	3	6	27	42	73	38	14	13	7	4	4
D. Manufacturing	25017	315	691	3199	4268	7285	4981	1916	1497	541	211	113
E. Electricity, gas and water supply	845	7	19	122	128	261	203	42	51	9	3	-
F. Construction	4249	64	137	496	558	1152	920	421	304	114	52	31
G. Wholesale and retail trade, repairs	54909	2757	4360	8740	7023	13406	9626	3962	3023	1205	513	294
H. Hotels and restaurants	18649	1087	1379	2545	1797	4624	3843	1522	1135	499	133	85
I. Transport, storage and communications	9669	124	346	1586	1881	2867	1628	623	382	147	55	30
J. Financial intermediaries	12227	93	333	2170	2353	3441	2797	589	325	87	28	11
K. Real estate, renting and business activities	23853	271	668	3498	4227	6550	4772	1776	1291	506	191	103
L. Public administration and defence, social security	26420	119	414	2332	3396	9381	6704	2077	1426	433	83	55
M. Education	42399	350	400	2481	4923	10851	12726	5443	3390	1349	317	169
N. Health and social work	71826	573	1372	5685	8566	21033	19362	7550	5101	1942	433	209
O,P,Q. Other	16055	561	871	2136	2328	4323	3072	1208	918	383	153	102

Notes:
1 The industry categorisation is based on the 'UK Standard Industrial Classifications of Economic Activities 1992' (SIC92).
2 'Other' industry includes other community, social and personal service activities, private households with employed persons and extra-territorial organisations and bodies.
3 'In employment' includes economically active full-time students in employment.

S036

Table S037: Sex and Former Industry by Age (UK Basis)

Table population: All persons aged 16 to 64 in not employment the week before the Census

	All persons	16 to 17	18 to 19	20 to 24	25 to 29	30 to 39	40 to 49	50 to 54	55 to 59	60 to 64
All persons	388157	38904	23855	34501	26260	68199	64052	37119	43512	51755
Unemployed in the week before the Census	52202	3049	4776	8378	6434	11999	9324	3953	3051	1238
A. Agriculture, hunting and forestry	848	14	34	107	110	259	196	72	36	20
B. Fishing	88	-	3	9	9	33	19	5	7	3
C. Mining and quarrying	139	6	9	24	25	35	16	12	7	5
D. Manufacturing	6413	178	540	1250	1022	1459	1045	409	351	159
E. Electricity, gas and water supply	203	-	7	20	12	39	36	43	34	12
F. Construction	5444	131	326	912	755	1482	1074	373	257	134
G. Wholesale and retail trade, repairs	7293	460	943	1696	1000	1537	888	398	276	95
H. Hotels and restaurants	2984	252	442	781	403	600	325	102	57	22
I. Transport, storage and communications	1992	63	122	299	258	540	377	159	117	57
J. Financial intermediaries	430	6	22	83	73	76	81	49	27	13
K. Real estate, renting and business activities	2234	68	144	399	437	529	368	137	114	38
L. Public administration and defence, social security	1424	28	37	240	164	275	301	199	123	57
M. Education	1785	40	125	244	232	403	353	182	152	54
N. Health and social work	2681	52	171	435	340	738	528	224	145	48
O,P,Q. Other	1921	63	166	381	273	435	361	119	90	33
Never worked or last worked before 1996	16323	1688	1685	1498	1321	3559	3356	1470	1258	488
Economically inactive in the week before the Census	335955	35855	19079	26123	19826	56200	54728	33166	40461	50517
A. Agriculture, hunting and forestry	1857	42	59	141	120	313	319	180	291	392
B. Fishing	162	3	3	6	6	32	35	13	39	25
C. Mining and quarrying	343	3	18	38	28	50	38	32	52	84
D. Manufacturing	16528	248	558	2214	2069	3601	2300	1347	1693	2498
E. Electricity, gas and water supply	923	3	6	41	20	91	117	178	243	224
F. Construction	7568	141	224	871	659	1640	1414	730	869	1020
G. Wholesale and retail trade, repairs	23962	1528	2137	4034	2647	4900	2930	1647	1844	2295
H. Hotels and restaurants	9553	758	929	1881	960	1885	1168	627	607	738
I. Transport, storage and communications	5003	110	142	488	412	997	843	539	664	808
J. Financial intermediaries	2330	13	31	253	238	476	372	241	358	348
K. Real estate, renting and business activities	7149	100	246	1159	794	1528	1020	603	724	975
L. Public administration and defence, social security	7376	30	67	364	361	1173	1263	1053	1318	1747
M. Education	9761	74	133	620	626	1544	1526	1150	1783	2305
N. Health and social work	16472	159	348	1470	1579	3548	2852	1716	2148	2652
O,P,Q. Other	5451	209	303	844	667	1263	736	443	406	580
Never worked or last worked before 1996	221517	32434	13875	11699	8640	33159	37795	22667	27422	33826

	All persons	16 to 17	18 to 19	20 to 24	25 to 29	30 to 39	40 to 49	50 to 54	55 to 59	60 to 64
Males	**155584**	**18959**	**10806**	**15142**	**9840**	**22737**	**24662**	**14682**	**17629**	**21127**
Unemployed in the week before the Census	**34479**	**1777**	**2831**	**5277**	**4235**	**7845**	**6358**	**2810**	**2232**	**1114**
A. Agriculture, hunting and forestry	764	11	27	91	98	239	181	64	33	20
B. Fishing	88	-	3	9	9	33	19	5	7	3
C. Mining and quarrying	121	3	6	19	21	32	16	12	7	5
D. Manufacturing	4909	137	405	949	775	1079	829	307	276	152
E. Electricity, gas and water supply	174	-	4	14	12	34	27	40	31	12
F. Construction	5257	126	311	881	723	1428	1041	360	253	134
G. Wholesale and retail trade, repairs	4240	225	501	981	590	898	535	246	182	82
H. Hotels and restaurants	1493	116	236	367	208	301	167	56	27	15
I. Transport, storage and communications	1574	40	90	219	179	433	320	138	101	54
J. Financial intermediaries	208	-	13	38	32	24	34	33	24	10
K. Real estate, renting and business activities	1362	36	72	224	276	336	215	87	78	38
L. Public administration and defence, social security	973	16	17	134	97	158	234	164	100	53
M. Education	760	33	60	99	88	149	140	83	74	34
N. Health and social work	828	13	41	107	120	233	165	67	56	26
O,P,Q. Other	1110	25	60	178	155	261	261	80	60	30
Never worked or last worked before 1996	10618	996	985	967	852	2207	2174	1068	923	446
Economically inactive in the week before the Census	**121105**	**17182**	**7975**	**9865**	**5605**	**14892**	**18304**	**11872**	**15397**	**20013**
A. Agriculture, hunting and forestry	1434	21	39	94	79	231	260	144	258	308
B. Fishing	151	3	3	6	6	29	30	13	36	25
C. Mining and quarrying	310	3	10	35	25	44	34	32	47	80
D. Manufacturing	7816	152	283	952	732	1315	1137	708	1004	1533
E. Electricity, gas and water supply	742	3	3	23	15	50	91	152	209	196
F. Construction	6720	112	193	769	564	1435	1289	657	773	928
G. Wholesale and retail trade, repairs	7328	618	741	1224	552	999	1028	530	712	924
H. Hotels and restaurants	2406	322	323	532	203	331	256	139	154	146
I. Transport, storage and communications	3278	76	70	231	184	532	608	416	527	634
J. Financial intermediaries	847	9	14	79	30	43	101	131	215	225
K. Real estate, renting and business activities	2746	53	87	468	283	375	374	273	338	495
L. Public administration and defence, social security	4091	17	27	153	126	428	656	748	925	1011
M. Education	2312	30	37	190	126	211	263	254	466	735
N. Health and social work	1878	44	63	196	133	316	347	199	256	324
O,P,Q. Other	1579	63	99	209	114	251	267	141	183	252
Never worked or last worked before 1996	77467	15656	5983	4704	2433	8302	11563	7335	9294	12197

S037

S037

Table S037: Sex and Former Industry by Age (UK Basis) (continued)

	All persons	16 to 17	18 to 19	20 to 24	25 to 29	30 to 39	40 to 49	50 to 54	55 to 59	60 to 64
Females	**232573**	**19945**	**13049**	**19359**	**16420**	**45462**	**39390**	**22437**	**25883**	**30628**
Unemployed in the week before the Census	**17723**	**1272**	**1945**	**3101**	**2199**	**4154**	**2966**	**1143**	**819**	**124**
A. Agriculture, hunting and forestry	84	3	7	16	12	20	15	8	3	-
B. Fishing	-	-	-	-	-	-	-	-	-	-
C. Mining and quarrying	18	3	3	5	4	3	-	-	-	-
D. Manufacturing	1504	41	135	301	247	380	216	102	75	7
E. Electricity, gas and water supply	29	-	3	6	-	5	9	3	3	-
F. Construction	187	5	15	31	32	54	33	13	4	-
G. Wholesale and retail trade, repairs	3053	235	442	715	410	639	353	152	94	13
H. Hotels and restaurants	1491	136	206	414	195	299	158	46	30	7
I. Transport, storage and communications	418	23	32	80	79	107	57	21	16	3
J. Financial intermediaries	222	6	9	45	41	52	47	16	3	3
K. Real estate, renting and business activities	872	32	72	175	161	193	153	50	36	4
L. Public administration and defence, social security	451	12	20	106	67	117	67	35	23	-
M. Education	1025	7	65	145	144	254	213	99	78	20
N. Health and social work	1853	39	130	328	220	505	363	157	89	22
O,P,Q. Other	811	38	106	203	118	174	100	39	30	3
Never worked or last worked before 1996	5705	692	700	531	469	1352	1182	402	335	42
Economically inactive in the week before the Census	**214850**	**18673**	**11104**	**16258**	**14221**	**41308**	**36424**	**21294**	**25064**	**30504**
A. Agriculture, hunting and forestry	423	21	20	47	41	82	59	36	33	84
B. Fishing	11	-	-	3	-	3	5	-	3	-
C. Mining and quarrying	33	-	8	3	3	6	4	-	5	4
D. Manufacturing	8712	96	275	1262	1337	2286	1163	639	689	965
E. Electricity, gas and water supply	181	-	3	18	5	41	26	26	34	28
F. Construction	848	29	31	102	95	205	125	73	96	92
G. Wholesale and retail trade, repairs	16634	910	1396	2810	2095	3901	1902	1117	1132	1371
H. Hotels and restaurants	7147	436	606	1349	757	1554	912	488	453	592
I. Transport, storage and communications	1725	34	72	257	228	465	235	123	137	174
J. Financial intermediaries	1483	4	17	174	208	433	271	110	143	123
K. Real estate, renting and business activities	4403	47	159	691	511	1153	646	330	386	480
L. Public administration and defence, social security	3285	13	40	211	235	745	607	305	393	736
M. Education	7449	44	96	430	500	1333	1263	896	1317	1570
N. Health and social work	14594	115	285	1274	1446	3232	2505	1517	1892	2328
O,P,Q. Other	3872	146	204	635	553	1012	469	302	223	328
Never worked or last worked before 1996	144050	16778	7892	6995	6207	24857	26232	15332	18128	21629

Notes:
1   The industry categorisation used is based on the 'UK Standard Industrial Classification of Economic Activities 1992' (SIC 92).
2   'Other' industry includes other community, social and personal service activities, private households with employed persons and extra-territorial organisations and bodies.
3   'Not in employment' includes all full-time students who are not in employment.
4   This table gives the former industry of all persons aged 16-64 who last worked between 1996 and 2001.

Table S335: Sex and Former Industry by Age (NI Basis)

Table population: All persons aged 16 to 74 not in employment the week before the Census

	All persons	16 to 17	18 to 19	20 to 24	25 to 29	30 to 39	40 to 49	50 to 54	55 to 59	60 to 64	65 to 69	70 to 74
All persons	500441	38904	23855	34501	26262	68198	64052	37119	43511	51753	58315	53971
Unemployed in the week before the Census	52492	3049	4776	8378	6436	11999	9324	3953	3050	1236	173	118
A. Agriculture, hunting and forestry	1062	14	34	108	128	317	252	103	62	38	3	3
B. Fishing	105	-	3	9	9	38	23	5	15	3	-	-
C. Mining and quarrying	195	6	9	24	27	42	41	27	12	7	-	-
D. Manufacturing	8419	178	540	1264	1158	1936	1668	736	621	280	24	14
E. Electricity, gas and water supply	264	-	7	20	17	43	52	47	48	27	3	-
F. Construction	7201	131	326	918	831	1903	1689	661	478	240	19	5
G. Wholesale and retail trade, repairs	8890	460	943	1713	1138	2032	1376	604	441	151	20	12
H. Hotels and restaurants	3507	252	442	793	454	761	474	164	121	43	3	-
I. Transport, storage and communications	2418	63	122	301	269	626	506	229	200	86	11	5
J. Financial intermediaries	515	6	22	84	79	92	111	58	41	19	-	3
K. Real estate, renting and business activities	2679	68	144	401	471	642	498	202	167	61	16	9
L. Public administration and defence, social security	1805	28	37	242	184	356	419	254	182	78	11	14
M. Education	2121	40	125	249	255	491	446	223	203	71	10	8
N. Health and social work	3336	52	171	436	390	942	741	304	212	58	14	16
O,P,Q. Other	2355	63	166	383	310	575	488	169	144	43	11	3
Never worked	7620	1688	1685	1433	716	1203	540	167	103	31	28	26
Economically inactive in the week before the Census	447949	35855	19079	26123	19826	56199	54728	33166	40461	50517	58142	53853
A. Agriculture, hunting and forestry	6680	42	59	144	156	583	783	474	709	1012	1347	1371
B. Fishing	449	3	3	6	7	60	73	54	70	57	63	53
C. Mining and quarrying	1139	3	18	38	33	87	114	79	132	198	228	209
D. Manufacturing	69770	248	558	2343	3111	9138	10091	6135	7408	9500	10970	10268
E. Electricity, gas and water supply	3733	3	6	41	25	150	313	340	512	745	866	732
F. Construction	24366	141	224	901	838	3030	3852	2451	2801	3236	3774	3118
G. Wholesale and retail trade, repairs	64181	1528	2137	4192	3778	10834	8857	5163	5713	6854	7808	7317
H. Hotels and restaurants	20519	758	929	1943	1285	3621	2799	1562	1638	2028	2061	1895
I. Transport, storage and communications	15422	110	142	493	490	1586	1957	1334	1863	2345	2711	2391
J. Financial intermediaries	6798	13	31	256	275	819	1102	573	827	943	1037	922
K. Real estate, renting and business activities	18352	100	246	1173	993	2693	2500	1445	1774	2248	2739	2441
L. Public administration and defence, social security	23493	30	67	366	477	2110	3012	2091	2840	3989	4485	4026
M. Education	27699	74	133	651	806	2446	2867	2241	3433	4785	5493	4770
N. Health and social work	47123	159	348	1521	2093	6410	6830	4351	5603	6691	7129	5988
O,P,Q. Other	15370	209	303	899	1041	2721	2137	1296	1404	1632	1968	1760
Never worked	102855	32434	13875	11156	4418	9911	7441	3577	3734	4254	5463	6592

Table S335: Sex and Former Industry by Age (NI Basis) (continued)

	All persons	16 to 17	18 to 19	20 to 24	25 to 29	30 to 39	40 to 49	50 to 54	55 to 59	60 to 64	65 to 69	70 to 74
Males	203850	18959	10806	15142	9840	22737	24662	14682	17629	21127	25760	22506
Unemployed in the week before the Census	34648	1777	2831	5277	4235	7845	6358	2810	2232	1114	114	55
A. Agriculture, hunting and forestry	954	11	27	92	114	293	230	87	59	38	-	3
B. Fishing	105	-	3	9	9	38	23	5	15	3	-	-
C. Mining and quarrying	174	3	6	19	23	39	38	27	12	7	-	-
D. Manufacturing	6227	137	405	955	860	1345	1212	547	474	266	19	7
E. Electricity, gas and water supply	230	-	4	14	14	37	42	44	45	27	3	-
F. Construction	6967	126	311	887	794	1833	1642	647	466	240	16	5
G. Wholesale and retail trade, repairs	5132	225	501	993	665	1135	792	378	290	132	14	7
H. Hotels and restaurants	1747	116	236	372	226	368	238	85	70	33	3	-
I. Transport, storage and communications	1938	40	90	221	187	506	425	200	173	83	8	5
J. Financial intermediaries	253	-	13	39	34	32	44	38	35	15	-	3
K. Real estate, renting and business activities	1654	36	72	225	296	398	302	133	118	56	12	6
L. Public administration and defence, social security	1227	16	17	135	106	209	307	206	147	72	7	5
M. Education	947	33	60	104	104	192	185	107	102	50	7	3
N. Health and social work	1012	13	41	107	131	284	231	93	77	29	3	3
O,P,Q. Other	1364	25	60	178	174	327	335	116	98	40	8	3
Never worked	4717	996	985	927	498	809	312	97	51	23	14	5
Economically inactive in the week before the Census	169202	17182	7975	9865	5605	14892	18304	11872	15397	20013	25646	22451
A. Agriculture, hunting and forestry	5154	21	39	95	104	440	617	377	602	759	1049	1051
B. Fishing	420	3	3	6	7	53	65	48	67	52	63	53
C. Mining and quarrying	1021	3	10	35	29	77	103	76	113	179	207	189
D. Manufacturing	26911	152	283	989	924	2320	3093	1967	2773	4041	5360	5009
E. Electricity, gas and water supply	2950	3	3	23	17	69	200	269	426	624	715	601
F. Construction	21928	112	193	796	717	2627	3469	2228	2528	2930	3527	2801
G. Wholesale and retail trade, repairs	18528	618	741	1257	697	1839	2300	1401	1707	2197	3066	2705
H. Hotels and restaurants	4475	322	323	542	261	565	575	316	373	380	431	387
I. Transport, storage and communications	10552	76	70	231	204	777	1259	958	1393	1771	2058	1755
J. Financial intermediaries	2401	9	14	79	32	74	192	190	343	458	538	472
K. Real estate, renting and business activities	6896	53	87	471	319	609	793	528	687	956	1289	1104
L. Public administration and defence, social security	11731	17	27	154	170	707	1292	1205	1636	2152	2441	1930
M. Education	7015	30	37	197	164	374	488	443	808	1265	1724	1485
N. Health and social work	5526	44	63	201	170	551	729	435	547	712	1083	991
O,P,Q. Other	4927	63	99	211	147	459	639	386	509	636	981	797
Never worked	38767	15656	5983	4578	1643	3351	2490	1045	885	901	1114	1121

S335

Table S335: Sex and Former Industry by Age (NI Basis) (continued)

	All persons	16 to 17	18 to 19	20 to 24	25 to 29	30 to 39	40 to 49	50 to 54	55 to 59	60 to 64	65 to 69	70 to 74
Females	**296591**	**19945**	**13049**	**19359**	**16422**	**45461**	**39390**	**22437**	**25882**	**30626**	**32555**	**31465**
Unemployed in the week before the Census	**17844**	**1272**	**1945**	**3101**	**2201**	**4154**	**2966**	**1143**	**818**	**122**	**59**	**63**
A. Agriculture, hunting and forestry	108	3	7	16	14	24	22	16	3	-	3	-
B. Fishing	-	-	-	-	-	-	-	-	-	-	-	-
C. Mining and quarrying	21	3	3	5	-	3	3	-	-	-	-	-
D. Manufacturing	2192	41	135	309	298	591	456	189	147	14	5	7
E. Electricity, gas and water supply	34	-	3	6	3	6	10	3	3	-	-	-
F. Construction	234	5	15	31	37	70	47	14	12	-	3	-
G. Wholesale and retail trade, repairs	3758	235	442	720	473	897	584	226	151	19	6	5
H. Hotels and restaurants	1760	136	206	421	228	393	236	79	51	10	-	-
I. Transport, storage and communications	480	23	32	80	82	120	81	29	27	3	3	-
J. Financial intermediaries	262	6	9	45	45	60	67	20	6	4	-	-
K. Real estate, renting and business activities	1025	32	72	176	175	244	196	69	49	5	4	3
L. Public administration and defence, social security	578	12	20	107	78	147	112	48	35	6	4	9
M. Education	1174	7	65	145	151	299	261	116	101	21	3	5
N. Health and social work	2324	39	130	329	259	658	510	211	135	29	11	13
O,P,Q. Other	991	38	106	205	136	248	153	53	46	3	3	-
Never worked	2903	692	700	506	218	394	228	70	52	8	14	21
Economically inactive in the week before the Census	**278747**	**18673**	**11104**	**16258**	**14221**	**41307**	**36424**	**21294**	**25064**	**30504**	**32496**	**31402**
A. Agriculture, hunting and forestry	1526	21	20	49	52	143	166	97	107	253	298	320
B. Fishing	29	-	-	-	-	7	8	6	3	5	-	-
C. Mining and quarrying	118	-	8	3	4	10	11	3	19	19	21	20
D. Manufacturing	42859	96	275	1354	2187	6818	6998	4168	4635	5459	5610	5259
E. Electricity, gas and water supply	783	-	3	18	8	81	113	71	86	121	151	131
F. Construction	2438	29	31	105	121	403	383	223	273	306	247	317
G. Wholesale and retail trade, repairs	45653	910	1396	2935	3081	8995	6557	3762	4006	4657	4742	4612
H. Hotels and restaurants	16044	436	606	1401	1024	3056	2224	1246	1265	1648	1630	1508
I. Transport, storage and communications	4870	34	72	262	286	809	698	376	470	574	653	636
J. Financial intermediaries	4397	4	17	177	243	745	910	383	484	485	499	450
K. Real estate, renting and business activities	11456	47	159	702	674	2084	1707	917	1087	1292	1450	1337
L. Public administration and defence, social security	11762	13	40	212	307	1403	1720	886	1204	1837	2044	2096
M. Education	20684	44	96	454	642	2072	2379	1798	2625	3520	3769	3285
N. Health and social work	41597	115	285	1320	1923	5859	6101	3916	5056	5979	6046	4997
O,P,Q. Other	10443	146	204	688	894	2262	1498	910	895	996	987	963
Never worked	64088	16778	7892	6578	2775	6560	4951	2532	2849	3353	4349	5471

Notes:

1　The industry categorisation used is based on the 'UK Standard Industrial Classification of Economic Activities 1992' (SIC 92).

2　'Other' industry includes other community, social and personal service activities, private households with employed persons and extra-territorial organisations and bodies.

3　'Not in employment' includes all full-time students who are not in employment.

4　This table gives the former industry of all persons aged 16–74 who have ever worked.

S 3 3 5

Table S038: Sex and Industry by Employment Status and Hours Worked

Table population: All persons aged 16 to 74 in employment the week before the Census

| | All persons | Employee | | Self-employed | | | |
| | | | | Without employees | | With employees | |
		Part-time	Full-time	Part-time	Full-time	Part-time	Full-time
All persons	**688642**	**137141**	**450941**	**11844**	**45158**	**4262**	**37296**
A. Agriculture, hunting and forestry	20066	1081	4345	1648	9779	282	2931
B. Fishing	656	27	166	23	229	13	198
C. Mining and quarrying	2571	121	2192	16	120	6	116
D. Manufacturing	97365	6413	82899	835	3311	350	3557
E. Electricity, gas and water supply	4775	183	4394	26	117	8	47
F. Construction	61751	3530	35298	1432	12783	457	8251
G. Wholesale and retail trade, repairs	114721	34480	62718	1457	6326	1122	8618
H. Hotels and restaurants	31033	12592	14136	385	882	402	2636
I. Transport, storage and communications	37206	3987	28104	671	2542	199	1703
J. Financial intermediaries	20386	3245	15719	244	572	70	536
K. Real estate, renting and business activities	53842	7880	36429	1520	3518	387	4108
L. Public administration and defence, social security	64025	6363	56821	232	349	42	218
M. Education	60490	18979	39699	810	582	93	327
N. Health and social work	87502	31291	50798	1318	1714	430	1951
O,P,Q. Other	30253	6969	17223	1227	2334	401	2099
Males	**377391**	**24296**	**273937**	**7022**	**39469**	**1736**	**30931**
A. Agriculture, hunting and forestry	17185	594	3772	1195	8832	168	2624
B. Fishing	633	19	154	23	226	13	198
C. Mining and quarrying	2341	76	2019	13	117	3	113
D. Manufacturing	72348	2221	63253	561	3032	141	3140
E. Electricity, gas and water supply	3931	71	3671	26	112	8	43
F. Construction	57502	2270	32835	1339	12679	310	8069
G. Wholesale and retail trade, repairs	59812	7470	38832	939	5419	377	6775
H. Hotels and restaurants	12384	2571	7221	150	578	112	1752
I. Transport, storage and communications	27537	1585	21392	570	2384	120	1486
J. Financial intermediaries	8159	225	6814	144	497	24	455
K. Real estate, renting and business activities	29989	1245	21122	881	2975	191	3575
L. Public administration and defence, social security	37605	1048	35941	146	280	26	164
M. Education	18091	2102	15091	328	358	25	187
N. Health and social work	15676	1315	12279	223	510	82	1267
O,P,Q. Other	14198	1484	9541	484	1470	136	1083

Table S038: Sex and Industry by Employment Status and Hours Worked (continued)

| | All persons | Employee | | Self-employed | | | |
| | | | | Without employees | | With employees | |
		Part-time	Full-time	Part-time	Full-time	Part-time	Full-time
Females	**309251**	**112845**	**177004**	**4822**	**5689**	**2526**	**6365**
A. Agriculture, hunting and forestry	2881	487	573	453	947	114	307
B. Fishing	23	8	12	-	3	-	-
C. Mining and quarrying	230	45	173	3	3	3	3
D. Manufacturing	25017	4192	19646	274	279	209	417
E. Electricity, gas and water supply	844	112	723	-	5	-	4
F. Construction	4249	1260	2463	93	104	147	182
G. Wholesale and retail trade, repairs	54909	27010	23886	518	907	745	1843
H. Hotels and restaurants	18649	10021	6915	235	304	290	884
I. Transport, storage and communications	9669	2402	6712	101	158	79	217
J. Financial intermediaries	12227	3020	8905	100	75	46	81
K. Real estate, renting and business activities	23853	6635	15307	639	543	196	533
L. Public administration and defence, social security	26420	5315	20880	86	69	16	54
M. Education	42399	16877	24608	482	224	68	140
N. Health and social work	71826	29976	38519	1095	1204	348	684
O,P,Q. Other	16055	5485	7682	743	864	265	1016

Notes:

1 The industry categorisation is based on the 'UK Standard Industrial Classifications of Economic Activities 1992' (SIC92).

2 'Other' industry includes other community, social and personal service activities, private households with employed persons and extra-territorial organisations and bodies.

3 For the Census, part-time is defined as working 30 hours or less a week. Full-time is defined as working 31 or more hours a week.

4 'In employment' includes economically active full-time students in employment.

S038

S336

Table S336: Sex and Industry by Ethnic Group

Table population: All persons aged 16 to 74 in employment the week before the Census

	All persons	White	Irish Traveller	Mixed	Indian	Pakistani	Bangladeshi	Other Asian	Black Caribbean	Black African	Other Black	Chinese	Other ethnic group
All persons	**686646**	**681653**	**269**	**837**	**746**	**226**	**91**	**97**	**135**	**197**	**151**	**1737**	**507**
A. Agriculture, hunting and forestry	20066	20030	10	5	6	-	-	-	3	-	3	6	3
B. Fishing	657	657	-	-	-	-	-	-	-	-	-	-	-
C. Mining and quarrying	2567	2561	3	3	-	-	-	-	-	-	-	-	-
D. Manufacturing	97367	96937	36	97	49	21	9	9	19	17	20	71	82
E. Electricity, gas and water supply	4781	4758	3	5	6	-	-	-	3	3	-	3	-
F. Construction	61754	61618	35	37	8	-	-	3	6	5	5	28	9
G. Wholesale and retail trade, repairs	114722	114137	49	132	126	59	16	12	16	12	10	122	31
H. Hotels and restaurants	31032	29648	11	85	58	43	44	3	11	13	6	1054	56
I. Transport, storage and communications	37203	37049	14	43	31	8	-	4	4	15	-	24	11
J. Financial intermediaries	20385	20299	3	13	16	3	7	-	3	3	3	35	-
K. Real estate, renting and business activities	53846	53453	23	87	78	15	3	11	14	17	7	97	41
L. Public administration and defence, social security	64024	63695	25	91	35	8	-	3	18	18	66	29	36
M. Education	60490	60114	17	72	76	15	6	9	9	15	8	106	43
N. Health and social work	87501	86604	20	125	228	51	3	39	19	69	20	141	182
O,P,Q. Other	30251	30093	20	42	29	3	3	4	10	10	3	21	13
Males	**377381**	**374380**	**175**	**470**	**471**	**166**	**66**	**38**	**84**	**123**	**107**	**1026**	**275**
A. Agriculture, hunting and forestry	17183	17159	10	5	3	-	-	-	-	-	-	3	3
B. Fishing	632	632	-	-	-	-	-	-	-	-	-	-	-
C. Mining and quarrying	2338	2332	3	3	-	-	-	-	-	-	-	-	-
D. Manufacturing	72348	72038	24	72	35	14	6	3	16	12	15	50	63
E. Electricity, gas and water supply	3933	3919	3	5	3	-	-	3	-	-	-	3	3
F. Construction	57503	57379	32	37	8	-	-	3	3	5	5	25	6
G. Wholesale and retail trade, repairs	59813	59499	31	65	74	42	13	3	10	5	3	54	14
H. Hotels and restaurants	12384	11489	5	49	38	43	37	-	8	5	6	660	44
I. Transport, storage and communications	27536	27420	14	27	24	5	-	4	4	15	-	12	11
J. Financial intermediaries	8158	8132	3	-	8	3	4	-	3	-	-	5	-
K. Real estate, renting and business activities	29990	29745	16	40	60	12	3	8	9	14	3	56	24
L. Public administration and defence, social security	37605	37368	13	65	22	5	-	3	12	14	63	16	24
M. Education	18092	17886	5	30	41	8	3	9	5	11	5	69	20
N. Health and social work	15674	15260	4	54	143	34	-	5	7	35	7	62	63
O,P,Q. Other	14192	14122	12	18	12	-	-	-	7	7	-	11	3

	All persons	White	Irish Traveller	Mixed	Indian	Pakistani	Bangladeshi	Other Asian	Black Caribbean	Black African	Other Black	Chinese	Other ethnic group
Females	**309265**	**307273**	**94**	**367**	**275**	**60**	**25**	**59**	**51**	**74**	**44**	**711**	**232**
A. Agriculture, hunting and forestry	2883	2871	-	-	3	-	-	-	3	-	3	3	-
B. Fishing	25	25	-	-	-	-	-	-	-	-	-	-	-
C. Mining and quarrying	229	229	-	-	-	-	-	-	-	-	-	-	-
D. Manufacturing	25019	24899	12	25	14	7	3	6	3	5	5	21	19
E. Electricity, gas and water supply	848	839	-	-	3	-	-	-	3	3	-	-	-
F. Construction	4251	4239	3	-	-	-	-	-	3	-	-	3	3
G. Wholesale and retail trade, repairs	54909	54638	18	67	52	17	3	9	6	7	7	68	17
H. Hotels and restaurants	18648	18159	6	36	20	-	7	3	3	8	-	394	12
I. Transport, storage and communications	9667	9629	-	16	7	3	-	-	-	-	-	12	-
J. Financial intermediaries	12227	12167	-	13	8	-	3	-	-	3	3	30	-
K. Real estate, renting and business activities	23856	23708	7	47	18	3	-	3	5	3	4	41	17
L. Public administration and defence, social security	26419	26327	12	26	13	3	-	-	6	4	3	13	12
M. Education	42398	42228	12	42	35	7	3	-	4	4	3	37	23
N. Health and social work	71827	71344	16	71	85	17	3	34	12	34	13	79	119
O,P,Q. Other	16059	15971	8	24	17	3	3	4	3	3	3	10	10

Notes:

1 The industry categorisation is based on the 'UK Standard Industrial Classifications of Economic Activities 1992' (SIC92).

2 'Other' industry includes other community, social and personal service activities, private households with employed persons and extra-territorial organisations and bodies.

3 'In employment' includes economically active full-time students in employment.

Table S337: Industry by Sex and Community Background (Religion or Religion Brought Up In)

Table population: All persons aged 16 to 74 in employment the week before the Census

	All persons	Males					Females				
		Total	Catholic	Protestant and Other Christian (including Christian related)	Other religions and philosophies	None	Total	Catholic	Protestant and Other Christian (including Christian related)	Other religions and philosophies	None
All persons	**686645**	**377391**	**149273**	**216776**	**1923**	**9419**	**309254**	**127253**	**175222**	**970**	**5809**
A. Agriculture, hunting and forestry	20068	17185	5458	11566	14	147	2883	754	2098	3	28
B. Fishing	659	632	184	437	-	11	27	10	14	3	-
C. Mining and quarrying	2572	2342	1080	1226	3	33	230	96	131	-	3
D. Manufacturing	97365	72348	26270	44446	211	1421	25017	9439	15107	66	405
E. Electricity, gas and water supply	4774	3931	1289	2559	11	72	843	367	460	-	16
F. Construction	61749	57502	30586	26152	47	717	4247	1863	2312	-	72
G. Wholesale and retail trade, repairs	114721	59812	22590	35692	257	1273	54909	21216	32537	143	1013
H. Hotels and restaurants	31033	12384	5757	5462	341	824	18649	8019	9861	135	634
I. Transport, storage and communications	37206	27537	10694	16051	103	689	9669	3707	5701	34	227
J. Financial intermediaries	20386	8159	2672	5271	26	190	12227	4704	7241	26	256
K. Real estate, renting and business activities	53842	29989	11189	17607	205	988	23853	9738	13532	75	508
L. Public administration and defence, social security	64025	37605	9973	25659	180	1793	26420	10538	15162	70	650
M. Education	60490	18091	8508	8914	156	513	42399	19223	22436	123	617
N. Health and social work	87502	15676	7371	7664	293	348	71826	30908	39704	221	993
O, P, Q. Other	30253	14198	5652	8070	76	400	16055	6671	8926	71	387

Notes:

1 The industry categorisation is based on the 'UK Standard Industrial Classification of Economic Activities 1992' (SIC92).

2 'Other' industry includes other community, social and personal service activities, private households with employed persons and extra-territorial organisations and bodies.

3 'In employment' includes economically active full-time students in employment.

4 The term 'Catholic' includes those respondents who gave their religion as Catholic or Roman Catholic.

S337

S338

Table S338: Sex and NS-SeC by Age

Table population: All persons aged 16 to 74

	All persons	16	17	18	19	20 to 24	25 to 29	30 to 34	35 to 39	40 to 44	45 to 49	50 to 54	55 to 59	60 to 64	65 to 69	70 to 74
All persons	**1187076**	**27183**	**26276**	**25392**	**23244**	**109385**	**114704**	**127517**	**129639**	**117335**	**102464**	**98426**	**88730**	**73588**	**65343**	**57850**
1. Higher managerial and professional occupations	**69977**	**26**	**70**	**116**	**188**	**3652**	**9472**	**9848**	**9804**	**8584**	**7312**	**6197**	**5061**	**3747**	**3240**	**2660**
.1 Large employers and higher managerial occupations	25059	9	20	43	70	785	2141	3392	3837	3463	3004	2523	2060	1496	1216	1000
L1 Employers in large organisations	3930	6	3	7	18	106	311	363	524	482	430	482	413	308	247	230
L2 Higher managerial	21129	3	17	36	52	679	1830	3029	3313	2981	2574	2041	1647	1188	969	770
.2 Higher professional occupations	44918	17	50	73	118	2867	7331	6456	5967	5121	4308	3674	3001	2251	2024	1660
L3.1 Higher professionals (traditional) - employees	27095	11	31	53	84	1782	4741	3905	3409	2937	2589	2281	1836	1324	1151	961
L3.2 Higher professionals (new) - employees	7620	3	16	20	31	958	1984	1447	1121	786	455	295	206	151	72	75
L3.3 Higher professionals (traditional) - self-employed	9493	3	3	-	3	101	526	1009	1314	1310	1173	1021	903	733	773	621
L3.4 Higher professionals (new) - self-employed	710	-	-	-	-	26	80	95	123	88	91	77	56	43	28	3
2. Lower managerial and professional occupations	**229612**	**88**	**368**	**483**	**875**	**12969**	**27239**	**30074**	**30260**	**28069**	**24854**	**21646**	**17517**	**13564**	**11707**	**9899**
L4.1 Lower professionals and higher technical (traditional) - employees	119002	45	232	214	383	6149	13594	14419	15165	14837	14153	11915	9225	7359	6211	5101
L4.2 Lower professionals and higher technical (new) - employees	9427	3	19	34	80	969	1830	1551	1153	819	647	593	581	402	433	313
L4.3 Lower professionals and higher technical (traditional) - self-employed	6811	-	-	4	7	169	561	777	914	925	841	836	718	514	349	196
L4.4 Lower professionals and higher technical (new) - self-employed	1996	-	3	3	3	27	81	158	192	186	216	298	287	219	168	155
L5 Lower managerial	49067	27	88	144	232	2993	6250	7406	6833	5824	4811	4358	3669	2608	2038	1786
L6 Higher supervisory	43309	13	26	84	170	2662	4923	5763	6003	5478	4186	3646	3037	2462	2508	2348
3. Intermediate occupations	**131679**	**151**	**699**	**1186**	**2028**	**15181**	**16349**	**16090**	**15631**	**14122**	**11411**	**10229**	**8899**	**7186**	**6616**	**5901**
L7.1 Intermediate clerical and administrative	65579	52	220	374	706	6497	7507	7582	7627	7185	5942	5362	4811	4142	3928	3644
L7.2 Intermediate sales and services	51037	70	383	691	1157	7183	6960	6901	6446	5395	3987	3475	2881	2118	1839	1551
L7.3 Intermediate technical and auxiliary	11318	20	39	77	113	1030	1414	1228	1236	1162	1002	1002	941	744	716	594
L7.4 Intermediate engineering	3745	9	57	44	52	471	468	379	322	380	480	390	266	182	133	112
4. Small employers and own account workers	**103644**	**20**	**78**	**108**	**251**	**3016**	**6991**	**11261**	**13455**	**12810**	**12023**	**12064**	**10966**	**8292**	**6891**	**5418**
L8.1 Employers in small organisations (non-professional)	37235	3	25	33	75	946	2426	4331	5171	4809	4483	4330	3881	2739	2194	1789
L8.2 Employers in small organisations (agriculture)	4506	3	6	3	6	119	221	317	438	448	461	553	541	479	478	433
L9.1 Own account workers (non-professional)	45154	11	41	56	147	1617	3418	5499	6224	5934	5433	5377	4541	3081	2247	1528
L9.2 Own account workers (agriculture)	16749	3	6	16	23	334	926	1114	1622	1619	1646	1804	2003	1993	1972	1668

Table S338: Sex and NS-SeC by Age (continued)

	All persons	16	17	18	19	20 to 24	25 to 29	30 to 34	35 to 39	40 to 44	45 to 49	50 to 54	55 to 59	60 to 64	65 to 69	70 to 74
5. Lower supervisory and technical occupations	**104088**	**205**	**1034**	**1308**	**1639**	**10348**	**11493**	**12063**	**11633**	**10488**	**8748**	**8453**	**7575**	**6750**	**6574**	**5777**
L10 Lower supervisory	63960	20	129	234	491	5198	7336	8094	7766	6616	5558	5399	4794	4166	4327	3832
L11.1 Lower technical craft	30682	176	855	1014	1015	4342	3337	2961	2892	2950	2395	2248	1931	1738	1508	1320
L11.2 Lower technical process operative	9446	9	50	60	133	808	820	1008	975	922	795	806	850	846	739	625
6. Semi-routine occupations	**183128**	**409**	**1872**	**2749**	**3649**	**19556**	**17999**	**19915**	**20084**	**17870**	**15336**	**16103**	**15004**	**12564**	**10618**	**9400**
L12.1 Semi-routine sales	54500	140	630	967	1452	7110	5746	6384	6014	4789	3997	4334	4003	3318	2899	2717
L12.2 Semi-routine service	63134	90	461	721	856	5062	5288	6427	7017	6534	5873	6423	5920	4983	4055	3424
L12.3 Semi-routine technical	11788	19	72	130	195	1007	1255	1346	1188	1099	946	889	1023	932	909	778
L12.4 Semi-routine operative	28080	93	450	545	667	3381	3101	3017	2863	2491	2194	2209	2164	1926	1561	1418
L12.5 Semi routine agriculture	3862	10	60	63	64	426	331	404	403	355	284	296	294	267	287	318
L12.6 Semi-routine clerical	13612	34	123	231	302	1634	1511	1469	1407	1355	1175	1250	1055	821	676	569
L12.7 Semi-routine childcare	8152	23	76	92	113	936	767	868	1192	1247	867	702	545	317	231	176
7. Routine occupations	**193186**	**604**	**2487**	**3037**	**3252**	**16484**	**16015**	**19252**	**19582**	**17752**	**16378**	**17738**	**17985**	**16397**	**14105**	**12118**
L13.1 Routine sales and service	19842	110	417	527	677	2980	2105	2174	1992	1639	1272	1459	1374	1147	1034	935
L13.2 Routine production	40356	64	290	396	513	3275	3716	4488	4131	3813	3511	3619	3497	3405	2950	2688
L13.3 Routine technical	57590	270	1086	1204	1140	5372	5316	6353	6317	5318	4956	4890	4801	4142	3557	2868
L13.4 Routine operative	73831	154	672	881	890	4685	4729	6071	6971	6824	6518	7628	8203	7595	6469	5541
L13.5 Routine agricultural	1567	6	22	29	32	172	149	166	171	158	121	142	110	108	95	86
8. Never worked and long-term unemployed	**77973**	**599**	**1463**	**1594**	**1703**	**7237**	**6828**	**7993**	**8450**	**7064**	**6002**	**5963**	**5723**	**5088**	**5589**	**6677**
L14.1 Never worked	58134	599	1428	1470	1464	5760	4680	5383	5553	4294	3529	3743	3837	4285	5491	6618
L14.2 Long-term unemployed	19839	-	35	124	239	1477	2148	2610	2897	2770	2473	2220	1886	803	98	59
Not classified	**93789**	**25081**	**18205**	**14811**	**9659**	**20942**	**2318**	**1021**	**740**	**576**	**400**	**33**	**-**	**-**	**3**	**-**
L15 Full-time students	93789	25081	18205	14811	9659	20942	2318	1021	740	576	400	33	-	-	3	-

S338

Table S338: Sex and NS-SeC by Age (continued)

S338

	All persons	16	17	18	19	20 to 24	25 to 29	30 to 34	35 to 39	40 to 44	45 to 49	50 to 54	55 to 59	60 to 64	65 to 69	70 to 74
Males	**581242**	**13861**	**13305**	**13000**	**11553**	**54913**	**56628**	**62487**	**63430**	**57432**	**51686**	**48484**	**43585**	**35401**	**30408**	**25069**
1. Higher managerial and professional occupations	**49493**	**19**	**59**	**103**	**141**	**2254**	**5796**	**6337**	**6603**	**6053**	**5513**	**4797**	**4042**	**2995**	**2653**	**2128**
1.1 Large employers and higher managerial occupations	18427	6	17	38	52	483	1322	2321	2767	2534	2322	1961	1638	1192	973	801
L1 Employers in large organisations	2897	3	3	7	10	71	173	284	409	360	319	365	291	246	185	171
L2 Higher managerial	15530	3	14	31	42	412	1149	2037	2358	2174	2003	1596	1347	946	788	630
1.2 Higher professional occupations	31066	13	42	65	89	1771	4474	4016	3836	3519	3191	2836	2404	1803	1680	1327
L3.1 Higher professionals (traditional) - employees	17859	7	27	49	65	1052	2759	2319	2063	1914	1836	1677	1425	1029	912	725
L3.2 Higher professionals (new) - employees	5053	3	12	16	21	621	1324	918	717	521	324	217	143	109	57	50
L3.3 Higher professionals (traditional) - self-employed	7546	3	3	-	3	76	318	699	952	1015	955	879	783	625	686	549
L3.4 Higher professionals (new) - self-employed	608	-	-	-	-	22	73	80	104	69	76	63	53	40	25	3
2. Lower managerial and professional occupations	**102822**	**67**	**260**	**296**	**467**	**5968**	**11526**	**13046**	**12963**	**12046**	**11174**	**10130**	**8404**	**6310**	**5558**	**4607**
L4.1 Lower professionals and higher technical - (traditional) - employees	40353	34	168	133	218	2515	4485	4668	4681	4770	4887	4236	3231	2479	2105	1743
L4.2 Lower professionals and higher technical - (new) - employees	6157	3	9	20	42	490	1066	903	744	519	431	461	459	344	390	276
L4.3 Lower professionals and higher technical - (traditional) - self-employed	4459	-	-	4	4	111	338	479	544	607	580	579	490	360	242	121
L4.4 Lower professionals and higher technical - (new) - self-employed	1733	-	3	3	3	21	63	126	165	158	186	261	253	202	149	140
L5 Lower managerial	28550	20	62	83	113	1543	3133	4041	3898	3390	2969	2703	2378	1679	1372	1166
L6 Higher supervisory	21570	10	18	53	87	1288	2441	2829	2931	2602	2121	1890	1593	1246	1300	1161
3. Intermediate occupations	**37837**	**59**	**285**	**456**	**696**	**5038**	**4832**	**4591**	**4500**	**3923**	**3344**	**2864**	**2397**	**1912**	**1647**	**1293**
L7.1 Intermediate clerical and administrative	13171	13	60	100	140	1526	1552	1360	1372	1306	1154	1079	1003	943	861	702
L7.2 Intermediate sales and services	18240	20	144	278	455	2664	2324	2557	2458	1978	1519	1225	1004	678	537	399
L7.3 Intermediate technical and auxiliary	2983	17	24	38	54	432	533	325	372	286	210	189	150	126	133	94
L7.4 Intermediate engineering	3443	9	57	40	47	416	423	349	298	353	461	371	240	165	116	98
4. Small employers and own account workers	**82031**	**17**	**66**	**96**	**213**	**2527**	**5677**	**8873**	**10538**	**10280**	**9687**	**9465**	**8520**	**6508**	**5432**	**4132**
L8.1 Employers in small organisations (non-professional)	27436	3	16	29	58	760	1814	3198	3792	3641	3419	3158	2752	1981	1576	1239
L8.2 Employers in small organisations (agriculture)	3966	3	6	3	6	110	210	288	387	394	402	491	467	403	421	375
L9.1 Own account workers (non-professional)	35872	8	38	48	126	1339	2760	4348	4879	4769	4387	4258	3619	2465	1747	1081
L9.2 Own account workers (agriculture)	14757	3	6	16	23	318	893	1039	1480	1476	1479	1558	1682	1659	1688	1437

Table S338: Sex and NS-SeC by Age (continued)

	All persons	16	17	18	19	20 to 24	25 to 29	30 to 34	35 to 39	40 to 44	45 to 49	50 to 54	55 to 59	60 to 64	65 to 69	70 to 74
5. Lower supervisory and technical occupations	**72078**	**184**	**958**	**1172**	**1332**	**7601**	**7978**	**8073**	**7852**	**7304**	**6054**	**5678**	**5049**	**4577**	**4355**	**3911**
L10 Lower supervisory	37942	7	83	130	252	2907	4384	4764	4619	4007	3305	3128	2817	2511	2618	2410
L11.1 Lower technical craft	28639	173	844	1002	980	4143	3088	2700	2664	2769	2252	2078	1779	1600	1372	1195
L11.2 Lower technical process operative	5497	4	31	40	100	551	506	609	569	528	497	472	453	466	365	306
6. Semi-routine occupations	**60119**	**242**	**1036**	**1323**	**1613**	**8254**	**6632**	**6403**	**5840**	**4915**	**4358**	**4430**	**4459**	**4095**	**3544**	**2975**
L12.1 Semi-routine sales	8432	62	244	329	464	2214	1144	828	606	462	389	393	393	349	299	256
L12.2 Semi-routine service	18822	53	230	308	343	1803	1645	1891	1908	1663	1528	1668	1689	1601	1396	1096
L12.3 Semi-routine technical	9454	19	67	120	179	903	1088	1144	991	876	748	695	803	689	635	497
L12.4 Semi-routine operative	17816	87	409	447	512	2580	2176	1940	1755	1439	1287	1245	1179	1096	880	784
L12.5 Semi-routine agriculture	3298	6	60	60	59	402	307	359	347	299	226	234	232	222	232	253
L12.6 Semi-routine clerical	2058	8	23	55	51	314	242	203	212	158	152	181	146	129	98	86
L12.7 Semi-routine childcare	239	7	3	4	5	38	30	38	21	18	28	14	17	9	4	3
7. Routine occupations	**102160**	**467**	**1928**	**2279**	**2313**	**10945**	**9804**	**10987**	**10878**	**9280**	**8366**	**8342**	**8337**	**7346**	**6019**	**4869**
L13.1 Routine sales and service	3524	23	69	108	188	734	336	275	246	229	195	225	244	217	227	208
L13.2 Routine production	9200	44	198	243	298	1525	1249	1197	951	732	611	581	507	490	322	252
L13.3 Routine technical	53407	267	1068	1178	1101	5093	5027	5930	5949	4964	4649	4517	4447	3728	3068	2421
L13.4 Routine operative	35048	127	576	739	715	3494	3099	3482	3632	3259	2831	2932	3056	2835	2342	1929
L13.5 Routine agricultural	981	6	17	11	11	99	93	103	100	96	80	87	83	76	60	59
8. Never worked and long-term unemployed	**32812**	**361**	**839**	**858**	**839**	**3400**	**3303**	**3727**	**3937**	**3403**	**2991**	**2768**	**2377**	**1658**	**1197**	**1154**
L14.1 Never worked	19115	361	811	776	702	2493	1894	2040	2042	1526	1214	1142	936	924	1128	1126
L14.2 Long-term unemployed	13697	-	28	82	137	907	1409	1687	1895	1877	1777	1626	1441	734	69	28
Not classified	41890	12445	7874	6417	3939	8926	1080	450	319	228	199	10	-	-	3	-
L15 Full-time students	41890	12445	7874	6417	3939	8926	1080	450	319	228	199	10	-	-	3	-

S338

Table S338: Sex and NS-SeC by Age (continued)

S338

	All persons	16	17	18	19	20 to 24	25 to 29	30 to 34	35 to 39	40 to 44	45 to 49	50 to 54	55 to 59	60 to 64	65 to 69	70 to 74
Females	**605834**	**13322**	**12971**	**12392**	**11691**	**54472**	**58076**	**65030**	**66209**	**59903**	**50778**	**49942**	**45145**	**38187**	**34935**	**32781**
1. Higher managerial and professional occupations	**20484**	**7**	**11**	**13**	**47**	**1398**	**3676**	**3511**	**3201**	**2531**	**1799**	**1400**	**1019**	**752**	**587**	**532**
1.1 Large employers and higher managerial occupations	6632	3	3	5	18	302	819	1071	1070	929	682	562	422	304	243	199
L1 Employers in large organisations	1033	3	-	-	8	35	138	79	115	122	111	117	122	62	62	59
L2 Higher managerial	5599	-	3	5	10	267	681	992	955	807	571	445	300	242	181	140
1.2 Higher professional occupations	13852	4	8	8	29	1096	2857	2440	2131	1602	1117	838	597	448	344	333
L3.1 Higher professionals (traditional) - employees	9236	4	4	4	19	730	1982	1586	1346	1023	753	604	411	295	239	236
L3.2 Higher professionals (new) - employees	2567	-	4	4	10	337	660	529	404	265	131	78	63	42	15	25
L3.3 Higher professionals (traditional) - self-employed	1947	-	-	-	-	25	208	310	362	295	218	142	120	108	87	72
L3.4 Higher professionals (new) - self-employed	102	-	-	-	-	4	7	15	19	19	15	14	3	3	3	-
2. Lower managerial and professional occupations	**126790**	**21**	**108**	**187**	**408**	**7001**	**15713**	**17028**	**17297**	**16023**	**13680**	**11516**	**9113**	**7254**	**6149**	**5292**
L4.1 Lower professionals and higher technical (traditional) - employees	78649	11	64	81	165	3634	9109	9751	10484	10067	9266	7679	5994	4880	4106	3358
L4.2 Lower professionals and higher technical (new) - employees	3270	-	10	14	38	479	764	648	409	300	216	132	122	58	43	37
L4.3 Lower professionals and higher technical (traditional) - self-employed	2352	-	-	-	3	58	223	298	370	318	261	257	228	154	107	75
L4.4 Lower professionals and higher technical (new) - self-employed	263	-	-	-	-	6	18	32	27	28	30	37	34	17	19	15
L5 Lower managerial	20517	7	26	61	119	1450	3117	3365	2935	2434	1842	1655	1291	929	666	620
L6 Higher supervisory	21739	3	8	31	83	1374	2482	2934	3072	2876	2065	1756	1444	1216	1208	1187
3. Intermediate occupations	**93842**	**92**	**414**	**730**	**1332**	**10143**	**11517**	**11499**	**11131**	**10199**	**8067**	**7365**	**6502**	**5274**	**4969**	**4608**
L7.1 Intermediate clerical and administrative	52408	39	160	274	566	4971	5955	6222	6255	5879	4788	4283	3808	3199	3067	2942
L7.2 Intermediate sales and services	32797	50	239	413	702	4519	4636	4344	3988	3417	2468	2250	1877	1440	1302	1152
L7.3 Intermediate technical and auxiliary	8335	3	15	39	59	598	881	903	864	876	792	813	791	618	583	500
L7.4 Intermediate engineering	302	-	-	4	5	55	45	30	24	27	19	19	26	17	17	14
4. Small employers and own account workers	**21613**	**3**	**12**	**12**	**38**	**489**	**1314**	**2388**	**2917**	**2530**	**2336**	**2599**	**2446**	**1784**	**1459**	**1286**
L8.1 Employers in small organisations (non-professional)	9799	-	9	4	17	186	612	1133	1379	1168	1064	1172	1129	758	618	550
L8.2 Employers in small organisations (agriculture)	540	-	-	-	-	9	11	29	51	54	59	62	74	76	57	58
L9.1 Own account workers (non-professional)	9282	3	3	8	21	278	658	1151	1345	1165	1046	1119	922	616	500	447
L9.2 Own account workers (agriculture)	1992	-	-	-	-	16	33	75	142	143	167	246	321	334	284	231

Table S338: Sex and NS-SeC by Age (continued)

	All persons	16	17	18	19	20 to 24	25 to 29	30 to 34	35 to 39	40 to 44	45 to 49	50 to 54	55 to 59	60 to 64	65 to 69	70 to 74
5. Lower supervisory and technical occupations	**32010**	**21**	**76**	**136**	**307**	**2747**	**3515**	**3990**	**3781**	**3184**	**2694**	**2775**	**2526**	**2173**	**2219**	**1866**
L10 Lower supervisory	26018	13	46	104	239	2291	2952	3330	3147	2609	2253	2271	1977	1655	1709	1422
L11.1 Lower technical craft	2043	3	11	12	35	199	249	261	228	181	143	170	152	138	136	125
L11.2 Lower technical process operative	3949	5	19	20	33	257	314	399	406	394	298	334	397	380	374	319
6. Semi-routine occupations	**123009**	**167**	**836**	**1426**	**2036**	**11302**	**11367**	**13512**	**14244**	**12955**	**10978**	**11673**	**10545**	**8469**	**7074**	**6425**
L12.1 Semi-routine sales	46068	78	386	638	988	4896	4602	5556	5408	4327	3608	3941	3610	2969	2600	2461
L12.2 Semi-routine service	44312	37	231	413	513	3259	3643	4536	5109	4871	4345	4755	4231	3382	2659	2328
L12.3 Semi-routine technical	2334	-	5	10	16	104	167	202	197	223	198	194	220	243	274	281
L12.4 Semi-routine operative	10264	6	41	98	155	801	925	1077	1108	1052	907	964	985	830	681	634
L12.5 Semi-routine agriculture	564	4	-	3	5	24	24	45	56	56	58	62	62	45	55	65
L12.6 Semi-routine clerical	11554	26	100	176	251	1320	1269	1266	1195	1197	1023	1069	909	692	578	483
L12.7 Semi-routine childcare	7913	16	73	88	108	898	737	830	1171	1229	839	688	528	308	227	173
7. Routine occupations	**91026**	**137**	**559**	**758**	**939**	**5539**	**6211**	**8265**	**8704**	**8472**	**8012**	**9396**	**9648**	**9051**	**8086**	**7249**
L13.1 Routine sales and service	16318	87	348	419	489	2246	1769	1899	1746	1410	1077	1234	1130	930	807	727
L13.2 Routine production	31156	20	92	153	215	1750	2467	3291	3180	3081	2900	3038	2990	2915	2628	2436
L13.3 Routine technical	4183	3	18	26	39	279	289	423	368	354	307	373	354	414	489	447
L13.4 Routine operative	38783	27	96	142	175	1191	1630	2589	3339	3565	3687	4696	5147	4760	4127	3612
L13.5 Routine agricultural	586	-	5	18	21	73	56	63	71	62	41	55	27	32	35	27
8. Never worked or long-term unemployed	**45161**	**238**	**624**	**736**	**864**	**3837**	**3525**	**4266**	**4513**	**3661**	**3011**	**3195**	**3346**	**3430**	**4392**	**5523**
L14.1 Never worked	39019	238	617	694	762	3267	2786	3343	3511	2768	2315	2601	2901	3361	4363	5492
L14.2 Long-term unemployed	6142	-	7	42	102	570	739	923	1002	893	696	594	445	69	29	31
Not classified	**51899**	**12636**	**10331**	**8394**	**5720**	**12016**	**1238**	**571**	**421**	**348**	**201**	**23**	-	-	-	-
L15 Full-time students	51899	12636	10331	8394	5720	12016	1238	571	421	348	201	23	-	-	-	-

Notes:
1 NS-SeC stands for National Statistics Socio-economic Classification.
2 In the NS-SeC classification all full-time students are recorded in the 'full-time students' category regardless of whether they are economically active or inactive.
3 For long-term unemployed, year last worked is 1999 or earlier.

S338

Table S339: Sex and Age and General Health by NS-SeC

Table population: All persons aged 16 to 74

	All persons	Large employers and higher managerial occupations	Higher professional occupations	Lower managerial and professional occupations	Intermediate occupations	Small employers and own account workers	Lower supervisory and technical occupations	Semi-routine occupations	Routine occupations	Never worked	Long-term unemployed	Full-time students
All persons	**1187073**	**25056**	**44917**	**229609**	**131679**	**103648**	**104088**	**183131**	**193187**	**58134**	**19941**	**93783**
16 to 24	**211482**	924	3123	14780	19245	3477	14534	28238	25865	10721	1877	88698
Good health	183205	834	2865	13075	16664	3069	12706	23345	21691	7089	1406	80461
Fairly good health	22468	82	226	1420	2189	337	1503	3990	3251	2076	406	6988
Not good health	**5809**	8	32	285	392	71	325	903	923	1556	65	1249
25 to 34	**242221**	5533	13787	57313	32439	18252	23556	37914	35267	10063	4758	3339
Good health	**189887**	4886	12565	48918	26069	14978	18605	27426	25344	5110	3225	2761
Fairly good health	**38560**	554	1033	6744	4865	2646	3639	7630	6928	2813	1249	459
Not good health	**13774**	93	189	1651	1505	628	1312	2858	2995	2140	284	119
35 to 49	**349438**	10304	15396	83183	41164	38288	30869	53290	53712	13376	8140	1716
Good health	**239055**	8492	12810	63581	28912	28457	20674	33362	31054	5581	4863	1269
Fairly good health	**72383**	1359	1993	14001	8384	6994	6487	12840	13402	4075	2550	298
Not good health	**38000**	453	593	5601	3868	2837	3708	7088	9256	3720	727	149
50 to 54	**98423**	2523	3674	21646	10229	12064	8453	16103	17738	3743	2220	30
Good health	**55852**	1857	2818	14532	6233	7630	4464	8247	7726	1201	1123	21
Fairly good health	**24947**	465	633	4610	2532	2909	2171	4562	5028	1215	813	9
Not good health	**17624**	201	223	2504	1464	1525	1818	3294	4984	1327	284	-
55 to 59	**88730**	2060	3001	17517	8899	10966	7575	15004	17985	3837	1886	-
Good health	**43854**	1370	2145	10548	4868	6213	3283	6793	6608	1144	882	-
Fairly good health	**24701**	424	566	4216	2380	2933	2153	4582	5473	1214	760	-
Not good health	**20175**	266	290	2753	1651	1820	2139	3629	5904	1479	244	-
60 to 64	**73587**	1496	2250	13564	7186	8292	6750	12564	16397	4285	803	-
Good health	**31873**	886	1522	7567	3476	4104	2431	5001	5142	1292	452	-
Fairly good health	**23714**	374	504	3833	2367	2567	2173	4225	5824	1572	275	-
Not good health	**18000**	236	224	2164	1343	1621	2146	3338	5431	1421	76	-
65 to 74	**123192**	2216	3686	21606	12517	12309	12351	20018	26223	12109	157	-
Good health	**45623**	1154	2166	10501	5271	5373	4061	6524	7164	3332	77	-
Fairly good health	**47821**	727	1107	7629	4878	4763	4859	8081	10742	4976	59	-
Not good health	**29748**	335	413	3476	2368	2173	3431	5413	8317	3801	21	-

S339

Table S339: Sex and Age and General Health by NS-SeC (continued)

	All persons	Large employers and higher managerial occupations	Higher professional occupations	Lower managerial and professional occupations	Intermediate occupations	Small employers and own account workers	Lower supervisory and technical occupations	Semi-routine occupations	Routine occupations	Never worked	Long-term unemployed	Full-time students
Males	**581230**	**18426**	**31062**	**102820**	**37837**	**82029**	**72078**	**60119**	**102160**	**19115**	**13698**	**41886**
16 to 24	106624	595	1976	7056	6534	2917	11247	12468	17932	5143	1155	39601
Good health	94327	550	1822	6358	5882	2611	10048	10724	15587	3419	898	36428
Fairly good health	9538	40	131	570	547	255	982	1406	1794	912	215	2686
Not good health	2759	5	23	128	105	51	217	338	551	812	42	487
25 to 34	119115	3643	8490	24572	9423	14550	16051	13035	20791	3934	3096	1530
Good health	96537	3320	7793	21290	7824	12060	13150	9981	15897	1800	2116	1306
Fairly good health	16627	285	596	2675	1217	2025	2185	2203	3411	1072	783	175
Not good health	5951	38	101	607	382	465	716	851	1483	1062	197	49
35 to 49	172548	7623	10546	36183	11767	30505	21210	15113	28524	4782	5549	746
Good health	121809	6383	8910	28091	8278	22742	14668	9493	17590	1774	3303	577
Fairly good health	33461	952	1265	5804	2364	5513	4203	3505	6508	1499	1733	115
Not good health	17278	288	371	2288	1125	2250	2339	2115	4426	1509	513	54
50 to 54	48483	1961	2836	10130	2864	9465	5678	4430	8342	1142	1626	9
Good health	28741	1476	2210	6875	1708	5981	3141	2227	3954	328	835	6
Fairly good health	11594	356	473	2102	685	2252	1375	1217	2159	388	584	3
Not good health	8148	129	153	1153	471	1232	1162	986	2229	426	207	-
55 to 59	43585	1638	2404	8404	2397	8520	5049	4459	8337	936	1441	-
Good health	22439	1114	1730	5091	1208	4810	2256	1951	3375	242	662	-
Fairly good health	11429	313	443	1982	651	2213	1407	1270	2268	290	592	-
Not good health	9717	211	231	1331	538	1497	1386	1238	2694	404	187	-
60 to 64	35401	1192	1803	6310	1912	6508	4577	4095	7346	924	734	-
Good health	15400	704	1223	3441	775	3118	1623	1508	2356	230	422	-
Fairly good health	10636	287	395	1675	616	2000	1418	1256	2419	321	249	-
Not good health	9365	201	185	1194	521	1390	1536	1331	2571	373	63	-
65 to 74	55474	1774	3007	10165	2940	9564	8266	6519	10888	2254	97	-
Good health	21700	944	1787	4930	1071	4153	2783	2115	3264	599	54	-
Fairly good health	20896	564	892	3565	1157	3692	3210	2500	4412	872	32	-
Not good health	12878	266	328	1670	712	1719	2273	1904	3212	783	11	-

S339

	All persons	Large employers and higher managerial occupations	Higher professional occupations	Lower managerial and professional occupations	Intermediate occupations	Small employers and own account workers	Lower supervisory and technical occupations	Semi-routine occupations	Routine occupations	Never worked	Long-term unemployed	Full-time students
Females	**605843**	**6630**	**13855**	**126789**	**93842**	**21619**	**32010**	**123012**	**91027**	**39019**	**6143**	**51897**
16 to 24	**104858**	329	1147	7724	12711	560	3287	15770	7933	5578	722	49097
Good health	**88878**	284	1043	6717	10782	458	2658	12621	6104	3670	508	44033
Fairly good health	**12930**	42	95	850	1642	82	521	2584	1457	1164	191	4302
Not good health	**3050**	3	9	157	287	20	108	565	372	744	23	762
25 to 34	**123106**	1890	5297	32741	23016	3702	7505	24879	14476	6129	1662	1809
Good health	**93350**	1566	4772	27628	18245	2918	5455	17445	9447	3310	1109	1455
Fairly good health	**21933**	269	437	4069	3648	621	1454	5427	3517	1741	466	284
Not good health	**7823**	55	88	1044	1123	163	596	2007	1512	1078	87	70
35 to 49	**176890**	2681	4850	47000	29397	7783	9659	38177	25188	8594	2591	970
Good health	**117246**	2109	3900	35490	20634	5715	6006	23869	13464	3807	1560	692
Fairly good health	**38922**	407	728	8197	6020	1481	2284	9335	6894	2576	817	183
Not good health	**20722**	165	222	3313	2743	587	1369	4973	4830	2211	214	95
50 to 54	**49940**	562	838	11516	7365	2599	2775	11673	9396	2601	594	21
Good health	**27111**	381	608	7657	4525	1649	1323	6020	3772	873	288	15
Fairly good health	**13353**	109	160	2508	1847	657	796	3345	2869	827	229	6
Not good health	**9476**	72	70	1351	993	293	656	2308	2755	901	77	-
55 to 59	**45145**	422	597	9113	6502	2446	2526	10545	9648	2901	445	-
Good health	**21415**	256	415	5457	3660	1403	1027	4842	3233	902	220	-
Fairly good health	**13272**	111	123	2234	1729	720	746	3312	3205	924	168	-
Not good health	**10458**	55	59	1422	1113	323	753	2391	3210	1075	57	-
60 to 64	**38186**	304	447	7254	5274	1784	2173	8469	9051	3361	69	-
Good health	**16473**	182	299	4126	2701	986	808	3493	2786	1062	30	-
Fairly good health	**13078**	87	109	2158	1751	567	755	2969	3405	1251	26	-
Not good health	**8635**	35	39	970	822	231	610	2007	2860	1048	13	-
65 to 74	**67718**	442	679	11441	9577	2745	4085	13499	15335	9855	60	-
Good health	**23923**	210	379	5571	4200	1220	1278	4409	3900	2733	23	-
Fairly good health	**26925**	163	215	4064	3721	1071	1649	5581	6330	4104	27	-
Not good health	**16870**	69	85	1806	1656	454	1158	3509	5105	3018	10	-

Notes:
1 NS-SeC stands for National Statistics Socio-economic Classification.
2 General health refers to health over the 12 months prior to Census day (29 April 2001).
3 In the NS-SeC classification, all full-time students are recorded in the 'full-time students' category regardless of whether they are economically active or inactive.
4 For long-term unemployed, year last worked is 1999 or earlier.

S339

Table S340: Sex and Age and Limiting Long-Term Illness by NS-SeC

Table population: All persons aged 16 to 74

	All persons	Large employers and higher managerial occupations	Higher professional occupations	Lower managerial and professional occupations	Intermediate occupations	Small employers and own account workers	Lower supervisory and technical occupations	Semi-routine occupations	Routine occupations	Never worked	Long-term unemployed	Full-time student
All persons	**1187079**	**25056**	**44917**	**229609**	**131679**	**103648**	**104088**	**183131**	**193187**	**58134**	**19841**	**93789**
16 to 24 years	211482	924	3123	14780	19245	3477	14534	28238	25865	10721	1877	88698
With limiting long-term illness	13688	29	91	667	860	156	712	1912	1917	2955	166	4223
Without limiting long-term illness	197794	895	3032	14113	18385	3321	13822	26326	23948	7766	1711	84475
25 to 34 years	242221	5533	13787	57313	32439	18252	23556	37914	35267	10063	4758	3339
With limiting long-term illness	24976	221	408	2947	2515	1270	2297	4881	5199	4343	614	281
Without limiting long-term illness	217245	5312	13379	54366	29924	16982	21259	33033	30068	5720	4144	3058
35 to 49 years	349438	10304	15396	83183	41164	38288	30869	53290	53712	13376	8140	1716
With limiting long-term illness	61409	731	1056	9131	6185	5000	5664	10867	14048	7019	1424	284
Without limiting long-term illness	288029	9573	14340	74052	34979	33288	25205	42423	39664	6357	6716	1432
50 to 59 years	187159	4583	6675	39163	19128	23030	16028	31107	35723	7580	4106	36
With limiting long-term illness	59456	835	949	9019	5164	5750	5841	10620	15546	4690	1036	6
Without limiting long-term illness	127703	3748	5726	30144	13964	17280	10187	20487	20177	2890	3070	30
60 to 64 years	73587	1496	2250	13564	7186	8292	6750	12564	16397	4285	803	-
With limiting long-term illness	32093	487	514	4601	2675	3174	3534	5680	8701	2533	194	-
Without limiting long-term illness	41494	1009	1736	8963	4511	5118	3216	6884	7696	1752	609	-
65 to 74 years	123192	2216	3686	21606	12517	12309	12351	20018	26223	12109	157	-
With limiting long-term illness	61152	860	1129	8546	5344	5366	6796	10416	15297	7344	54	-
Without limiting long-term illness	62040	1356	2557	13060	7173	6943	5555	9602	10926	4765	103	-
Males	**581232**	**18426**	**31062**	**102820**	**37837**	**82029**	**72078**	**60119**	**102160**	**19115**	**13698**	**41888**
16 to 24 years	106624	595	1976	7056	6534	2917	11247	12468	17932	5143	1155	39601
With limiting long-term illness	7176	16	63	348	285	121	506	815	1271	1596	107	2048
Without limiting long-term illness	99448	579	1913	6708	6249	2796	10741	11653	16661	3547	1048	37553
25 to 34 years	119915	3643	8490	24572	9423	14550	16051	13035	20791	3934	3096	1530
With limiting long-term illness	12076	134	253	1295	753	990	1394	1644	2776	2272	439	126
Without limiting long-term illness	107039	3509	8237	23277	8670	13560	14657	11391	18015	1662	2657	1404
35 to 49 years	172548	7623	10546	36183	11767	30505	21210	15113	28524	4782	5549	746
With limiting long-term illness	29391	497	678	3966	1941	3999	3627	3363	6967	3178	1058	117
Without limiting long-term illness	143157	7126	9868	32217	9826	26506	17583	11750	21557	1604	4491	629
50 to 59 years	92070	3599	5240	18534	5261	17985	10727	8889	16679	2078	3067	11
With limiting long-term illness	28471	609	724	4269	1703	4653	3743	3334	7030	1606	797	3
Without limiting long-term illness	63599	2990	4516	14265	3558	13332	6984	5555	9649	472	2270	8
60 to 64 years	35401	1192	1803	6310	1912	6508	4577	4095	7346	924	734	-
With limiting long-term illness	16371	401	413	2385	1001	2663	2486	2103	4042	706	171	-
Without limiting long-term illness	19030	791	1390	3925	911	3845	2091	1992	3304	218	563	-
65 to 74 years	55474	1774	3007	10165	2940	9564	8266	6519	10888	2254	97	-
With limiting long-term illness	27529	692	899	4188	1502	4292	4577	3636	6183	1534	26	-
Without limiting long-term illness	27945	1082	2108	5977	1438	5272	3689	2883	4705	720	71	-

Table S340: Sex and Age and Limiting Long-Term Illness by NS-SeC (continued)

	All persons	Large employers and higher managerial occupations	Higher professional occupations	Lower managerial and professional occupations	Intermediate occupations	Small employers and own account workers	Lower supervisory and technical occupations	Semi-routine occupations	Routine occupations	Never worked	Long-term unemployed	Full-time student
Females	**605847**	**6630**	**13855**	**126789**	**93842**	**21619**	**32010**	**123012**	**91027**	**39019**	**6143**	**51901**
16 to 24 years	104858	329	1147	7724	12711	560	3287	15770	7933	5578	722	49097
With limiting long-term illness	6512	13	28	319	575	35	206	1097	646	1359	59	2175
Without limiting long-term illness	98346	316	1119	7405	12136	525	3081	14673	7287	4219	663	46922
25 to 34 years	123106	1890	5297	32741	23016	3702	7505	24879	14476	6129	1662	1809
With limiting long-term illness	12900	87	155	1652	1762	280	903	3237	2423	2071	175	155
Without limiting long-term illness	110206	1803	5142	31089	21254	3422	6602	21642	12053	4058	1487	1654
35 to 49 years	176890	2681	4850	47000	29397	7783	9659	38177	25188	8594	2591	970
With limiting long-term illness	32018	234	378	5165	4244	1001	2037	7504	7081	3841	366	167
Without limiting long-term illness	144872	2447	4472	41835	25153	6782	7622	30673	18107	4753	2225	803
50 to 59 years	95089	984	1435	20629	13867	5045	5301	22218	19044	5502	1039	25
With limiting long-term illness	30985	226	225	4750	3461	1097	2098	7286	8516	3084	239	3
Without limiting long-term illness	64104	758	1210	15879	10406	3948	3203	14932	10528	2418	800	22
60 to 64 years	38186	304	447	7254	5274	1784	2173	8469	9051	3361	69	-
With limiting long-term illness	15722	86	101	2216	1674	511	1048	3577	4659	1827	23	-
Without limiting long-term illness	22464	218	346	5038	3600	1273	1125	4892	4392	1534	46	-
65 to 74 years	67718	442	679	11441	9577	2745	4085	13499	15335	9855	60	-
With limiting long-term illness	33623	168	230	4358	3842	1074	2219	6780	9114	5810	28	-
Without limiting long-term illness	34095	274	449	7083	5735	1671	1866	6719	6221	4045	32	-

S340

Notes:
1 NS-SeC stands for National Statistics Socio-economic Classification.
2 In the NS-SeC classification, all full-time students are recorded in the 'full-time students' category regardless of whether they are economically active or inactive.
3 For long-term unemployed, year last worked is 1999 or earlier.
4 Limiting long-term illness covers any long-term illness, health problem or disability which limits daily activities or work.

Table S341: Sex and NS-SeC by Economic Activity

Table population: All persons aged 16 to 74

	All persons	Economically active				Economically inactive				
		Employee	Self-employed	Unemployed	Full-time students	Retired	Student	Looking after home/family	Permanently sick/disabled	Other
All persons	**1187075**	**563770**	**98230**	**49098**	**28032**	**130313**	**67623**	**88207**	**110787**	**51015**
1. Higher managerial and professional occupations	69973	46600	11772	772	-	6493	59	1222	2109	946
1.1 Large employers and higher managerial occupations	25056	17056	2902	350	-	2892	11	403	1064	378
1.2 Higher professional occupations	44917	29544	8870	422	-	3601	48	819	1045	568
2. Lower managerial and professional occupations	229609	162612	7227	3455	-	29547	178	9943	12085	4562
3. Intermediate occupations	131679	90587	93	2181	-	15568	133	11066	8418	3633
4. Small employers and own account workers	103648	-	79138	1492	-	8867	21	3083	8089	2958
5. Lower supervisory and technical occupations	104086	67183	-	2655	-	13100	52	5602	11559	3935
6. Semi-routine occupations	183131	103569	-	5577	-	21689	237	22473	19710	9876
7. Routine occupations	193185	93219	-	6961	-	26492	158	22180	30923	13252
8. Never worked and long-term unemployed	77975	-	-	26005	-	8557	1028	12638	17894	11853
L14.1 Never worked	58134	-	-	6164	-	8557	1028	12638	17894	11853
L14.2 Long-term unemployed	19841	-	-	19841	-	-	-	-	-	-
Not classified	93789	-	-	-	28032	-	65757	-	-	-
L15 Full-time students	93789	-	-	-	28032	-	65757	-	-	-
Males	**581231**	**288285**	**78946**	**32957**	**11846**	**53408**	**30894**	**8398**	**56421**	**20076**
1. Higher managerial and professional occupations	49488	32190	9324	590	-	5052	35	182	1538	577
1.1 Large employers and higher managerial occupations	18426	12534	2219	270	-	2290	4	86	791	232
1.2 Higher professional occupations	31062	19656	7105	320	-	2762	31	96	747	345
2. Lower managerial and professional occupations	102820	74014	5200	2115	-	12920	58	764	5910	1839
3. Intermediate occupations	37837	28889	73	965	-	3862	27	281	2873	867
4. Small employers and own account workers	82029	-	64349	1310	-	6309	11	985	6864	2201
5. Lower supervisory and technical occupations	72078	50366	-	2073	-	8228	27	1122	7897	2365
6. Semi-routine occupations	60119	39952	-	2931	-	5975	77	1256	7237	2691
7. Routine occupations	102159	62874	-	5289	-	9734	54	2781	15912	5515
8. Never worked and long-term unemployed	32813	-	-	17684	-	1328	563	1027	8190	4021
L14.1 Never worked	19115	-	-	3986	-	1328	563	1027	8190	4021
L14.2 Long-term unemployed	13698	-	-	13698	-	-	-	-	-	-
Not classified	41888	-	-	-	11846	-	30042	-	-	-
L15 Full-time students	41888	-	-	-	11846	-	30042	-	-	-

	All persons	Economically active				Economically inactive				
		Employee	Self-employed	Unemployed	Full-time students	Retired	Student	Looking after home/family	Permanently sick/disabled	Other
Females	**605844**	**275485**	**19284**	**16141**	**16186**	**76905**	**36729**	**79809**	**54366**	**30939**
1. Higher managerial and professional occupations	20485	14410	2448	182	-	1441	24	1040	571	369
1.1 Large employers and higher managerial occupations	6630	4522	683	80	-	602	7	317	273	146
1.2 Higher professional occupations	13855	9888	1765	102	-	839	17	723	298	223
2. Lower managerial and professional occupations	126789	88598	2027	1340	-	16627	120	9179	6175	2723
3. Intermediate occupations	93842	61698	20	1216	-	11706	106	10785	5545	2766
4. Small employers and own account workers	21619	-	14789	182	-	2558	10	2098	1225	757
5. Lower supervisory and technical occupations	32008	16817	-	582	-	4872	25	4480	3662	1570
6. Semi-routine occupations	123012	63617	-	2646	-	15714	160	21217	12473	7185
7. Routine occupations	91026	30345	-	1672	-	16758	104	19399	15011	7737
8. Never worked and long-term unemployed	45162	-	-	8321	-	7229	465	11611	9704	7832
L14.1 Never worked	39019	-	-	2178	-	7229	465	11611	9704	7832
L14.2 Long-term unemployed	6143	-	-	6143	-	-	-	-	-	-
Not classified	51901	-	-	-	16186	-	35715	-	-	-
L15 Full-time students	51901	-	-	-	16186	-	35715	-	-	-

Notes:

1 NS-SeC stands for National Statistics Socio-economic Classification.

2 In the NS-SeC classification all full-time students are recorded in the 'full-time students' category regardless of whether they are economically active or inactive.

3 For long-term unemployed, year last worked is 1999 or earlier.

S 3 4 1

Table S342: Sex and NS-SeC by Method of Travel to Work

Table population: All persons aged 16 to 74 in employment the week before the Census

	All persons	Work mainly at or from home	Train	Bus, minibus or coach	Motorcycle, scooter or moped	Driving a car or van	Passenger in a car or van	Car or van pool	Taxi	Bicycle	On foot	Other method
All persons	**686644**	**60404**	**5920**	**41259**	**5527**	**383728**	**61670**	**39335**	**10873**	**5959**	**66831**	**5138**
1. Higher managerial and professional occupations	58372	5256	869	1851	323	41268	1788	3125	234	527	2799	332
1.1 Large employers and higher managerial occupations	19958	1121	175	389	87	15102	622	1086	104	163	977	132
1.2 Higher professional occupations	38414	4135	694	1462	236	26166	1166	2039	130	364	1822	200
2. Lower managerial and professional occupations	169839	8934	1734	6872	868	119666	8626	10504	1545	1180	9288	622
3. Intermediate occupations	90680	3103	1610	9121	526	51712	8598	5879	1322	485	7920	404
4. Small employers and own account workers	79138	32971	104	484	143	35981	2296	2648	808	155	2607	941
5. Lower supervisory and technical occupations	67185	2265	373	3370	1076	40071	7109	4431	1113	851	6122	404
6. Semi-routine occupations	103569	3780	566	9156	1125	48157	11923	6137	2870	1238	18315	302
7. Routine occupations	93221	3418	320	7208	1216	41169	14843	5619	1883	1279	14206	2060
8. Never worked and long-term unemployed	-	-	-	-	-	-	-	-	-	-	-	-
L14.1 Never worked	-	-	-	-	-	-	-	-	-	-	-	-
L14.2 Long-term unemployed	-	-	-	-	-	-	-	-	-	-	-	-
Not classified	24640	677	344	3197	250	5704	6487	992	1098	244	5574	73
L15 Full-time students	24640	677	344	3197	250	5704	6487	992	1098	244	5574	73
Males	**377391**	**42800**	**3149**	**16534**	**4857**	**216675**	**30375**	**21889**	**4065**	**4960**	**27538**	**4549**
1. Higher managerial and professional occupations	41514	4281	634	1154	298	29325	867	2112	151	462	1935	295
1.1 Large employers and higher managerial occupations	14753	844	118	237	80	11326	290	766	73	150	753	116
1.2 Higher professional occupations	26761	3437	516	917	218	17999	577	1346	78	312	1182	179
2. Lower managerial and professional occupations	79214	5780	882	2864	686	54574	2922	4790	553	998	4682	483
3. Intermediate occupations	28962	894	572	2416	400	16853	1723	2098	231	371	3099	305
4. Small employers and own account workers	64349	25994	80	351	127	30321	1859	2123	684	133	1778	899
5. Lower supervisory and technical occupations	50366	1740	313	1978	1018	31653	5133	3520	506	784	3354	367
6. Semi-routine occupations	39952	1506	276	3045	958	20047	4690	2597	814	964	4841	214
7. Routine occupations	62875	2205	233	3558	1147	31313	10833	4177	824	1056	5581	1948
8. Never worked and long-term unemployed	-	-	-	-	-	-	-	-	-	-	-	-
L14.1 Never worked	-	-	-	-	-	-	-	-	-	-	-	-
L14.2 Long-term unemployed	-	-	-	-	-	-	-	-	-	-	-	-
Not classified	10159	400	159	1168	223	2589	2348	472	302	192	2268	38
L15 Full-time students	10159	400	159	1168	223	2589	2348	472	302	192	2268	38

	All persons	Work mainly at or from home	Train	Bus, minibus or coach	Motorcycle, scooter or moped	Driving a car or van	Passenger in a car or van	Car or van pool	Taxi	Bicycle	On foot	Other method
Females	**309253**	**17604**	**2771**	**24725**	**670**	**167053**	**31295**	**17446**	**6808**	**999**	**39293**	**589**
1. Higher managerial and professional occupations	16858	975	235	697	25	11943	921	1013	83	65	864	37
1.1 Large employers and higher managerial occupations	5205	277	57	152	7	3776	332	320	31	13	224	16
1.2 Higher professional occupations	11653	698	178	545	18	8167	589	693	52	52	640	21
2. Lower managerial and professional occupations	90625	3154	852	4008	182	65092	5704	5714	992	182	4606	139
3. Intermediate occupations	61718	2209	1038	6705	126	34859	6875	3781	1091	114	4821	99
4. Small employers and own account workers	14789	6977	24	133	16	5660	437	525	124	22	829	42
5. Lower supervisory and technical occupations	16819	525	60	1392	58	8418	1976	911	607	67	2768	37
6. Semi-routine occupations	63617	2274	290	6111	167	28110	7233	3540	2056	274	13474	88
7. Routine occupations	30346	1213	87	3650	69	9856	4010	1442	1059	223	8625	112
8. Never worked and long-term unemployed	-	-	-	-	-	-	-	-	-	-	-	-
L14.1 Never worked	-	-	-	-	-	-	-	-	-	-	-	-
L14.2 Long-term unemployed	-	-	-	-	-	-	-	-	-	-	-	-
Not classified	14481	277	185	2029	27	3115	4139	520	796	52	3306	35
L15 Full-time students	14481	277	185	2029	27	3115	4139	520	796	52	3306	35

Notes:
1 NS-SeC stands for National Statistics Socio-economic Classification.
2 In the NS-SeC classification, all full-time students are recorded in the 'full-time students' category regardless of whether they are economically active or inactive.
3 For long-term unemployed, year last worked is 1999 or earlier.
4 'Other method' includes no fixed place of work, working at an offshore installation, working outside the UK.

S342

S 3 4 3

Table S343: NS-SeC by Tenure

Table population: All persons in households aged 16 to 74

	All persons	Owner occupied			Social rented		Private rented			Other
		Owns outright	Owns with a mortgage or loan	Shared ownership	Rented from NIHE	Other social rented	Private landlord or letting agency	Employer of a household member	Relative or friend of a household member	
All persons	**1171801**	**330185**	**552290**	**8967**	**173759**	**17173**	**66550**	**6850**	**11165**	**4862**
1. Higher managerial and professional occupations	**69093**	**21205**	**39173**	**262**	**1953**	**346**	**3598**	**1215**	**577**	**764**
1.1 Large employers and higher managerial occupations	24449	7238	14633	95	910	122	807	395	167	82
L1 Employers in large organisation	3892	1635	1712	14	292	33	155	9	35	7
L2 Higher managerial	20557	5603	12921	81	618	89	652	386	132	75
1.2 Higher professional occupations	44644	13967	24540	167	1043	224	2791	820	410	682
L3.1 Higher professionals (traditional) - employees	26885	8035	14748	113	726	148	1764	684	264	403
L3.2 Higher professionals (new) - employees	7604	1686	4820	32	191	43	706	22	77	27
L3.3 Higher professionals (traditional) - self-employed	9442	4014	4561	19	104	33	279	114	69	249
L3.4 Higher professionals (new) -self-employed	713	232	411	3	22	-	42	-	-	3
2. Lower managerial and professional occupations	**227400**	**68659**	**129186**	**1360**	**11579**	**1828**	**9666**	**2247**	**1983**	**892**
L4.1 Lower professionals and higher technical (traditional) - employees	118506	37756	66425	616	5639	900	4979	714	1056	421
L4.2 Lower professionals and higher technical (new) - employees	9407	2385	5824	72	488	59	449	22	95	13
L4.3 Lower professionals and higher technical (traditional) - self-employed	6771	2249	3602	27	232	53	477	21	87	23
L4.4 Lower professionals and higher technical (new) - self-employed	1992	785	1044	9	55	9	76	3	11	-
L5 Lower managerial	48942	12841	29178	364	3036	455	2303	226	420	119
L6 Higher supervisory	41782	12643	23113	272	2129	352	1382	1261	314	316
3. Intermediate occupations	**129486**	**37689**	**69675**	**1123**	**11034**	**1471**	**5951**	**944**	**1181**	**418**
L7.1 Intermediate clerical and administrative	65399	21022	34148	542	5192	691	2674	308	619	203
L7.2 Intermediate sales and services	49081	12497	27739	426	4288	567	2394	593	403	174
L7.3 Intermediate technical and auxiliary	11277	3190	5596	111	1287	192	690	40	139	32
L7.4 Intermediate engineering	3729	980	2192	44	267	21	193	3	20	9
4. Small employers and own account workers	**103392**	**44443**	**47068**	**465**	**5610**	**616**	**3607**	**134**	**1178**	**271**
L8.1 Employers in small organisations (non-professional)	37135	13972	19369	117	1722	230	1258	31	358	78
L8.2 Employers in small organisations (agriculture)	4494	3147	1071	9	91	7	82	10	61	16
L9.1 Own account workers (non-professional)	45044	14686	23372	321	3562	372	2024	68	516	123
L9.2 Own account workers (agriculture)	16719	12638	3256	18	235	7	243	25	243	54
5. Lower supervisory and technical occupations	**103496**	**27264**	**51555**	**1039**	**15203**	**1599**	**5071**	**486**	**911**	**368**
L10 Lower supervisory	63582	16467	32015	642	8720	1083	3403	400	587	265
L11.1 Lower technical craft	30533	8360	15304	294	4536	362	1275	69	253	80
L11.2 Lower technical process operative	9381	2437	4236	103	1947	154	393	17	71	23

Table S343: NS-SeC by Tenure (continued)

	All persons	Owner occupied			Social rented		Private rented			Other
		Owns outright	Owns with a mortgage or loan	Shared ownership	Rented from NIHE	Other social rented	Private landlord or letting agency	Employer of a household member	Relative or friend of a household member	
6. Semi-routine occupations	**182418**	**46608**	**79834**	**1796**	**36626**	**3582**	**10828**	**811**	**1645**	**688**
L12.1 Semi-routine sales	54349	13713	23678	563	10800	1064	3515	286	517	213
L12.2 Semi-routine service	62836	15879	26584	661	13363	1419	3813	285	575	257
L12.3 Semi-routine technical	11741	2874	5275	112	2611	232	504	16	84	33
L12.4 Semi-routine operative	27945	6761	12128	266	6377	519	1573	45	200	76
L12.5 Semi-routine agriculture	3827	1537	979	15	843	48	257	51	73	24
L12.6 Semi-routine clerical	13572	3825	6752	120	1676	189	769	65	126	50
L12.7 Semi-routine childcare	8148	2019	4438	59	956	111	397	63	70	35
7. Routine occupations	**192247**	**47749**	**74187**	**1756**	**50814**	**4151**	**10576**	**525**	**1799**	**690**
L13.1 Routine sales and service	19764	4341	7433	160	5122	475	1800	138	200	95
L13.2 Routine production	40198	8823	14298	399	12878	980	2281	70	347	122
L13.3 Routine technical	57287	15641	25687	519	11059	911	2690	74	526	180
L13.4 Routine operative	73439	18499	26290	672	21322	1757	3686	226	704	283
L13.5 Routine agricultural	1559	445	479	6	433	28	119	17	22	10
8. Never worked and long-term unemployed	**74567**	**17969**	**14969**	**578**	**30120**	**2621**	**6880**	**164**	**924**	**342**
L14.1 Never worked	54797	14748	10093	408	21984	1997	4435	115	745	272
L14.2 Long-term unemployed	19770	3221	4876	170	8136	624	2445	49	179	70
Not classified	**89702**	**18599**	**46643**	**588**	**10820**	**959**	**10373**	**324**	**967**	**429**
L15 Full-time students	89702	18599	46643	588	10820	959	10373	324	967	429

Notes:
1 The terms used to describe tenure are defined as:
   Shared ownership: pays part rent and part mortgage.
   Rented from NIHE: rented from Northern Ireland Housing Executive.
   Other social rented: rented from Registered Social Landlord, Housing Association, Housing Co-operative or Charitable Trust.
(2) 'Social rented' and 'Private rented' include living in the household rent free.
(3) NS-SeC stands for National Statistics Socio-economic Classification.
(4) In the NS-SeC classification all full-time students are recorded in the 'full-time students' category regardless of whether they are economically active or inactive.
(5) For long-term unemployed, year last worked is 1999 or earlier'.

S343

Table S344: Sex and NS-SeC of Household Reference Person (HRP) by Tenure

Table population: All household reference persons (HRPs) aged 16 to 74

	All households	Owner occupied	Rented from NIHE	Other social rented	Private rented
ALL HRPs	**563970**	**399115**	**101767**	**11574**	**51514**
1. Higher managerial and professional occupations	45136	39121	1319	268	4428
1.1 Large employers and higher managerial occupations	17110	15264	650	91	1105
1.2 Higher professional occupations	28026	23857	669	177	3323
2. Lower managerial and professional occupations	119579	101434	7384	1381	9380
3. Intermediate occupations	53126	40836	6468	1035	4787
4. Small employers and own account workers	69098	60726	4065	484	3823
5. Lower supervisory and technical occupations	58125	42680	9796	1175	4474
6. Semi-routine occupations	79242	46116	22464	2410	8252
7. Routine occupations	99081	55910	31638	2926	8607
8. Never worked or long-term unemployed	36651	11387	18087	1779	5398
L14.1 Never worked	24688	7950	12139	1282	3317
L14.2 Long-term unemployed	11963	3437	5948	497	2081
Not classified	3932	905	546	116	2365
L15 Full-time students	3932	905	546	116	2365
Males	**351133**	**271988**	**46158**	**5384**	**27603**
1. Higher managerial and professional occupations	37524	32840	922	201	3561
1.1 Large employers and higher managerial occupations	14498	13080	445	67	906
1.2 Higher professional occupations	23026	19760	477	134	2655
2. Lower managerial and professional occupations	73054	63459	3572	647	5376
3. Intermediate occupations	22672	18594	1902	318	1858
4. Small employers and own account workers	61520	54694	3306	378	3142
5. Lower supervisory and technical occupations	45701	35496	6435	732	3038
6. Semi-routine occupations	34061	22670	7635	926	2830
7. Routine occupations	59985	39295	14722	1423	4545
8. Never worked or long-term unemployed	15045	4527	7487	718	2313
L14.1 Never worked	6486	1925	3280	386	895
L14.2 Long-term unemployed	8559	2602	4207	332	1418
Not classified	1571	413	177	41	940
L15 Full-time students	1571	413	177	41	940

S 3 4 4

208

© Crown copyright 2003

	All households	Owner occupied	Rented from NIHE	Other social rented	Private rented
Females	**212837**	**127127**	**55609**	**6190**	**23911**
1. Higher managerial and professional occupations	7612	6281	397	67	867
1.1 Large employers and higher managerial occupations	2612	2184	205	24	199
1.2 Higher professional occupations	5000	4097	192	43	668
2. Lower managerial and professional occupations	46525	37975	3812	734	4004
3. Intermediate occupations	30454	22242	4566	717	2929
4. Small employers and own account workers	7578	6032	759	106	681
5. Lower supervisory and technical occupations	12424	7184	3361	443	1436
6. Semi-routine occupations	45181	23446	14829	1484	5422
7. Routine occupations	39096	16615	16916	1503	4062
8. Never worked or long-term unemployed	21606	6860	10600	1061	3085
L14.1 Never worked	18202	6025	8859	896	2422
L14.2 Long-term unemployed	3404	835	1741	165	663
Not classified	2361	492	369	75	1425
L15 Full-time students	2361	492	369	75	1425

Notes:
1 NS-SeC stands for National Statistics Socio-economic Classification.
2 In the NS-SeC classification all full-time students are recorded in the 'full-time students' category regardless of whether they are economically active or inactive.
3 The terms used to describe tenure are defined as:
   Owner occupied: either owns outright, owns with a mortgage or loan, or pays part rent and part mortgage (shared ownership).
   Rented from NIHE: rented from Northern Ireland Housing Executive.
   Other social rented: rented from Registered Social Landlord, Housing Association, Housing Co-operative or Charitable Trust.
   Private rented: rented from a private landlord or letting agency, employer of a household member, or relative or friend of a household member or other person.
4 'Rented from NIHE', 'Other social rented' and 'Private rented' include living in the household rent free.
5 For long-term unemployed, year last worked is 1999 or earlier.
6 The Household Reference Person may not be the oldest person in a household, as economic activity is given priority over age.

S344

Table S345: Sex and NS-SeC of Household Reference Person (HRP) by Household Composition

Table population: All household reference persons (HRPs) aged 16 to 74

| | All households | One person | | One family and no others | | | | | | | | Other households | | | | |
| | | Pensioner | Other | Couple households | | | | | Lone parent households | | | With one dependent child | With two or more dependent children | All student | All pensioner | Other |
				All pensioner	No children	With one dependent child	With two or more dependent children	All children non-dependent	With one dependent child	With two or more dependent children	All children non-dependent					
ALL HRPs	**563968**	**39978**	**91055**	**30896**	**79623**	**55289**	**106720**	**49510**	**24516**	**25949**	**21190**	**7270**	**8363**	**1732**	**2707**	**19170**
1. Higher managerial and professional occupations	45136	1257	7544	2562	8648	5499	12264	3236	529	405	415	350	472	-	116	1839
1.1 Large employers and higher managerial occupations	17110	436	2169	1000	3344	2271	5048	1509	228	159	191	147	200	-	35	373
1.2 Higher professional occupations	28026	821	5375	1562	5304	3228	7216	1727	301	246	224	203	272	-	81	1466
2. Lower managerial and professional occupations	119579	7058	20357	6607	20234	13446	25643	9283	3542	3113	2938	1253	1288	-	561	4256
3. Intermediate occupations	53126	4709	9308	2888	8040	4876	8176	3623	3020	2673	2077	716	653	-	279	2088
4. Small employers and own account workers	69098	2410	7030	3640	9812	8733	20066	9214	798	776	1505	959	1406	-	384	2365
5. Lower supervisory and technical occupations	58125	3295	8477	3798	9251	6890	12205	5876	1605	1546	1602	751	814	-	233	1782
6. Semi-routine occupations	79242	7409	12542	4440	9737	5864	9722	6677	6248	6756	4284	1269	1321	-	430	2543
7. Routine occupations	99081	8967	15466	5547	12094	8628	15376	9867	5197	5878	5539	1372	1574	-	519	3057
8. Never worked or long-term unemployed	36651	4873	9462	1414	1677	1252	3066	1731	3252	4568	2813	504	747	-	185	1107
L14.1 Never worked	24688	4796	4846	1382	807	470	1164	1061	2330	3729	2332	357	547	-	179	688
L14.2 Long-term unemployed	11963	77	4616	32	870	782	1902	670	922	839	481	147	200	-	6	419
Not classified	3930	-	869	-	130	101	202	3	325	234	17	96	88	1732	-	133
L15 Full-time students	3930	-	869	-	130	101	202	3	325	234	17	96	88	1732	-	133
Males	**351133**	**10119**	**55970**	**19888**	**58565**	**45515**	**92724**	**37674**	**2333**	**1566**	**4621**	**3712**	**4843**	**660**	**1181**	**11762**
1. Higher managerial and professional occupations	37524	650	5059	2320	7471	4994	11510	3018	143	103	227	255	398	-	65	1311
1.1 Large employers and higher managerial occupations	14498	202	1443	908	2918	2097	4754	1404	63	39	118	109	174	-	13	256
1.2 Higher professional occupations	23026	448	3616	1412	4553	2897	6756	1614	80	64	109	146	224	-	52	1055
2. Lower managerial and professional occupations	73054	1420	10153	4479	14011	10262	20874	6924	377	258	675	621	787	-	165	2048
3. Intermediate occupations	22672	571	3940	1079	4194	3111	5863	2062	130	88	257	210	242	-	54	871
4. Small employers and own account workers	61520	1396	6013	3130	8968	8305	19324	8511	343	258	815	827	1253	-	302	2075
5. Lower supervisory and technical occupations	45701	1481	6601	3096	7917	6301	11450	5136	290	170	666	510	620	-	122	1341
6. Semi-routine occupations	34061	1507	6469	2050	5717	4007	7087	3844	255	210	553	385	461	-	163	1353
7. Routine occupations	59985	2478	10798	3350	9119	7445	13860	7180	487	314	1054	738	866	-	250	2046
8. Never worked or long-term unemployed	15045	616	6495	384	1085	1011	2597	996	290	152	371	146	195	-	60	647
L14.1 Never worked	6486	580	2738	369	364	327	862	407	116	50	144	73	86	-	57	313
L14.2 Long-term unemployed	8559	36	3757	15	721	684	1735	589	174	102	227	73	109	-	3	334
Not classified	1571	-	442	-	83	79	159	3	18	13	3	20	21	660	-	70
L15 Full-time students	1571	-	442	-	83	79	159	3	18	13	3	20	21	660	-	70

Table S345: Sex and NS-SeC of Household Reference Person (HRP) by Household Composition (continued)

| | All households | One person | | One family and no others | | | | | | | | Other households | | | | |
| | | | | Couple households | | | | | Lone parent households | | | | | | | |
		Pensioner	Other	All pensioner	No children	With one dependent child	With two or more dependent children	All children non-dependent	With one dependent child	With two or more dependent children	All children non-dependent	With one dependent child	With two or more dependent children	All student	All pensioner	Other
Females	**212835**	**29859**	**35085**	**11008**	**21058**	**9774**	**13996**	**11836**	**22183**	**24383**	**16569**	**3558**	**3520**	**1072**	**1526**	**7408**
1. Higher managerial and professional occupations	7612	607	2485	242	1177	505	754	218	386	302	188	95	74	-	51	528
1.1 Large employers and higher managerial occupations	2612	234	726	92	426	174	294	105	165	120	73	38	26	-	22	117
1.2 Higher professional occupations	5000	373	1759	150	751	331	460	113	221	182	115	57	48	-	29	411
2. Lower managerial and professional occupations	46525	5638	10204	2128	6223	3184	4769	2359	3165	2855	2263	632	501	-	396	2208
3. Intermediate occupations	30454	4138	5368	1809	3846	1765	2313	1561	2890	2585	1820	506	411	-	225	1217
4. Small employers and own account workers	7578	1014	1017	510	844	428	742	703	455	518	690	132	153	-	82	290
5. Lower supervisory and technical occupations	12424	1814	1876	702	1334	589	755	740	1315	1376	936	241	194	-	111	441
6. Semi-routine occupations	45181	5902	6073	2390	4020	1857	2635	2833	5993	6546	3731	884	860	-	267	1190
7. Routine occupations	39096	6489	4668	2197	2975	1183	1516	2687	4710	5564	4485	634	708	-	269	1011
8. Never worked or long-term unemployed	21606	4257	2967	1030	592	241	469	735	2962	4416	2442	358	552	-	125	460
L14.1 Never worked	18202	4216	2108	1013	443	143	302	654	2214	3679	2188	284	461	-	122	375
L14.2 Long-term unemployed	3404	41	859	17	149	98	167	81	748	737	254	74	91	-	3	85
Not classified	2359	-	427	-	47	22	43	-	307	221	14	76	67	1072	-	63
L15 Full-time students	2359	-	427	-	47	22	43	-	307	221	14	76	67	1072	-	63

Notes:
1 NS-SeC stands for National Statistics Socio-economic Classification.
2 In the NS-SeC classification, all full-time students are recorded in the 'full-time students' category regardless of whether they are economically active or inactive.
3 A dependent child is a person in a household aged 0 to 15 (whether or not in a family) or a person aged 16 to 18 who is a full-time student in a family with parent(s).
4 For long-term unemployed, year last worked is 1999 or earlier.
5 A family consists of a couple (married or cohabiting) with or without children, or a lone parent and their children.
   It also includes a married or cohabiting couple with their grandchildren or a lone grandparent with his or her grandchildren, if there is no parent in the intervening generation in the household.
   A family will also include step-children when their parent is part of the couple.
6 Pensionable age at the time of the Census (29 April 2001) was 65 for men and 60 for women

S345

S 3 4 6

Table S346: Sex and NS-SeC of Household Reference Person (HRP) by Age (of HRP)

Table population: All household reference persons (HRPs) aged 16 to 74

	ALL HRPs	16 to 24	25 to 34	35 to 44	45 to 49	50 to 54	55 to 59	60 to 64	65 to 74
ALL HRPs	**563969**	**21233**	**107033**	**135633**	**59242**	**57086**	**52703**	**44001**	**87038**
1. Higher managerial and professional occupations	45136	656	10028	12796	5610	4773	3901	2716	4656
1.1 Large employers and higher managerial occupations	17110	139	3076	5328	2386	1916	1533	1006	1726
1.2 Higher professional occupations	28026	517	6952	7468	3224	2857	2368	1710	2930
2. Lower managerial and professional occupations	119579	2243	24920	31502	14293	12944	10461	7815	15401
3. Intermediate occupations	53126	2443	11497	13024	5256	4688	4402	3560	8256
4. Small employers and own account workers	69098	476	10003	18134	8654	8629	7820	5838	9544
5. Lower supervisory and technical occupations	58125	1844	12021	14342	5925	5598	5048	4308	9039
6. Semi-routine occupations	79242	4597	15047	16647	6976	7452	7730	7066	13727
7. Routine occupations	99081	3656	16442	21174	9255	9812	10261	9870	18611
8. Never worked or long-term unemployed	36651	2712	6379	7534	3139	3175	3080	2828	7804
L14.1 Never worked	24688	2200	3981	4120	1401	1536	1596	2175	7679
L14.2 Long-term unemployed	11963	512	2398	3414	1738	1639	1484	653	125
Not classified	3931	2606	696	480	134	15	-	-	-
L15 Full-time students	3931	2606	696	480	134	15	-	-	-
Males	**351133**	**8374**	**66499**	**92460**	**41280**	**38807**	**34468**	**26016**	**43229**
1. Higher managerial and professional occupations	37524	439	7625	10738	4893	4181	3416	2339	3893
1.1 Large employers and higher managerial occupations	14498	77	2434	4560	2086	1692	1351	865	1433
1.2 Higher professional occupations	23026	362	5191	6178	2807	2489	2065	1474	2460
2. Lower managerial and professional occupations	73054	1145	14973	20353	9283	8313	6613	4477	7897
3. Intermediate occupations	22672	752	5088	6567	2679	2197	1828	1296	2265
4. Small employers and own account workers	61520	388	8998	16636	7924	7806	6932	5085	7751
5. Lower supervisory and technical occupations	45701	1237	9513	11859	4904	4553	3992	3242	6401
6. Semi-routine occupations	34061	1269	6619	7731	3323	3447	3512	3084	5076
7. Routine occupations	59985	1581	10734	14508	6335	6486	6501	5362	8478
8. Never worked or long-term unemployed	15045	574	2642	3872	1865	1819	1674	1131	1468
L14.1 Never worked	6486	368	1139	1448	535	563	512	529	1392
L14.2 Long-term unemployed	8559	206	1503	2424	1330	1256	1162	602	76
Not classified	1571	989	307	196	74	5	-	-	-
L15 Full-time students	1571	989	307	196	74	5	-	-	-

Table S346: Sex and NS-SeC of Household Reference Person (HRP) by Age (of HRP) (continued)

	ALL HRPs	16 to 24	25 to 34	35 to 44	45 to 49	50 to 54	55 to 59	60 to 64	65 to 74
Females	**212836**	**12859**	**40534**	**43173**	**17962**	**18279**	**18235**	**17985**	**43809**
1. Higher managerial and professional occupations	7612	217	2403	2058	717	592	485	377	763
1.1 Large employers and higher managerial occupations	2612	62	642	768	300	224	182	141	293
1.2 Higher professional occupations	5000	155	1761	1290	417	368	303	236	470
2. Lower managerial and professional occupations	46525	1098	9947	11149	5010	4631	3848	3338	7504
3. Intermediate occupations	30454	1691	6409	6457	2577	2491	2574	2264	5991
4. Small employers and own account workers	7578	88	1005	1498	730	823	888	753	1793
5. Lower supervisory and technical occupations	12424	607	2508	2483	1021	1045	1056	1066	2638
6. Semi-routine occupations	45181	3328	8428	8916	3653	4005	4218	3982	8651
7. Routine occupations	39096	2075	5708	6666	2920	3326	3760	4508	10133
8. Never worked or long-term unemployed	21606	2138	3737	3662	1274	1356	1406	1697	6336
L14.1 Never worked	18202	1832	2842	2672	866	973	1084	1646	6287
L14.2 Long-term unemployed	3404	306	895	990	408	383	322	51	49
Not classified	2360	1617	389	284	60	10	-	-	-
L15 Full-time students	2360	1617	389	284	60	10	-	-	-

Notes:

1 NS-SeC stands for National Statistics Socio-economic Classification.

2 In the NS-SeC classification all full-time students are recorded in the 'full-time students' category regardless of whether they are economically active or inactive.

3 For long-term unemployed, year last worked is 1999 or earlier.

S346

Table S347: NS-SeC of Household Reference Person (HRP) by Households with Full-time Students Living Away From Home and Age of Student

Table population: All households with students in full-time education whose home address is in the area, but they live away from home during term-time

	All households with students 'living away from home'	Households with 1 student living away from home		Households with 2 students living away from home			Households with 3 or more students living away from home		
		Aged under 18	Aged 18 or over	Both aged under 18	One aged under 18 and one aged 18 or over	Both aged 18 or over	All aged under 18	Combination of students aged under 18, and 18 and over	All aged 18 or over
All household reference persons (HRPs)	**20202**	**536**	**16132**	**98**	**86**	**2995**	**25**	**20**	**310**
1. Higher managerial and professional occupations	2884	81	2143	26	17	542	3	7	65
1.1 Large employers and higher managerial occupations	1068	35	795	19	6	184	3	3	23
1.2 Higher professional occupations	1816	46	1348	7	11	358	-	4	42
2. Lower managerial and professional occupations	6066	120	4781	30	22	999	8	5	101
3. Intermediate occupations	1494	38	1261	4	4	173	3	-	11
4. Small employers and own account workers	4241	82	3372	13	27	666	3	8	70
5. Lower supervisory and technical occupations	1482	48	1233	7	7	170	-	-	17
6. Semi-routine occupations	1594	62	1320	8	3	177	4	-	20
7. Routine occupations	1827	61	1525	7	6	204	4	-	20
8. Never worked and long-term unemployed	459	36	373	3	-	44	-	-	3
L14.1 Never worked	202	21	166	-	-	12	-	-	3
L14.2 Long-term unemployed	257	15	207	3	-	32	-	-	-
Not classified	155	8	124	-	-	20	-	-	3
L15 Full-time students	74	5	55	-	-	11	-	-	3
L17 Not classifiable for other reasons	81	3	69	-	-	9	-	-	-

Notes:

1   The term 'student living away from home' refers to students and schoolchildren in full-time education who would be resident in the household if they were not living elsewhere during term-time. They are counted as residents at their term-time address.

2   NS-SeC stands for National Statistics Socio-economic Classification.

3   In the NS-SeC classification, all full-time students are recorded in the 'full-time students' category regardless of whether they are economically active or inactive.

4   For long-term unemployed, year last worked is 1999 or earlier.

5   'Not classifiable for other reasons' includes HRPs not aged 16-74.

S348

Table S348: Sex and NS-SeC by Ethnic Group

Table population: All persons aged 16 to 74

	All persons	White	Irish Traveller	Mixed	Indian	Pakistani	Bangladeshi	Other Asian	Black Caribbean	Black African	Other Black	Chinese	Other ethnic group
All persons	**1187073**	**1177608**	**1076**	**1534**	**1217**	**428**	**154**	**160**	**204**	**344**	**295**	**3048**	**1005**
1. Higher managerial and professional occupations	69965	68788	24	130	384	70	10	32	14	74	15	271	153
1.1 Large employers and higher managerial occupations	25051	24878	9	27	37	6	-	4	6	10	4	35	35
1.2 Higher professional occupations	44914	43910	15	103	347	64	10	28	8	64	11	236	118
2. Lower managerial and professional occupations	229609	228405	71	265	166	44	21	54	48	49	45	197	244
3. Intermediate occupations	131676	131086	41	142	67	17	10	9	22	28	81	109	64
4. Small employers and own account workers	103648	102326	85	105	188	84	25	3	23	14	11	728	56
5. Lower supervisory and technical occupations	104091	103586	68	104	39	23	12	6	16	17	13	156	51
6. Semi-routine occupations	183130	181996	119	198	88	45	23	8	27	37	40	462	87
7. Routine occupations	193187	192518	176	153	44	16	14	8	19	29	29	119	62
8. Never worked and long-term unemployed	77978	76713	424	114	138	84	32	11	18	39	38	258	109
L14.1 Never worked	58135	57010	386	93	125	79	29	11	11	26	31	239	95
L14.2 Long-term unemployed	19843	19703	38	21	13	5	3	-	7	13	7	19	14
Not classified	93789	92190	68	323	103	45	7	29	17	57	23	748	179
L15 Full-time students	93789	92190	68	323	103	45	7	29	17	57	23	748	179
Males	**581225**	**576253**	**587**	**775**	**651**	**251**	**84**	**60**	**113**	**194**	**173**	**1640**	**444**
1. Higher managerial and professional occupations	49485	48642	19	86	276	52	7	24	8	65	15	184	107
1.1 Large employers and higher managerial occupations	18423	18296	9	19	25	6	-	4	-	6	4	23	31
1.2 Higher professional occupations	31062	30346	10	67	251	46	7	20	8	59	11	161	76
2. Lower managerial and professional occupations	102820	102285	47	110	75	30	12	11	27	24	23	93	83
3. Intermediate occupations	37834	37609	21	52	20	5	-	-	15	13	59	15	25
4. Small employers and own account workers	82030	81117	72	73	131	66	21	3	14	10	11	472	40
5. Lower supervisory and technical occupations	72078	71734	49	78	31	17	9	3	13	11	8	93	32
6. Semi-routine occupations	60118	59611	48	79	29	25	17	-	9	16	16	246	27
7. Routine occupations	102160	101843	95	88	14	8	8	-	8	14	19	44	17
8. Never worked and long-term unemployed	32812	32403	190	47	24	17	7	3	10	14	12	60	25
L14.1 Never worked	19116	18795	162	36	17	12	7	3	6	4	9	48	17
L14.2 Long-term unemployed	13696	13608	28	11	7	5	-	-	4	10	3	12	8
Not classified	41888	41009	46	162	51	31	3	16	9	30	10	433	88
L15 Full-time students	41888	41009	46	162	51	31	3	16	9	30	10	433	88

	All persons	White	Irish Traveller	Mixed	Indian	Pakistani	Bangladeshi	Other Asian	Black Caribbean	Black African	Other Black	Chinese	Other ethnic group
Females	**605848**	**601355**	**489**	**759**	**566**	**177**	**70**	**100**	**91**	**150**	**122**	**1408**	**561**
1. Higher managerial and professional occupations	20480	20146	5	44	108	18	3	8	6	9	-	87	46
1.1 Large employers and higher managerial occupations	6628	6582	-	8	12	-	-	-	6	4	-	12	4
1.2 Higher professional occupations	13852	13564	5	36	96	18	3	8	-	5	-	75	42
2. Lower managerial and professional occupations	126789	126120	24	155	91	14	9	43	21	25	22	104	161
3. Intermediate occupations	93842	93477	20	90	47	12	10	9	7	15	22	94	39
4. Small employers and own account workers	21618	21209	13	32	57	18	4	-	9	4	-	256	16
5. Lower supervisory and technical occupations	32013	31852	19	26	8	6	3	3	3	6	5	63	19
6. Semi-routine occupations	123012	122385	71	119	59	20	6	8	18	26	24	216	60
7. Routine occupations	91027	90675	81	65	30	8	6	8	11	13	10	75	45
8. Never worked and long-term unemployed	45166	44310	234	67	114	67	25	8	8	25	26	198	84
L14.1 Never worked	39019	38215	224	57	108	67	22	8	5	22	22	191	78
L14.2 Long-term unemployed	6147	6095	10	10	6	-	3	-	3	3	4	7	6
Not classified	51901	51181	22	161	52	14	4	13	8	27	13	315	91
L15 Full-time students	51901	51181	22	161	52	14	4	13	8	27	13	315	91

Notes:
1 NS-SeC stands for National Statistics Socio-economic Classification.
2 In the NS-SeC classification, all full-time students are recorded in the 'full-time students' category regardless of whether they are economically active or not.
3 For long-term unemployed, year last worked is 1999 or earlier.

S348

Table S349: NS-SeC by Sex and Community Background (Religion or Religion Brought Up In)

Table population: All persons aged 16 to 74

	All persons	Males					Females				
		Total	Catholic	Protestant and Other Christian (including Christian related)	Other religions and philosophies	None	Total	Catholic	Protestant and Other Christian (including Christian related)	Other religions and philosophies	None
All persons	1187079	581232	245374	319199	2936	13723	605847	263590	329659	2136	10462
1. Higher managerial and professional occupations	69973	49488	17393	29877	658	1560	20485	8805	10867	246	567
1.1 Large employers and higher managerial occupations	25056	18426	5958	11871	103	494	6630	2743	3696	32	159
1.2 Higher professional occupations	44917	31062	11435	18006	555	1066	13855	6062	7171	214	408
2. Lower managerial and professional occupations	229609	102820	38234	61272	458	2856	126789	54194	70142	383	2070
3. Intermediate occupations	131679	37837	11663	24669	154	1351	93842	35184	56778	215	1665
4. Small employers and own account workers	103648	82029	36830	43305	481	1413	21619	7747	13199	179	494
5. Lower supervisory and technical occupations	104088	72078	27687	42749	226	1416	32010	12973	18444	77	516
6. Semi-routine occupations	183131	60119	24166	34256	280	1417	123012	49692	71243	275	1802
7. Routine occupations	193187	102160	48077	52535	156	1392	91027	42004	47909	127	987
8. Never worked and long-term unemployed	77975	32813	19738	12238	135	702	45162	25153	18837	334	838
L14.1 Never worked	58134	19115	11758	6874	71	412	39019	21770	16218	316	715
L14.2 Long-term unemployed	19841	13698	7980	5364	64	290	6143	3383	2619	18	123
Not classified	93789	41888	21586	18298	388	1616	51901	27838	22240	300	1523
L15 Full-time students	93789	41888	21586	18298	388	1616	51901	27838	22240	300	1523

Notes:

1 NS-SeC stands for National Statistics Socio-economic Classification.
2 In the NS-SeC classification, all full-time students are recorded in the 'full-time students' category regardless of whether they are economically active or inactive.
3 For long-term unemployed, year last worked is 1999 or earlier.
4 The term 'Catholic' includes those respondents who gave their religion as Catholic or Roman Catholic.

Table S066: Sex and Approximated Social Grade by Age

Table population: All persons aged 16 and over in households

	All persons	16	17	18	19	20 to 24	25 to 29	30 to 34	35 to 39	40 to 44	45 to 49	50 to 54	55 to 59	60 to 64	65 to 69	70 to 74	75 and over
All persons	**1261257**	**27080**	**26075**	**24725**	**21202**	**105729**	**112934**	**126402**	**128847**	**116727**	**101915**	**97817**	**88132**	**72985**	**64594**	**56634**	**89459**
AB. Higher and intermediate managerial / administrative / professional	213530	4810	4607	4221	3133	14647	19729	23696	26091	24467	21919	19201	15088	11540	9987	7942	2452
C1. Supervisory, clerical, junior managerial / administrative / professional	383889	7101	7123	6525	5448	29438	33182	37002	37913	35487	30918	28832	25240	18888	16505	14464	49823
C2. Skilled manual workers	262048	6183	5969	5768	4705	24576	26617	29154	28985	25502	22344	21466	19249	15293	13710	10100	2427
D. Semi-skilled and unskilled manual workers	298486	6959	6605	6423	5942	28992	27253	29367	28690	25222	21857	23630	24127	22568	18988	17209	4654
E. On state benefit, unemployed, lowest grade workers	103304	2027	1771	1788	1974	8076	6153	7183	7168	6049	4877	4688	4428	4696	5404	6919	30103
Males	**605288**	**13803**	**13183**	**12631**	**10629**	**52456**	**55254**	**61614**	**62841**	**57045**	**51331**	**48113**	**43241**	**35082**	**30036**	**24562**	**33467**
AB. Higher and intermediate managerial / administrative / professional	106186	2423	2261	2222	1626	7656	9569	11654	12624	11854	11068	9787	7676	5574	4824	4060	1308
C1. Supervisory, clerical, junior managerial / administrative / professional	180141	3650	3712	3334	2893	14795	15944	17640	18159	17156	15437	13957	12192	8977	7629	6132	18534
C2. Skilled manual workers	142902	3109	3029	3015	2525	13128	14075	15477	15573	13751	12338	11627	10556	8619	8182	7062	836
D. Semi-skilled and unskilled manual workers	137929	3584	3316	3264	2855	14011	13141	13875	13360	11499	10128	10585	10906	10219	7923	6036	3227
E. On state benefit, unemployed, lowest grade workers	38130	1037	865	796	730	2866	2525	2968	3125	2785	2360	2157	1911	1693	1478	1272	9562
Females	**655969**	**13277**	**12892**	**12094**	**10573**	**53273**	**57680**	**64788**	**66006**	**59682**	**50584**	**49704**	**44891**	**37903**	**34558**	**32072**	**55992**
AB. Higher and intermediate managerial / administrative / professional	107344	2387	2346	1999	1507	6991	10160	12042	13467	12613	10851	9414	7412	5966	5163	3882	1144
C1. Supervisory, clerical, junior managerial / administrative / professional	203748	3451	3411	3191	2555	14643	17238	19362	19754	18331	15481	14875	13048	9911	8876	8332	31289
C2. Skilled manual workers	119146	3074	2940	2753	2180	11448	12542	13677	13412	11751	10006	9839	8693	6674	5528	3038	1591
D. Semi-skilled and unskilled manual workers	160557	3375	3289	3159	3087	14981	14112	15492	15330	13723	11729	13045	13221	12349	11065	11173	1427
E. On state benefit, unemployed, lowest grade workers	65174	990	906	992	1244	5210	3628	4215	4043	3264	2517	2531	2517	3003	3926	5647	20541

Notes:

1   Social Grade is the socio-economic classification used by the Market Research and Marketing Industries, most often in the analysis of spending habits and consumer attitudes. Although it is not possible to allocate Social Grade precisely from information collected by the 2001 Census, the Market Research Society has developed a method for using Census information to provide a good approximation of Social Grade.

2   In this table, persons are classified by the Approximated Social Grade of their Household Reference Person, as agreed with the Market Research Society.

S066

Table S067: Age of Household Reference Person (HRP) and Dependent Children by Approximated Social Grade

Table population: All households

	All households	AB. Higher and intermediate managerial/ administrative/ professional	C1. Supervisory, clerical, junior managerial/ administrative/ professional	C2. Skilled manual workers	D. Semi-skilled and unskilled manual workers	E. On state benefit, unemployed, lowest grade workers
All households	**625718**	**101117**	**193467**	**114921**	**148412**	**68801**
Age of HRP under 25	**21296**	**1499**	**5170**	**3109**	**6970**	**4548**
- youngest dependent child aged 0 to 4	8456	233	1530	964	3185	2544
- youngest dependent child aged 5 to 11	788	27	179	76	299	207
- youngest dependent child aged 12 to 18	105	4	28	20	31	22
- no dependent children	11947	1235	3433	2049	3455	1775
Age of HRP 25 to 34	**107033**	**19875**	**32059**	**22232**	**24956**	**7911**
- youngest dependent child aged 0 to 4	40555	6293	10929	9774	10423	3136
- youngest dependent child aged 5 to 11	15411	1135	3698	2750	5580	2248
- youngest dependent child aged 12 to 18	1591	107	344	247	629	264
- no dependent children	49476	12340	17088	9461	8324	2263
Age of HRP 35 to 49	**194875**	**40446**	**57245**	**41280**	**44745**	**11159**
- youngest dependent child aged 0 to 4	37877	9458	10963	8757	7092	1607
- youngest dependent child aged 5 to 11	55188	11763	15980	12161	12382	2902
- youngest dependent child aged 12 to 18	37226	6798	10988	7789	9631	2020
- no dependent children	64584	12427	19314	12573	15640	4630
Age of HRP 50 and over	**303514**	**39297**	**98993**	**48300**	**71741**	**45183**
- youngest dependent child aged 0 to 4	3073	447	771	774	848	233
- youngest dependent child aged 5 to 11	7174	1441	1935	1803	1578	417
- youngest dependent child aged 12 to 18	21105	4735	5717	5002	4703	948
- no dependent children	272162	32674	90570	40721	64612	43585

Notes:

1 The Household Reference Person may not be the oldest person in a household, as economic activity is given priority over age.

2 A dependent child is a person in a household aged 0 to 15 (whether or not in a family) or a person aged 16 to 18 who is a full-time student in a family with parent(s). The dependent child may or may not be a child of the Household Reference Person.

3 Social Grade is the socio-economic classification used by the Market Research and Marketing industries, most often in the analysis of spending habits and consumer attitudes. Although it is not possible to allocate Social Grade precisely from information collected by the 2001 Census, the Market Research Society has developed a method for using Census information to provide a good approximation of Social Grade.

4 In this table, persons are classified by the Approximated Social Grade of their Household Reference Person, as agreed with the Market Research Society.

Table S118: Number of Employed Persons and Method of Travel to Work by Number of Cars or Vans in Household

Table population: All households with at least one person working in the week before the Census

	All households	Number of cars or vans in household				
		None	1	2	3	4 or more
All households with at least one person working	**395348**	**44922**	**179994**	**136271**	**25853**	**8308**
One employed person in household	**179018**	**33719**	**103326**	**37055**	**4077**	**841**
- Driving a car or van	98668	3167	65186	26919	2844	552
- 'Other' method of travel to work	64176	29131	29294	5101	544	106
- Works at home	16174	1421	8846	5035	689	183
Two employed persons in household	**166014**	**8950**	**64067**	**80745**	**10089**	**2163**
- Both driving cars or vans	65852	222	10472	48535	5561	1062
- Both taking 'other' method of travel to work	21128	7414	10164	3118	349	83
- Both working at home	4670	102	1572	2333	466	197
- One driving a car or van, one by 'other' method	55696	849	36724	15966	1824	333
- One driving a car or van, one working at home	13858	57	2748	9014	1614	425
- One by 'other' method, one working at home	4810	306	2387	1779	275	63
Three or more employed persons in household	**50316**	**2253**	**12601**	**18471**	**11687**	**5304**
- All driving cars or vans	6834	23	304	1783	3207	1517
- All taking 'other' method of travel to work	4857	1741	2031	797	233	55
- All working at home	668	17	104	258	182	107
- Mixture of driving a car or van and 'other'	27858	323	8615	12151	5048	1721
- Mixture of driving a car or van and working at home	4385	18	329	1191	1685	1162
- Mixture of 'other' and working at home	1730	111	614	632	275	98
- Mixture of driving a car or van, 'other' and working at home	3984	20	604	1659	1057	644

Notes:
1. Driving a car or van includes sharing driving and car-pooling.
2. 'Other' in method of travel is any other means of travel to work.
3. The number of cars or vans in a household only includes a company car or van if it is available for private use.

S118

Table S350: Sex and Age by Method of Travel to Work

Table population: All persons aged 16 to 74 working in the week before the Census

	All persons	Work mainly at or from home	Train	Bus, minibus or coach	Motorcycle, scooter or moped	Driving a car or van	Passenger in a car or van	Car or van pool	Taxi	Bicycle	On foot	Other method
All persons	**686644**	**60404**	**5920**	**41259**	**5527**	**383728**	**61670**	**39335**	**10873**	**5959**	**66831**	**5138**
16 to 19	39343	1196	439	5913	790	7098	11898	1849	1874	405	7605	276
20 to 24	74884	2753	1199	7882	732	31575	11475	4828	2513	634	10836	457
25 to 29	88442	4508	1040	5886	766	51274	8006	5820	1443	877	8166	656
30 to 34	94813	6393	781	4384	882	59512	6522	5987	1187	959	7463	743
35 to 39	94145	7966	645	4036	803	59480	5601	5682	1012	947	7248	725
40 to 44	84292	7834	546	3631	582	53044	4923	4978	865	627	6637	625
45 to 49	71455	7380	472	3207	365	44402	4374	3934	726	442	5658	495
50 to 54	61307	7439	386	2755	304	36534	3907	3052	574	435	5460	461
55 to 59	45222	6562	275	2173	171	25362	3081	1957	406	339	4493	403
60 to 64	21835	4250	97	963	91	11384	1361	874	199	201	2210	205
65 to 69	7026	2570	21	253	29	2770	350	245	46	54	632	56
70 to 74	3880	1553	19	176	12	1293	172	129	28	39	423	36
Males	**377391**	**42800**	**3149**	**16534**	**4857**	**216675**	**30375**	**21889**	**4065**	**4960**	**27538**	**4549**
16 to 19	21950	883	233	2582	715	4570	6774	1229	684	361	3694	225
20 to 24	39771	1976	565	3005	606	17468	6197	2880	874	526	5296	378
25 to 29	46788	3212	501	2339	652	27149	4073	3244	528	724	3793	573
30 to 34	51731	4426	417	1814	804	32372	3250	3340	431	843	3356	678
35 to 39	51449	5443	366	1659	726	32704	2831	3042	391	829	2806	652
40 to 44	45294	5500	318	1391	519	29186	2161	2531	309	541	2269	569
45 to 49	39162	5230	278	1245	316	25161	1806	2114	303	358	1902	449
50 to 54	33802	5176	222	1065	261	21272	1475	1607	261	327	1720	416
55 to 59	25956	4570	161	829	142	15847	1080	1124	176	251	1416	360
60 to 64	14276	3171	64	443	80	8178	531	557	86	140	846	180
65 to 69	4647	1998	14	92	24	1910	135	143	14	34	240	43
70 to 74	2565	1215	10	70	12	858	62	78	8	26	200	26
Females	**309253**	**17604**	**2771**	**24725**	**670**	**167053**	**31295**	**17446**	**6808**	**999**	**39293**	**589**
16 to 19	17393	313	206	3331	75	2528	5124	620	1190	44	3911	51
20 to 24	35113	777	634	4877	126	14107	5278	1948	1639	108	5540	79
25 to 29	41654	1296	539	3547	114	24125	3933	2576	915	153	4373	83
30 to 34	43082	1967	364	2570	78	27140	3272	2647	756	116	4107	65
35 to 39	42696	2523	279	2377	77	26776	2770	2640	621	118	4442	73
40 to 44	38998	2334	228	2240	63	23858	2762	2447	556	86	4368	56
45 to 49	32293	2150	194	1962	49	19241	2568	1820	423	84	3756	46
50 to 54	27505	2263	164	1690	43	15262	2432	1445	313	108	3740	45
55 to 59	19266	1992	114	1344	29	9515	2001	833	230	88	3077	43
60 to 64	7559	1079	33	520	11	3206	830	317	113	61	1364	25
65 to 69	2379	572	7	161	5	860	215	102	32	20	392	13
70 to 74	1315	338	9	106	-	435	110	51	20	13	223	10

Notes:
1 'Other method' includes no fixed place of work, working at offshore installation, working outside the UK.

4. Housing and Transport

4. Housing and Transport

Access to a Car or Van

Tenure and Accommodation Type

Central Heating and Occupancy Rating

Table S059: Accommodation Type and Car or Van Availability by Number of Persons Aged 17 or Over in the Household

Table population: All households

	All households	Number of persons aged 17 or over in household				
		None	1	2	3	4 or more
All households	**626717**	**102**	**213262**	**285056**	**80467**	**47830**
No car or van	164949	74	114902	37754	8489	3730
1 car or van	278579	20	94199	141636	29876	12848
2 cars or vans	147880	5	3580	98193	30870	15232
3 cars or vans	26814	-	450	6079	9818	10467
4 or more cars or vans	8495	3	131	1394	1414	5553
Detached house or bungalow	**230408**	**35**	**45556**	**123856**	**37401**	**23560**
No car or van	21148	15	15195	4561	977	400
1 car or van	90393	12	28492	48920	9412	3557
2 cars or vans	92753	5	1632	64632	18408	8076
3 cars or vans	19329	-	169	4667	7401	7092
4 or more cars or vans	6785	3	68	1076	1203	4435
Semi-detached house or bungalow	**174781**	**21**	**55723**	**85413**	**21701**	**11923**
No car or van	37558	21	25144	9469	2082	842
1 car or van	93771	-	29468	50282	9929	4092
2 cars or vans	37486	-	961	24475	7927	4123
3 cars or vans	4877	-	125	979	1630	2143
4 or more cars or vans	1089	-	25	208	133	723
Terraced house or bungalow (including end-terrace)	**169433**	**22**	**72424**	**64979**	**20221**	**11787**
No car or van	74372	17	47241	19762	5044	2308
1 car or van	76839	5	24422	37280	10122	5010
2 cars or vans	15351	-	650	7500	4275	2926
3 cars or vans	2329	-	89	353	714	1173
4 or more cars or vans	542	-	22	84	66	370
Flat, maisonette or apartment	**50335**	**21**	**38877**	**9908**	**1037**	**492**
No car or van	31489	21	27007	3913	372	176
1 car or van	16675	-	11468	4655	384	168
2 cars or vans	1875	-	322	1255	212	86
3 cars or vans	235	-	64	66	63	42
4 or more cars or vans	61	-	16	19	6	20
Caravan or other mobile or temporary structure	**1760**	**3**	**682**	**900**	**107**	**68**
No car or van	382	-	315	49	14	4
1 car or van	901	3	349	499	29	21
2 cars or vans	415	-	15	331	48	21
3 cars or vans	44	-	3	14	10	17
4 or more cars or vans	18	-	-	7	6	5

S059

Notes:

1   Car or van includes company car or van if available for private use.

227

S062

Table S062: Household Composition by Number of Cars or Vans Available

Table population: All households

	All households	Number of cars or vans available				
		None	1	2	3	4 or more
All households	**626718**	**164949**	**278580**	**147880**	**26815**	**8494**
One person	**171573**	**90599**	**77471**	**2988**	**403**	**112**
- pensioner	80486	52654	27297	439	81	15
- other	91087	37945	50174	2549	322	97
One family and no others	**413706**	**63951**	**185446**	**134265**	**22937**	**7107**
All pensioner	40769	7802	27109	5531	256	71
Couple family households	293310	20056	124029	121216	21280	6729
- no children	79766	6994	39672	30407	2227	466
- with dependent child(ren)	162118	9432	68843	71493	9337	3013
- all children non-dependent	51426	3630	15514	19316	9716	3250
Lone parent households	79627	36093	34308	7518	1401	307
- with dependent child(ren)	50641	27555	20927	1768	313	78
- all children non-dependent	28986	8538	13381	5750	1088	229
Other households	**41439**	**10399**	**15663**	**10627**	**3475**	**1275**
- with dependent child(ren)	15755	3420	5980	4278	1554	523
- all student	1732	927	453	240	83	29
- all pensioner	4295	1681	2011	539	51	13
- other	19657	4371	7219	5570	1787	710

Notes:

1 Couple family households include both married and cohabiting couple family households.

2 A dependent child is a person in a household aged 0 to 15 (whether or not in a family) or a person aged 16 to 18 who is a full-time student in a family with parent(s).

3 Car or van availability includes any company car or van if available for private use.

4 A family consists of a couple (married or cohabiting) with or without children, or a lone parent and their children. It also includes a married or cohabiting couple with their grandchildren or a lone grandparent with his or her grandchildren, if there is no parent in the intervening generation in the household. A family will also include step-children when their parent is part of the couple.

5 Pensionable age at the time of the Census (29 April 2001) was 65 for men and 60 for women

Table S351: Tenure and Number of Cars or Vans by Ethnic Group of Household Reference Person (HRP)

Table population: All households

	All HRPs	White	Irish Traveller	Mixed	Indian	Pakistani	Bangladeshi	Other Asian	Black Caribbean	Black African	Other Black	Chinese	Other ethnic group
All households	**626720**	**622346**	**665**	**647**	**603**	**178**	**74**	**69**	**126**	**186**	**122**	**1288**	**416**
Cars or vans													
None	164949	163687	326	219	82	27	20	31	54	62	58	251	132
1	278582	276618	275	302	273	85	44	24	59	90	48	599	165
2 or more	183189	182041	64	126	248	66	10	14	13	34	16	438	119
Owner occupied	**436217**	**433718**	**259**	**327**	**445**	**130**	**54**	**33**	**61**	**78**	**58**	**859**	**195**
Cars or vans													
None	54008	53726	82	43	20	6	11	4	22	7	15	53	19
1	211041	209836	132	181	191	61	33	15	29	40	31	404	88
2 or more	171168	170156	45	103	234	63	10	14	10	31	12	402	88
Social rented	**132934**	**132131**	**264**	**168**	**42**	**19**	**13**	**6**	**32**	**35**	**26**	**153**	**45**
Cars or vans													
None	86305	85806	173	114	18	14	6	3	19	22	21	80	29
1	42357	42093	77	49	21	5	7	3	10	13	5	62	12
2 or more	4272	4232	14	5	3	-	-	-	3	-	-	11	4
Private rented	**57569**	**56497**	**142**	**152**	**116**	**29**	**7**	**30**	**33**	**73**	**38**	**276**	**176**
Cars or vans													
None	24636	24155	71	62	44	7	3	24	13	33	22	118	84
1	25184	24689	66	72	61	19	4	6	20	37	12	133	65
2 or more	7749	7653	5	18	11	3	-	-	-	3	4	25	27

Notes:
1   The terms used to describe tenure are defined as:
    Owner occupied: either owns outright, owns with a mortgage or loan, or pays part rent and part mortgage (shared ownership).
    Social rented: rented from Northern Ireland Housing Executive, Registered Social Landlord, Housing Association, Housing Co-operative or Charitable Trust.
    Private rented: rented from a private landlord or letting agency, employer of a household member, or relative or friend of a household member or other person.
2   'Social rented' and 'Private rented' include living in the household rent free.
3   Cars or vans includes company cars or vans if available for private use.

S 3 5 1

Table S352: Tenure and Number of Cars or Vans by Community Background (Religion or Religion Brought Up In) of Household Reference Person (HRP)

Table population: All households

	All HRPs	Catholic	Protestant and Other Christian (including Christian related)	Other religions and philosophies	None
All households	**626717**	**247568**	**364767**	**2666**	**11716**
Cars or vans					
None	**164949**	70943	90303	629	3074
1	**278580**	110298	161527	1241	5514
2	**147880**	53436	91153	648	2643
3 or more	**35308**	12891	21784	148	485
Owner occupied	**436217**	**166884**	**260401**	**1706**	**7226**
Cars or vans					
None	**54008**	22928	30159	161	760
1	**211041**	82321	124191	814	3715
2	**137756**	49529	85327	590	2310
3 or more	**33412**	12106	20724	141	441
Social rented	**132930**	**56412**	**74051**	**345**	**2122**
Cars or vans					
None	**86305**	36609	48129	206	1361
1	**42355**	18018	23536	130	671
2	**3737**	1536	2110	9	82
3 or more	**533**	249	276	-	8
Private rented	**57570**	**24272**	**30315**	**615**	**2368**
Cars or vans					
None	**24636**	11406	12015	262	953
1	**25184**	9959	13800	297	1128
2	**6387**	2371	3716	49	251
3 or more	**1363**	536	784	7	36

Notes:

1. The terms used to describe tenure are defined as:
   Owner occupied: either owns outright, owns with a mortgage or loan, or pays part rent and part mortgage (shared ownership).
   Social rented: rented from Northern Ireland Housing Executive, Registered Social Landlord, Housing Association, Housing Co-operative or Charitable Trust.
   Private rented: rented from a private landlord or letting agency, employer of a household member, or relative or friend of a household member or other person.
2. 'Social rented' and 'Private rented' include living in the 'household rent free.
3. Cars or vans includes company cars or vans if available for private use.
4. The term 'Catholic' includes those respondents who gave their religion as Catholic or Roman Catholic.

Table S353: Dwelling Type and Accommodation Type by Tenure

Table population: All occupied household spaces

	Total	Owner occupied			Social rented		Private rented			Other
		Owns outright	Owns with a mortgage or loan	Shared ownership	Rented from NIHE	Other social rented	Private landlord or letting agency	Employer of a household member	Relative or friend of a household member	
All occupied household spaces	**626718**	**184090**	**247182**	**4945**	**116477**	**16454**	**41676**	**3405**	**9355**	**3134**
In an unshared dwelling	**626658**	**184086**	**247182**	**4945**	**116474**	**16451**	**41626**	**3405**	**9355**	**3134**
House or bungalow	574620	178622	243145	4525	94100	7624	32368	3095	8670	2471
Detached	230406	100638	105053	514	8702	803	8076	1294	4104	1222
Semi-detached	174781	45134	85422	2464	26005	2927	8771	1109	2268	681
Terraced (including end terrace)	169433	32850	52670	1547	59393	3894	15521	692	2298	568
Flat, maisonette or apartment	50278	4321	3907	416	22242	8824	9059	300	586	623
In a purpose built block of flats or tenement	42830	3615	3432	363	21541	8363	4479	209	324	504
Part of a converted or shared house (includes bed-sits)	5674	414	311	50	570	413	3620	29	192	75
In a commercial building	1774	292	164	3	131	48	960	62	70	44
Caravan or other mobile or temporary structure	1760	1143	130	4	132	3	199	10	99	40
In a shared dwelling	**60**	**4**	**-**	**-**	**3**	**3**	**50**	**-**	**-**	**-**

Notes:

1 The terms used to describe tenure are defined as:
   Shared ownership: pays part rent and part mortgage.
   Rented from NIHE: rented from Northern Ireland Housing Executive.
   Other social rented: rented from Registered Social Landlord, Housing Association, Housing Co-operative or Charitable Trust.

2 'Social rented' and 'Private rented' include living in the household rent free.

3 In general, a household's accommodation is defined as an unshared dwelling if all the rooms are behind a door that only that household can use.

4 'In a commercial building' includes in an office building, or hotel, or over a shop.

S353

Table S354: Dwelling Type and Accommodation Type by Tenure (Persons)

Table population: All persons in households

	Total	Owner occupied			Social rented		Private rented			Other
		Owns outright	Owns with a mortgage or loan	Shared ownership	Rented from NIHE	Other social rented	Private landlord or letting agency	Employer of a household member	Relative or friend of a household member	
All persons	**1658813**	**430431**	**790289**	**12900**	**266452**	**28783**	**94694**	**10363**	**17908**	**6993**
In an unshared dwelling	**1658744**	**430424**	**790289**	**12900**	**266448**	**28777**	**94642**	**10363**	**17908**	**6993**
House or bungalow	1583418	421271	783754	12323	235177	18285	80103	9739	16768	5998
Detached	694840	260169	372301	1472	21355	2012	21988	4148	8389	3006
Semi-detached	463906	94913	259749	7179	63079	7390	22298	3400	4182	1716
Terraced (including end terrace)	424672	66189	151704	3672	150743	8883	35817	2191	4197	1276
Flat, maisonette or apartment	70897	6209	6144	572	30969	10488	14094	609	920	892
In a purpose built block of flats or tenement	58468	4885	5107	479	29782	9852	6791	429	476	667
Part of a converted or shared house (includes bed-sits)	9246	703	573	85	940	559	5882	57	317	130
In a commercial building	3183	621	464	8	247	77	1421	123	127	95
Caravan or other mobile or temporary structure	4429	2944	391	5	302	4	445	15	220	103
In a shared dwelling	**69**	**7**	**-**	**-**	**4**	**6**	**52**	**-**	**-**	**-**

Notes:

1 The terms used to describe tenure are defined as:
   Shared ownership: pays part rent and part mortgage.
   Rented from NIHE: rented from Northern Ireland Housing Executive.
   Other social rented: rented from Registered Social Landlord, Housing Association, Housing Co-operative or Charitable Trust.

2 'Social rented' and 'Private rented' include living in the household rent free.

3 In general, a household's accommodation is defined as an unshared dwelling if all the rooms are behind a door that only that household can use.

4 'In a commercial building' includes in an office building, or hotel, or over a shop.

Table S355: Tenure and Household Size by Number of Rooms

Table population: All households

	All households	1 room	2 rooms	3 rooms	4 rooms	5 rooms	6 rooms	7 rooms	8 or more rooms
All households	**626717**	**2335**	**10490**	**35676**	**83573**	**198470**	**136047**	**67903**	**92223**
1 person	171573	1704	7234	23471	43467	49431	28817	9379	8070
2 persons	176180	394	2264	6999	26289	58958	41426	18377	21473
3 persons	103629	103	616	2472	8332	37434	25225	12626	16821
4 persons	95315	56	244	1490	3610	29937	23215	14339	22424
5 persons	49930	39	93	712	1191	14487	10908	8217	14283
6 persons	21914	26	34	391	504	6151	4698	3554	6556
7 persons	5344	9	5	96	111	1439	1146	897	1641
8 or more persons	2832	4	-	45	69	633	612	514	955
Owner occupied	**436217**	**624**	**2507**	**9710**	**34147**	**129704**	**112345**	**60507**	**86673**
1 person	91157	292	1333	4287	15870	31593	23093	7854	6835
2 persons	127708	171	713	2705	11211	40521	35382	16779	20226
3 persons	77131	72	264	1231	3883	23684	20666	11371	15960
4 persons	77350	40	126	847	2045	20166	19512	13125	21489
5 persons	40011	25	48	382	738	9100	8879	7201	13638
6 persons	16851	17	18	196	300	3540	3590	3047	6143
7 persons	4014	3	5	43	65	797	831	741	1529
8 or more persons	1995	4	-	19	35	303	392	389	853
Rented from NIHE	**116476**	**898**	**3863**	**14834**	**33304**	**47723**	**11948**	**2624**	**1282**
1 person	48002	724	2630	10744	19239	11312	2503	463	387
2 persons	29003	139	901	2309	9625	12352	2859	562	256
3 persons	16704	16	224	835	2897	9689	2360	493	190
4 persons	11187	9	76	484	1031	7172	1874	382	159
5 persons	6487	4	22	245	313	4242	1214	321	126
6 persons	3497	3	10	159	146	2132	740	220	87
7 persons	968	3	-	35	29	536	226	99	40
8 or more persons	628	-	-	23	24	288	172	84	37

Table S355: Tenure and Household Size by Number of Rooms (continued)

	All households	1 room	2 rooms	3 rooms	4 rooms	5 rooms	6 rooms	7 rooms	8 or more rooms
Other social rented	**16456**	**294**	**2022**	**5649**	**4105**	**3053**	**793**	**354**	**186**
1 person	10165	266	1746	4876	2354	640	151	72	60
2 persons	3279	19	234	674	1324	758	173	64	33
3 persons	1336	3	32	49	309	667	177	70	29
4 persons	844	-	7	26	81	523	128	58	21
5 persons	481	3	3	18	21	300	77	45	14
6 persons	246	3	-	6	8	122	56	32	19
7 persons	66	-	-	-	5	33	17	8	3
8 or more persons	39	-	-	-	3	10	14	5	7
Private rented	**57568**	**519**	**2098**	**5483**	**12017**	**17990**	**10961**	**4418**	**4082**
1 person	22249	422	1525	3564	6004	5886	3070	990	788
2 persons	16190	65	416	1311	4129	5327	3012	972	958
3 persons	8458	12	96	357	1243	3394	2022	692	642
4 persons	5934	7	35	133	453	2076	1701	774	755
5 persons	2951	7	20	67	119	845	738	650	505
6 persons	1320	3	6	30	50	357	312	255	307
7 persons	296	3	-	18	12	73	72	49	69
8 or more persons	170	-	-	3	7	32	34	36	58

Notes:

1 The terms used to describe tenure are defined as:

Owner occupied: either owns outright, owns with a mortgage or loan, or pays part rent and part mortgage (shared ownership).

Rented from NIHE: rented from Northern Ireland Housing Executive.

Other social rented: rented from Registered Social Landlord, Housing Association, Housing Co-operative or Charitable Trust.

Private rented: rented from a private landlord or letting agency, employer of a household member, or relative or friend of a household member or other person.

2 'Rented from NIHE', 'Other social rented' and 'Private rented' include living in the household rent free.

3 The number of rooms available to the household excludes bathrooms, toilets, halls or landings, and rooms that can only be used for storage. It also does not include any rooms shared with another household such as a shared kitchen.

S355

Table S356: Tenure and Persons Per Room by Accommodation Type

Table population: All households

	All households	House or bungalow			Flat, maisonette or apartment			Caravan or other mobile or temporary structure
		Detached	Semi-detached	Terraced (including end-terraced)	In a purpose built block of flats or tenement	Part of a converted or shared house	In a commercial building	
All households	**626720**	**230406**	**174781**	**169433**	**42830**	**5734**	**1776**	**1760**
up to 0.5 persons per room	418101	158307	109897	106285	37112	4291	1372	837
over 0.5 and up to 1.0 persons per room	191712	67574	59854	56613	5311	1320	356	684
over 1.0 and up to 1.5 persons per room	13734	3654	4161	5460	247	56	36	120
over 1.5 persons per room	3173	871	869	1075	160	67	12	119
Owner occupied	**436217**	**206205**	**133020**	**87067**	**7410**	**779**	**459**	**1277**
up to 0.5 persons per room	288901	142222	83328	55188	6647	621	330	565
over 0.5 and up to 1.0 persons per room	137499	60514	46554	28936	713	126	113	543
over 1.0 and up to 1.5 persons per room	8180	2844	2641	2542	35	9	13	96
over 1.5 persons per room	1637	625	497	401	15	23	3	73
Rented from NIHE	**116479**	**8702**	**26005**	**59393**	**21541**	**573**	**133**	**132**
up to 0.5 persons per room	76157	5248	16299	35288	18755	411	96	60
over 0.5 and up to 1.0 persons per room	34901	2844	8278	21002	2559	138	30	50
over 1.0 and up to 1.5 persons per room	4300	447	1154	2532	138	16	4	9
over 1.5 persons per room	1121	163	274	571	89	8	3	13
Other social rented	**16454**	**803**	**2927**	**3894**	**8363**	**416**	**48**	**3**
up to 0.5 persons per room	12551	477	1749	2564	7395	324	39	3
over 0.5 and up to 1.0 persons per room	3545	282	1047	1206	923	82	5	-
over 1.0 and up to 1.5 persons per room	279	32	106	108	25	4	4	-
over 1.5 persons per room	79	12	25	16	20	6	-	-
Private rented	**57570**	**14696**	**12829**	**19079**	**5516**	**3966**	**1136**	**348**
up to 0.5 persons per room	40492	10360	8521	13245	4315	2935	907	209
over 0.5 and up to 1.0 persons per room	15767	3934	3975	5469	1116	974	208	91
over 1.0 and up to 1.5 persons per room	975	331	260	278	49	27	15	15
over 1.5 persons per room	336	71	73	87	36	30	6	33

Notes:

1 The terms used to describe tenure are defined as:
Owner occupied: either owns outright, owns with a mortgage or loan, or pays part rent and part mortgage (shared ownership).
Rented from NIHE: rented from Northern Ireland Housing Executive.
Other social rented: rented from Registered Social Landlord, Housing Association, Housing Co-operative or Charitable Trust.
Private rented: rented from a private landlord or letting agency, employer of a household member, or relative or friend of a household member or other person.

2 'Rented from NIHE', 'Other social rented' and 'Private rented' include living in the household rent free.

3 'In a commercial building' includes in an office building, or hotel, or over a shop.

4 The number of rooms available to the household excludes bathrooms, toilets, halls or landings, and rooms that can only be used for storage. It also does not include any rooms shared with another household such as a shared kitchen.

Table S357: Household Composition by Tenure and Occupancy Rating

Table population: All households

	All households	Owner occupied				Rented from NIHE				Other social rented				Private rented			
		+2 or more	+1	0	-1 or less	+2 or more	+1	0	-1 or less	+2 or more	+1	0	-1 or less	+2 or more	+1	0	-1 or less
All households	626717	284025	87933	42934	21325	26141	41962	32651	15723	1875	4254	7287	3037	23659	16498	11741	5672
One person	171573	69375	15870	4287	1625	14665	19239	10744	3354	923	2354	4876	2012	10734	6004	3564	1947
- pensioner	80486	33351	7273	1976	751	6528	9411	5164	1529	422	1325	3616	1236	4553	1947	950	454
- other	91087	36024	8597	2311	874	8137	9828	5580	1825	501	1029	1260	776	6181	4057	2614	1493
One family and no others	413705	203843	65380	33326	15603	10953	21170	19512	9848	871	1790	2206	806	11443	8824	5681	2449
All pensioner	40769	28444	3064	757	241	2331	1949	598	247	136	312	398	95	1577	425	137	58
Married couple households	269087	149580	46594	24748	12058	4773	6759	6159	4088	411	627	587	281	5949	3429	2060	984
- no children	66484	51806	3732	1033	316	3148	1549	464	184	253	270	110	54	2438	796	244	87
- with dependent child(ren)	152218	74300	30475	18031	9208	947	3232	4356	3138	116	273	388	186	2968	2272	1563	765
- all children non dependent	50385	23474	12387	5684	2534	678	1978	1339	766	42	84	89	41	543	361	253	132
Cohabiting couple households	24222	10719	3748	1317	456	758	1569	1208	518	56	141	134	48	1373	1217	706	254
- no children	13282	7949	1254	231	65	496	549	204	61	34	61	36	17	1018	785	385	137
- with dependent child(ren)	9900	2464	2236	966	331	228	930	936	424	22	77	92	28	336	415	305	110
- all children non dependent	1040	306	258	120	60	34	90	68	33	-	3	6	3	19	17	16	7
Lone parent households	79627	15100	11974	6504	2848	3091	10893	11547	4995	268	710	1087	382	2544	3753	2778	1153
- with dependent child(ren)	50641	5978	5244	3571	1713	2120	8032	9143	3999	223	590	875	304	2139	3280	2425	1005
- all children non dependent	28986	9122	6730	2933	1135	971	2861	2404	996	45	120	212	78	405	473	353	148
Other households	41439	10807	6683	5321	4097	523	1553	2395	2521	81	110	205	219	1482	1670	2496	1276
- with dependent child(ren)	15755	3442	2195	2678	2674	162	447	1145	1783	14	27	66	92	158	225	308	339
- all student	1732	22	35	78	24	3	4	-	5	4	5	5	6	251	322	692	276
- all pensioner	4295	1645	805	457	176	83	220	329	129	12	11	43	36	120	107	80	42
- other	19657	5698	3648	2108	1223	275	882	921	604	51	67	91	85	953	1016	1416	619

Notes:
1 The terms used to describe tenure are defined as:
   Owner occupied: either owns outright, owns with a mortgage or loan, or pays part rent and part mortgage (shared ownership).
   Rented from NIHE: rented from Northern Ireland Housing Executive.
   Other Social rented: rented from Registered Social Landlord, Housing Association, Housing Co-operative or Charitable Trust.
   Private rented: rented from a private landlord or letting agency, employer of a household member, or relative or friend of a household member or other person.
2 'Rented from NIHE', 'Other social rented' and 'Private rented' include living in the household rent free.
3 The occupancy rating provides a measure of under-occupancy and overcrowding. For example a value of -1 implies that there is one room too few and that there is overcrowding in the household.
   The occupancy rating assumes that every household, including one person households, requires a minimum of two common rooms (excluding bathrooms).
4 A dependent child is a person in a household aged 0 to 15 (whether or not in a family) or person aged 16 to 18 who is a full-time student in a family with parent(s).
5 A family consists of a couple (married or cohabiting) with or without children, or a lone parent and their children. It also includes a married or cohabiting couple with their grandchildren or a lone grandparent with his or her grandchildren,
   if there is no parent in the intervening generation in the household. A family will also include step-children when their parent is part of the couple.
6 Pensionable age at the time of the Census (29 April 2001) was 65 for men and 60 for women.

S 3 5 8

238

Table S358: Dwelling Type and Accommodation Type and Central Heating (and Amenities for Shared Dwellings) by Tenure

Table population: All households

	All households	Owner occupied			Social rented		Private rented
		Owns outright	Owns with a mortgage or loan	Shared ownership	Rented from NIHE	Other social rented	
All households	**626705**	**184089**	**247182**	**4942**	**116474**	**16447**	**57571**
Central heating	596090	173320	244080	4759	106305	16066	51560
No central heating	30615	10769	3102	183	10169	381	6011
In an unshared dwelling	**626651**	**184086**	**247182**	**4942**	**116474**	**16447**	**57520**
Detached house or bungalow	**230406**	**100638**	**105053**	**514**	**8702**	**803**	**14696**
Central heating	221728	95428	104406	485	7402	777	13230
No central heating	8678	5210	647	29	1300	26	1466
Semi-detached house or bungalow	**174781**	**45134**	**85422**	**2464**	**26005**	**2927**	**12829**
Central heating	168574	43212	84527	2402	23568	2857	12008
No central heating	6207	1922	895	62	2437	70	821
Terraced house or bungalow (including end-terrace)	**169433**	**32850**	**52670**	**1547**	**59393**	**3894**	**19079**
Central heating	157402	29689	51242	1471	54547	3735	16718
No central heating	12031	3161	1428	76	4846	159	2361
In a purpose built block of flats or tenement	**42830**	**3615**	**3432**	**363**	**21541**	**8363**	**5516**
Central heating	40528	3500	3333	353	20079	8254	5009
No central heating	2302	115	99	10	1462	109	507
Part of a converted or shared house (including bed-sits)	**5674**	**414**	**311**	**50**	**570**	**413**	**3916**
Central heating	5025	384	302	44	507	396	3392
No central heating	649	30	9	6	63	17	524

Table S358: Dwelling Type and Accommodation Type and Central Heating (and Amenities for Shared Dwellings) by Tenure (continued)

	All households	Owner occupied			Social rented		Private rented
		Owns outright	Owns with a mortgage or loan	Shared ownership	Rented from NIHE	Other social rented	
In a commercial building	**1770**	**292**	**164**	**-**	**131**	**47**	**1136**
Central heating	1547	255	156	-	114	47	975
No central heating	223	37	8	-	17	-	161
Caravan or other mobile or temporary structure	**1757**	**1143**	**130**	**4**	**132**	**-**	**348**
Central heating	1255	849	114	4	88	-	200
No central heating	502	294	16	-	44	-	148
In a shared dwelling	**54**	**3**	**-**	**-**	**-**	**-**	**51**
Sole use of bath/shower and toilet	15	3	-	-	-	-	12
Central heating	12	3	-	-	-	-	9
No central heating	3	-	-	-	-	-	3
Not sole use of bath/shower and toilet	39	-	-	-	-	-	39
Central heating	19	-	-	-	-	-	19
No central heating	20	-	-	-	-	-	20

Notes:
1   The terms used to describe tenure are defined as:
    Shared ownership: pays part rent and part mortgage.
    Rented from NIHE: rented from Northern Ireland Housing Executive.
    Other social rented: rented from Registered Social Landlord, Housing Association, Housing Co-operative or Charitable Trust.
2   'Social rented' and 'Private rented' include living in the household rent free.
3   In general, a household's accommodation is defined as an unshared dwelling if all the rooms are behind a door that only that household can use.
4   'In a commercial building' includes an office building, or hotel, or over a shop.

S358

239

S359

Table S359: Tenure and Amenities by Household Composition

Table population: All households

	All households	One person: Pensioner	One person: Other	One family and no others: All pensioner	Couple households: No children	Couple households: With dependent child(ren)	Couple households: All children non-dependent	Lone parent households: With dependent child(ren)	Lone parent households: All children non-dependent	Other households: With dependent child(ren)	Other households: All student	Other households: All pensioner	Other households: Other
All households	**626719**	**80484**	**91086**	**40770**	**79766**	**162118**	**51425**	**50641**	**28986**	**15757**	**1735**	**4295**	**19656**
With sole use of bath/shower and toilet	622236	79375	90120	40565	79429	161437	51178	50351	28791	15652	1728	4172	19438
With central heating	593343	72345	83445	38793	77465	158560	49521	47537	26914	15025	1688	3713	18337
Without central heating	28893	7030	6675	1772	1964	2877	1657	2814	1877	627	40	459	1101
Without sole use of bath/shower and toilet	4483	1109	966	205	337	681	247	290	195	105	7	123	218
With central heating	2757	423	457	136	292	631	197	238	142	90	7	37	107
Without central heating	1726	686	509	69	45	50	50	52	53	15	-	86	111
Owner occupied	**436217**	**43351**	**47806**	**32506**	**66386**	**138011**	**44823**	**16506**	**19920**	**10989**	**159**	**3083**	**12677**
With sole use of bath/shower and toilet	433296	42685	47292	32360	66128	137450	44616	16407	19795	10920	155	2986	12502
With central heating	420410	38957	45029	31185	65120	136294	43540	16119	18752	10671	143	2676	11924
Without central heating	12886	3728	2263	1175	1008	1156	1076	288	1043	249	12	310	578
Without sole use of bath/shower and toilet	2921	666	514	146	258	561	207	99	125	69	4	97	175
With central heating	1752	207	178	101	229	531	172	73	90	60	4	29	78
Without central heating	1169	459	336	45	29	30	35	26	35	9	-	68	97
Rented from NIHE	**116481**	**22632**	**25370**	**5125**	**6655**	**14191**	**4986**	**23294**	**7232**	**3539**	**14**	**761**	**2682**
With sole use of bath/shower and toilet	115802	22480	25240	5100	6613	14114	4955	23170	7186	3513	14	750	2667
With central heating	105776	20828	22724	4790	6086	12808	4554	21112	6586	3210	11	680	2387
Without central heating	10026	1652	2516	310	527	1306	401	2058	600	303	3	70	280
Without sole use of bath/shower and toilet	679	152	130	25	42	77	31	124	31	26	-	11	15
With central heating	530	109	95	20	31	66	25	106	25	23	-	5	10
Without central heating	149	43	35	5	11	11	6	18	6	3	-	6	5

	All households	One person		One family and no others						Other households			
		Pensioner	Other	All pensioner	Couple households			Lone parent households		With dependent child(ren)	All student	All pensioner	Other
					No children	With dependent child(ren)	All children non-dependent	With dependent child(ren)	All children non-dependent				
Other social rented	**16448**	**6597**	**3565**	**942**	**835**	**1182**	**269**	**1992**	**455**	**198**	**20**	**100**	**293**
With sole use of bath/shower and toilet	16314	6551	3508	939	829	1176	269	1982	452	198	20	100	290
With central heating	15936	6460	3378	927	807	1154	264	1921	439	187	20	100	279
Without central heating	378	91	130	12	22	22	5	61	13	11	-	-	11
Without sole use of bath/shower and toilet	**134**	46	57	3	6	6	-	10	3	-	-	-	3
With central heating	**134**	46	57	3	6	6	-	10	3	-	-	-	3
Without central heating	**-**	-	-	-	-	-	-	-	-	-	-	-	-
Private rented	**57573**	**7904**	**14345**	**2197**	**5890**	**8734**	**1347**	**8849**	**1379**	**1031**	**1542**	**351**	**4004**
With sole use of bath/shower and toilet	56824	7659	14080	2166	5859	8697	1338	8792	1358	1021	1539	336	3979
With central heating	51221	6100	12314	1891	5452	8304	1163	8385	1137	957	1514	257	3747
Without central heating	5603	1559	1766	275	407	393	175	407	221	64	25	79	232
Without sole use of bath/shower and toilet	**749**	245	265	31	31	37	9	57	21	10	3	15	25
With central heating	**341**	61	127	12	26	28	-	49	9	7	3	3	16
Without central heating	**408**	184	138	19	5	9	9	8	12	3	-	12	9

Notes:

1 The terms used to describe tenure are defined as:

Owner occupied: either owns outright, owns with a mortgage or loan, or pays part rent and part mortgage (shared ownership).

Rented from NIHE: rented from Northern Ireland Housing Executive.

Other social rented: rented from Registered Social Landlord, Housing Association, Housing Co-operative or Charitable Trust.

Private rented: rented from a private landlord or letting agency, employer of a household member, or relative or friend of a household member or other person.

2 'Rented from NIHE', 'Other social rented' and 'Private rented' include living in the household rent free.

3 A dependent child is a person in a household aged 0 to 15 (whether or not in a family) or a person aged 16 to 18 who is a full-time student in a family with parent(s).

4 A family consists of a couple (married or cohabiting) with or without children, or a lone parent and their children. It also includes a married or cohabiting couple with their grandchildren or a lone grandparent with his or her grandchildren, if there is no parent in the intervening generation in the household. A family will also include step-children when their parent is part of the couple.

5 Pensionable age at the time of the Census (29 April 2001) was 65 for men and 60 for women.

S359

241

Table S360: Tenure and Lowest Floor Level by Household Composition

Table population: All households

		One person		One family and no others							Other households			
					Couple households			Lone parent households						
	All households	Pensioner	Other	All pensioner	No children	With dependent child(ren)	All children non-dependent	With dependent child(ren)	All children non-dependent	With dependent child(ren)	All student	All pensioner	Other
All households	**626713**	**80486**	**91087**	**40769**	**79766**	**162117**	**51426**	**50644**	**28986**	**15751**	**1728**	**4297**	**19656**
Basement or semi-basement	5167	518	671	330	736	1635	440	312	181	160	3	28	153
Ground floor (street level)	587670	72567	77249	39004	76169	157875	50097	47857	27762	15128	1547	4068	18347
First floor	25920	5632	9049	1190	2260	2424	839	2054	864	424	141	164	879
Second floor	4809	1150	2394	157	359	98	31	262	109	26	21	17	185
Third or fourth floor	1867	376	1006	43	143	48	16	107	38	7	16	11	56
Fifth floor or higher	1280	243	718	45	99	37	3	52	32	6	-	9	36
Owner occupied	**436220**	**43351**	**47806**	**32506**	**66386**	**138010**	**44823**	**16509**	**19920**	**10990**	**157**	**3084**	**12678**
Basement or semi-basement	4115	300	360	284	671	1518	411	155	147	131	-	25	113
Ground floor (street level)	422129	41319	44875	31503	64498	134801	43769	16003	19371	10653	154	2964	12219
First floor	8822	1499	2000	656	1071	1655	629	331	374	203	3	92	309
Second floor	802	157	411	42	93	27	10	14	20	-	-	3	25
Third or fourth floor	235	40	118	11	35	9	4	3	3	3	-	-	9
Fifth floor or higher	117	36	42	10	18	-	-	3	5	-	-	-	3
Rented from NIHE	**116476**	**22632**	**25370**	**5125**	**6655**	**14191**	**4986**	**23294**	**7232**	**3537**	**11**	**761**	**2682**
Basement or semi-basement	440	88	115	23	11	45	17	87	30	16	-	-	8
Ground floor (street level)	102834	19999	18934	4787	5887	13603	4799	21687	6714	3313	11	702	2398
First floor	9538	1835	4269	233	564	473	154	1227	378	172	-	44	189
Second floor	1919	358	1054	39	102	35	10	179	58	26	-	6	52
Third or fourth floor	779	156	437	11	35	16	3	71	28	4	-	4	14
Fifth floor or higher	966	196	561	32	56	19	3	43	24	6	-	5	21

Table S360: Tenure and Lowest Floor Level by Household Composition (continued)

	All households	One person		One family and no others — Couple households				One family and no others — Lone parent households		Other households			
		Pensioner	Other	All pensioner	No children	With dependent child(ren)	All children non-dependent	With dependent child(ren)	All children non-dependent	With dependent child(ren)	All student	All pensioner	Other
Other social rented	**16448**	**6599**	**3566**	**941**	**835**	**1182**	**269**	**1992**	**456**	**197**	**18**	**101**	**292**
Basement or semi-basement	154	72	52	3	15	4	-	8	-	-	-	-	-
Ground floor (street level)	11906	4160	2225	682	689	1128	250	1861	395	190	8	72	246
First floor	3066	1747	800	188	91	41	12	95	37	7	4	16	28
Second floor	947	502	291	53	29	6	4	19	17	-	3	5	18
Third or fourth floor	327	110	165	15	11	3	3	9	4	-	3	4	-
Fifth floor or higher	48	8	33	-	-	-	-	-	3	-	-	4	-
Private rented	**57569**	**7904**	**14345**	**2197**	**5890**	**8734**	**1348**	**8849**	**1378**	**1027**	**1542**	**351**	**4004**
Basement or semi-basement	458	58	144	20	39	68	12	62	4	13	3	3	32
Ground floor (street level)	50801	7089	11215	2032	5095	8343	1279	8306	1282	972	1374	330	3484
First floor	4494	551	1980	113	534	255	44	401	75	42	134	12	353
Second floor	1141	133	638	23	135	30	7	50	14	-	18	3	90
Third or fourth floor	526	70	286	6	62	20	6	24	3	-	13	3	33
Fifth floor or higher	149	3	82	3	25	18	-	6	-	-	-	-	12

Notes:

1 The terms used to describe tenure are defined as:
Owner occupied: either owns outright, owns with a mortgage or loan, or pays part rent and part mortgage (shared ownership).
Rented from NIHE: rented from Northern Ireland Housing Executive.
Other social rented: rented from Registered Social Landlord, Housing Association, Housing Co-operative or Charitable Trust.
Private rented: rented from a private landlord or letting agency, employer of a household member, or relative or friend of a household member or other person.

2 'Rented from NIHE', 'Other social rented' and 'Private rented' include living in the household rent free.

3 A dependent child is a person in a household aged 0 to 15 (whether or not in a family) or a person aged 16 to 18 who is a full-time student in a family with parent(s).

4 A family consists of a couple (married or cohabiting) with or without children, or a lone parent and their children. It also includes a married or cohabiting couple with their grandchildren or a lone grandparent with his or her grandchildren, if there is no parent in the intervening generation in the household. A family will also include step-children when their parent is part of the couple.

5 Pensionable age at the time of the Census (29 April 2001) was 65 for men and 60 for women.

Table S361: Tenure and Car or Van Availability by Number of Persons Aged 17 or Over in the Household

Table population: All households

	All households	Number of persons aged 17 or over in household				
		None	1	2	3	4 or more
All households	**626717**	**100**	**213263**	**285057**	**80467**	**47830**
No car or van	164949	74	114902	37754	8489	3730
1 car or van	278580	21	94199	141636	29876	12848
2 cars or vans	147880	5	3580	98193	30870	15232
3 cars or vans	26814	-	450	6079	9818	10467
4 or more cars or vans	8494	-	132	1395	1414	5553
Owner occupied	**436217**	**26**	**102889**	**227196**	**66423**	**39683**
No car or van	54008	8	34536	14903	3350	1211
1 car or van	211041	13	65172	112773	23491	9592
2 cars or vans	137756	5	2764	92431	28843	13713
3 cars or vans	25336	-	318	5785	9381	9852
4 or more cars or vans	8076	-	99	1304	1358	5315
Rented from NIHE	**116476**	**43**	**68033**	**33809**	**9538**	**5053**
No car or van	75116	40	52897	16618	3941	1620
1 car or van	37453	3	14777	15790	4559	2324
2 cars or vans	3406	-	285	1329	948	844
3 cars or vans	427	-	63	54	82	228
4 or more cars or vans	74	-	11	18	8	37
Other social rented	**16455**	**5**	**11938**	**3584**	**638**	**290**
No car or van	11189	5	9322	1532	240	90
1 car or van	4902	-	2558	1893	315	136
2 cars or vans	331	-	51	150	75	55
3 cars or vans	25	-	7	6	8	4
4 or more cars or vans	8	-	-	3	-	5
Private rented	**57569**	**26**	**30403**	**20468**	**3868**	**2804**
No car or van	24636	21	18147	4701	958	809
1 car or van	25184	5	11692	11180	1511	796
2 cars or vans	6387	-	480	4283	1004	620
3 cars or vans	1026	-	62	234	347	383
4 or more cars or vans	336	-	22	70	48	196

Notes:

1   Car or van includes company car or van if available for private use.

2   The terms used to describe tenure are defined as:
Owner occupied: either owns outright, owns with a mortgage or loan, or pays part rent and part mortgage (shared ownership).
Rented from NIHE: rented from Northern Ireland Housing Executive.
Other social rented: rented from Registered Social Landlord, Housing Association, Housing Co-operative or Charitable Trust.
Private rented: rented from a private landlord or letting agency, employer of a household member, or relative or friend of a household member or other person.

3   'Rented from NIHE', 'Other social rented' and 'Private rented' include living in the household rent free.

Table S362: Tenure and Car or Van Availability by Economic Activity

Table population: All persons aged 16 to 74 in households

	All persons	Economically active				Economically inactive				
		Employee	Self-employed	Unemployed	Full-time student	Retired	Student	Looking after home/family	Permanently sick/disabled	Other
All households	**1171798**	**558846**	**98096**	**48928**	**26563**	**129620**	**64952**	**88135**	**106796**	**49862**
No car or van	193566	53132	2417	17826	4251	30757	10012	23117	33348	18706
1 car or van	496690	235404	28838	20496	9555	68722	23865	38459	50792	20559
2 cars or vans	359669	205379	45996	7824	8664	24416	21495	20513	17456	7926
3 cars or vans	88456	47229	14089	2086	3023	4578	7033	4468	4038	1912
4 or more cars or vans	33417	17702	6756	696	1070	1147	2547	1578	1162	759
Owner occupied	**891441**	**471758**	**90248**	**24110**	**19285**	**100386**	**47640**	**51611**	**60313**	**26090**
No car or van	60508	23286	1270	3172	818	14381	2009	3650	8076	3846
1 car or van	380827	194157	24888	11725	6934	57184	17084	23875	32091	12889
2 cars or vans	334500	192766	43794	6648	7761	23312	19685	18363	15279	6892
3 cars or vans	83703	44675	13678	1915	2797	4394	6510	4213	3763	1758
4 or more cars or vans	31903	16874	6618	650	975	1115	2352	1510	1104	705
Rented from NIHE	**173759**	**46180**	**2903**	**16969**	**2692**	**20043**	**8575**	**25287**	**34185**	**16925**
No car or van	93824	19864	673	10525	1311	12347	4221	14602	19173	11108
1 car or van	68654	21309	1555	5712	1150	7060	3733	9531	13427	5177
2 cars or vans	9583	4172	560	632	192	541	535	1005	1387	559
3 cars or vans	1437	717	92	83	31	82	72	126	163	71
4 or more cars or vans	261	118	23	17	8	13	14	23	35	10
Other social rented	**17173**	**4172**	**312**	**1372**	**230**	**2986**	**768**	**1971**	**4038**	**1324**
No car or van	9245	1717	55	848	106	1780	359	1079	2406	895
1 car or van	7029	2035	189	479	110	1161	349	825	1496	385
2 cars or vans	816	375	63	38	14	45	57	61	132	31
3 cars or vans	55	33	5	4	-	-	3	3	4	3
4 or more cars or vans	28	12	-	3	-	-	3	3	-	10
Private rented	**89425**	**36736**	**4633**	**6477**	**4356**	**6205**	**7969**	**9266**	**8260**	**5523**
No car or van	29989	8265	419	3281	2016	2249	3423	3786	3693	2857
1 car or van	40180	17903	2206	2580	1361	3317	2699	4228	3778	2108
2 cars or vans	14770	8066	1579	506	697	518	1218	1084	658	444
3 cars or vans	3261	1804	314	84	195	102	448	126	108	80
4 or more cars or vans	1225	698	115	26	87	19	181	42	23	34

Notes:

1 Car or van includes company car or van if available for private use.

2 The terms used to describe tenure are defined as:

Owner occupied: either owns outright, owns with a mortgage or loan, or pays part rent and part mortgage (shared ownership).

Rented from NIHE: rented from Northern Ireland Housing Executive.

Other social rented: rented from Registered Social Landlord, Housing Association, Housing Co-operative or Charitable Trust.

Private rented: rented from a private landlord or letting agency, employer of a household member, or relative or friend of a household member or other person.

3 'Rented from NIHE', 'Other social rented' and 'Private rented' include living in the household rent free.

S 3 6 3

Table S363: Dwelling Type and Accommodation Type by Household Space Type

Table population: All household spaces

	Total	Occupied	Unoccupied	
			Second residence/ Holiday accommodation	Vacant
All household spaces	**658426**	**626718**	**4992**	**26716**
In an unshared dwelling	**658317**	**626658**	**4975**	**26684**
House or bungalow	600356	574620	4056	21680
Detached	240137	230406	2229	7502
Semi-detached	179903	174781	856	4266
Terraced (including end terrace)	180316	169433	971	9912
Flat, maisonette or apartment	56090	50278	869	4943
In a purpose built block of flats or tenement	47215	42830	700	3685
Part of a converted or shared house (includes bed-sits)	6618	5674	144	800
In a commercial building	2257	1774	25	458
Caravan or other mobile or temporary structure	1871	1760	50	61
In a shared dwelling	**109**	**60**	**17**	**32**

Notes:

1 In general, a household's accommodation is defined as an unshared dwelling if all the rooms are behind a door that only that household can use.

2 'In a commercial building' includes in an office building, or hotel, or over a shop.

Table S364: Tenure by Ethnic Group of Household Reference Person (HRP)

Table population: All households

	All HRPs	White	Irish Traveller	Mixed	Indian	Pakistani	Bangladeshi	Other Asian	Black Caribbean	Black African	Other Black	Chinese	Other ethnic group
All households	**626719**	**622346**	**665**	**647**	**602**	**175**	**75**	**71**	**129**	**185**	**119**	**1289**	**416**
Owner occupied	**436218**	**433718**	**259**	**327**	**445**	**128**	**55**	**33**	**62**	**78**	**58**	**860**	**195**
Owns outright	184090	183204	162	99	171	24	15	8	17	17	33	281	59
Owns with a mortgage or loan	247182	245602	90	224	268	104	37	25	42	57	25	576	132
Shared ownership	4946	4912	7	4	6	-	3	-	3	4	-	3	4
Social rented	**132926**	**132131**	**264**	**168**	**41**	**19**	**11**	**3**	**31**	**36**	**24**	**153**	**45**
Rented from NIHE	116476	115784	237	150	32	16	11	-	27	32	24	127	36
Other social rented	16450	16347	27	18	9	3	-	3	4	4	-	26	9
Private rented	**57575**	**56497**	**142**	**152**	**116**	**28**	**9**	**35**	**36**	**71**	**37**	**276**	**176**
Private landlord or letting agency	41676	40889	103	117	72	21	3	26	30	61	18	209	127
Employer of a household member	3407	3295	3	14	24	7	-	3	3	5	15	15	23
Relative or friend of a household member	9357	9280	13	13	6	-	3	3	3	-	-	27	9
Other	3135	3033	23	8	14	-	3	3	-	5	4	25	17

Notes:

1 The terms used to describe tenure are defined as:

   Shared ownership: pays part rent and part mortgage.

   Rented from NIHE: rented from Northern Ireland Housing Executive.

   Other social rented: rented from Registered Social Landlord, Housing Association, Housing Co-operative or Charitable Trust.

2 'Social rented' and 'Private rented' include living in the household rent free.

S364

247

Table S365: Tenure and Occupancy Rating by Community Background (Religion or Religion Brought Up In)

Table population: All persons in households

Persons living in:	All persons	Catholic	Protestant and Other Christian (including Christian related)	Other religions and philosophies	None
All households	**1658813**	**728477**	**879361**	**6239**	**44736**
+2 or more	805208	299565	481208	3129	21306
+1	386046	167894	204758	1306	12088
0	286397	143630	133871	955	7941
-1 or less	181162	117388	59524	849	3401
Owner occupied households	**1233620**	**526648**	**672849**	**4208**	**29915**
+2 or more	712617	263763	428400	2661	17793
+1	261226	115213	138202	792	7019
0	159896	81594	74258	419	3625
-1 or less	99881	66078	31989	336	1478
Social rented households	**295235**	**144776**	**142650**	**629**	**7180**
+2 or more	46053	18689	26227	113	1024
+1	88226	36927	48623	204	2472
0	96019	46939	46261	199	2620
-1 or less	64937	42221	21539	113	1064
Private rented households	**129958**	**57053**	**63862**	**1402**	**7641**
+2 or more	46538	17113	26581	355	2489
+1	36594	15754	17933	310	2597
0	30482	15097	13352	337	1696
-1 or less	16344	9089	5996	400	859

Notes:

1 The occupancy rating provides a measure of under-occupancy and overcrowding. For example a value of -1 implies that there is one room too few and that there is overcrowding in the household. The occupancy rating assumes that every household, including one person households, requires a minimum of two common rooms (excluding bathrooms).

2 The terms used to describe tenure are defined as:
    Owner occupied: either owns outright, owns with a mortgage or loan, or pays part rent and part mortgage (shared ownership).
    Social rented: rented from Northern Ireland Housing Executive, Registered Social Landlord, Housing Association, Housing Co-operative or Charitable Trust.
    Private rented: rented from a private landlord or letting agency, employer of a household member, or relative or friend of a household member or other person.

3 'Social rented' and 'Private rented' include living in the household rent free.

4 The term 'Catholic' includes those respondents who gave their religion as Catholic or Roman Catholic.

Table S366: Tenure by Community Background (Religion or Religion Brought Up In) of Household Reference Person (HRP)

Table population: All households

	All HRPs	Catholic	Protestant and Other Christian (including Christian related)	Other religions and philosophies	None
All households	**626718**	**247568**	**364767**	**2667**	**11716**
Owner occupied	**436217**	**166884**	**260401**	**1706**	**7226**
Owns outright	184090	63716	117690	618	2066
Owns with a mortgage or loan	247182	101091	140002	1062	5027
Shared ownership	4945	2077	2709	26	133
Social rented	**132931**	**56412**	**74051**	**346**	**2122**
Rented from NIHE	116477	50126	64251	275	1825
Other social rented	16454	6286	9800	71	297
Private rented	**57570**	**24272**	**30315**	**615**	**2368**
Private landlord or letting agency	41676	18964	20458	466	1788
Employer of a household member	3405	605	2417	66	317
Relative or friend of a household member	9355	3624	5554	36	141
Other	3134	1079	1886	47	122

Notes:
1 The terms used to describe tenure are defined as:
   Shared ownership: pays part rent and part mortgage.
   Rented from NIHE: rented from Northern Ireland Housing Executive.
   Other social rented: rented from Registered Social Landlord, Housing Association, Housing Co-operative or Charitable Trust.
2 'Social rented' and 'Private rented' include living in the household rent free.
3 The term 'Catholic' includes those respondents who gave their religion as Catholic or Roman Catholic.

S366

249

Table S367: Central Heating and Occupancy Rating by Age

Table population: All persons in households

	All persons	0 to 2	3 to 4	5 to 7	8 to 9	10 to 14	15	16 to 17	18 to 19	20 to 24	25 to 49	50 to 59	60 to 64	65 to 74	75 to 84	85 to 94	95 and over
All persons	**1658813**	**67275**	**47917**	**72314**	**50670**	**132379**	**27001**	**53155**	**45927**	**105729**	**586825**	**185949**	**72985**	**121228**	**71791**	**16878**	**790**
Central heating	**1596705**	**65222**	**46610**	**70474**	**49354**	**128675**	**26198**	**51522**	**44252**	**101571**	**569146**	**178613**	**69512**	**114066**	**65944**	**14873**	**673**
+2 or more	785012	29418	21378	31295	20833	48961	9777	17152	13553	33858	286647	106241	45553	73954	38543	7529	320
+1	369792	17864	12446	17871	11899	28105	5549	10281	9337	24846	137595	37642	13576	23638	15286	3705	152
0	272807	11796	8741	14307	10790	30816	5976	11796	10469	23301	93536	21416	6899	11402	8730	2687	145
-1 or less	169094	6144	4045	7001	5832	20793	4896	12293	10893	19566	51368	13314	3484	5072	3385	952	56
No central heating	**62108**	**2053**	**1307**	**1840**	**1316**	**3704**	**803**	**1633**	**1675**	**4158**	**17679**	**7336**	**3473**	**7162**	**5847**	**2005**	**117**
+2 or more	20196	282	200	262	184	412	91	186	216	800	4708	2884	1680	3768	3261	1194	68
+1	16254	657	411	542	329	819	154	306	357	1078	4899	2007	905	1807	1473	481	29
0	13590	627	378	563	440	1170	250	435	466	1097	4365	1359	511	975	714	229	11
-1 or less	12068	487	318	473	363	1303	308	706	636	1183	3707	1086	377	612	399	101	9

Note:

1 The occupancy rating provides a measure of under-occupancy and overcrowding. For example a value of -1 implies that there is one room too few and that there is overcrowding in the household. The occupancy rating assumes that every household, including one person households, requires a minimum of two common rooms (excluding bathrooms).

250

Table S368: Central Heating and Occupancy Rating by Ethnic Group

Table population: All persons in households

	All persons	White	Irish Traveller	Mixed	Indian	Pakistani	Bangladeshi	Other Asian	Black Caribbean	Black African	Other Black	Chinese	Other ethnic group
All persons	**1658809**	**1645345**	**1671**	**3226**	**1514**	**647**	**246**	**176**	**239**	**468**	**332**	**3775**	**1170**
Central heating	**1596705**	**1584230**	**1271**	**3080**	**1457**	**633**	**231**	**172**	**215**	**429**	**315**	**3563**	**1109**
+2 or more	785012	779777	286	1305	925	309	65	61	88	152	92	1492	460
+1	369792	367011	255	758	238	115	55	31	52	85	81	880	231
0	272807	270633	277	655	154	64	52	28	53	91	65	517	218
-1 or less	169094	166809	453	362	140	145	59	52	22	101	77	674	200
No central heating	**62104**	**61115**	**400**	**146**	**57**	**14**	**15**	**4**	**24**	**39**	**17**	**212**	**61**
+2 or more	20195	20083	25	39	8	-	-	-	8	3	4	16	9
+1	16254	16082	30	40	14	-	15	-	6	18	4	33	12
0	13588	13383	40	39	25	3	-	4	3	12	4	57	18
-1 or less	**12067**	11567	305	28	10	11	-	-	7	6	5	106	22

Note:

1 The occupancy rating provides a measure of under-occupancy and overcrowding. For example a value of -1 implies that there is one room too few and that there is overcrowding in the household. The occupancy rating assumes that every household, including one person households, requires a minimum of two common rooms (excluding bathrooms).

S368

Table S369: Central Heating and Occupancy Rating by Ethnic Group of Household Reference Person (HRP)

Table population: All households

	All HRPs	White	Irish Traveller	Mixed	Indian	Pakistani	Bangladeshi	Other Asian	Black Caribbean	Black African	Other Black	Chinese	Other ethnic group
All households	**626719**	**622346**	**665**	**647**	**603**	**176**	**73**	**69**	**125**	**188**	**123**	**1288**	**416**
Central heating	**596099**	**592092**	**517**	**605**	**578**	**173**	**68**	**66**	**112**	**169**	**114**	**1217**	**388**
+2 or more	323046	321216	170	252	384	95	23	23	53	63	37	561	169
+1	142202	141308	115	163	89	32	18	14	27	39	30	287	80
0	88958	88313	113	119	54	14	13	12	21	33	26	169	71
-1 or less	41893	41255	119	71	51	32	14	17	11	34	21	200	68
No central heating	**30620**	**30254**	**148**	**42**	**25**	**3**	**5**	**3**	**13**	**19**	**9**	**71**	**28**
+2 or more	12658	12593	21	13	3	-	-	-	7	3	3	10	5
+1	8443	8379	17	9	7	-	5	-	3	5	-	13	5
0	5654	5571	23	9	10	-	-	3	-	8	3	19	8
-1 or less	3865	3711	87	11	5	3	-	-	3	3	3	29	10

Notes:

1 The occupancy rating provides a measure of under-occupancy and overcrowding. For example a value of -1 implies that there is one room too few and that there is overcrowding in the household.
The occupancy rating assumes that every household, including one person households, requires a minimum of two common rooms (excluding bathrooms).

Table S370: Central Heating and Occupancy Rating by Community Background (Religion or Religion Brought Up In)

Table population: All persons in households

	All persons	Catholic	Protestant and Other Christian (including Christian related)	Other religions and philosophies	None
All persons	**1658813**	**728477**	**879361**	**6239**	**44736**
Central heating	**1596705**	**702764**	**844897**	**5955**	**43089**
+2 or more	785012	293710	467358	3069	20875
+1	369792	161613	195380	1221	11578
0	272807	137372	127018	883	7534
-1 or less	169094	110069	55141	782	3102
No central heating	**62108**	**25713**	**34464**	**284**	**1647**
+2 or more	20196	5855	13850	60	431
+1	16254	6281	9378	85	510
0	13590	6258	6853	72	407
-1 or less	**12068**	7319	4383	67	299

Notes:

1   The occupancy rating provides a measure of under-occupancy and overcrowding. For example a value of -1 implies that there is one room too few and that there is overcrowding in the household.
    The occupancy rating assumes that every household, including one person households, requires a minimum of two common rooms (excluding bathrooms).

2   The term 'Catholic' includes those respondents who gave their religion as Catholic or Roman Catholic.

S 3 7 0

Table S371: Central Heating and Occupancy Rating by Community Background (Religion or Religion Brought Up In) of Household Reference Person (HRP)

Table population: All households

	All HRPs	Catholic	Protestant and Other Christian (including Christian related)	Other religions and philosophies	None
All households	**626718**	**247568**	**364767**	**2667**	**11716**
Central heating	**596099**	**236117**	**346382**	**2526**	**11074**
+2 or more	323046	113200	202697	1362	5787
+1	142202	57132	81579	526	2965
0	88958	41155	45780	352	1671
-1 or less	41893	24630	16326	286	651
No central heating	**30619**	**11451**	**18385**	**141**	**642**
+2 or more	12654	3623	8795	35	201
+1	8445	3179	5019	44	203
0	5656	2503	2975	31	147
-1 or less	3864	2146	1596	31	91

Notes:

1   The occupancy rating provides a measure of under-occupancy and overcrowding. For example a value of -1 implies that there is one room too few and that there is overcrowding in the household.
    The occupancy rating assumes that every household, including one person households, requires a minimum of two common rooms (excluding bathrooms).

2   The term 'Catholic' includes those respondents who gave their religion as Catholic or Roman Catholic.

Table S054: Shared/Unshared Dwelling and Central Heating and Occupancy Rating by Age

Table population: All persons in households

	All persons	0 to 2	3 to 4	5 to 7	8 to 9	10 to 14	15	16 to 17	18 to 19	20 to 24	25 to 49	50 to 59	60 to 64	65 to 74	75 to 84	85 to 94	95 and over
All persons	1658809	67275	47917	72313	50670	132379	27003	53155	45924	105729	586824	185949	72985	121227	71791	16878	790
In a shared dwelling	65	3	-	-	-	-	3	3	3	4	40	9	-	-	-	-	-
Central heating	38	3	-	-	-	-	3	-	-	4	25	3	-	-	-	-	-
+2 or more	-	-	-	-	-	-	-	-	-	-	-	-	-	-	-	-	-
+1	9	-	-	-	-	-	3	-	-	-	6	-	-	-	-	-	-
0	29	3	-	-	-	-	-	-	-	4	19	3	-	-	-	-	-
-1 or less	-	-	-	-	-	-	-	-	-	-	-	-	-	-	-	-	-
No central heating	27	-	-	-	-	-	-	3	3	-	15	6	-	-	-	-	-
+2 or more	-	-	-	-	-	-	-	-	-	-	-	-	-	-	-	-	-
+1	-	-	-	-	-	-	-	-	-	-	-	-	-	-	-	-	-
0	6	-	-	-	-	-	-	-	-	-	-	6	-	-	-	-	-
-1 or less	21	-	-	-	-	-	-	3	3	-	15	-	-	-	-	-	-
In an unshared dwelling	1658744	67272	47917	72313	50670	132379	27000	53152	45921	105725	586784	185940	72985	121227	71791	16878	790
Central heating	1596660	65219	46610	70473	49354	128675	26197	51520	44249	101567	569119	178610	69512	114065	65944	14873	673
+2 or more	785011	29418	21378	31295	20833	48961	9777	17152	13553	33858	286646	106241	45553	73954	38543	7529	320
+1	369791	17864	12446	17871	11899	28105	5549	10281	9337	24846	137594	37642	13576	23638	15286	3705	152
0	272797	11796	8741	14307	10790	30816	5975	11796	10468	23301	93530	21415	6899	11401	8730	2687	145
-1 or less	169061	6141	4045	7000	5832	20793	4896	12291	10891	19562	51349	13312	3484	5072	3385	952	56
No central heating	62084	2053	1307	1840	1316	3704	803	1632	1672	4158	17665	7330	3473	7162	5847	2005	117
+2 or more	20196	282	200	262	184	412	91	186	216	800	4708	2884	1680	3768	3261	1194	68
+1	16254	657	411	542	329	819	154	306	357	1078	4899	2007	905	1807	1473	481	29
0	13586	627	378	563	440	1170	250	435	464	1097	4363	1359	511	975	714	229	11
-1 or less	12048	487	318	473	363	1303	308	705	635	1183	3695	1080	377	612	399	101	9

Notes:

1 The occupancy rating provides a measure of under-occupancy and overcrowding. For example a value of -1 implies that there is one room too few and that there is overcrowding in the household.
   The occupancy rating assumes that every household, including one person households, requires a minimum of two common rooms (excluding bathrooms).

2 In general a household's accommodation is defined as an unshared dwelling if all the rooms are behind a door that only that household can use.

S 0 5 4

S058

Table S058: Households in a Shared Dwelling and Amenities and Household Size by Central Heating and Number of Rooms

Table population: All households in a shared dwelling

	All households in a shared dwelling	Central heating				No central heating			
		1 room	2 rooms	3 rooms	4 or more rooms	1 room	2 rooms	3 rooms	4 or more rooms
All households in a shared dwelling	**51**	**14**	**11**	**4**	**-**	**16**	**3**	**3**	**-**
1 person	48	14	8	4	-	16	3	3	-
2 persons	3	-	3	-	-	-	-	-	-
3 persons	-	-	-	-	-	-	-	-	-
4 persons	-	-	-	-	-	-	-	-	-
5 persons	-	-	-	-	-	-	-	-	-
6 persons	-	-	-	-	-	-	-	-	-
7 persons	-	-	-	-	-	-	-	-	-
8 or more persons	-	-	-	-	-	-	-	-	-
Sole use of bath/shower and toilet	**14**	**4**	**3**	**4**	**-**	**-**	**-**	**3**	**-**
1 person	14	4	3	4	-	-	-	3	-
2 persons	-	-	-	-	-	-	-	-	-
3 persons	-	-	-	-	-	-	-	-	-
4 persons	-	-	-	-	-	-	-	-	-
5 persons	-	-	-	-	-	-	-	-	-
6 persons	-	-	-	-	-	-	-	-	-
7 persons	-	-	-	-	-	-	-	-	-
8 or more persons	-	-	-	-	-	-	-	-	-
Does not have sole use of bath/shower and toilet	**37**	**10**	**8**	**-**	**-**	**16**	**3**	**-**	**-**
1 person	34	10	5	-	-	16	3	-	-
2 persons	3	-	3	-	-	-	-	-	-
3 persons	-	-	-	-	-	-	-	-	-
4 persons	-	-	-	-	-	-	-	-	-
5 persons	-	-	-	-	-	-	-	-	-
6 persons	-	-	-	-	-	-	-	-	-
7 persons	-	-	-	-	-	-	-	-	-
8 or more persons	-	-	-	-	-	-	-	-	-

Note:

1   The number of rooms available to the household excludes bathrooms, toilets, halls or landings and rooms that can only be used for storage. It also does not include any rooms shared with another household such as a shared kitchen.

5. Irish Language

5. Irish Language

© Crown copyright 2003

Table S372: Sex and Age by Knowledge of Irish

Table population: All persons aged 3 and over

	All persons	Understands spoken Irish but cannot read, write or speak Irish	Speaks but does not read or write Irish	Speaks and reads but does not write Irish	Speaks, reads, writes and understands Irish	Other combination of skills	Has some knowledge of Irish	Has no knowledge of Irish
All persons	**1617957**	**36479**	**24536**	**7183**	**75125**	**24167**	**167490**	**1450467**
3 to 11	223130	2626	3878	577	5100	1529	13710	209420
12 to 15	107616	2550	1752	709	15341	5310	25662	81954
16 to 24	211482	5949	3946	1360	17808	4811	33874	177608
25 to 39	371860	9847	5896	2100	16645	5296	39784	332076
40 to 59	406957	10000	5823	1730	14389	4830	36772	370185
60 to 74	196780	3873	2285	537	4335	1705	12735	184045
75 and over	100132	1634	956	170	1507	686	4953	95179
Males	**786896**	**18044**	**11741**	**3363**	**35265**	**11445**	**79858**	**707038**
3 to 11	114514	1322	1808	235	2493	762	6620	107894
12 to 15	55194	1304	846	353	7425	2835	12763	42431
16 to 24	106624	3132	1845	597	7571	2260	15405	91219
25 to 39	182545	4975	2897	951	7759	2322	18904	163641
40 to 59	201187	4962	2949	885	7213	2219	18228	182959
60 to 74	90876	1750	1054	276	2184	773	6037	84839
75 and over	35956	599	342	66	620	274	1901	34055
Females	**831061**	**18435**	**12795**	**3820**	**39860**	**12722**	**87632**	**743429**
3 to 11	108616	1304	2070	342	2607	767	7090	101526
12 to 15	52422	1246	906	356	7916	2475	12899	39523
16 to 24	104858	2817	2101	763	10237	2551	18469	86389
25 to 39	189315	4872	2999	1149	8886	2974	20880	168435
40 to 59	205770	5038	2874	845	7176	2611	18544	187226
60 to 74	105904	2123	1231	261	2151	932	6698	99206
75 and over	64176	1035	614	104	887	412	3052	61124

Note:
1 An ability to speak, read or write Irish does not imply an ability to understand spoken Irish unless stated. Persons in these categories may or may not have the ability to understand Irish.

Table S373: Sex and Age by Knowledge of Irish and Country of Birth

Table population: All persons aged 3 and over

	All persons	Some knowledge of Irish					No knowledge of Irish				
		Total	Persons born in Northern Ireland	Persons born in Republic of Ireland	Persons born in Ireland - part not specified	Persons born elsewhere	Total	Persons born in Northern Ireland	Persons born in Republic of Ireland	Persons born in Ireland - part not specified	Persons born elsewhere
All persons	1617957	167490	143535	15322	2136	6497	1450467	1325596	23418	932	100521
3 to 11	223130	13710	12669	208	289	544	209420	198132	1046	196	10046
12 to 15	107616	25662	24418	370	171	703	81954	77275	503	30	4146
16 to 24	211482	33874	30069	2258	390	1157	177608	163267	1738	124	12479
25 to 39	371860	39784	32453	4384	620	2327	332076	295982	2981	226	32887
40 to 59	406957	36772	30375	4588	521	1288	370185	337643	6770	214	25558
60 to 74	196780	12735	10055	2236	84	360	184045	168604	5729	66	9646
75 and over	100132	4953	3496	1278	61	118	95179	84693	4651	76	5759
Males	786896	79858	70256	5200	1227	3175	707038	645910	9174	501	51453
3 to 11	114514	6620	6086	105	145	284	107894	101926	587	122	5259
12 to 15	55194	12763	12151	176	84	352	42431	40088	271	16	2056
16 to 24	106624	15405	13871	751	229	554	91219	83642	820	78	6679
25 to 39	182545	18904	15961	1463	382	1098	163641	145405	1270	113	16853
40 to 59	201187	18228	15639	1605	317	667	182959	166581	2727	113	13538
60 to 74	90876	6037	5036	782	47	172	84839	77853	2172	29	4785
75 and over	35956	1901	1512	318	23	48	34055	30415	1327	30	2283
Females	831061	87632	73279	10122	909	3322	743429	679686	14244	431	49068
3 to 11	108616	7090	6583	103	144	260	101526	96206	459	74	4787
12 to 15	52422	12899	12267	194	87	351	39523	37187	232	14	2090
16 to 24	104858	18469	16198	1507	161	603	86389	79625	918	46	5800
25 to 39	189315	20880	16492	2921	238	1229	168435	150577	1711	113	16034
40 to 59	205770	18544	14736	2983	204	621	187226	171062	4043	101	12020
60 to 74	105904	6698	5019	1454	37	188	99206	90751	3557	37	4861
75 and over	64176	3052	1984	960	38	70	61124	54278	3324	46	3476

Note:
1 Knowledge of Irish is any of the following: understanding spoken Irish, reading Irish, speaking Irish or writing Irish.

Table S374: Sex and Highest Level of Qualification by Knowledge of Irish

Table population: All persons aged 16 to 74

	All persons	Understands spoken Irish but cannot read, write or speak Irish	Speaks but does not read or write Irish	Speaks and reads but does not write Irish	Speaks, reads, writes and understands Irish	Other combination of skills	Has some knowledge of Irish	Has no knowledge of Irish
All persons	**1187079**	**29669**	**17950**	**5727**	**53177**	**16642**	**123165**	**1063914**
No qualifications	494277	10301	6138	1178	9324	3291	30232	464045
Level 1	204478	5431	3191	844	6563	2361	18390	186088
Level 2	194265	5320	3261	1160	11641	3771	25153	169112
Level 3	106548	2964	1957	801	8212	2246	16180	90368
Level 4	129741	3693	2228	1135	10878	3128	21062	108679
Level 5	57770	1960	1175	609	6559	1845	12148	45622
Males	**581232**	**14819**	**8745**	**2709**	**24727**	**7574**	**58574**	**522658**
No qualifications	255134	5664	3320	657	4892	1689	16222	238912
Level 1	100064	2778	1572	410	3300	1159	9219	90845
Level 2	82703	2341	1384	497	4937	1512	10671	72032
Level 3	47868	1343	844	306	3429	907	6829	41039
Level 4	64019	1728	1010	538	4862	1396	9534	54485
Level 5	31444	965	615	301	3307	911	6099	25345
Females	**605847**	**14850**	**9205**	**3018**	**28450**	**9068**	**64591**	**541256**
No qualifications	239143	4637	2818	521	4432	1602	14010	225133
Level 1	104414	2653	1619	434	3263	1202	9171	95243
Level 2	111562	2979	1877	663	6704	2259	14482	97080
Level 3	58680	1621	1113	495	4783	1339	9351	49329
Level 4	65722	1965	1218	597	6016	1732	11528	54194
Level 5	26326	995	560	308	3252	934	6049	20277

Notes:
1 An ability to speak, read or write Irish does not imply an ability to understand spoken Irish unless stated. Persons in these categories may or may not have the ability to understand Irish.
2 The levels for 'Highest level of qualification' are defined as follows:
No qualifications : No qualifications
Level 1 : GCSE (grades D-G), CSE (grades 2-5), 1-4 CSEs (grade 1), 1-4 GCSEs (grades A-C), 1-4 'O' level passes, NVQ level 1, GNVQ Foundation or equivalents
Level 2 : 5+ CSEs (grade 1), 5+ GCSEs (grades A-C), 5- 'O' level passes, Senior Certificate, 1 'A' level, 1-3 AS levels, Advanced Senior Certificate, NVQ level 2, GNVQ Intermediate or equivalents
Level 3 : 2+ 'A' levels, 4+ AS levels, NVQ level 3, GNVQ Advanced or equivalents
Level 4 : First Degree, NVQ level 4, HNC, HND or equivalents
Level 5 : Higher Degree, NVQ level 5 or equivalents

Table S375: Sex and Age by Knowledge of Irish and Community Background (Religion or Religion Brought Up In)

Table population: All persons aged 3 and over

	All persons	Some knowledge of Irish					No knowledge of Irish				
		Total	Catholic	Protestant and Other Christian (including Christian related)	Other religions and philosophies	None	Total	Catholic	Protestant and Other Christian (including Christian related)	Other religions and philosophies	None
All persons	1617956	167489	154622	10987	415	1465	1450467	549827	855777	5886	38977
3 to 11	223130	13710	12253	1140	29	288	209420	98208	98898	744	11570
12 to 15	107616	25662	24676	747	30	209	81954	30069	47862	271	3752
16 to 24	211482	33874	31958	1618	88	210	177608	74714	95952	766	6176
25 to 39	371860	39784	36459	2784	133	408	332076	131120	189330	1928	9698
40 to 59	406957	36772	33509	2855	118	290	370185	132592	230142	1555	5896
60 to 74	196780	12735	11472	1197	17	49	184045	57140	124980	467	1458
75 and over	100131	4952	4295	646	-	11	95179	25984	68613	155	427
Males	786896	79858	73943	4851	253	811	707038	266641	415513	3319	21565
3 to 11	114514	6620	5840	594	18	168	107894	50498	50798	398	6200
12 to 15	55194	12763	12285	366	11	101	42431	15823	24511	139	1958
16 to 24	106624	15405	14580	662	55	108	91219	38680	48804	398	3337
25 to 39	182545	18904	17484	1119	84	217	163641	62379	94763	1118	5381
40 to 59	201187	18228	16629	1351	73	175	182959	63932	114542	932	3553
60 to 74	90876	6037	5452	539	12	34	84839	26238	57419	264	918
75 and over	35956	1901	1673	220	-	8	34055	9091	24676	70	218
Females	831060	87631	80679	6136	162	654	743429	283186	440264	2567	17412
3 to 11	108616	7090	6413	546	11	120	101526	47710	48100	346	5370
12 to 15	52422	12899	12391	381	19	108	39523	14246	23351	132	1794
16 to 24	104858	18469	17378	956	33	102	86389	36034	47148	368	2839
25 to 39	189315	20880	18975	1665	49	191	168435	68741	94567	810	4317
40 to 59	205770	18544	16880	1504	45	115	187226	68660	115600	623	2343
60 to 74	105904	6698	6020	658	5	15	99206	30902	67561	203	540
75 and over	64175	3051	2622	426	-	3	61124	16893	43937	85	209

Notes:

1 The term 'Catholic' includes those respondents who gave their religion as Catholic or Roman Catholic.
2 Knowledge of Irish is any of the following: understanding spoken Irish, reading Irish, speaking Irish or writing Irish.

Annex A:
Geographical Level of Tables

Annex A: Availability of Standard Tables at lower geographical levels.

		Northern Ireland	District Council	Electoral Ward
S001	Age by Sex and Whether Living in a Household or Communal Establishment	✓	✓	✓
S002	Age by Sex and Marital Status	✓	✓	✓
S003	Age of Household Reference Person (HRP) by Sex and Marital Status ('Headship')	✓	✓	✓
S005	Age of Household Reference Person (HRP) by Sex and Living Arrangements	✓	✓	✓
S006	Age of Family Reference Person (FRP) and Age of Dependent Children by Family Type	✓	✓	✓
S007	Age of Family Reference Person (FRP) and Number and Age of Dependent Children by Family Type	✓	✓	✓
S011	Family Composition by Age of Family Reference Person (FRP)	✓	✓	✓
S012	Schoolchildren and Students in Full-time Education Living Away From Home in Term-Time: Sex by Age	✓	✓	✓
S014	Age and Dependent Children by Household Type (Adults)	✓	✓	✓
S015	Country of Birth by Sex and Age	✓	✓	✓
S016	Sex and Age by General Health and Limiting Long-Term Illness (Household Residents)	✓	✓	✓
S018	Sex and Amenities and Central Heating by General Health and Limiting Long-Term Illness	✓	✓	✓
S019	General Health and Limiting Long-Term Illness and Occupancy Rating by Age	✓	✓	✓
S020	Limiting Long-Term Illness and Age by Accommodation Type and Lowest Floor Level of Accommodation	✓	✓	✓
S021	Economic Activity and Hours Worked by Sex and Limiting Long-Term Illness	✓	✓	✓
S022	Sex and Number of Cars or Vans in Household by General Health and Limiting Long-Term Illness	✓	✓	✓
S025	Sex and Age by General Health and Provision of Unpaid Care	✓	✓	✓
S026	Sex and Economic Activity by General Health and Provision of Unpaid Care	✓	✓	✓
S027	Households with a Person with a Limiting Long-Term Illness (LLTI) and Their Age by Number of Carers in Household and Economic Activity	✓	✓	✓
S028	Sex and Age by Economic Activity	✓	✓	✓
S029	Sex and Age by Hours Worked	✓	✓	✓
S030	Sex and Economic Activity by Living Arrangements	✓	✓	✓
S031	Family Composition and Number of Dependent Children by Sex and Economic Activity	✓	✓	✓
S032	Sex and Age and Level of Qualifications by Economic Activity	✓	✓	✓
S033	Sex and Occupation by Age	✓	✓	
S034	Sex and Former Occupation by Age (UK Basis)	✓	✓	
S035	Sex and Occupation by Employment Status and Hours Worked	✓	✓	
S036	Sex and Industry by Age	✓	✓	
S037	Sex and Former Industry by Age (UK Basis)	✓	✓	
S038	Sex and Industry by Employment Status and Hours Worked	✓	✓	
S039	Occupation by Industry	✓	✓	
S040	Sex and Occupation by Hours Worked	✓	✓	
S041	Sex and Economic Activity and Year Last Worked by Age	✓	✓	✓
S054	Shared/Unshared Dwelling and Central Heating and Occupancy Rating by Age	✓		
S058	Households in a Shared Dwelling and Amenities and Household Size by Central Heating and Number of Rooms	✓		
S059	Accommodation Type and Car or Van Availability by Number of Persons Aged 17 or Over in the Household	✓	✓	✓
S062	Household Composition by Number of Cars or Vans Available	✓	✓	✓
S065	Sex and Age by General Health and Limiting Long-Term Illness (Communal Establishment Residents)	✓	✓	

		Northern Ireland	District Council	Electoral Ward
S066	Sex and Approximated Social Grade by Age	✓	✓	✓
S067	Age of Household Reference Person (HRP) and Dependent Children by Approximated Social Grade	✓	✓	✓
S068	Age and Dependent Children by Household Type (Household Reference Persons)	✓	✓	✓
S118	Number of Employed Persons and Method of Travel to Work by Number of Cars or Vans in Household	✓	✓	✓
S301	Sex and Type of Communal Establishment by Type of Resident and Age	✓	✓	✓
S302	Type of Communal Establishment by Type of Resident and Whether or Not Resident One Year Ago	✓	✓	
S303	Sex and Age by Ethnic Group	✓	✓	
S304	Sex and Type of Communal Establishment by Ethnic Group	✓		
S305	Age by Sex and Community Background (Religion or Religion Brought Up In)	✓	✓	✓
S305A	Age by Sex and Religion	✓	✓	✓
S306	Age by Community Background (Religion or Religion Brought Up In)	✓	✓	✓
S306A	Age by Religion	✓	✓	✓
S307	Sex and Type of Communal Establishment by Community Background (Religion or Religion Brought Up In)	✓	✓	
S308	Religion by Sex	✓		
S309	Age by Sex and Living Arrangements	✓	✓	✓
S310	Age of Full-time Schoolchildren and Students Aged 18 and Under by Household Type	✓	✓	
S311	Household Composition by Ethnic Group of Household Reference Person (HRP)	✓	✓	
S312	Household Composition by Community Background (Religion or Religion Brought Up In) of Household Reference Person (HRP)	✓	✓	✓
S313	Living Arrangements and Community Background (Religion or Religion Brought Up In) by Sex and Age	✓	✓	✓
S314	Country of Birth by Ethnic group	✓	✓	
S315	Tenure and Age by General Health and Limiting Long-Term Illness	✓	✓	✓
S316	Limiting Long-Term Illness and Age by Number of Floor Levels and Tenure	✓	✓	✓
S317	Sex and Limiting Long-Term Illness and Type of Communal Establishment by Age (Residents (Non-Staff) in Communal Establishments)	✓	✓	
S318	Age and Limiting Long-Term Illness and General Health by Ethnic Group	✓	✓	
S319	Sex and Age and Limiting Long-Term Illness and General Health by Community Background (Religion or Religion Brought Up In)	✓	✓	✓
S320	Sex and Age by Highest Level of Qualification	✓	✓	✓
S321	Sex and NS-Sec by Highest Level of Qualification	✓	✓	✓
S322	Sex and Highest Level of Qualification by Ethnic Group	✓		
S323	Age and Highest Level of Qualification by Ethnic Group	✓		
S324	Sex and Highest Level of Qualification by Community Background (Religion or Religion Brought Up In)	✓	✓	✓
S325	Age and Highest Level of Qualification by Sex and Community Background (Religion or Religion Brought Up In)	✓	✓	
S325A	Age and Highest Level of Qualification by Sex and Religion	✓	✓	
S326	Sex and Occupation by Highest Level of Qualification	✓	✓	
S327	Age of Household Reference Person (HRP) and Tenure by Economic Activity of HRP	✓	✓	✓
S328	Economic Activity by Ethnic Group	✓	✓	
S329	Sex and Economic Activity by Community Background (Religion or Religion Brought Up In)	✓	✓	✓
S330	Age and Economic Activity by Sex and Community Background (Religion or Religion Brought Up In)	✓	✓	

		Northern Ireland	District Council	Electoral Ward
S330A	Age and Economic Activity by Sex and Religion	✓	✓	
S331	Economic Activity and Age of Full-time Students by Household Type and Tenure	✓	✓	
S332	Sex and Former Occupation by Age (NI Basis)	✓	✓	
S333	Sex and Occupation by Ethnic Group	✓		
S334	Occupation by Sex and Community Background (Religion or Religion Brought Up In)	✓	✓	
S335	Sex and Former Industry by Age (NI Basis)	✓	✓	
S336	Sex and Industry by Ethnic Group	✓		
S337	Industry by Sex and Community Background (Religion or Religion Brought Up In)	✓	✓	
S338	Sex and NS-SeC by Age	✓	✓	
S339	Sex and Age and General Health by NS-SeC	✓	✓	✓
S340	Sex and Age and Limiting Long-Term Illness by NS-SeC	✓	✓	✓
S341	Sex and NS-SeC by Economic Activity	✓	✓	✓
S342	Sex and NS-SeC by Method of Travel to Work	✓	✓	✓
S343	NS-SeC by Tenure	✓	✓	
S344	Sex and NS-SeC of Household Reference Person (HRP) by Tenure	✓	✓	✓
S345	Sex and NS-SeC of Household Reference Person (HRP) by Household Composition	✓	✓	✓
S346	Sex and NS-SeC of Household Reference Person (HRP) by Age (of HRP)	✓	✓	✓
S347	NS-Sec of Household Reference Person (HRP) by Households with Full-time Students Living Away From Home and Age of Student	✓		
S348	Sex and Ns-Sec by Ethnic Group	✓		
S349	NS-Sec by Sex and Community Background (Religion or Religion Brought Up In)	✓	✓	✓
S350	Sex and Age by Method of Travel to Work	✓	✓	✓
S351	Tenure and Number of Cars or Vans by Ethnic Group of Household Reference Person (HRP)	✓		
S352	Tenure and Number of Cars or Vans by Community Background (Religion or Religion Brought Up In) of Household Reference Person (HRP)	✓	✓	✓
S353	Dwelling Type and Accommodation Type by Tenure	✓	✓	✓
S354	Dwelling Type and Accommodation Type by Tenure (Persons)	✓	✓	✓
S355	Tenure and Household Size by Number of Rooms	✓	✓	✓
S356	Tenure and Persons Per Room by Accommodation Type	✓	✓	✓
S357	Household Composition by Tenure and Occupancy Rating	✓	✓	✓
S358	Dwelling Type and Accommodation Type and Central Heating (and Amenities for Shared Dwellings) by Tenure	✓	✓	✓
S359	Tenure and Amenities by Household Composition	✓	✓	✓
S360	Tenure and Lowest Floor Level by Household Composition	✓	✓	
S361	Tenure and Car or Van Availability by Number of Persons Aged 17 or Over in the Household	✓	✓	✓
S362	Tenure and Car or Van Availability by Economic Activity	✓	✓	✓
S363	Dwelling Type and Accommodation Type by Household Space Type	✓	✓	✓
S364	Tenure by Ethnic Group of Household Reference Person (HRP)	✓		
S365	Tenure and Occupancy Rating by Community Background (Religion or Religion Brought Up In)	✓	✓	✓
S366	Tenure by Community Background (Religion or Religion Brought Up In) of Household Reference Person (HRP)	✓	✓	✓
S367	Central Heating and Occupancy Rating by Age	✓	✓	✓
S368	Central Heating and Occupancy Rating by Ethnic Group	✓	✓	

		Northern Ireland	District Council	Electoral Ward
S369	Central Heating and Occupancy Rating by Ethnic Group of Household Reference Person (HRP)	✓	✓	
S370	Central Heating and Occupancy Rating by Community Background (Religion or Religion Brought Up In)	✓	✓	✓
S371	Central Heating and Occupancy Rating by Community Background (Religion or Religion Brought Up In) of Household Reference Person (HRP)	✓	✓	✓
S372	Sex and Age by Knowledge of Irish	✓	✓	
S373	Sex and Age by Knowledge of Irish and Country of Birth	✓	✓	✓
S374	Sex and Highest Level of Qualification by Knowledge of Irish	✓	✓	✓
S375	Sex and Age by Knowledge of Irish and Community Background (Religion or Religion Brought Up In)	✓	✓	✓

Notes:
Tables available for District Councils will also be available for Health and Social Services Boards, Education and Library Boards, NUTS Level III Areas and Parliamentary Constituencies.
Tables for lower geographical levels can be found in the Census section of www.nisra.gov.uk

270

Annex B:
Suggested Alternatives to UK Standard Tables

Annex B: Suggested alternative tables for UK tables not produced in Northern Ireland

UK Table Number	Available in NI?	Alternative Table	Table Name
S001	✓		Age by Sex and Whether Living in a Household or Communal Establishment
S002	✓		Age by Sex and Marital Status
S003	✓		Age of Household Reference Person (HRP) by Sex and Marital Status ('Headship')
S004	✓	S309	Age by Sex and Living Arrangements
S005	✓		Age of Household Reference Person (HRP) by Sex and Living Arrangements
S006	✓		Age of Family Reference Person (FRP) and Age of Dependent Children by Family Type
S007	✓		Age of Family Reference Person (FRP) and Number and Age of Dependent Children by Family Type
S008	Migration table		Type of Residency and Sex and Age by Migration (People)
S009	Migration table		Age of Household Reference Person and Number of Dependent Children by Migration of Households
S010	Migration table		Household Composition by Migration of Households
S011	✓		Family Composition by Age of Family Reference Person (FRP)
S012	✓		Schoolchildren and Students in Full-time Education Living Away From Home in Term-Time: Sex by Age
S013	✓	S327	Age of Household Reference Person (HRP) and Tenure by Economic Activity of HRP
S014	✓		Age and Dependent Children by Household Type (Adults)
S015	✓		Country of Birth by Sex and Age
S016	✓		Sex and Age by General Health and Limiting Long-Term Illness (Household Residents)
S017	✓	S315	Tenure and Age by General Health and Limiting Long-Term Illness
S018	✓		Sex and Amenities and Central Heating by General Health and Limiting Long-Term Illness
S019	✓		General Health and Limiting Long-Term Illness and Occupancy Rating by Age
S020	✓		Limiting Long-Term Illness and Age by Accommodation Type and Lowest Floor Level of Accommodation
S021	✓		Economic Activity and Hours Worked by Sex and Limiting Long-Term Illness
S022	✓		Sex and Number of Cars or Vans in Household by General Health and Limiting Long-Term Illness
S023	✓	S339	Sex and Age and General Health by NS-SeC
S024	✓	S340	Sex and Age and Limiting Long-Term Illness by NS-SeC
S025	✓		Sex and Age by General Health and Provision of Unpaid Care
S026	✓		Sex and Economic Activity by General Health and Provision of Unpaid Care
S027	✓		Households with a Person with a Limiting Long-Term Illness (LLTI) and Their Age by Number of Carers in Household and Economic Activity
S028	✓		Sex and Age by Economic Activity
S029	✓		Sex and Age by Hours Worked
S030	✓		Sex and Economic Activity by Living Arrangements
S031	✓		Family Composition and Number of Dependent Children by Sex and Economic Activity
S032	✓		Sex and Age and Level of Qualifications by Economic Activity
S033	✓		Sex and Occupation by Age
S034	✓		Sex and Former Occupation by Age (UK Basis)
S035	✓		Sex and Occupation by Employment Status and Hours Worked
S036	✓		Sex and Industry by Age

UK Table Number	Available in NI?	Alternative Table	Table Name
S037	✓		Sex and Former Industry by Age (UK Basis)
S038	✓		Sex and Industry by Employment Status and Hours Worked
S039	✓		Occupation by Industry
S040	✓		Sex and Occupation by Hours Worked
S041	✓		Sex and Economic Activity and Year Last Worked by Age
S042	✓	S338	Sex and NS-SeC by Age
S043	✓	S341	Sex and NS-SeC by Economic Activity
S044	✓	S345	Sex and NS-SeC of Household Reference Person (HRP) by Household Composition
S045	✓	S346	Sex and NS-SeC of Household Reference Person (HRP) by Age (of HRP)
S046	✓	S344	Sex and NS-SeC of Household Reference Person (HRP) by Tenure
S047	✓	S343	NS-SeC by Tenure
S048	✓	S363	Dwelling Type and Accommodation Type by Household Space Type
S049	✓	S353	Dwelling Type and Accommodation Type by Tenure
S050	✓	S354	Dwelling Type and Accommodation Type by Tenure (Persons)
S051	✓	S355	Tenure and Household Size by Number of Rooms
S052	✓	S356	Tenure and Persons Per Room by Accommodation Type
S053	✓	S357	Household Composition by Tenure and Occupancy Rating
S054	✓		Shared/Unshared Dwelling and Central Heating and Occupancy Rating by Age
S055	✓	S358	Dwelling Type and Accommodation Type and Central Heating (and Amenities for Shared Dwellings) by Tenure
S056	✓	S359	Tenure and Amenities by Household Composition
S057	✓	S360	Tenure and Lowest Floor Level by Household Composition
S058	✓		Households in a Shared Dwelling and Amenities and Household Size by Central Heating and Number of Rooms
S059	✓		Accommodation Type and Car or Van Availability by Number of Persons Aged 17 or Over in the Household
S060	✓	S361	Tenure and Car or Van Availability by Number of Persons Aged 17 or Over in the Household
S061	✓	S362	Tenure and Car or Van Availability by Economic Activity
S062	✓		Household Composition by Number of Cars or Vans Available
S063	✓	S331	Economic Activity and Age of Full-time Students by Household Type and Tenure
S064	✓	S347	NS-SeC of Household Reference Person (HRP) by Households with Full-time Students Living Away From Home and Age of Student
S065	✓		Sex and Age by General Health and Limiting Long-Term Illness (Communal Establishment Residents)
S066	✓		Sex and Approximated Social Grade by Age
S067	✓		Age of Household Reference Person (HRP) and Dependent Children by Approximated Social Grade
S068	✓		Age and Dependent Children by Household Type (Household Reference Persons)

Note:
Migration and distance to place of work tables will be included in a future publication.